T0350869

Harvest Wobblies

Harvest Wobblies

The Industrial Workers of the World
and Agricultural Laborers in the American West,
1905-1930

⌘⌘⌘

GREG HALL

Oregon State University Press
Corvallis

The paper in this book meets the guidelines for permanence and durability of the Committee on Production Guidelines for Book Longevity of the Council on Library Resources and the minimum requirements of the American National Standard for Permanence of Paper for Printed Library Materials Z39.48-1984.

Library of Congress Cataloging-in-Publication Data
Hall, Greg, 1961-
 Harvest Wobblies : the Industrial Workers of the World and
agricultural laborers in the American West, 1905-1930 / by Greg Hall.—
1st ed.
     p. cm.
Includes bibliographical references and index.
 ISBN 0-87071-532-1 (alk. paper)
 1. Agricultural Workers' Industrial Union. 2. Industrial Workers of
the World. 3. Agricultural laborers—Labor unions—United
States—History. I. Title.
 HD6515.A292 A394 2001
 331.88'6--dc21
                                    2001002296

Oregon State University Press
101 Waldo Hall
Corvallis OR 97331-6407
541-737-3166 •fax 541-737-3170
OREGON STATE   http://.osu.orst.edu/dept/press
UNIVERSITY

Contents

For my Grandparents

Who taught me the value of labor

⌘

Acknowledgments

This book began as a paper for a United States history seminar on the topic of agriculture and rural life. Like many graduate students, I was taking the course primarily to fulfill a requirement so that I could hurry up and take my preliminary examinations and get on with finding a dissertation topic. To my surprise, I enjoyed David Coon's seminar and discovered that I found the labor systems that made industrial agriculture possible in the American West fascinating and somewhat neglected by labor and Western historians. David encouraged me to pursue my interest in farm labor and union organizing efforts. I chose a less researched, underrated effort by the Industrial Workers of the World to organize farm workers as my topic. Beginning with that paper and its various incarnations as a conference paper, dissertation and finally, a monograph, David offered his support, direction, knowledge of U.S. agricultural history and editing skills. Along the way, LeRoy Ashby and Raymond Sun offered me advice and acted as readers. To all three, I am indebted for making the dissertation process as painless as possible.

Researching my topic was an eventful experience and could not have happened without financial support and expert assistance. Therefore, I want to express my gratitude to Washington State University for a 1997 Summer Graduate Research Assistantship and to the university's Department of History for awarding me the 1997 Pettyjohn Graduate Research Fellowship in Pacific Northwest history. I must also thank my father, David Hall, for his familial financial assistance. With cash in hand, I traveled throughout the West and Midwest, visiting more than two-dozen research sites. To make my limited funds last the entire summer, I have my mother, family members, and friends to thank for providing me with food, lodging, and encouragement. At the research sites themselves, I want to thank all of the patient and helpful archivists, reference librarians, and historical society workers, who guided me through their material. I especially want to thank Bill LeFevre at Walter P. Reuther Library, Archives of Labor and Urban Affairs, which houses most of the existing IWW documents. Bill helped me find the relevant material for *Harvest Wobblies* out of a mountain of documents.

Transforming *Harvest Wobblies* from a dissertation to a monograph required incredible patience. Luckily, the good people at Oregon State

University Press gave me direction and simultaneously the freedom to make this book my own; therefore, I want to thank especially Warren Slesinger, Mary Braun, Jo Alexander, and Judith Lipsett for helping me publish my book.

Most of the participants in this history left little tangible evidence of their lives and even fewer images of themselves. However, the photographs, illustrations, and map used in the book helped to make *Harvest Wobblies* more personal and better located in space and time. I want to thank Glen Curtis for sharing photos of his family's ranch and farm in eastern Washington and the folks at the Reuther Library, the Institute for Regional Studies at North Dakota State University, the Bancroft Library, the California State Archives, the Charles H. Kerr Publishing Company, and Joy Werlink at the Washington State Historical Society. I also want to thank Eric King for his artful map of the West.

Finally, I would like to thank Liza Rognas, my partner and fellow historian. Liza read and critiqued this manuscript, patiently listened to my never-ending concerns, and gave me the necessary support to carry this project to completion.

G.H.
Olympia, Washington
July 2001

Introduction

⌘⌘⌘

In summer 1923, the Agricultural Workers' Industrial Union (AWIU) was at a high point in membership and exercised significant influence within the Industrial Workers of the World (IWW). It was also at near-maximum strength across the North American wheat belt that stretched from West Texas to the Canadian prairies. In a small but significant portion of the western wheat-growing country, AWIU members, whom I call "harvest Wobblies," saw an opportunity to gain an organizational foothold and to reassert themselves in an area they had long contested with employers. At first a small group of harvest Wobblies met with several bankers and a Whitman County official at the Farmers' National Bank in Washington's wheat town of Palouse, named after the state's rich wheat-growing region. The conference participants, however, could not agree on a standard wage for harvest or threshing work. Yet harvest Wobblies believed that they had the advantage. Area farmers were enjoying a bumper wheat crop, but they lacked an adequate supply of labor. The AWIU members considered themselves strong enough to hold up the harvest and threshing of the valuable wheat with a strike, thereby achieving their demands.[1]

Harvest Wobblies fanned out among independent harvest workers in the Palouse country, taking their message to small eastern Washington towns. Back in Spokane, they created a Whitman County Strike Committee. In August 1923, the Wobblies urged their fellow harvest workers to strike. The strike call was not only for recognition of the AWIU but for improvements in local wages and working conditions and for the release of political prisoners held in state and federal prisons. Although a majority of farm workers in eastern Washington's wheat country had been independent, the AWIU was successful in gaining support. By the end of August, a region-wide agricultural strike gripped eastern Washington. Workers honored IWW picket lines at the downtown Spokane municipal employment bureau, temporarily shutting down the flow of harvesters to sites in the Palouse. In addition, some threshing workers refused employment offered to them in Spokane by Whitman County farmers who would not provide beds but expected their hired hands to bring their own blankets for sleeping in straw stacks or in barns on their farms. In the countryside, harvest Wobblies instigated work stoppages among a number of threshing crews, some as far south as Uniontown, at the southern end of the Palouse.

Organizing a strike at a worksite had its consequences, as Al Cook and E. Preager discovered in Uniontown when the local sheriff arrested them and took them to the county jail. Opposition to their strike efforts only emboldened harvest Wobblies, however, for they soon took their message to the streets of Colfax, the county seat. Within the next several days, sheriff's deputies arrested seven more IWW members. Among them, John Murphy and Frank Shields faced the most serious charge of criminal syndicalism, under a law designed to suppress the IWW. A. Steward, Joe Murray, and several other men sat in jail on lesser charges awaiting appeal. Keeping these men company were Fred McGarrahan and J. Perry, serving thirty days for passing out strike handbills on the streets of Colfax. The handbill they distributed was probably the one issued by the Strike Committee for circulation among harvest and threshing workers. In part it read:

Leave the jobs!

Tell the boss you are not going to return until the Class-War Prisoners of America are released.

In you lies the power to force the issue. Without your work the boss will starve. You do all the work and the boss gets all the money.

It is time that we, the workers, get a little of what we produce.

Keep out of Whitman County!
Boost for the general strike![2]

Fortunately for harvesters in eastern Washington, the strike brought about a one-dollar-a-day increase in wages for a variety of agricultural jobs. In Whitman County, though, law enforcement officials continued to arrest Wobblies. In mid-September, the AWIU members in the Colfax County jail escalated the confrontation with a hunger strike and a noise campaign. Most of the members joined the hunger strike, and all participated in the noise-making strategy to disrupt the jailhouse and the local neighborhood. According to John Kelley, who spent thirty-two days in the county facility, "The big show starts at 11 o'clock and continues [until] 20 minutes after the hour, then silence until the clock strikes the next hour." The noise usually subsided in the small hours of the morning. According to Kelley, Sheriff William Cole, the keeper of this crew of rambunctious prisoners, greeted them in the morning with,

"Boys, please don't do that." Joe Murray, an occasional spokesman for the jailed Wobblies, deemed the hunger strike and noise campaign successful. Prosecutors eventually dropped criminal syndicalism charges against Murphy and Shields. Within a week of Murray's prison update in the *Industrial Worker*, the sheriff released the rest of the jailed harvest Wobblies.[3]

No mass release of state-held prisoners held on criminal syndicalism charges followed the incident in eastern Washington, however, until December, when President Calvin Coolidge decided to release all remaining IWW federal prisoners who had been serving sentences since the mass wartime trials. In doing so, Coolidge was bowing to pressure from within his own government and to growing nationwide sentiment that the war and postwar antiradical hysteria had resulted in serious excesses of federal power. Throughout this period, but especially in 1922 and 1923, branches of the IWW in agriculture, mining, construction, marine transportation, and logging continually pressed federal authorities to release their members from prison through strikes, boycotts, and petition campaigns. Most of the IWW strikes during the early 1920s combined a demand for the release of political prisoners with improvements in local wage and working conditions and union recognition.[4]

The harvest Wobblies of eastern Washington followed this pattern of combining the effort to improve the work lives of laborers with larger goals that were significant for the life of their revolutionary union. Furthermore, they displayed their solidarity in the face of repression with innovative strategies and with humor. Though these particular IWW members passed quickly from the public consciousness, they are part of the history not only of the IWW but also of agriculture in the American West. The story of the work lives and unionizing efforts of the IWW members who labored in agriculture is one that has not been told in its entirety.[5]

Harvest Wobblies, in the form of the Agricultural Workers' Organization (AWO) and later the AWIU, eventually became one of the largest and most dynamic constituencies of the IWW. Their greatest organizational achievements were in the West. From the founding of the IWW in 1905 until the mid-1920s, harvest Wobblies had to face challenges to their organizing efforts from unions affiliated with the American Federation of Labor (AFL) on the Pacific Coast and from ethnic associations of Asian and Hispanic farm workers that focused on immigrants. State and federal farm labor exchanges contested the IWW's efforts to supply and distribute farm labor as well. Despite these obstacles, the IWW's agricultural branch grew by leaps and bounds, even after the repression the union faced during World War I and in the immediate postwar era. From 1915 to 1925, over half of the IWW's finances originated with the AWO or the AWIU.

Moreover, the agricultural branch of the IWW became a proving ground for many of the best organizers and leaders of the union. Even more important, harvest Wobblies personified some of the most indelible features of the union membership. They were the militant casual laborers of the American West, riding the rails, living in makeshift camps known as "jungles," and preaching industrial unionism and revolution in the workplace. They, along with other Wobblies of the West, created the footloose, masculine, rebel worker culture of the IWW. They migrated across the country, working in agriculture, construction, mining, logging, and marine transportation on a seasonal basis. They were part of what historian Carlos A. Schwantes refers to as the "wageworkers' frontier," the workforce that industrialized the West and built its infrastructure during the late nineteenth and early twentieth centuries. Overall, the IWW proved to be most successful at organizing these western workers, with harvest Wobblies playing a significant role. In doing so, harvest Wobblies spread the union's message to some of the most exploited workers in American industry, those in agriculture (fig. 1).[6]

The workers among whom harvest Wobblies traveled, worked, and lived during the first few decades of the twentieth century in the American West have been chronicled by historians, sociologists, ethnographers, novelists, and others. Yet this period remains largely unexplored by historians of western farm labor.[7] These workers represented a new phenomenon in American agriculture at the close of the nineteenth century, as farming in the West moved to an over-whelmingly market-oriented enterprise. Many farmers were forced to turn to monocrop agriculture in order to survive economically. With technological innovations, farming became increasingly more mech-anized, making it possible for farmers to plant thousands of acres. In the Great Plains, these acres tended to be planted in wheat. Yet even small farmers who had to plant several hundred acres of wheat to remain economically solvent could not harvest the crop without seasonal help. Migrant and seasonal farm labor became as indispensable for wheat farmers to harvest their crops as the railroad was for getting those crops to market. In California and Washington, and in other parts of the West, railroad expansion, irrigation, and new refrigeration technology were the

Figure 1. Appearing in the *Industrial Worker*, 23 April 1910, the "Blanket Stiff" epitomized the worklife of the western laborer, his exploitation, and his marginal status in the West.
(Courtesy, Charles H. Kerr Publishing Company, Chicago, 1998)

forces that drove the development of commercial agriculture, but migrant and seasonal farm labor were essential to the harvest of the grains, fruit, vegetables, potatoes, sugar beets, and many other crops grown in these regions.

In the mid-nineteenth century, when farms were more diverse, farmers used local farmhands as seasonal labor. The farmhand was a kind of apprentice farmer, whose goal was to save enough of his earnings and buy a farm for himself one day. This was known as the "agricultural ladder." But this ladder broke down as arable land filled up with farms, and prices for land and equipment rose beyond what a worker could hope to save. By the turn of the twentieth century, American farming, particularly in the West, relied on the agricultural labor of migrant and local seasonal workers who would never become farmers.[8]

These were the workers that the IWW tried to organize, making the first effort in U.S. history to bring all agricultural laborers into one all-inclusive industrial union. Though the West is a vast area with many different subregions, I am using the ninety-eighth meridian to define where the West begins. Therefore, for this study, the West comprises the Dakotas, Nebraska, Kansas, Oklahoma, and Texas, and extending west to the Pacific Coast states of California, Oregon, and Washington (fig. 2). The ninety-eighth meridian is a geographic demarcation based on aridity, but it also denotes the beginning of a subregion of the West called the Great Plains. Here, where the North American wheat belt extends from West Texas to the Canadian prairies, as many as a quarter of a million migrant and seasonal workers traversed the plains, harvesting and threshing wheat, until the advent of the combine in the second half of the 1920s. But there are also other significant subregions of the West where farmers developed extensive and intensive agriculture. Eastern Washington's Palouse and the fruit-growing areas of the Yakima and Wenatchee Valleys were some of the earliest western agricultural zones to require tens of thousands of seasonal workers every harvest and packing season during the early decades of the twentieth century. And as early as the 1870s, the farms of California's central river valleys required seasonal laborers. California's agribusiness would eventually become the largest user of migrant farm labor in the American West.[9]

The IWW, between 1909 and 1925, was uniquely suited to organizing the tens of thousands of migrant and seasonal workers essential to western agriculture. When activists formed the union in 1905, they had two simultaneous goals, one practical and one revolutionary. First, the union would organize the masses of industrial American workers who were not members of the more conservative AFL-affiliated unions, regardless of the workers' skill level, industry, gender, race, ethnicity, or nationality. Within a few years, therefore, agricultural workers were actively sought after as IWW members.

The second goal of the IWW was to emancipate American workers from the exploitation of employers and the capitalist system by ushering in an egalitarian society in which workers controlled the means of production through their unions and received the full fruits of their labor. Wobblies would accomplish this goal through their unique union structure and the use of the general strike. In short, the IWW was a very different kind of labor association than the trade unionism of the AFL. While the AFL organized based on craft or trade within the industry, Wobblies organized based on the industry as a whole. Therefore they attempted to organize all workers in agriculture, construction, transportation, logging, or mining into constituent industrial unions. By organizing all of the nation's industries, Wobblies hoped to displace the

Figure 2. The American West circa 1900.
(Courtesy, King Illustration and Design)

AFL and eventually control the entire U.S. economy. From this position of economic power, the IWW could call a general strike and bring down the edifices of capitalism and the state. With an industrial union system in place, the IWW would be the foundation of a new classless, wageless, and socioeconomically just society. The IWW's revolutionary industrial unionism bore a striking similarity to European syndicalism, though few Wobblies labeled themselves syndicalists, or, for that matter, socialists. They were Wobblies, and they sought to bring together a disparate assemblage of the American left and every type of American worker into one great house of labor.[10]

These were, of course, distant goals. Until the IWW and the American working class achieved their ultimate victory over capitalism and its servant, the state, committed Wobblies strove to "build the new society within the shell of the old" by organizing the unaffiliated worker. They also sought to export their concept of revolutionary industrial unionism abroad, where it took root in Australia, Canada, and briefly in Mexico. But it was among western agricultural workers that the IWW acquired its greatest number of adherents, primarily in the Great Plains. What accounts for this success in the West, especially in the nation's wheat belt? The answer lies in the harvest Wobblies' cultural appeal as a band of unionized workingmen migrating through the countryside. They appeared on the scene sometime between 1905 and 1909 and began to forge a bond with underskilled itinerant laborers that developed into collective historical agency. Many of the harvest workers who joined the AWO and later the AWIU wanted to put an end to their exploitation at the hands of farmers, law enforcement officials, and business interests through collective means. These workers were attempting something that had not been attempted in American agriculture up to that time: to address economic hardships and social marginality with the power of a union open to all agricultural wage workers. This would be the first of many efforts by agricultural laborers over the course of the twentieth century to improve their socioeconomic circumstances by union action. Through trial and error, harvest Wobblies eventually implemented the industrial union concept in agriculture, making them a force to be reckoned with by agricultural employers.

During the first few decades of the twentieth century, the vast majority of migrant and seasonal laborers working in western agriculture were white, native-born men. Among these predominantly unmarried workers, traveling by rail from job to job and living in "jungles," harvest Wobblies developed a distinctive culture of work and of life on the road, which I have termed their "worklife culture." They shared much of this culture with other migrant and seasonal agricultural laborers of the day. Yet the Wobblies embodied a unique camaraderie in the jungles, worksites, union halls, skid rows, jails, and freight cars of the American West. Their common experiences forged a sociocultural bond that was further strengthened by aggressive opposition to employers, law enforcement officers, and "hi-jacks," the robbers and confidence men who preyed on migrant harvest workers. Harvest Wobblies expressed themselves through an impressive outpouring of writing, impassioned speeches, union organizing, humor, and song. Sustained through several decades by a common sense of identity and purpose, they created a worklife culture that appealed to Great Plains migrant and seasonal workers, bringing tens of thousands of them into their union.[11]

This is the story of the harvest Wobblies, and the rise and fall of their revolutionary industrial union. It is also an investigation into the dramatic changes in western American agriculture during the early decades of the twentieth century, changes that propelled this union's growth. What was the nature of the agricultural industries that the IWW sought to control? Who were the men and women that Wobblies wanted to organize, and why were they so essential and yet so exploited within the agricultural industries of the West? The history of the harvest Wobblies begins with the answers to these questions.

Chapter One

Working for Wages in the West

⌘⌘⌘

During the last decades of the nineteenth century, farms in the Great Plains, the central and southern valleys of California, and areas of the Pacific Northwest evolved into "factories in the field," a term coined by Carey McWilliams for his seminal work on California farm labor. The phrase appropriately describes the industrial form that agriculture took in the West soon after farmers turned to commercial farming. Between 1900 and 1925, the use of temporary wage labor to harvest crops reached its historic peak among western farmers and ranchers. Thousands of farmers, compromising their agrarian identity as self-sufficient producers, adapted new management practices and marketing strategies to the unique features of their regions. Farmers in the plains states, for example, grew wheat as the crop best suited to the region's climate and soil. With the use of rail systems, new farm machinery, and a steady supply of labor for harvesting and threshing, these single-crop producers could supply grain to ever-expanding domestic and international markets. Farms in California and Washington, though more agriculturally diverse, experienced similar changes. With government-supported irrigation projects and innovations in refrigeration, canning, and rail systems, industrial agriculture thrived in these two states. Moreover, as the populations of the United States and Europe became primarily urban, the market for California's and Washington's fruits, vegetables, and other crops continued to grow. [1]

Whether on the plains or in fertile valleys, the West's agricultural factories became the seasonal workplaces of several hundred thousand people. Many of these workers, mostly men, migrated from county to county and state to state in search of work; others rarely left their home counties. Some considered themselves agricultural workers by trade, while others, due to economic circumstances or discrimination, worked on western farms solely to earn wages. Their work experiences varied, as did their reasons for working in agriculture. Still, a common worklife culture developed among a large segment of this population of workers. Ultimately, the attributes that they shared, which the Wobblies hoped to make the most of, were their common class position, the nature of their work, and their exploitation at the hands of farmers.

The Fortunes of Western Farms

The last three decades of the nineteenth century were difficult years for American farmers. Prices for their products languished in a chronically depressed state. At the end of the 1890s, however, their fortunes began to change. From 1900 to 1910, the value of agricultural commodities climbed to $9 billion. According to agricultural historian Gilbert C. Fite, this was almost double the value of the previous decade's farm products. Prosperity on American farms proceeded unabated, so that by 1919, agricultural commodities achieved a value of nearly $24 billion. For this reason, most agricultural scholars consider the era from 1900 to World War I as the "Golden Age" of American farming. Demand for agricultural products outstripped supply during these years as Americans and Europeans became increasingly urban. The Great War further stimulated demand for American farm products. Domestic consumption, exports, and prices did not level off until after 1920.

Another factor that benefited farmers during this "Golden Age" was the increasing value of farmland. Farmers found, according to Fite, that "between 1900 and 1910 the per acre value of land and buildings rose about 100 percent and then climbed another 90 percent by 1920." At least three Great Plains states, Nebraska, Kansas, and South Dakota, witnessed significant increases in the value of farmland and subsequent capital gains for land-owning farmers. Higher crop yields and greater productivity due to advances in agricultural science and technological innovations also contributed to the farmers' economic well-being. Farmers were now able to purchase tractors, new machinery, automobiles, and trucks, and acquire electrical service and telephones.

California agriculturalists led the way in creating the modern industrial farm, and their collective prosperity continued throughout the Roaring Twenties to a degree comparable to that of urban industrialists. Yet for most other American farmers, the 1920s held an entirely different economic experience. These postwar years signaled the beginning of a depression in agriculture that would bottom out a long decade later. At the end of 1920, prices for wheat, cotton, and meat products fell as European farmers were once more able to meet their population's agricultural needs. Furthermore, with their economies in tatters, Europeans had difficulty purchasing imported agricultural products. American farmers also faced significant competition from Argentina, Canada, and Australia. The downturn in international demand for American farm products was accompanied by a reduction in demand for American manufactured goods, which had an impact on domestic urban demand for farm products. But the fall in prices for farm commodities fell faster than those for manufactured goods, reducing the farmer's purchasing power while increasing farm costs. The combination of declining farm prices and declining land prices created desperate economic circumstances for American farmers, particularly those in the wheat belt who had expanded production to keep up with demand. These farmers now found themselves overproducing and in debt after borrowing funds to support their expanding enterprises. By the end of the 1920s, farmers, especially in the Great Plains, were experiencing their worst economic situation in over thirty years.[2]

Farming the Great Plains

Farmers had settled the Great Plains in the last third of the nineteenth century with a sharp eye toward cheap land and economic opportunity. They quickly discovered that several different strains of wheat and other small grains such as oats, rye, barley, and buckwheat grew best in the rather arid climate. This region, which became known in these decades as the wheat belt, can be broken down into two basic areas divided by a corn belt that runs from west to east through the state of Nebraska. The southern region of small-grain-growing states, including northern Texas, western Oklahoma, Kansas, eastern New Mexico, and Colorado, is characterized climatically by mild winters, devastatingly hot summers, and low levels of precipitation. Southern plains wheat farmers generally planted strains of hard winter wheat in the fall and harvested it in late spring. The wheat-growing region to the north of the Nebraska corn belt includes the western areas of Iowa and Minnesota and the plains states of the Dakotas, eastern Wyoming, and Montana, as well as southern Canada. Summers in the northern region of the wheat belt can be as hot as those in the southern, although they tend to be less so. The winters, however, offer a greater contrast, as winter temperatures in the northern regions are among the lowest in the United States. In the north plains, farmers planted hard spring wheat, and other strains, in the mid-spring months and harvested in middle to late summer.[3]

From the end of the nineteenth century through the 1920s, the wheat belt became the breadbasket of the United States. The growing urban demand for wheat and other grain crops such as oats, rye, barley, and buckwheat stimulated large-scale agriculture: as of 1899, the wheat belt had nearly sixty thousand farms with five hundred or more acres of land.

More than twenty-one thousand of these farms were one thousand acres or more. The success of these large farms depended heavily on access to rail systems. For example, with the penetration of the Northern Pacific, St. Paul, Minneapolis, and Manitoba railroad companies into the Red River valley of western Minnesota and eastern North Dakota in the 1880s, settlement accelerated and farming expanded rapidly. Western historian William Robbins, in *Colony and Empire,* argues that the railroad companies, with their aggressive promotion of the West for agricultural development, became the most important impetus for the increase in settlement and commercial agriculture. Between 1870 and the early 1900s, the number of transcontinental rail lines increased from one to five. Robbins further argues that by the first decade of the twentieth century, the plains became an "integral yet dependent component of an Atlantic-dominated agricultural marketing system" that fed the grain needs of the U.S. domestic market and that of Europe.[4]

The bonanza farm was part of this explosion in western commercial agriculture and a prime example of its industrial character. According to agricultural historian Hiram M. Drache, the bonanza farm represented a new type of farming, one that saw some of its most spectacular development in North Dakota. These farms were highly mechanized, and the labor force employed required little specialized knowledge due to the use of machinery and intense supervision. Such farms had a distinct factory-like quality. Drache is quick to point out, in *The Day of the Bonanza,* that bonanza farms were not the only kind of agriculture in North Dakota. While there were many farms totaling seven thousand acres or more each, most farms in the state covered hundreds, rather than thousands, of acres. Regardless of farm size, however, farmers required seasonal wage labor for harvesting and threshing.[5]

The Dalrymple family's agribusiness in North Dakota epitomized the large-scale farm operation. The family began acquiring land in the 1870s, and after 1900 owned approximately one hundred thousand acres, tens of thousands of which were planted in wheat. The land was divided into several farms and ranches with a variety of agricultural uses. Alfred N. Terry, the Dalrymples' bookkeeper, commented that in 1919, farm number one, where he and his family resided, possessed close to twenty-five thousand acres subdivided into eight sections of around three thousand to thirty-five hundred acres each. The farm technology of the era made cultivating large tracts of land in wheat, oats, barley, and hay possible, but it did not eliminate the need for temporary wage labor. In the 1880s, Dalrymple managers reported employing one thousand men in a single harvest season. Mrs. O. L. Ferguson, daughter of one of the Dalrymples' farm managers, remembers helping her mother serve breakfast and supper to one hundred men a day during the harvest season. Like other Great Plains farms, the Dalrymple farm's labor needs gradually decreased as farm technology required fewer laborers. Yet the overall need for these workers throughout the wheat belt did not abate significantly until after 1930.[6]

In the southern plains, which were settled concurrently with the north, railroad companies again helped stimulate commercial agricultural development. The Santa Fe railroad connected Topeka, Kansas, and Pueblo, Colorado, in the 1870s. In the 1880s, the Santa Fe linked Kansas with the Pacific coast. Kansas's population almost tripled between 1870 and 1880, and practically doubled again by 1890. Its agriculture also included bonanza farms. Eastern investors owned one such farming operation in Ellsworth County, Kansas, and hired M. M. Sherman to manage it. In 1902, the operation held forty thousand acres of land, with some devoted to livestock, but most under cultivation. The farm, or ranch as it was called, was intensively managed from a centralized headquarters, to the point that a writer in the periodical *The World's Work* suggested that "no factory was ever operated in a more systematic manner than this farm." There were similar operations in Oklahoma. The Miller "101" Ranch outside of Ponca City, Oklahoma, had five thousand acres of wheat under cultivation in 1894 which produced seventy thousand bushels. In later seasons, as the ranch expanded, managers employed as many as five hundred laborers to work nine thousand acres of wheat.

While most wheat farms on the plains were not bonanza-size farms, wheat tended to be the primary if not the sole crop small farmers produced for market. In 1900, the half-dozen counties in eastern North Dakota's so-called "bonanza belt" had farms that averaged slightly over three hundred acres of cultivated land apiece. In Kansas at the turn of the century, approximately two hundred acres per farm were under cultivation. As an aggregate of farms both large and small, the wheat-growing industry in the United States produced almost 236 million bushels of wheat in 1870, more than double that amount in 1898, and 763 million bushels in 1913. As of 1909, approximately three-quarters of the nation's wheat crop grew in the central states of the country — the Great Plains and a few Midwestern states east of the Mississippi River.[7]

Laboring on Great Plains Farms

Despite the increasing mechanization of agriculture, harvesting and threshing wheat tended to be two separate operations, each requiring temporary wage laborers. As early as the 1870s, wheat farmers used automatic binders that drastically reduced, but did not eliminate, the need for hand labor. These machines, pulled by two or four horses and operated by a single farmer, could cut wheat, bind it into bundles with wire or twine, and drop the bundles to the side. One farmer could cut hundreds of acres of wheat in a matter of days. The convenience and affordability of the device made it a standard feature of Great Plains farming until well after the turn of the century. Men no longer needed to rake wheat gavels or stalks and bind them into sheaves before shocking— that is, placing the automatically bound bundles in an upright position in groups of four or six. Shocking, which required several workers per binder, was the one major harvest task that remained. Jack Spiese, a migrant harvester who worked the northern plains in the 1910s, recalled that shocking the wheat was very important because grain had to stand for a time until it was cured. Later, workers loaded the sheaves of wheat onto a wagon to be taken for threshing (fig. 3).

Until 1919, most wheat in the United States was harvested with an automatic binder. In the West, however, some wheat farmers used the header, another laborsaving harvest machine. Headers, as their name

Figure 3. Harvest workers shocking wheat bundles in North Dakota, 1911. (Courtesy, The Fred Hultstrand History in Pictures Collection, Institute for Regional Studies, NDSU, Fargo, N.D.)

implies, cut only the head of the grain. A horse-drawn barge accompanied the header, and a grain elevator linked the header to the barge, transporting the wheat heads into the barge's bed. One of the advantages of the header was that it removed the need for shocking wheat, thereby eliminating another hand-labor task. Shocking allowed the wheat to dry out before threshing, but in areas of the West that experienced dry harvest seasons, this step was not necessary, and farmers preferred the header. Yet harvesting with a header still required workers to operate the machine, tend the horses, operate the barge, and thresh and stack the wheat. Regardless of whether farmers used binders or headers, they needed migrant or resident temporary wage laborers because of the limits of the laborsaving farm machinery and because of the sheer volume of their single-crop harvest.[8]

Threshing crews were another seasonal labor need; this part of the harvest operation separated the grain from the straw. Steam-powered threshing machines arrived on the Great Plains in the 1880s, and although horse-powered machines persisted after the turn of the century, their steam-powered rivals were commonplace by that time, and continued to be until being displaced by gasoline-powered threshers in the 1920s. Threshermen tended to be independent contractors who owned their own threshing machinery and who hired engineers and separatormen to operate it. The threshing crew—those who performed the more unskilled work—could be local or migrant harvesters. Many of those in the crews were men who followed the harvest and, if possible, accepted the offer to stay on in an area for the higher wages and the extended employment of threshing. The engineer and separatormen had higher-skilled jobs. The engineer operated the threshing machine, and the separatormen performed the necessary maintenance to keep the temperamental machines, with their long belts, running. The threshing crew brought shocked wheat to the threshing area and pitched the bundles into the machine. Later, they sacked the grain, which other workers eventually transported to a warehouse to await shipment. Depending on the size of the threshing operation, several to several dozen men could be employed during the process (fig. 4).[9]

Even though farm machinery reduced the need for many hand-labor tasks, the steady expansion of agricultural land use, particularly due to dry-farming techniques, increased the need for temporary wage laborers. The expanding wheat belt required tens of thousands of migrant and seasonal agricultural laborers to harvest and thresh the crop. One of the most comprehensive federal government studies regarding farm labor in the United States noted that in 1870 there were 2,885,996 wage earners

Figure 4. North Dakota threshing scene, circa 1900. (Courtesy, The Fred Hultstrand History in Pictures Collection, Institute for Regional Studies, NDSU, Fargo, N.D.)

employed in agriculture. In 1900, the number of such workers had increased by over fifty percent to 4,410,877. Although these increases occurred nationwide, they were especially dramatic in the Great Plains states, particularly in the western counties. According to a study by Eldon E. Shaw and John A. Hopkins for the Works Progress Administration, hired labor in the small-grain-producing region—North and South Dakota, Montana, Nebraska, and Kansas—remained fairly constant between 1909 and 1921. Farmers employed approximately one hundred eighty thousand agricultural laborers annually during these years. Family labor also remained constant during the same time period at six hundred thousand annually employed in agriculture. Hired labor peaked in 1927 at two hundred sixteen thousand, then began to steadily decline in the early 1930s due to the introduction of the combine, a period of drought, and lower production levels. (Employment specifically in wheat harvesting actually began to decline as early as 1925, due to increased use of the combine.) Still, whether their wheat farms were large or small, farmers relied on some form of seasonal labor to harvest their crop during the 1910s and 1920s. For example, in 1912 Kansas's farm owners drew eighty-five percent of their harvest labor force from outside the state. On one mid-size central Kansas farm in 1920, a wheat farmer needed ninety days of extra harvest and threshing labor to process his crop. In Oklahoma, the state's Commissioner of Labor reported in 1921 that the state employment offices provided 11,296 harvest workers to Oklahoma's wheat farmers.[10]

The wage laborers who migrated in massive numbers through the wheat belt and the resident workers who labored seasonally for wages on local farms were profiled by the federal government in a series of studies in the early 1920s. Donald D. Lescohier, an economics scholar and former superintendent of the Public Employment Office in Minneapolis, worked on these studies with the U.S. Department of Agriculture and the U.S. Department of Labor. Lescohier, with the help of a small team of assistants, produced several government publications and several articles for the general public. His studies contain a wealth of information, and like a good progressive, he displayed a great deal of empathy for the difficult working and living conditions of migrant laborers.

Lescohier's studies document the intense uncertainty of harvest and threshing employment, which was unlike any other agricultural labor system in the country. The demand for temporary wage labor in the plains, whether supplied by locals or migrants, lacked consistency throughout the region and from year to year. Moreover, just getting to harvest areas could be problematic. For example, when the southern plains harvest ended, only a fraction of the harvest workers in the area would travel north to join the northern plains harvest because trains— the primary mode of transportation for migrant wheat belt harvest labor—did not travel from south to north with the same frequency as from west to east. For railroad corporations, getting grain to market was the major criterion used to determine the placement of rail lines and scheduling of service. Some workers managed to continue to work the wheat harvest as it moved north, making use of haphazard northbound connecting rail lines. Once they arrived, however, they could find the labor market saturated, especially in parts of Nebraska and South Dakota, due to the influx of so many harvesters from the East. In some years, on the other hand, migrants from the southern plains, could get a jump on the harvesters from the East, for they were following the ripening wheat cycle that differed slightly each year due to climatic conditions.[11]

Lescohier and his team discovered that the number of resident laborers in a given county and the type of crops under cultivation helped determine the need for migrant laborers by area farmers. Some counties had enough resident labor to accommodate the seasonal nature of harvest work. In others, farmers recruited predominantly migrant workers to harvest local crops. In Kansas and Oklahoma, more than fifty percent of the harvest workforce migrated from county to county to bring in the winter wheat. Nebraska and South Dakota had much more diverse agriculture, which included corn, barley, rye, and oats along with wheat. These other crops did not require as large a harvest labor force because of their size and their staggered harvest periods. Therefore, farmers could harvest these other grains using only family or resident seasonal labor.

The need for harvest hand-labor hours for these crops was further reduced by agricultural technology. In fact, Nebraska and South Dakota farmers planted only half of their cropland in wheat, the primary grain crop requiring harvest and threshing labor.[12]

Harvest labor demands were also influenced by climatic conditions. Heavy rains during the growing season stimulated the growth of longer straw. On farms that used a binder, more labor was necessary in such years, due to the difficulty in handling the longer straw. A dry growing season could result in such a poor crop that farmers would not even harvest it. For instance, the 1921 harvest season was so poor in north-central South Dakota, eastern North Dakota, and in northwestern Kansas counties that farmers harvested little of their wheat crop. Counties that had required substantial extra labor in previous years did not need any extra labor at all in 1921. Rain during the harvest itself posed problems for the farmer and the harvester, delaying the harvest until the weather cleared. Few farmers were willing to keep migrants or seasonal workers on hand during the waiting period, so workers would arrive in a region and have to remain idle until the rains ended. In addition, farmers could lose part of a crop due to rain, reducing the amount of labor needed that particular season.[13]

Following the harvest, threshing could begin immediately or within several weeks. The size of a farm, the amount of labor on hand, the harvesting equipment used, and weather conditions all factored into the process of threshing. On large farms, many harvesters stayed on for threshing work. In Kansas, when a header was used during the harvest, it was common for the harvest and threshing to be combined into almost one operation. Instead of shocking grain cut by a binder and letting the sheaves dry, the heads of the wheat cut by a header could be hauled directly to a threshing machine.

Most farmers in the wheat belt, although they may have owned a binder or header, did not own their own threshing machine or even own one collectively. Over three-quarters of the farms in the 1921 threshing season used contract-threshing outfits, although the responsibility for hiring, feeding, and housing a threshing crew was not uniform. In Oklahoma and Kansas, the farmer usually had to hire the entire crew. In Nebraska and Minnesota, where it was more common for groups of farmers to collectively own threshing machines, a farmer usually had to hire only the engineer, a separatorman, and perhaps a waterman, who managed the water needs of the steam-powered machines. Local farmers volunteered the rest of the labor with the expectation that each farmer would help with his neighbors' threshing needs. In the Dakotas, while some threshing outfits supplied a cook car and boarded the crew that they supplied, the vast majority of threshing laborers were fed and housed by farmers themselves. The number of men used in threshing was only a small percentage of the overall seasonal labor workforce in the wheat belt, but these jobs were highly prized because the pay was higher than for general harvest labor.[14]

The Worklife Culture of Wheat Belt Wage Laborers

Lescohier and his investigative team of four men and one woman had a keen interest in the personal histories of the workers who harvested the nation's wheat crop. They wanted to explain who they were, where they came from, their motivation to become harvest hands, and the conditions of their employment. In a two-part series for the progressive magazine *The Survey*, Lescohier described the sources of his team's data for this series and his USDA reports. Throughout the wheat belt, Lescohier and his staff interviewed approximately thirty-six hundred harvest hands in 1919, 1920, and 1921. They interviewed workers in migrant labor camps, in wheat-town railroad yards, at employment offices, on the trains, and on the farms. They gathered information on thirteen hundred farms, ranging in size from eighty acres to one hundred ten thousand acres. One hundred and fifteen threshing crews, who worked on eight hundred farms, provided valuable information, as did a host of wheat farmers. Lescohier also made use of state and federal reports, especially the U.S. Employment Services data collected from twenty-nine thousand harvest workers in 1920 and 1921.

According to Lescohier, Great Plains farm workers, particularly those who followed the harvest from county to county and from state to state as migratory laborers, shared a common cultural experience that could be attributed to their age, gender, race, regional origin, trades, motives, mobility, employment experiences, wages, working conditions, and life on the road. The "bindle stiffs" or "harvest stiffs" in the Great Plains, as migrant agricultural laborers were sometimes called, tended to be young, unmarried white men in their twenties and thirties. To maintain a nearly all-white workforce in the southern plains, some advertisements for harvest labor actively discouraged black workers with the words "cannot use colored." Foreign-born workers were also a rare sight. In the northern plains, on the other hand, especially in the Dakotas, one could encounter Germans, Finns, and Scandinavians in the harvest. While the percentage of these foreign workers barely exceeded ten percent, they made up one-third of those workers who had no permanent residence, despite the fact that few of them had been in the country for less than ten years.[15]

Wage laborers involved in the wheat belt harvest came from all over the country, but the vast majority were from the Mississippi Valley, with Kentucky, Tennessee, Indiana, Ohio, and Michigan serving as the eastern border of the labor supply. Around fifty percent of the migrant workers interviewed in 1920 and 1921 had a residence in Kansas, Oklahoma, Arkansas, Iowa, Indiana, or Missouri, with the largest number from Missouri. Colorado and Montana were the only two states to the west of the wheat belt that provided a sizable contingent of migrant workers in the plains; small farmers and miners from Montana sought work during the harvest and threshing season in North Dakota, while Colorado migrants tended to journey to the western counties of Kansas and Nebraska on a seasonal basis to profit from the wheat crop.[16]

Lescohier's studies serve as a snapshot of the immediate postwar years and offer reasonably accurate descriptions of the early-twentieth-century seasonal farm labor workforce in the wheat belt. He and his team identified three basic categories of harvest laborers. One-third of the workers were farm workers by trade. These men and boys were either farmers or members of farm families who worked to supplement their limited farm incomes. The majority of this group were farmhands working in their home communities or nearby. Farmers preferred these workers because of their agricultural skills and their work ethic. A second third were laborers who lacked a specific trade. These workers tended to work the wheat belt harvest as part of a migratory pattern of employment. Such laborers worked not only in agriculture but also in construction, mining, and logging. The final third of the seasonal labor force comprised skilled or semiskilled workers largely from urban areas. These workers included mechanics, miners, railroad men, factory operatives, construction workers, professionals, office clerks, and students. This latter third of the workforce usually had more education than agricultural workers or common laborers, whether high school, trade school, or college.[17]

Seasonal and migrant workers participated in the wheat belt harvest for a variety of reasons. Those who primarily worked in agriculture, either as farmers or farmhands, looked upon the harvest as a means to supplement their incomes or as an annual part of their work cycle. If a small farmer could not sustain his family with earnings from his crops, helping other farmers in the region could make up the difference. Farmers whose crops failed due to disease or weather conditions also found the harvest a lifesaver. Skilled and semiskilled urban workers sought harvest employment during economic downturns. If un-employed, one could at least find work during the harvest season, even without much knowledge of farm work. Shocking wheat bundles or feeding a threshing machine did not require expertise, only stamina and a strong back. Workers who had no particular trade but who worked the harvest as part of a cycle of employment viewed it as an opportunity to earn a winter stake, that is, enough money to sustain them through the general underemployment of the winter months. Many of these workers spent their winters renting hotel rooms or staying in flophouses in such places as Kansas City, Minneapolis, or Chicago; those who went on to work the harvests of the Far West would spend their winters in cities such as Seattle or San Francisco. Some men and boys found motivation in the romantic adventure and the mystique associated with migrant or hobo life. Riding the freight trains through the Great Plains, living in the makeshift jungle camps, and finding camaraderie with other men in the western countryside probably sparked the imagination of many, especially those in the urban workforce.[18]

Despite sporadic efforts by well-intentioned railroad company owners, federal government officials, employment office officials, and farmers' organizations, no coordinated labor supply system to distribute labor to needed areas by rail ever existed in the United States. Canada, on the other hand, had an extensive employment recruitment system and a reduced-fare program for the harvest worker population moving through the western prairies of that country. Canada thus offered farmers and workers a more coordinated system of labor distribution than did the U.S., which presented haphazard harvest and threshing opp-ortunities. The search for work by U.S. harvesters was one experience these agricultural laborers shared.[19]

Harvesters with experience in the fields usually knew when the harvest season began, and journeyed to nearby wheat farms or to the wheat country itself if they were from other regions. Inexperienced harvesters found out about employment through family members who had been on the harvest before, or through acquaintances, handbills, or, most commonly, newspapers, which ran advertisements for employment as well as reports on the season's expected harvest. In early summer 1901, for example, the *New York Sun* reported that farmers needed five thousand extra harvesters in Kansas's wheat fields. In summer 1915, the *Minneapolis Morning Tribune* noted that the projected bumper crop in the wheat belt would require a much larger army of harvesters than in previous years. Unfortunately, reporters were sometimes misinformed about the actual need for extra labor. Some regions of the wheat belt ended up with more laborers than farmers needed. In other cases, employers could not hire enough seasonal labor. Most workers had been to the harvest at least once and based their search for work on experience and word of mouth. In one study by Lescohier and his staff, two-thirds of the workers interviewed had previous harvest experience, with the largest number having been on the harvest four or more times.[20]

Transportation to the harvest was almost exclusively by railroad, making this one of the most significant shared experiences of wheat belt harvesters. In the early 1920s, ninety-five percent of harvesters traveled throughout the wheat belt by freight trains or passenger trains. Because of the expense of "riding the cushions," as passenger train travel was referred to by harvesters, only about one-third of migrants paid a fare. The rest rode freight trains. Railroad companies knew the important role they played in supplying labor to the small-grain-producing regions. During peak harvest periods, railroad officials and brakemen looked the other way when literally thousands of harvesters climbed aboard freight trains headed for Kansas or Dakota wheat towns. As railroad companies were the major means by which farmers transported their produce to market, they had a vested interest in a successful harvest. Despite this symbiotic relationship, however, during slack periods, train crews frequently ejected harvesters; it was also not uncommon for brakemen to extort payment from migrants who hitched a ride on the train, even if they were traveling in large groups.[21]

Riding the rails could be quite a dangerous means of travel. Harvesters en route through the wheat belt shared their accommodations with a criminal element that preyed on any workers with cash in their pockets. As a worker accumulated wages over the course of many weeks, he was vulnerable to robbery and even murder. And although brakemen usually only aimed their guns over the heads of harvesters running to catch slow-moving trains, it was possible to get shot trying to board. Even the ride itself could be risky, as there were far more derailments and wrecks of freight trains than passenger trains. Riding the rods of a train, that is, underneath a boxcar, was a dangerous but sometimes necessary means of travel for men who needed to work the harvest but could not find an empty and unlocked boxcar. Accidents were unfortunately very common among migrants hitching rides on trains. For example, between 1901 and 1905, twenty-five thousand injures and fatalities occurred among this population on the U.S. railroad network.[22]

Freight train travel was not the most effective means of distributing harvest labor. Freights moved slowly, making it difficult to time one's arrival to a harvest. Either too many workers would arrive or not enough. Railroad officials would inform employment agencies in the wheat belt about the number of workers proceeding to a given community. The best that the U.S. Employment Service could do regarding freight train travel was to send out scouts to estimate the number of workers heading to a particular destination.[23]

Most harvesters experienced some frustration when searching for work. The two most common ways to find work were to use public employment offices or to wait in a railroad yard or on a city street for prospective employers. Public employment services were established in several states, with Nebraska acting first in 1897, and Kansas following in 1901. In 1904, representatives from South Dakota, Minnesota, Iowa, Nebraska, Missouri, and Kansas tried to solve the problem of poor and haphazard distribution by coordinating their need for labor during the harvest. The representatives designated Kansas City, which had a well-established employment bureau, as the distribution center for extra wheat belt labor. Yet state governments lacked the funds and the political will to see this project through. Even though state agricultural experts enthusiastically advocated such a coordinated harvest labor distribution effort, political leaders preferred to rely on the state labor commissioner's office and other state and local employment bureaus to disseminate harvest and threshing employment information.

Only after the creation of the wartime United States Employment Service in 1918 did an agency exist that could help channel harvest labor to needed areas. But even this service received minimal funding and had no means to distribute labor. Workers could find out where work was available, either through the U.S. Employment Service offices or through a state's labor commission, but it was up to the individual to get to the worksite and find an employer, a process that could take days. Once a worker had completed the job, he then needed to find information about more employment, and once again required transportation to reach it— usually involving a ride on the nearest freight train going in the direction where the worker assumed work could be found. In this way, workers lost many days of employment and chewed up their earnings searching for jobs.[24]

The earnings of harvesters varied, depending on the state or county in which they found employment and on the health of the agricultural economy. Overall wages for harvest labor steadily rose from the 1890s through the 1910s, peaking in 1920. Throughout the 1920s and into the

Great Depression, wages for farm labor fell below those for factory labor and remained below the cost of living at least through the mid-1920s. This trend can be attributed to a decrease in agricultural prices as depression gripped the wheat country during the decade. Farmers were no longer able to pay wages at the scale they had during the war and postwar years.

Few harvesters earned wages comparable to those of workers in more stable industries. In a 1921 government study, the only agricultural workers who earned $6 a day or more were threshermen, with engineers and separatormen the highest-paid. For basic harvest labor, Kansas paid the highest wage at $5 a day in the central and western portions of the state. Minnesota, North and South Dakota, and Nebraska averaged between $3 and $4 a day for harvest work in 1921. But 1921 was not a good year for wheat growers. Prices for wheat were falling after reaching record levels because of high demand during the war years and immediate postwar years. By 1921, however, net earnings for seasonal workers were only one-fourth or one-fifth what they were for factory workers or office clerks with steady full-time employment. These figures sharply contrast to those of the 1919 and 1920 seasons, in which a general harvest worker earned $8 a day in some wheat belt counties.

Regardless of patterns in wage rates, harvesters and threshermen had to bargain for a wage with farmers. In the end, few workers made their winter stake or the large amount of cash that they expected on the harvest or threshing circuit. In some cases, a hundred dollars, the clothes on one's back, and a pouch of tobacco were all a worker could claim at the end of the harvest.[25]

Working conditions in the wheat belt for the seasonal or migrant worker also varied to a considerable degree. When a worker did find employment, he would put in between ten and sixteen hours a day, despite summer heat that could reach 110 degrees. Farmers needed their grain harvested and threshed as quickly as possible. Poor weather, such as a heavy rain, could damage the crop, causing it to rot. Also, if farmers did not cut the grain fast enough, wheat heads would shatter, scattering seed on the ground. For these reasons, farmers wanted their wage laborers to work long hours to complete tasks in as few days as possible. Another factor determining the length of the workday was tradition. Some farmers had always worked ten-, twelve-, or sixteen-hour days during the harvest and threshing season, so workers, too, had to put in these hours if they wanted employment and a full day's pay, as they were paid by the day. Given that many workers went days between jobs, they welcomed any work they could find.

Overall, the work was arduous at best. Jack Miller, a migrant laborer who worked the wheat harvest for several seasons during the 1910s, remembered men passing out from heat exhaustion, including the "boss" on one particular farm in Kansas. Though incidents of men and horses dying of heat exhaustion were rare, they did occur. Miller also recalled that "working on the header barges, the wagons that hauled the grain, was so hard you never saw any fat men." Nels Peterson, a harvest worker who joined the IWW before the outbreak of World War I, described threshing work as difficult because of its long hours, poor food, and lack of adequate sleeping accommodations.[26]

Along with a wage, harvesters expected farmers to provide them with adequate food. Some workers complained about mediocre fare, while others raved about the meals they were given by a particular farmer, or more specifically, by a farmer's wife. The quality of the food often depended on the wealth of the farmer. For example, in the Red River Valley of the North, with its wealthy bonanza farms, cooks could and did provide memorable meals for harvesters. Harvester Jack Spiese reported that he was well fed in eastern North Dakota, but as he moved west, the farms became poorer and the food less memorable, though he was compensated by a slightly higher wage. He reasoned that the farms in western North Dakota, as well as those in Saskatchewan that he also harvested, faced "very uncertain crops" because of unpredictable weather conditions. Other harvest hands had a different theory for the varying quality of food: the ethnic background of the farmer was the determining factor. In Kansas, Joe Murphy, an itinerant worker and a man of many trades, noted that he and his fellow workers were fed five times a day during the harvest season. He asserted that the German farmers in Kansas fed workers well because they knew that a good diet made for an energetic worker.[27]

Next to low wages, the most common complaints of harvesters concerned the lack of affordable lodging and bathing facilities, and the treatment they received from wheat belt townspeople. On wealthier farms, a harvester or thresher could expect lodging in a bunkhouse with a bed and a relatively clean blanket. But most farmers could not afford to offer temporary housing for workers who labored in their fields for such short periods of time. It was not uncommon for a harvester to bring his own blanket and spend the night sleeping on a straw stack in the field. Usually, however, those farmers who did not have a bunkhouse gave migrant workers the use of their barns along with a blanket; in some cases, farmers provided tents for workers to spend their evenings in during the harvest. It was rare, though, for an employer to offer any bathing facilities. A worker may have had access to a cleaned-out horse trough with fresh water in the morning to wash up in, but a thorough bath had to wait until the worker could find a hotel or a migrant camp with an adjacent stream.[28]

Between jobs, it was up to each migrant to find a place to spend the night or to wait until employment became available. Thus, migrant workers could find themselves perceived as unwanted outsiders in a town, especially when employers in the area did not need itinerant workers. The terms *harvester, migrant, tramp, hobo,* and *bum* were sometimes used interchangeably by townspeople to describe migrant laborers. For those who took the time to consider the differences between these groups, it would have been apparent that harvesters, migrants, and hoboes were terms for men who worked, while tramp and bum described those who tended to avoid work. One harvester noted that he always carried a clean outfit to wear in town so that he would not look like he was unemployed. At the time, a worker's trade could be identified by what he wore. Therefore, to wear the clothing of a harvester when the harvest was over could pose a problem.

Being arrested for vagrancy—being unemployed and homeless—was a common concern for harvest workers. Migrants such as Jack Miller, Jack Spiese, Nels Peterson, Joe Murphy, and others sincerely believed that the police and municipal governments were operating a racket: to make revenue for the town, police would arrest men and fine them for being unemployed. In other instances, the threat of jail time for vagrancy could be used as a means to get undesirable elements out of a town. A more dangerous technique for keeping towns free of unwanted workers was the formation of vigilante parties. These groups of townspeople and local farmers ran migrants out of town or prevented them from disembarking from trains passing through when the workers were not needed. Incidents of severe beatings unleashed on groups of itinerant workers illustrate the ambivalence with which wheat belt communities viewed migrant labor.[29]

The only relatively safe haven for migrant agricultural laborers who did not have enough cash to spend on a downtown hotel room was the migrant labor camp, better known at the time as a "jungle." Jungles existed throughout the United States from the closing decades of the nineteenth century until the end of the Great Depression. But the kind of jungles used by agricultural laborers predominated in the West from roughly the 1890s to the 1920s. Jungles were simply makeshift communities for workers on the road. They were situated well outside of towns, though most were near a railroad line and a few were actually adjacent to railroad yards. Most important, a jungle needed to be close to a water source such as a stream or a creek. In these camps, a worker could make a meal, sleep, bathe, clean his clothing, socialize, and learn about employment opportunities. Jungles provided a worker with a comfortable place to reside between jobs, wait for the harvest season to begin, or set up a temporary home while he worked in a nearby wheat field as a harvester or thresher. Some jungles were secure enough that a worker could leave his belongings there without fear that they would be stolen. At times, cookware and cooking utensils would remain at jungles for succeeding groups of itinerant laborers to use. Cleaning such items and leaving them for other workers was part of the etiquette of the jungle.[30]

A distinctive camaraderie existed in these camps. Many of the road-weary laborers who inhabited them had limited skills and little in the way of resources, and had to sell their labor at whatever rate a farmer decided to pay. Frequently, workers would pool their resources in order to adequately feed each other. A "mulligan" or jungle stew often resulted, made of whatever a group of workers could contribute. Not all food items that went into the pot had actually been purchased, however. Begging in a nearby town was sometimes an option for hungry and penniless workers. And one reason that police "encouraged" unemployed and homeless workers to leave town was that theft of food was a frequent occurrence during the harvest period. Many a mulligan stew, with its mixture of chicken, carrots, potatoes, onions, and canned goods, also contained items stolen from local farms or warehouses.[31]

Not all jungles were safe havens for migrants. In some, a serious criminal element was present. Pilfering from a neighboring farm, though obviously a crime, did not compare to the armed robbery and, at times, outright murder committed by the men known as hi-jacks or highwaymen who preyed on migrant workers. This more serious criminal element sometimes spread to nearby communities as well. The approaches that local law enforcement took to address this problem could take extreme forms. Raiding jungle camps, destroying the site, and arresting men for vagrancy were common means of removing a real or imagined criminal threat.[32]

Of course, not all of the laborers who traversed the North American wheat belt had identical experiences, nor did they have the same reasons for engaging in harvest work. Workers with the resources to find adequate lodging in wheat towns between jobs did not have to stay in jungles. These workers may also have "ridden the cushions" rather than stealing rides on freight trains. Still other agricultural workers rarely traveled outside of their home counties in the wheat belt. Harvesters and threshermen came from a variety of backgrounds that informed their reasons for laboring for wages on Great Plains farms and the frequency with which they returned to the fields in subsequent harvest and threshing seasons.

Nevertheless, the evidence suggests that most wage laborers on the plains shared some attributes of a common worklife culture, one of the most important of which was the work itself. Harvesting and threshing were difficult hand-labor jobs performed over long hours under the searing summer sun. Here endurance was more important than skill. Moreover, a shared class position defined the relationships these men had with employers. Whether a worker was local or migrant, he had to market his labor and determine the acceptability of the wages and working conditions offered by farmers; a significant corollary to this common class experience was social homogeneity and mobility. And while these workers had different personal experiences in this vast region, many of them had to adapt to the ambivalent attitudes that farmers and townspeople had towards them.

Creating Industrial Farms in California

Unlike the Great Plains states, California never had an equal mix of large- and small-scale agriculture. From the beginning, when the United States took possession of the region from Mexico in the 1840s, large-scale agriculture predominated. Through fraud and manipulation, American settlers in California successfully gained control of vast tracts of Mexican land holdings. Due to this monopolistic control of the state's most arable land by large landowners, the small family farm venture never took hold to the extent that it did in other regions of the country. According to Carey McWilliams in *Factories in the Field*, as early as 1871 approximately five hundred families owned almost nine million acres of land in California. It was not uncommon for families and corporations, other than railroads, to own hundreds of thousands of acres of land. The bonanza farm grew out of these large land holdings and became a common feature of California agriculture from the mid-nineteenth century up to the present day. At first, the major California bonanza farms in the fertile regions of the centrally located Sacramento and San Joaquin Valleys grew wheat. California wheat farmers in 1889 produced forty million bushels, making them the nation's second-largest wheat producers.[33]

Like wheat growers in the plains states, California's wheat farmers fed the growing urban domestic and foreign markets for small grains, and railroads made the access to these markets possible. Unfortunately for the state's wheat growers, the Panic of 1873 caused profits in California wheat to decline precipitously. By the beginning of the next decade, wheat producers were experiencing only a four-percent return on average. During the 1880s, several factors converged to steer California agriculture towards fruit and vegetable production over wheat. Central and southern regions of the state possessed exceptionally fertile land, ample sunshine, and a long growing season; water was the only thing missing. With irrigation, California's agricultural development would change dramatically. Irrigation increased the value of land, making land speculators wealthy and making agricultural diversity possible for those with the capital to develop the soil. The expansion of railroads and the invention of the refrigerated rail car made transportation of fresh fruits and vegetables to eastern markets feasible. Once California agricultural industrialists moved in this direction, they discovered not only that their products were in great demand, but also that they had little competition outside of the state. Progress in canning and in dried fruit production further contributed to the success of the industry. By the turn of the century, California was the largest fruit- and-vegetable-producing state in the nation.[34]

In 1900, although the annual increase of new lands under cultivation began to slow, the amount of irrigated land increased, leading to the further expansion of vegetable and fruit production. The direct consequence of this trend was a greater need for seasonal wage laborers and the displacement of the traditional farmhand. In 1860, California farmers employed 13,541 agricultural laborers. By 1929, the number of agricultural laborers had reached 196,812, or 59.3 per cent of individuals working in California's agricultural industry. In no other state was the proportion this high. California agribusiness led the nation in the employment of farm workers and also in employing immigrant agricultural wage laborers.

Farming in California, as in many other western states, was an expensive undertaking during the first few decades of the century. Farm machinery, seed, storage, and railroad fees were all expensive fixed costs from the farmers' point of view. However, they considered labor a variable cost, one that they could manipulate. Therefore, they went out of their way to find the most inexpensive labor source possible. In California, "cheap labor" meant immigrants, particularly Asians and Hispanics.

California fruit and vegetable farmers successfully mechanized much of their cultivation and planting by the 1910s. Machinery, especially the increased use of the tractor, allowed them to cultivate vast acres of a single crop. For example, John D. Spreckles, a sugar beet grower and a member of the "Sugar Trust," had twenty thousand acres of land devoted solely to sugar beet production. According to McWilliams, almost the entire field labor workforce in sugar beets consisted of immigrant workers, mostly Japanese and Mexicans. McWilliams categorized such operations as plantations that relied on "coolie labor." Despite the innovative use of technology in California agriculture throughout the first few decades of the twentieth century, harvesting and certain other aspects of cultivation remained intensive, hand-labor tasks. Mechanized farming actually *increased* the need for temporary wage laborers, while reducing the need for year-round farm work in the form of permanent farmhands. These highly skilled agricultural workers had been essential to diverse farming operations. Traditionally, the farmhand had been an apprentice farmer who would eventually earn enough from his wages to purchase his own farm. Unfortunately for aspiring farmers, the industrial farms of California required large numbers of temporary wage laborers, and supervisors to manage the workforce. They had little need for apprentice farmers.

Farmers in the state tended to focus on one or two crops, depending on the size of their farms. But the nature of agricultural work on these farms could only offer laborers at most several months of employment each year. California's agricultural industry could not support many full-time, year-round farm workers. Furthermore, the San Joaquin and Sacramento valleys, and other such areas, had very small resident populations. Therefore, migrant seasonal labor systems proved necessary to harvest and process the state's produce.[35]

California's Immigrant Farm Laborers

Even before the transition to vegetable and fruit growing, the use of thousands of low-paid migrant and seasonal agricultural laborers in the wheat-growing bonanza farms of the Sacramento River Valley disturbed politicians, trade union leaders, university agricultural scholars, and associations of small farmers. Few of these migrant workers had land of their own, permanent residences, high-level skills, or steady year-round employment that could keep them out of poverty. Many competed for jobs in urban areas during the winter and spring months when farm work was scarce or nonexistent. Though a majority of these early agricultural workers were young white men, a substantial minority were Asian immigrants.

The use of such workers concerned those who advocated agrarianism. For many Americans in the late nineteenth century, the small family farm embodied agrarian values. This value system, which emphasized independence, virtue, and political engagement, was thought to provide the foundation upon which the American Republic rested. Those who promoted fruit and vegetable growing in the 1880s and 1890s thought not only that California could be hugely successful in this industry, but also that such enterprises would lend themselves to smaller farms, thereby mitigating the farm labor problems of large wheat farms. Yet when fruit and vegetable farming took on the same contours that wheat farming had a generation earlier—large-scale farms with little crop diversity that required large numbers of temporary agricultural workers—profits were far too great to make the agrarianist's vision of the small family farm viable.[36]

One of the unique features of California's agricultural labor force was its ethnic and racial diversity. Waves of immigrants from in the mid-nineteenth century onward supplied farm owners with the inexpensive labor that they needed. The first group of immigrants to secure farm labor jobs was the Chinese. They replaced many of the Far West's surviving American Indians who had worked as agricultural laborers. Originally, the Chinese found employment in railroad building and mining, but once construction of the Central Pacific's transcontinental railroad was complete, thousands of these laborers lost their jobs. When they were also excluded from mine work by whites, the Chinese began to work in agriculture as farm laborers, with many aspiring to be farm owners themselves.[37]

At first, farmers considered the Chinese to be better farm workers than American Indians and in some respects better than white laborers. Chinese workers proved to be efficient and reliable. They also were willing to work in a gang-labor system, under the supervision of contractors who could insure a dependable supply of labor. Chinese laborers worked for lower wages than any other group of workers, and did not require year-round support on farms, as they were hired as temporary labor. Those defending the use of Chinese labor claimed that these Asian workers did not aspire to the same living conditions as whites nor did they seek to own their own land. They were content, according to California's large landholders, to live as a permanent agricultural labor force. Therefore, they were the perfect workers, especially on California's wheat, fruit, and vegetable bonanza farms of the late nineteenth century, at least according to California's large landholders.

Creating such a dependent class of laborers with little social connection to the mainstream of California society proved extraordinarily valuable to those who desired a cheap, docile, and exploitable labor supply. But the California labor movement, advocates of agrarianism, and racist elements of the electorate successfully pushed for the passage of the Chinese Exclusion Act of 1882. The belief, however, that excluding further Chinese immigration would aid the agrarians' goal of bringing an end to massive farming operations in California and their dependent labor force proved erroneous. The vision of white farmhands who would work only long enough at farm labor to be able to purchase their own farms failed to materialize. Farm owners continued to employ wage laborers on a temporary basis only. Furthermore, the cost of starting a farm in California was beyond the reach of most farm laborers, whether they were American-born whites or Chinese immigrants. And the fresh immigration of Japanese workers in the 1890s simply replaced one exploitable immigrant agricultural labor force with another.

Of course, despite the Chinese Exclusion Act, Chinese laborers still worked in agriculture. Some became farmers in their own right, and the rest did not behave as a docile workforce. In fact, the Chinese developed labor associations, called *tongs* or "the six companies," to channel employment opportunities for the Chinese community. Farmers were hostile to *tongs* because of their secretive nature, initiation fees, and membership dues. They seemed disquietingly similar to labor unions, although they functioned more like mutual-aid societies, aiding sick or injured workers and providing burial services to members. Because most economic opportunities were closed to the Chinese in California, farm work continued to be a significant source of employment that they tried to manipulate to their best advantage under difficult circumstances.[38]

With the restrictions on further immigration from China and the very high male-to-female ratio of those Chinese already living in California, Japanese workers eventually superseded Chinese. As of 1910, Japanese immigrants outnumbered Chinese in the California population and in employment in agriculture. Like their Chinese counterparts, most Japanese agricultural laborers were men in their teens, twenties, and thirties. They, too, formed labor associations, often worked as gang laborers, and provided their own housing and food. All the employer needed to do was to pay them a wage. Farmers soon found, though, that the Japanese were not a docile workforce either, and that they, too, tended to strive for farm ownership.[39]

A substantial portion of the Japanese workers who immigrated to California from Japan and those who immigrated from Hawaii were farmers or farm laborers by trade. These workers congregated in a number of agricultural enterprises and attempted to control the labor market in those industries. They accepted wages lower than the Chinese, a practice that initially endeared them to white farmers. The Japanese labor associations, however, proved to be different from the Chinese *tongs*. A common tactic they employed was to focus on a particular agricultural enterprise and undercut other labor-supply companies. Once they dominated the workforce in that industry or on a number of farms, they would threaten to strike at a critical period during the harvest season. The labor association boss would present the employer with a list of demands of the workers under his supervision. This collective bargaining strategy worked in many instances, forcing farmers to raise wages and improve working conditions.

Japanese workers, though, did not form labor associations solely for the promotion of workers' interests. Most Japanese immigrants in agriculture wished to have their own farms, or at least make the transition from farm laborer to farm tenant. For this reason, instead of considering Japanese farm workers as agrarian comrades, white farmers saw them as a serious threat. As willing tenant farmers, and as farmers who employed their countrymen when possible, the Japanese grew to dominate several sectors of California's fruit and vegetable industries. By 1907, Californians overwhelmingly supported federal restrictions on Japanese immigration, and several years later the state legislature passed an Alien Land Act designed to prevent Japanese and other immigrant groups who were ineligible for citizenship due to their race from owning their own farms.[40]

Another means by which farmers tried to thwart Japanese successes as organized farm workers or as small farmers involved using immigrant workers from India. These workers, mostly young men, began turning up in California in noticeable numbers around 1906 after originally arriving in British Columbia and working their way down the Pacific Coast. Most of them found employment in railroad construction, but quickly took up farm work when the opportunity presented itself. Farmers had mixed opinions regarding this group of workers, whom they tended to refer to as Hindus. Some considered them less physically fit than Japanese or Chinese workers, not as intelligent, and not as effective as other Asian agricultural laborers. But others, particularly cotton growers in southern California's Imperial Valley, found Indians to be skilled agriculturalists. Indian workers developed labor associations similar to those of the Japanese and Chinese, and at times successfully bargained for higher wages or better working conditions using collective action and the labor contractor as a collective bargaining agent. And like the Japanese and Chinese, some Indians achieved land ownership or farm tenancy. The Alien Land Act had the same impact on these workers as it did on other immigrants, keeping many employed only as farm workers, or in some instances as foremen. Moreover, the Asiatic Exclusion League (a West Coast organization devoted to preventing further Asian immigration) successfully supported legislation limiting Indian immigration.[41]

Despite exclusionist legislation and discrimination, Chinese, Japanese, and Indian workers continued to find employment in agriculture. Yet their collective presence within the California agricultural workforce paled in comparison to that of Hispanic workers. Hispanics, who came almost exclusively from Mexico, would make up the majority of immigrant agricultural laborers in California soon after the United States entered World War I. From that point through the rest of the twentieth century, Hispanics, whether born in the United States or immigrating from Latin America, would grow to dominate the farm labor supply.[42]

In 1900, few Mexican immigrants resided more than one hundred miles north of the U.S.-Mexico border. At that time, most resident Hispanics were born in the United States. But over the next two decades, Mexican immigration increased from a trickle to a steady stream. Some were fleeing their country due to revolutionary upheaval, but many journeyed to the U.S. to take advantage of wartime agricultural employment opportunities, especially in the Southwest. California farmers readily employed Mexican workers because they did not have labor associations and they worked for lower wages than Chinese, Japanese, or Indian laborers. At first most Mexican workers were young, single men. They either traveled the rail systems like migrant laborers in the Great Plains or found employment though labor contractors from many industries, including agriculture. These recruited workers had their transportation paid for and worked in gangs for a variety of American employers, from a railroad construction company in Kansas to a large cotton grower in Texas to a fruit farmer in California.[43]

During the 1910s, Mexican laborers distinguished themselves from other immigrant farm worker groups by increasingly coming to the U.S. as families. These families could be found in most of California's agricultural regions. They settled in the Sacramento, San Joaquin, and Imperial Valleys and in the citrus-growing region of Southern California, working for white as well as Asian farmers. Mexicans became a favored workforce in agriculture during the war years and over the course of the 1920s because they tended to work as individuals or as family units rather than as gangs of young single men. Japanese, Chinese, and Indian workers tended to arrive as a group, starting and stopping work together. Such groups always presented the possibility of a strike, although a coordinated strike by more than one social group was rare before 1930. Mexican workers, especially during the war years, arrived as recruited workers. They were dependent on their employer not only for wages, but also for housing, food, and other amenities of life. Collective action proved difficult for Mexican workers because of their dependency and the very real threat of swift deportation.[44]

Making the Least with White Male Privilege

The crucial shared experience of these social groups of workers involved their common class position in California farming. Filipino and Korean agricultural workers, as well as southern and eastern European workers such as Portuguese, Italian, Greek, and Armenian immigrants were also included in this mix. All of these groups found a niche in California's agricultural labor systems during the first three decades of the twentieth century. European immigrants, though they faced prejudice and stereotyping, had greater access to the limited agricultural ladder in California than did immigrants from other areas, and some attained farm ownership, thereby transcending their class position. They also had more economic opportunities in urban areas, not to mention educational opportunities for their children. Therefore, Europeans did not usually find themselves forced into agricultural labor or menial employment in cities to the same degree as racial minorities. But those who worked as agricultural laborers remained in the same class as non-white immigrants.[45]

Until World War I, white agricultural workers could be found in almost any agricultural enterprise in California, and accounted for the simple majority of farm laborers in the state. Because of racial prejudices, employers considered them more intelligent and capable of more personal initiative than their Asian or Mexican counterparts. Many employers believed that only white workers were capable of working without supervision. Jobs available for white workers paid by the hour, day, week, or month, whereas those offered to Asians, Mexicans, and the small number of African Americans in agriculture paid by the day or by piece rate. Even so, there were many agricultural laborers working in the fields or in the orchards who were white, and many workers not of European descent, particularly Chinese and Japanese women and girls, could be found in packing houses. The agricultural industry was so vast and varied that generalizations about which group worked in what capacity cannot be made without acknowledging numerous exceptions.[46]

The white farm labor force can be broken down into several types of workers with differing motivations for seeking agricultural employment. Those most sought-after by the dominant white farmer population were workers who intended to become farmers themselves, or at least to secure permanent employment in agriculture. A small but preferred group were local families and single women working seasonally. Another group of white workers were those who worked in agriculture only when not employed in their given trade. The economic panics of 1893, 1907, and 1913 forced urban white male workers into farm labor and other forms of seasonal labor such as construction, canning, and logging. These workers would return to their trades once the opportunity presented itself. The fourth and most numerous group of white workers in agriculture comprised migrant and seasonal workers. These agricultural laborers did not endear themselves to farmers, because they were undependable. The rapid turnover of white labor, despite their higher wages, "forced" employers to hire Chinese, Japanese, and Mexican workers.

It is common to find, in congressional testimony and contemporary studies of the era, employers expressing resentment toward white workers. They held migrant white laborers responsible for the presence of foreign-born workers and the low wages for farm work in comparison to other forms of employment. Time and again employers commented on white migrant labor's heavy turnover in contrast to the reliable work of Asian and Mexican workers. Asian and Mexican workers would simply work for a lower wage than white workers would. Yet these employers shed crocodile tears over having to employ low-wage immigrants, and that was why they hired them. However, the only reason these immigrants worked for such low wages was because they lacked the same employment opportunities that white workers had. Many urban employers simply would not hire them for anything but the most menial jobs. Actually, in some rare instances white employers admitted that they preferred to hire immigrant gang labor even if that required negotiating a wage and working conditions with the labor contractor, who in some instances worked as a foreman. Here, at least, employers felt they were assured of reliable, hard-working, supervised laborers.[47]

California's white migrants who worked as farm laborers, packing-house workers, or common laborers were largely under the age of forty, with a significant number in their twenties. Few had a high level of education or trade skills. Most were not California residents, and considered themselves part of the floating labor force in the American West. They rode the rails singly or in small groups throughout California, and occasionally to worksites in the Great Plains and Pacific Northwest. They carried their belongings on their backs in the form of a bindle, and resided in California's jungles between jobs if they could not afford to stay in a skid row hotel in San Francisco, Los Angeles, Sacramento, Fresno, or any of the smaller towns in the state. Some worked in California's logging or mining industries or in one of many enterprises such as railroad or highway construction. Working through the spring and summer months, they hoped to earn enough of a stake to last them through the underemployment of the winter months which largely shut down the state's agriculture, construction, logging, and mining industries.[48]

During the 1910s, as many as one hundred fifty thousand migrant and seasonal workers roamed California in search of agricultural employment. White workers tended to migrate over larger distances, while Asian and Mexican workers tended to work within a particular region, valley, or industry, creating a socioeconomic network to support their fellow immigrants. For example, Japanese workers were known for traveling to distant harvest fields using bicycles or motorcycles. Once the day's work was completed, they returned each evening to their home community. Though the majority of workers were young, single, and male, immigrant workers, especially Mexicans, tried to establish families and use agricultural labor as their primary source of income. Whole families of Mexican workers could be found in the farm fields that surrounded their communities performing harvest and other farm work. Like most immigrants, Mexicans aspired to land ownership or other forms of more permanent work. Whites, on the other hand, generally tended to maintain a solitary, itinerant lifestyle.

White workers, of course, had many more economic opportunities than non-whites. They did not fear deportation. Even newly arrived white immigrant workers had the right to naturalization, the opportunity to own land, and few restrictions on housing as long as their income was adequate. When confronted with difficult working conditions, low pay, or an abusive supervisor, whites usually left in protest to seek another job. Asian and Mexican workers had to put up with such problems because their employment options were limited. They would leave employment collectively at times over poor working conditions or initiate an actual strike, but the latter was not common.[49]

The working conditions and pay for California's migrant labor workforce depended largely on the national origin, skin color, gender, and age of the worker. White workers could experience preferential treatment in the form of a secure job for the season and higher pay. Farmers reserved the higher-paying packinghouse, teamster, foreman, and farmhand jobs for white males. These jobs paid board along with the wage. Farmers preferred to give piece-rate jobs, such as fieldwork, canning, and some packinghouse work, to women, children, and Asian and Hispanic workers. These jobs usually did not come with a board option. Consequently, non-white workers, who were paid less and forced to live in segregated labor camps and communities, endured a very low standard of living.[50]

Even though white workers in California received higher pay from farmers because of their race, those who worked in the fields, orchards, and packinghouses experienced many of the same working, traveling, and living conditions as the migrant labor force in the Great Plains. Although there were contract labor companies to manage the labor of minority groups in the California agriculture industry, few employment agencies linked whites with harvest labor jobs. Workers could make use of some agencies for other kinds of temporary employment, such as construction, but they had to pay a fee for such job placement services, which caused resentment and sometimes discouraged their use. Farm workers could find out about harvest work in newspapers and circulars, through word of mouth and past experience, and by congregating in agricultural towns. Traveling to find work involved the precarious practice of hitching rides on freight trains and avoiding detection by a brakeman. For those workers who could not afford hotel or boarding room costs, living in a jungle proved a primary alternative. Unlike Japanese, Chinese, Indian, and Mexican workers, white harvest workers were occasionally provided with sleeping accommodations by farmers. These usually consisted of a haystack in the field or a bed of straw in a barn. Finally, as in the case of other itinerant workers hoping to earn an adequate winter stake, farm workers tended to fall short of their income goals, despite a variety of employment opportunities.[51]

In California, these disparate farm labor social groups were not united by a common culture. Their cultures were unique to their labor and community-building experiences. As each successive wave of immigrants arrived and sought a niche in the agricultural economy of California, and as each seasonal migration of white laborers moved through the state, distinctive living and working patterns found reinforcement. The only truly shared feature of the lives of those who worked in California agriculture that crossed cultural boundaries was their class position. Selling one's labor in an industry that rarely paid enough for workers to save for their own farms locked many into permanent wage labor status. But while they had social class in common, there was little class unity. Race, ethnicity, and gender divided the state's agricultural workers. Racism among white workers, isolation of immigrant groups, language barriers, and employers who pitted one ethnic or racial group against another to reduce their labor costs prevented farm workers from coming together as a class.

Pockets of Industrial Agriculture in the Pacific Northwest

The use of farm labor in the Pacific Northwest and the worklife culture of the workers there, like California and the Great Plains, were tied intimately to the course of agricultural development. Settlement in the Pacific Northwest, though concurrent with the plains and California, grew at a slower rate than those regions during the last third of the nineteenth century. Unlike the vast growing areas of the plains states and California's central valleys, there were forests, mountain ranges, and stretches of arid plateaus that divided the arable land in the Pacific Northwest. Agriculture, therefore, tended to develop in pockets.

Wheat and fruit were significant crops in the early agricultural history of the region. The Willamette Valley of western Oregon, the Oregon Trail's primary termination point, led the development of a significant farming economy. Dry-land farming took hold in the Walla Walla Valley several decades later, making this area, in what eventually became the state of Washington, highly prosperous. In the Palouse region of southeastern Washington, wheat farmers turned the rolling hills of Whitman County into the highest-yielding wheat-producing county in the United States by 1910. In the early decades of the twentieth century, fruit growing also developed rapidly in the region, especially as irrigation became available in the 1880s. The irrigated valleys of the Snake River in present-day Idaho, the Hood River and Rogue River Valleys of Oregon, and the Okanogan, Wenatchee, and Yakima Valleys in Washington became centers of commercial orchard agriculture. The Yakima and Wenatchee Valleys, by the first decade of the twentieth century, produced huge quantities of fruits, especially apples, for markets both domestic and foreign. By 1917, Washington had become the nation's largest apple producer.[52]

As in other areas of the West, access to market proved crucial to commercial agriculture. Expansion of local rail lines on the Columbia Plateau and completion of a northern transcontinental rail line linked farmers and ranchers to domestic and international markets. The Northern Pacific, in particular, created a link between eastern Washington and the Puget Sound region. Access to the port facilities of the Sound allowed Pacific Northwest wheat to be sold in European and Asian markets. The eastern Washington counties of Adams, Columbia, Garfield, Lincoln, Walla Walla, and Whitman formed the contours of Washington's wheat belt, with the city of Spokane to the north serving as the region's political, economic, and financial locus. A Northern Pacific rail line linking the wheat ranching operations of southeast Washington to Spokane ensured that city's dominance over the area.

Even though Washington's wheat industry produced some of the same varieties of wheat as the Great Plains, its agricultural practices differed from that area's in several ways. The higher levels of precipitation and the higher elevation led farmers to experiment with different grains and practices to suit the region. For example, eastern Washington farmers tended to grow soft wheat and Great Plains farmers tended to grow hard wheat. While Great Plains farmers embraced silos and grain elevators to store and transport grain, these were slow to take hold in the Northwest because farmers there believed that sacking the grain prevented spoilage. In addition, the very hilly Palouse region stimulated farmers to experiment with equipment that could adapt to steep terrain; farmers in the region used either headers or binders, depending on their preference.[53]

The railroad companies played a key role in developing the irrigation projects necessary for large farming operations in the Yakima and Wenatchee Valleys. Like the central valleys of California, the southern region of the Columbia Basin possessed fertile soil, abundant sunshine, and a long growing season. And, like California's fruit and vegetable farming regions, all that was lacking was water. After a modest initial effort by farmers' associations, irrigation projects accelerated with subsidies from the Northern Pacific. The Sunnyside district along the southern portion of the Yakima River was eventually irrigated under the auspices of the Washington Irrigation Company. According to Robert E. Ficken and Charles P. LeWarne, in *Washington: A Centennial History*, "[B]y

1904 the Sunnyside project included seven hundred miles of canals and laterals irrigating thirty-six-thousand acres." No other reclamation project in the Pacific Northwest reached these proportions at the time.

Yet farmers quickly found that they needed even more water than that provided by this major project, so despite their ideology of rugged individualism, the farm owners of this portion of eastern Washington benefited from one of the era's largest federally sponsored reclamation projects. With help from the Department of the Interior, the Yakima project got underway at the end of 1905. By 1910, the Yakima Valley had more than two hundred thousand acres of irrigated land. Irrigation raised the price for an acre of land dramatically. An acre in Yakima County, for example, cost around $126, compared to $47 in nearby Whitman County. Though farm sizes remained relatively small in Yakima, averaging 96 acres, irrigated orchard agriculture proved to be highly successful. Though the expansion of irrigated and cultivated acreage leveled off in 1918, apple production steadily increased due to advances in growing methods. In 1913, the area's farmers produced over twenty-

Figure 5. Birchmount Orchard picking crew pose for a photograph in Wenatchee, Washington, circa 1925. (A. G. Simmer, Washington State Historical Society, Tacoma)

Figure 6. Apple packers sorting and packing fruit in Yakima, Washington, 1908. (Asahel Curtis Collection, #11303, Washington State Historical Society, Tacoma)

six million pounds of apples. On the same acreage, these farmers produced over one hundred thirty million pounds of apples only eight years later. The value of their produce peaked during this period at more than three million dollars in 1921.[54]

The Industrial Labor Component of Washington's Commercial Agriculture

Washington's wheat belt, coupled with its extensive fruit orchards, made the state the largest user of migrant agricultural labor in the Pacific Northwest. In the 1920s, two-thirds of Washington's agricultural income derived from wheat and apples, crops that required tens of thousands of migrant and seasonal farm laborers. Though apple growers used some year-round farmhands, their primary labor needs arose at harvest time, when seasonal workers were required to pick, haul, and pack huge quantities of apples quickly for shipment to market (figs. 5 and 6). Wheat-producing regions also required a large seasonal labor force, like that in the Great Plains, because wheat-harvest work in Washington included the labor-intensive task of sacking the wheat after threshing (figs. 7 and 8). One of the largest agricultural operations in Washington was the McGregor family's wheat-growing enterprise in Whitman County. During

Figure 7. Harvest workers transport wheat bundles to the threshing
site at the Herman Curtis Ranch, Garfield, Washington, 1915.
(Courtesy, Glen Curtis)

Figure 8. Aftermath of a day of threshing wheat on the Herman
Curtis Ranch, Garfield, Washington, 1909. Note grain is sacked
rather than stored in a grain silo. (Courtesy, Glen Curtis)

the harvest and threshing seasons before 1920, the family usually needed 120 workers and 320 mules and horses to harvest, thresh, sack, and transport their crop to warehouse. Only in the mid-1920s would the use of combines and other laborsaving technology begin to displace these temporary workers.[55]

Migrant farm labor systems in Washington bore similarities to those of both the Great Plains and California, but with key differences. In the first three decades of the twentieth century, Washington farmers annually employed approximately thirty-five thousand migrant and seasonal agricultural laborers. This number pales in comparison to the numbers used in the Great Plains or in California. The micro-agricultural pockets of Washington prevented the same kind of large-scale enterprises that were so common in the other regions of the West. Moreover, family and community labor made up a substantial component of the overall seasonal harvest labor force required in early summer and through the fall. Still, Washington's cash-crop agriculture needed migrants to help with the wheat harvest in the southeastern portion of the state and the fruit harvest in the Yakima and Wenatchee Valleys.[56]

The overwhelming majority of the migrant agricultural workers in Washington and the Pacific Northwest were white, native-born, single men under the age of forty. Nevertheless, it was not uncommon to find African Americans, Filipinos, Chinese, and Pacific Northwest Indians working as agricultural laborers, too, and by the end of the 1910s and early 1920s, women and families of harvesters made up ever-larger segments of this workforce. Like other agricultural workers in the West, those in the Pacific Northwest came from a variety of backgrounds, but, especially before 1920, they tended to be itinerant laborers by trade, rather than the regionally based farm workers one might have found on an asparagus farm in California or the out-of-work tradesmen working on a Dakota wheat farm. They rode the rails from job site to job site, spending most of their labor time in Washington because the state had a much greater use for migrant and seasonal farm labor than did Oregon or Idaho. Like most agricultural workers in the West, few could afford to "ride the cushions," so most hopped a freight train when they could get away with it. An empty side-door Pullman boxcar was the favored mode of transportation. A considerable number also worked in whatever seasonal jobs were available, including construction, mining, and logging. Many traveled to Washington from outside the state, stopping to work the wheat harvest in the Palouse and moving on to the apple harvest in Yakima. Some would continue down to California for more work or head back to their home states. Others would hole up in Seattle, Spokane, Portland, or in another Pacific Northwest city with their winter stake. Those who were residents of the state and had a trade returned home to work, whether as a longshoreman in Tacoma or as a shingle weaver in Everett.[57]

Frequently, workers had to wait in a jungle until the harvest began. Like their counterparts in the Great Plains, if they were short of money and could not buy food or were insulted by the cost, they sometimes resorted to stealing from farmers. Thomas Horland, in a letter to the *Industrial Worker*, noted just such an experience. He and another man left Spokane late one evening by freight train and got off at a spot just south of the city. Early the next morning they went looking for work, but the farmers had no need for them and made them feel unwelcome. Together with a third man they bought what they considered an expensive and rather small loaf of bread from a local farmer for fifteen cents. Still hungry, and with no freight train departing soon, they decided to visit the farmer's chicken coop and enjoyed chicken stew later that day. Horland noted that following their meal, with no train heading deeper into the wheat country, they "considered it best to hike." They walked the eleven miles to Spangle, Washington, and headed to the local jungle to wait for work. There they found out from resident "bums" and a "cow puncher" which farmer had an oversupply of chickens. They enjoyed another meal at a farmer's expense, then waited for the expected harvest work, which was to begin a week later.[58]

To find work, migrants—whether in Colfax, Washington; Fresno, California; or Fargo, North Dakota—usually made themselves visible in the center of town and waited for local farmers to offer them a job. When they were needed, farmers, townspeople, and small business owners welcomed their presence. The farmers needed their labor to harvest their crops, and small businesses could profit by providing harvesters with food, drink, clothing, and lodging. Nevertheless, when temporary workers were no longer needed, when petty criminal activity arose among the migrants living in nearby jungles, or when townspeople simply grew tired of a wandering element, law enforcement could take drastic action. For example, in January 1911, a city marshal dynamited two cave-like jungles along the banks of the Yakima River near Prosser, Washington. Even though a nearby construction project probably employed some of the migrants living there, their presence was not welcome by the local community.[59]

Worklife Culture

The worklife culture of the seasonal and migrant portion of Washington's agricultural labor force had a great deal in common with that of the workers in the Great Plains and of the white male workers of California. Though the agricultural industries depended on these largely under-skilled workers for the mass production of grains, fruits, and vegetables, few received adequate compensation for their work or had satisfactory living and working conditions. Migrant workers also found themselves, socially and culturally, outside the mainstream resident community.

Of course, not all of the West's migrant and seasonal farm laborers shared this experience. California's diverse agricultural labor population, for example, made cultural unity impossible. The large number of local or "home guard" workers did not share the life of the migrant, but lived and worked among their employers year round. Moreover, even within the cohort of migrant laborers, differences in needs and desires diluted a common worklife culture.

Nevertheless, a common class experience did exist. For example, most white workers, whether men or women, could not secure year-round farm work nor attain farm ownership in California or other western states any more than could Japanese or Mexican immigrants. Farmers may have hired whites over Asian or Hispanic workers, and even paid them a higher wage, but the work was generally the same regardless of the worker's race or ethnicity. Field and packinghouse jobs required long hours, repetitive tasks, and heavy lifting under a hot sun or in a poorly ventilated warehouse. These low-paying jobs were temporary and did not translate into permanent employment, whether the employee was a resident seasonal worker or a migrant. In short, agricultural laborers in the American West could find unity in their class position, the nature of their labor, and in their common exploitation at the hands of farmers. In the years following the founding of the Industrial Workers of the World, harvest workers who joined the union—harvest Wobblies—would draw on these shared experiences of class, work, and exploitation to build an inclusive union of agricultural workers that bridged the workers' cultural differences.

Chapter Two

Organizing Workers in the Streets and on the Farms

⌘⌘⌘

The IWW's first opportunity to bridge the divisions created by a multiracial and multiethnic agricultural workforce took place in Wheatland, California, a small town near Marysville in the Sacramento River Valley. There, Ralph Durst and his brother owned a large farm and ranch that produced a variety of cash crops. Ralph Durst, the farm and ranch manager, supervised the production of hops, the Dursts' most significant crop. For a couple of years, the farm produced an abundant crop of hops that fetched a high price. In 1913, however, the price of hops fell. For the Durst brothers to continue making a profit, they determined that harvest labor costs had to be cut. At the same time, workers would have to harvest every single hop flower to get as much of the crop to market as possible. For the August harvest, Ralph Durst advertised in fliers throughout the region and in newspapers in California, Oregon, and Nevada for workers to journey to his farm to pick hops. In one flier, he promised a job to every white picker who arrived at his farm by August 5. Though he did not need more than fifteen hundred workers—and could not even accommodate that many—almost three thousand men, women, and children answered his call. These workers represented the gamut of the California farm labor workforce: Cubans, Puerto Ricans, Mexicans, Hawaiians, Syrians, Japanese, Indians, Poles, Greeks, Italians, and Lithuanians made up the largest contingents of foreign-born workers; in all, the workers spoke twenty-seven different languages. Native-born workers included migrant white males, resident seasonal day laborers, small farmers from the Sierra foothills, and a number of local white families who regularly participated in the harvest season in the valley (fig. 9).

When the workers arrived, they discovered that the labor camp was not rent-free. Individuals or families could rent a tent and space on the campsite for seventy-five cents a week, but there were not enough tents available for the number of workers. Some had to construct shelters out of poles and gunnysacks, and others had to sleep in the open on piles of straw. Durst provided no blankets for the chilly evenings. If workers

Figure 9. Harvest workers pose for a photograph at the Durst Hop Ranch at the time of the 1913 strike. (Courtesy, Walter P. Reuther Library, Wayne State University)

chose not to buy food at the grocery store on Durst's property, from which he received a percentage of the profits, they had to walk to town, as Durst would not allow groceries to be delivered to the ranch. Durst also provided little in the way of toilet facilities, leaving the workers to make do with nine crudely built toilets. The California Commission of Immigration and Housing (CCIH), a committee charged with investigating working and living conditions throughout the state, reported that these toilets "were also used as receptacles for the garbage from the camp, as well as for the offal of slaughtered animals, and swarmed with blue flies and were alive with maggots." Worse still, the drinking water supply was inadequate and dangerous. Those wells that were not dry contained stagnant water and were situated near garbage and toilet areas. Consequently, diseases such as typhoid, dysentery, and malaria circulated among the workers.[1]

The wages Durst offered his workers also demonstrate the depths to which California farm owners would sink when cutting agricultural labor costs. In his fliers, Durst promised that pickers would receive the going rate of one dollar for one hundred pounds of picked hops. But this was deceptive. The hops were excessively cleaned before weighing, and no hop-pickers were present on the inspection crew. Durst also withheld ten cents per hundred pounds of picked hops until the end of the harvest. In this way, he coerced pickers into staying until the end of the harvest or their withheld pay would be forfeited. Workers ended up making less that $1.50 a day—and a workday on the Durst farm was twelve hours long. Even though most other hop ranches also required a twelve-hour day, the usual pay on these ranches resulted in a common standard day's wage of $3. Despite temperatures reaching over 110 degrees, workers who wanted water had to leave the field and walk a considerable distance. Of course, Durst knew that piece-rate workers would avoid leaving the field, so he provided, at a cost of five cents a glass, powdered lemonade. One more egregious aspect of the working conditions at Durst's ranch was the absence of high-pole men. It was common in hop fields for men using poles to bring down the high-growing vines of the hop plants so that women and children could reach the flowers. It was also common for these men to help women and children load the eighty- to one-hundred-pound hopsacks into wagons. Without pole men, the work was far more difficult for women and children than on other hop ranches.[2]

The harvest commenced on 29 July 1913, and by 1 August discontent over the poor working and living conditions permeated the entire camp. Working among these hop-pickers were current and former members of the IWW. True to the spontaneous nature of the organization, approx- imately thirty of these men created a temporary local and began organizing the hop-pickers. With the participation of the vast majority of the workers in several mass meetings, the Wobblies established a committee whose elected members included former Wobbly Richard "Blackie" Ford as chief spokesman for the hop-pickers and current Wobbly Herman Suhr as the committee secretary. The committee approached Durst with a list of worker demands that included a flat rate of $1.25 per hundred pounds of picked hops, drinking water in the fields, inspection of picked hops by the pickers themselves, high-pole men, separate toilets for women, improvement of camp toilets, and lemonade made from real lemons, not powdered citric acid.[3]

Durst would only agree to improve toilet facilities, provide water in the fields, and add one worker to the picked hop inspection team. The workers' committee warned Durst that the hop-pickers would strike if their demands were not fully met. Durst broke off the negotiations when he struck Ford with his glove and fired him and the rest of the committee, ordering them to pick up their pay and leave his ranch. When Ford and the committee refused, Durst asked Deputy Sheriff Henry Daken to arrest Ford. Workers intervened on Ford's behalf when Daken could not produce a warrant. Later that day, the workers organized a mass meeting in which Ford and Suhr addressed the crowd. The Wobblies urged the workers to strike to force Durst to address their grievances. At one point in his speech, Ford lifted a sick child up before the crowd and said, "It's for the life of the kids we're doing this." In order to persuade as many as possible to join in the strike, speakers in German, Greek, Italian, Arabic, and Spanish addressed the crowd. A show of hands confirmed that the vast majority of hop-pickers favored a strike. Yet despite the conditions and the impending strike, according to subsequent trial testimony, the workers were peaceful and sang Wobbly songs that afternoon.[4]

Durst summoned District Attorney Edward Manwell, who was also his lawyer, and Marysville Sheriff George Voss, who brought along a number of deputies, to arrest Ford and to break up the workers' gathering. When the party approached Ford, who was standing on a platform before the assembly, the workers again intervened on his behalf. Voss, Deputy Sheriff Lee Anderson, or Deputy Daken—it is not clear who— fired a shot into the air to disperse the crowd. The shot only enraged the workers, who fell upon Manwell and Anderson. Manwell, Deputy Eugene Reardon, a Puerto Rican hop-picker, and an English hop-picker died in the ensuing violence and gunfire. Many in the crowd suffered bullet wounds from the twenty or so rounds fired during the melee. One worker had his arm blown off by a shotgun blast from Deputy Daken. The crowd, however, was unarmed. By most accounts, the deaths of Manwell and Reardon resulted from Reardon and perhaps another member of the posse having their guns taken away and used against them. After this outbreak of violence, many hop workers immediately left the ranch, heading in all directions. The writer Jack London met a number of these workers as they streamed into nearby Sonoma County, and commented that they reminded him of the survivors of the San Francisco earthquake. Fearing more disturbances, Wheatland and Marysville municipal officials requested units of the National Guard from Governor Hiram Johnson. Soldiers and area law enforcement arrested approximately one hundred workers who remained at the camp.[5]

Soon after the August 3 event, a Marysville coroner's inquest concluded that the IWW strike leadership had caused a riot that led to the death of District Attorney Manwell. An extensive manhunt ensued throughout the state to arrest Wobblies involved in the Wheatland affair. Law enforcement officials issued arrest warrants for Ford and Suhr for murder. A coalition of deputy sheriffs and Burns detectives—a private detective agency known for its antiradical and antilabor tendencies— arrested a number of workers. Most of those arrested were either present at Wheatland at the time of the incident or lived nearby. The incarcerated workers were subjected to the civil rights abuses of John Doe warrants, which gave law enforcement officers the ability to write in the arrested person's name *after* the arrest, and of secret police blotters, which allowed law enforcement to keep lawyers in the dark as to where their clients had been detained. In an effort to force information from the arrested men, deputy sheriffs and Burns detectives resorted to beating, starving, bribery, and kidnapping. The torture proved so psychologically damaging that one man hanged himself in his prison cell, another attempted suicide, and still another had to be committed to a mental hospital. But their methods served their ends: eventually, law enforcement officials arrested Ford, Suhr, and fellow Wheatland hop workers Walter Bagan and William Beck for murder.[6]

The IWW immediately provided a legal defense for the accused men, and published an interpretation of the events surrounding the Wheatland strike in the pages of the *Industrial Worker* and *Solidarity*, the union's western and eastern newspapers. The causes of the strike, the mass arrests, and the subsequent trial also gained support for Ford, Suhr, Bagen, and Beck from other labor organizations, trades unions, socialists, religious leaders, and women's associations. During the trial, the brutal handling of those under arrest came to light. For example, Suhr suffered severe food and sleep deprivation early in his incarceration, which led to a confession that he later recanted. The trial also revealed the outrageous nature of the hop camp conditions, stirring public condemnation of Durst's behavior, and heightening public interest and concern over the plight of migrant agricultural workers.[7] Two organizations emerged to help with the workers' defense, the IWW's Wheatland Hop Picker's Defense League and a coalition group, the International Workers' Defense League. Their primary goals were to generate public support for the men on trial and raise funds for their defense.

Austin Lewis, a socialist, journalist, friend to the IWW, and lawyer by profession, represented the workers. With little hope for a fair trial in Marysville, Lewis motioned for a different venue. Judge E. P. McDaniel, who, like one of the prosecutors, Edward B. Stanwood, was a longtime friend of Manwell, denied the motion. Contributing to the anti-IWW atmosphere surrounding the trial, California's newspapers demonized the defendants and connected Wobblies with violence in the public's mind. Never in the course of the trial could the prosecutors demonstrate that Ford and Suhr either fired a weapon or encouraged others to use violence. The entire case of the prosecution rested on establishing a conspiracy by Ford and Suhr to murder Manwell. In the reasoning of the prosecution, Ford and Suhr led the strike, which brought about the death of Manwell. Despite Lewis's spirited defense and appeals to simple justice, the jury, eight of twelve of whom were farmers, found Ford and

Figure 10. Hop strike leaders, Herman D. Suhr and Richard
"Blackie" Ford, beginning their life sentences for murder.
(Courtesy, California State Archives)

Suhr guilty of second-degree murder after one day's deliberation. Ford
and Suhr received life sentences. On the same day, 31 January 1914, the
jury acquitted Bagan and Beck, due to their lack of a leadership role in
the strike and the inability of the prosecution to link them to any violence
(fig. 10).[8]

Following the Wheatland strike and the convictions of Ford and Suhr,
the IWW emerged as the primary labor organization among the state's
migrant laborers. Its reputation as the defender of migrant, seasonal,
unskilled, and agricultural laborers' interests spread throughout
California's jungle camps, according to F. C. Mills, a field agent of the
California Commission of Immigration and Housing, who spent part of
1914 living and working among the state's itinerant workforce. Mills, in
conversations with construction, packinghouse, and agricultural
workers, and with other itinerants, discovered that these workers looked
to the IWW rather than to the AFL for leadership. This opinion was
confirmed by Carleton Parker, director of the CCIH, who based his view
on the findings of his agents as well as on his own research among
California's casual labor population. Furthermore, not only did Ford and
Suhr have ample support among many California labor organizations,
but the IWW generated respect in labor circles for the work the union
did on behalf of migrant labor. The number of Wobblies in California rose

to five thousand in 1914, with a total of forty locals throughout the state. With this increase in membership and number of locals, and with a no serious competition from other labor unions, Wobblies found the door wide open to establish a farm workers' union that transcended race, ethnicity, and gender in California's "factories in the field."[9]

The IWW and Agricultural Laborers

Harvest Wobblies, those IWW members who worked in agriculture and occasionally paid their dues during a given year, did not suddenly appear on the scene at the Wheatland tragedy in 1913. The union had been active in the state since the founding of the organization in Chicago in 1905. Yet it took several years for Wobblies to arrive at a position of authority among agricultural laborers. The union suffered two serious problems during the initial phase of organizing farm workers. First, it needed time to adjust to the unique features of the West's industrial laborers. Unlike the East, the West had a large migrant and seasonal workforce. To recruit this mobile and largely male contingent of workers, the Wobblies created mixed locals that allowed any person to join, regardless of occupation. Traditionally, union locals centered on one trade or industry. Though the mixed local was important in creating an open recruiting station, it was not the most efficient way to organize farm workers. Furthermore, it catered to the migrant white male worker, diminishing its appeal to workers with different cultural backgrounds and sensibilities. Second, the union needed to enhance its visibility among the region's workers. Notable in this regard were the street-speaking campaigns in western towns that led to dramatic free-speech fights in cities such as Spokane, Washington; Fresno, California; and Minot, North Dakota. Despite the tenacity of IWW members, these free-speech fights did not lead to a significant degree of farm-labor organizing.[10]

While the mixed local and free-speech fights endured as part of Wobbly organizing practices and as part of the worklife culture of many western Wobblies, organizers also moved haltingly during these early years toward more effective methods. In particular, the violent and tragic Wheatland incident demonstrated that practical organizing on the job site was more useful than organizing out of a mixed local or through the propaganda efforts of free-speech fights. Among California Wobblies, however, tension between soapbox organizing and job site organizing continued through 1914 and later. Yet over time, the union's experience in California, Washington, and the northern Great Plains would culminate in a call for a coordinated strategy with a central admin-istration to organize all farm workers, particularly the tens of thousands of migrant and seasonal harvest laborers in the West.

IWW organizing among these migrant farm laborers began in 1909, and proceeded in fits and starts. California and Washington experienced the earliest Wobbly efforts, but by 1910 the Great Plains wheat belt witnessed them as well. Wobblies viewed migrant farm labor within the context of general migrant labor in the West. In the East, Wobblies sought to enlist in their ranks unskilled and semiskilled workers neglected by other trade unions: textile workers, machine operatives, transportation workers, and miners. In the West, Wobblies sought these same workers, but they also wanted to recruit the region's class of largely unskilled, underemployed, seasonal and migrant laborers who worked in agricultural harvests, fruit packing, canning, construction, logging, and milling. For the IWW, these seasonal workers, but especially migrant laborers, represented a revolutionary class of workers who lived and worked at the margins of the labor movement despite their indispens-able role in the West's major industries. Their working conditions and wages prevented them from attaining any semblance of an adequate existence as workers, according to the contributing writers and editors of the *Industrial Worker* and *Solidarity*.[11]

Putting together a concerted and efficient organizing effort among agricultural laborers in the West took the Wobblies a considerable amount of time. They found it difficult to establish bona fide industrial unions outside of cities such as San Francisco, Los Angeles, and San Diego. Ben H. Williams, an early Wobbly organizer and industrial union theorist, argued that part of the problem lay in the nature of industrial development in the western countryside. The West's large migrant labor force usually worked in a variety of industries and resided only temporarily in any one location. Therefore, he argued, the mixed local offered a temporary approach to initial organizing efforts until IWW organizers could replace them with locals representing specific industries. The flexibility of the mixed local allowed workers to join regardless of occupation or residence. The IWW chartered mixed locals throughout the West as all-purpose recruiting stations. Yet because of the transient nature of western workers, mixed locals were not the temporary approach that Williams had envisioned; instead, they became a permanent feature of the western IWW's structure. The practice of issuing union cards and not charging fees for transfer from one occupation to another further validated the purpose of mixed locals in the minds of many itinerant Wobblies. Unfortunately, efforts to organize agricultural workers by the harvesters, loggers, construction workers, miners, and variety of other workers represented in the mixed locals made it difficult to create an organizing strategy that targeted only area farm workers.[12]

Difficult, but not altogether impossible. It was in the mixed locals that agricultural organizing efforts first emerged, particularly in the West Coast states. In Washington, several Spokane locals provided a center for organizing activity. Spokane was not only located adjacent to the rich wheat-growing region of eastern Washington, but it was a major railroad hub, making it appealing to migrant workers, especially those in agriculture but in logging and mining as well. California Wobblies also spawned locals in agricultural regions. Brawley, in the southern Imperial Valley; Redlands, in the citrus region east of Los Angeles; Fresno, in the heart of the San Joaquin Valley; and the jungle local of Stockton near the Sacramento River Valley provided the first steps towards establishing a permanent Wobbly presence in the state. The Portland, Oregon, local had migrant farm workers attached to it by 1910. These laborers worked to the south in the Willamette Valley and in the Hood River Valley to the east.[13]

Before the IWW tried its hand at organizing farm labor, the AFL had made tentative organizational efforts among migrant farm laborers in California as early as 1903, according to historian Cletus Daniel. For example, the Central Labor Council of Los Angeles—and in subsequent years the California State Federation of Labor—drafted resolutions approving migrant farm labor organizing without regard to race or national origin. Daniel contends that, more than anything else, the purpose of such efforts was not to create an inclusive union for the benefit of all farm workers but to control the rising tide of non-white agricultural laborers. The primary concern of California labor union leaders and many California rank-and-file union members was the scabbing potential of non-white workers. After the formation of the IWW, the AFL tried to prevent the more inclusive IWW from achieving any success in California. Austin Lewis, writing in 1911 on the migrant organizing situation in California for the *International Socialist Review*, noted that the struggle between the AFL and the IWW over organizing unskilled workers exemplified the differences between the two movements. The AFL wanted solely to protect the interests of organized white labor, while the IWW hoped to organize *all* unskilled workers, including agricultural workers.[14]

From the beginning of their unionization efforts, AFL organizers, specifically J. B. Dale, the leader of the state federation's organizing drive, tended to view migrant farm workers as a social problem rather than as true members of the working class in need of union representation. Even when the total membership of the AFL-affiliated United Laborers of America, a union devoted to migratory laborers, reached five thousand, most of the members were not farm workers. AFL organizers focused only on recruiting farm workers on their off time or in the off-season in towns and cities in the state, revealing a poor understanding of how to reach migrant labor. In fact, even during the height of the effort from 1910 to 1914, union leaders argued for government intervention to ameliorate poor working conditions. The AFL organizers did not have faith that California's multicultural farm laborers could effectively function as trade union members and address these issues through union action.[15]

Confronting the Barriers Posed by Race

One of the early difficulties Wobblies faced in organizing the multiracial and ethnically diverse California agricultural labor force was white racism. Some of the strongest supporters of foreign exclusionist legislation were labor union members. One way that IWW writers refuted the racist attitudes of some Wobblies and other workers and to set the union apart from the rest of the labor movement was to explicitly acknowledge the IWW's official stand in favor of Asian immigration and union membership. The editors of the *Industrial Union Bulletin*, an early IWW newspaper, commented in a March 1907 editorial that Japanese workers already held IWW membership cards and were welcome in the union and as citizens of the country. Wobbly writers also hoped to educate white workers about the solidarity exhibited by Japanese workers. A report from Brawley, California, explained that local growers did not want to hire Japanese workers, not necessarily out of racial discrimination, but because Japanese laborers refused to accept the going wages and working conditions. One contributor to the *Bulletin* remarked that the Japanese had a keen sense of collective action to better their working conditions in comparison to white casual agricultural laborers, who were more interested in battling Japanese and Mexican workers than in joining forces in industrial solidarity. According to Wobbly organizer J. H. Walsh, Japanese and Chinese union members were among the most loyal and dependable dues-paying members. They also had developed an effective strategy of striking for higher wages. Walsh, in an April 1908 issue of the *Bulletin*, cited the California labor commissioner's observation that Japanese workers, in certain instances, would work under any conditions until all non-Japanese labor had left the field, leaving only Japanese workers. When the crop required immediate harvesting, the Japanese workers would strike, forcing the employer to improve working conditions and/or wages. The employer was likely to give in as the Japanese had eliminated the scabbing potential of other area workers.[16]

Wobblies, though, wanted white workers to do more than just admire Asian workers' collectivist sensibilities. They wanted to create a multiracial and multiethnic union in agricultural industries. IWW newspapers made a continual effort to argue that all workers, regardless of race or ethnicity, had a place in the IWW's industrial unions. Just as trade unions could be used to scab on each other, Wobblies argued, different races and ethnic groups could be used by agribusinessmen to divide workers by exploiting their prejudices. California's mixed locals, using Japanese, Chinese, and Mexican IWW organizers when possible, occasionally recruited members from these immigrant communities. Wobblies with a Japanese, Chinese, or Spanish surname surfaced in the pages of IWW newspapers, indicating their membership and activity, but this was not common. Japanese and Chinese workers, especially, preferred their own labor associations to the IWW. One major exception was the case of a Hawaiian IWW local that had a significant number of Japanese members.

The primary reason that Asian workers hesitated to join the IWW was that they would have to abandon their own successful labor associations, which were culturally their own. The fledgling and rhetorically multicultural IWW had little that was tangible to offer Japanese and Chinese workers during these years, though, IWW locals and branches supported alliances with Asian labor associations. For example, Wobblies from the Fresno branch of the IWW, which in 1909 gained an official charter as Local 66, held a joint rally with representatives from the two-thousand-member Japanese Labor League in 1909 in Fresno's Japanese neighborhood. Here the speakers, including Italian and Mexican Wobblies, advocated cross-racial and cross-ethnic worker solidarity. Beginning that year, Southern California Wobblies had better luck recruiting Hispanic workers. Immigrants from Mexico had arrived more recently than those from China or Japan; therefore, they lacked well-developed labor associations of their own. Mexican IWW members established a Spanish-language IWW newspaper and were an important contingent of Los Angeles and San Diego IWW locals for many years. Moreover, the IWW actively supported the Mexican revolution and worked closely with Mexican exiles in California.

In an effort to promote labor solidarity, the Wobbly press frequently addressed the commonality of labor experiences among white, Asian, Hispanic, and African American workers. Whether reporting on the difficult working experiences of Mexican construction laborers in San Diego, the exploitation of white, Chinese, and Japanese farm workers in California's central valleys, or the plight of impoverished white and African American loggers in Louisiana's pine forests, the Wobbly press sought to encourage workers to see past race to their common struggle against the employer who controlled the means of production. One of the best examples of the Wobbly perspective on employers' use of race or ethnicity to divide workers and reduce wages can be found in Ernest Riebe's cartoon panels in the *Industrial Worker* featuring a character named Mr. Block. These cartoons of the mid-teens placed Mr. Block, the hapless, non-class-conscious worker, in situations in which exploitive employers constantly manipulated him (fig. 11).[17]

Early Organizing in Washington

Within a few years of the IWW's founding, organizers attempted a two-pronged strategy to organize farm laborers. First, Wobblies reasoned that the best way to recruit new members involved educating workers in the virtues of industrial unionism, revolution, and the proposed cooperative commonwealth of the working class. Second, they tried to recruit members at the work site, though initially this part of the strategy lacked the concerted effort that would come in later years.[18] These two approaches, however, did not work in harmony with each other. The former would lead to free-speech fights and the latter would lead to the Wheatland strike. Eventually, organizing on the job site, as exhibited at Wheatland, would bring inspiration to harvest Wobblies, job delegates, and to the union as a whole. But it took trial and error for the harvest Wobblies to find an organizing strategy and industrial union structure that worked for agricultural job sites.

Reading the *Industrial Worker* or *Solidarity* over a period of months, or visiting a mixed local and discussing the message and goals of the IWW with resident Wobblies were probably the best ways for western migrant workers to decide whether they wanted to join the union. Of course, few of these workers had a residence to which a publication could be mailed, and few even knew of the existence of IWW mixed locals. To reach these workers, then, whether farm laborers, construction workers, or other itinerant day laborers, and to let them know that a labor union existed for their unique interests, Wobblies set out to articulate the

Figure 11. Ernest Riebe, through his Mr. Block character, explains to the reader how employers used race and ethnicity to divide workers. (Courtesy, Charles H. Kerr Publishing Company, Chicago, 1998)

union's philosophy on street corners in many western cities. Though street speaking proved to be of limited value for labor organizing, the practice engendered one of the most significant battles for free speech in American history, the legendary Wobbly free-speech fights that lasted from 1909 to 1916.[19]

One of the earliest of these fights took place in Spokane, Washington. The sheer number of itinerant laborers in Spokane seeking work in logging, construction, mining, and agriculture during the 1900s stimulated the creation of thirty or more private employment agencies. The Wobbly press called these employment agencies "employment sharks," as they charged workers for job placement and transportation to a job site. The fees and the not-uncommon practice of selling jobs that no longer existed once a laborer reached the job site caused workers to despise the agencies. In late 1908, IWW organizers held public demonstrations outside such agencies, calling on workers to avoid this system of employment and calling on employers to hire only through union halls, such as the local IWW halls in Spokane. In response, city officials, with the help of employment agency representatives, drafted ordinances prohibiting public street speaking unless it was by such religious organizations as the Salvation Army.[20]

The IWW launched the battle against these prohibitive ordinances in spring 1909. The strategy was simple. A speaker would stand upon a small platform, usually an overturned wooden crate, and begin to address an audience. City police would arrest the speaker for violating the ordinances, and another speaker would step in and take over. Such actions took on impressive proportions in November with one hundred and fifty Wobblies arrested for violating the city ordinances. Soon, the call went out in the IWW press for Wobblies to descend upon Spokane to fight for free speech and the union's right to openly recruit new members. As hundreds of Wobblies hopped freight trains to Spokane, city officials not only continued to arrest street speakers, but they closed down the offices of the *Industrial Worker* and raided and closed the IWW's main union hall. But this was a fight the city fathers would lose. The jail and courtroom costs generated by arresting hundreds of Wobblies strained the city treasury. Moreover, public opinion shifted in favor of the free-speech fighters, particularly as information about their treatment in jail—especially that of Elizabeth Gurley Flynn, the best-known female Wobbly—reached the public. Wobblies also found support in such unexpected sources as the *Spokane Press*, local women's civic groups, AFL affiliates, influential socialists, and German societies. Eventually, municipal officials rescinded the ordinances.[21]

In the end, the IWW free-speech fight secured the Wobblies' right to organize in the city and the chance to experiment with organizing techniques among the region's farm laborers. The Spokane Wobbly locals and the larger headquarters were important centers of agitation. The headquarters, especially, was a source of great pride for the union, and was located "right in the center of the slave market" where workers sold themselves into wage slavery. It had a large lecture hall that could seat hundreds of workers, and offices for the *Industrial Worker* staff. For five cents, members and visitors could watch an entertaining film and thereby help support the local's treasury. The headquarters also offered workers a library, smoke-free reading room, newsstand, and cigar shop. By late spring 1909, the Spokane IWW counted fifteen hundred members in good standing and as many as thirty-five hundred "on the books" altogether. The union could even afford to offer its members a medical insurance plan. Despite these achievements, the Wobblies' effort to organize migrant workers on the job site was sporadic at best.[22]

The first attempts at organizing farm workers in the Spokane vicinity hinged on the issues of wages and the length of the workday. Members from Spokane locals 222 and 434 circulated copies of the *Industrial Worker* in Palouse-area towns and jungles. Soon after, one optimistic IWW organizer reported—apparently without any evidence—that the men of the jungles were with the IWW. Opposing the efforts of the IWW organizers were local farmers, whose anti-union sentiments were well known. Contributing writers to the *Industrial Worker* in summer 1909 warned workers to be on their guard, or to avoid outright, the agriculturally rich Palouse town of Pullman: "Of all the places in the Northwest, Pullman is the worst by the story of every worker who has been there. All workingmen should keep away from Pullman, and let the crop rot on the ground. The farmers around there are religious and therefore mean. A word to the wise is enough. Keep away from Pullman at all costs!"[23]

That summer, southeastern Washington farmers were receiving a good price for their wheat, ninety-nine cents a bushel. Harvest Wobblies decided that this was an opportune time to institute a ten-hour day at $3 per day. Reports sent in from the field by members or sympathizers of the union, some using prepaid postcards available from IWW locals for this purpose, noted that wages peaked at $2.50 a day for a fourteen- to seventeen-hour day. Charles Grant, one of the union's first harvest Wobbly organizers, sent an extensive report to the *Industrial Worker*, explaining that workers had to hold back their labor just to get $2.50 a day in such towns as Lacrosse. Moreover, he wrote, "grub is said to be very poor on the ranches. Pork: morning, noon and night." One of the problems most galling to Grant was the large presence in the region of what were known as hoosiers or farm boys; these were workers who not only lacked class consciousness but also were considered rather dim-witted by the Wobblies. In the end, the Spokane *Spokesman-Review* deemed the strike in the Palouse region a complete failure, as farmers reported that there were so many idle men in towns such as Pullman and Colfax that they had no trouble finding people to work from sunup to sundown for $2.00 to $2.50 a day. In fact, a sign reportedly erected by Palouse jungle residents proclaiming "that good men would be furnished for $3 a day for 10 hours" subsequently disappeared.[24]

According to contributions to the *Industrial Worker*, Wobblies were experimenting with different organizing techniques among the harvest stiffs, as migrant farm workers were called, in the summer harvest season of 1910, particularly in eastern Washington. C. A. McCauley, writing in a spring issue, argued that the Spokane and Minneapolis locals should be used as command centers to improve labor conditions on Palouse and Dakota farms. He noted that the means to reach migrant workers should include plastering stickers on town buildings, water tanks, and coal chutes throughout the wheat country, "stating a minimum wage, hours to be worked, good food and blankets" for workers. He also suggested that street speakers with plenty of IWW literature should be in wheat towns on Saturday nights to address harvest workers. He concluded his article by asking fellow workers for suggestions on how to reach the homeguard, the term used for resident seasonal workers who wanted to establish themselves in a community and perhaps start a family of their own.[25]

Sabotage was another, more aggressive tactic proposed in the *Industrial Worker* to improve workers' wages and working conditions on Palouse farms. Walker C. Smith, chief editor of the paper, advised that during the harvest, workers who found wages and conditions of employment unsatisfactory and an employer unwilling to make improvements should resort to this strategy. Poorly sewn grain sacks, loads of produce spilled on the way to the barn, and broken-down machinery could all be forms of sabotage. From the Wobbly point of view, this was striking on the job. But the sabotage should not be severe enough to shut down production, because that would end up hurting the workers. It needed to be irritating enough and untraceable to have the effect of convincing the employer to improve conditions and/or wages. Such tactics had been part of the labor movement in the United States for decades, but during the 1910s and early 1920s, the public came to associate sabotage specifically with the IWW, to the union's detriment.[26]

By June 1910, an elected Harvest Committee set up shop in Spokane. They "request[ed] that all harvesters, etc., communicate with them, giving suggestions, information, etc., with a view to organizing and going after the goods in the harvest this summer." The mission of the Harvest Committee was simple and pragmatic. As members of the IWW, organized harvest workers could control the labor supply in eastern Washington, enabling them to raise wages, reduce working hours, and demand better accommodations. The Harvest Committee considered it extremely important to disabuse non-union harvesters of the myth that they could get fair treatment from an employer on their own. Because of the glut of harvesters in the labor market, farmers could keep wages very low. Therefore, the committee argued, organization was the only means to better the life of the harvester.

Charles Grant and the committee directed this message to the thousands of workers who made their way through Spokane and on to Washington's wheat country. The Spokane Harvest Committee described to harvesters its plan to establish locals, either temporary or permanent, in the Palouse country and the Big Bend area west of Spokane. Grant, chairman of the committee, explained it this way to his fellow Wobblies: "Boasting, quoting Karl Marx, predicting the fall of capitalism and the abolition of the wage system will not be worth a d— unless you do the constructing of the new and the busting of the old system right on the job—the point of production and exploitation."

It is important to note that even at this early date in organizing harvest workers, Wobblies emphasized a strategy that appealed less to revolutionary fervor than to industrial unionism, that is, to improving wages, working conditions, and accommodations in the present as organized workers within their industry. Take over the industry first, and the revolution will follow, was the pragmatic strategy of these early harvest Wobblies. [27]

The Harvest Committee explained in the pages of the *Industrial Worker* how to establish new locals or expand existing locals with "camp delegates." Delegates could be any members in good standing who entered the harvest fields. Locals were to supply such workers with dues books, stamps, literature, songbooks, and stickers. As far as organizing on the job, the Harvest Committee advised delegates to advocate for whatever wage a given local had set for harvest labor, but to make sure that obtaining the job was the highest priority. That meant that if holding out for a particular wage proved futile, then delegates needed to urge harvest Wobblies to take the job at the employer's offer. If possible, they should encourage the workers at the job site to strike for the wage set by the IWW local, but at the same time be alert to the number of unemployed workers in the area, because farmers could easily break a strike if unemployed harvesters were nearby.

The Harvest Committee also stressed the importance of communication, especially regarding tactics, over the course of the season. At least one harvest Wobbly at any organized job site needed to maintain contact with a camp delegate by mail. In addition, camp delegates had to maintain communication with their locals about job conditions, improvements, and organizing in general. In the end, the harvest organizing campaign of 1910 brought more workers into the IWW, educated workers on the advantages of industrial unionism, raised wages on a few work sites, and served as an example in the Wobbly press for organizing farm laborers in other regions of the West. This early harvest Wobbly campaign was not an overwhelming success, but it was a first step.[28]

Summer 1910 also brought news of harvest conditions and organizing in Kansas, Oregon, and California in the *Industrial Worker*. For example, Thomas Brown, a southern plains IWW organizer, reported that in Kansas, workers who struck for $3 a day got their demands met, though he admitted that the short supply of harvesters helped force wages up. From Portland, Oregon, IWW camp delegates fanned out to harvest fields in search of new members to educate workers about industrial unionism. Still, the vast majority of union action that summer took place in Washington, east of the Cascades, in the Palouse country, Walla Walla, and North Yakima. In Walla Walla, Wobblies arrived early for the harvest with literature and stickers to help spread their message. At a street-speaking event in early July, Walla Walla police officers arrested two Wobblies, L. W. Fourune and H. C. Parris, as they addressed a large crowd of harvest workers who were waiting for the harvest to begin. Chief of Police Davis promised that more arrests would follow if Wobblies continued their organizing campaign on the city's streets. The *Industrial Worker* reported that the police concentrated their numbers in the "troubled district" and that farmers attempted to employ workers only through an employment agency to ensure that they would not have to pay more than $1.50 a day for a worker.[29]

In the pages of the *Industrial Worker*, editors and writers directed Wobblies to organize on the job rather than on the street corner. This advice was not always heeded, however. On a summer Sunday evening, John W. Foss and Joseph Gordon held a street meeting on Front Street in downtown North Yakima. Although they had acquired a permit to speak, the two Wobblies were arrested for violating the terms of the permit. Instead of paying their fines of $40 and $25, Foss and Gordon took jail time, which paid off their fines at a rate of $3 a day. In North Yakima, jail time included work on a chain gang, which the men refused to do, convincing several other prisoners to refuse as well. Police Captain William Kelly put the men on a diet of bread and water until they agreed to work. When that strategy failed, Captain Kelly forced Foss and Gordon to carry a ball and chain in the hot summer sun. Staying in the cool cell during the day was no longer an option. This severe reaction on the part of the North Yakima police, which was supported by the local press, may have been inspired by fear of a repeat of the Spokane free-speech fight. It may also have been a response to the fear that Wobblies such as Foss and Gordon could gain an influence over migrant labor. Yakima valley farmers had great anxiety over the scarcity of labor for the summer harvest. By the end of July, however, farmers expressed relief that they had adequate labor for the season.[30]

In the agricultural region surrounding Walla Walla, in southeastern Washington, harvest Wobblies found that the control that farmers had over the labor supply was difficult to break. The Farmers Union in that area procured their labor through an employment agency. Edwin F.

Figure 12. Edwin Doree and Walter Nef with their wives Ida and Feige and Doree's son Bucky in 1921. Doree and Nef provided indispensable leadership to harvest Wobblies before World War One. (Courtesy, Walter P. Reuther Library, Wayne State University)

Doree, a twenty-one-year-old Wobbly organizer, led the drive to organize Walla Walla's agricultural workers (fig. 12). Despite his youth, Doree had already had years of migrant labor experience, including work in a railroad car factory and as a miner. After losing several fingers in a workplace accident, he headed to Washington, where he became a member of the Western Federation of Miners in 1906, and through the WFM's affiliation with the IWW, a Wobbly. However, it was not until 1910 that he became an active organizer. From Walla Walla, he reported in the *Industrial Worker* that Wobblies were few in number in the area and that they found their ability to organize seriously hampered by local law enforcement. Doree noted that as soon as they began to agitate for higher wages or for workers to avoid buying jobs through the employment agency "we had the can tied to us and were spotted to the police." Once identified as IWW members, they could find little employment. Doree and other Wobblies eventually had to settle for isolated warehouse or haying jobs, which kept them at a distance from the bulk of the migrant and seasonal workforce employed in the area. They found some modest organizing success, though, when they brought twenty-five new men into the union.[31]

In the Palouse region, the IWW had fared somewhat better. In Garfield and Steptoe, two towns in the heart of this rich wheat-growing area, the IWW gained more members and successfully struck for higher wages. Andrew Benson reported to chairman Grant and the Harvest Committee that workers in local jungle camps were eager to join the union. The level of organization was such that farmers went directly to the jungle camps and offered the Wobbly rate of $3 a day for ten hours of work. Benson asked for more literature from Spokane, especially copies of the *Industrial Worker* and *Solidarity*. His most urgent request was for an organizer to take advantage of this positive turn of events. Though organizers did arrive in Garfield and in other area towns to sign up new members, they did not establish a permanent local and news from the region disappeared from the Wobbly press at the close of the season (fig. 13).[32]

Although the IWW demonstrated a clear desire to organize farm laborers in eastern Washington, they had yet to discover an effective strategy. One factor that stood in their way was that resident seasonal workers, the homeguard, did not flock to join the union or accept its leadership in pressing for higher wages and improved conditions. These workers did not want to disrupt relationships with employers in the communities that they called home, recognizing that they would suffer the long-term consequences that conflict with employers could

Figure 13. Harvest Wobblies photographed at a jungle near Garfield,
Washington. This photo, headlined "A Business Meeting in the
Jungle," appeared in the *Industrial Worker*, 20 August, 1910.
(Courtesy, Walter P. Reuther Library, Wayne State University)

engender. They depended on farmers for year-round farmhand jobs,
help in starting their own farms, or recommendations for other
employment in their small communities.

Migrants, on the other hand, could simply leave the region. Thus, the
success that harvest Wobblies had as agitators and organizers was
primarily with migrant workers. In fact, IWW members and organizers
tended to be migrants themselves. They lived in jungles and rode the rails
well beyond eastern Washington. Migrant workers did not dominate the
seasonal labor workforce in the region, however, and when they
departed, so too did any temporary locals that harvest Wobbly organizers
had established. These factors help explain the inability of the union to
capitalize on its initial success in the Palouse. Another explanation is that
the unusually large number of laborers during the 1910 harvest season
in the wheat-growing areas and fruit-producing regions gave farmers the
edge, as it was an employers' labor market.[33]

Groping Towards an Organizing Strategy

Meanwhile, the summer of 1910 witnessed another important organizing
effort, this one in California's San Joaquin Valley. Yet this one, too,
developed primarily into a free-speech fight. Organizing California's

agricultural laborers fell to several IWW mixed locals. Except for periodic reports in Wobbly newspapers on working conditions, wages, living conditions, the types of workers employed, and confrontations with employers, no significant unionizing effort emerged in the state before 1910. Most organizing activity involved making the local union halls attractive to migrant workers. In many ways these facilities resembled jungles, and therefore white migrant male workers, who made up the overwhelming majority of jungle tenants, felt welcome and subsequently sought membership. Unfortunately for the IWW, these workers would stay only for the harvest season, and then hop a freight train to other employment. Few would maintain their IWW membership. A small number of Wobblies remained at each local in the hope of organizing migrants during the next harvest season. This low level of union activity and high degree of cultural exclusiveness go a long way towards explaining why male Asian, Hispanic, and homeguard farm workers, let alone women, did not find the IWW attractive. At a very early stage in farm labor organizing, harvest Wobblies demonstrated a marked dichotomy between inclusive rhetoric that appealed to all agricultural workers regardless of race, ethnicity, or gender and an exclusive worklife culture that appealed to white migrant male workers.

Initially, the only notable agricultural branches of the IWW in California were Local 419 in Redlands, near the western slope of the San Bernardino Mountains, and Brawley Local 437 and the Holtville jungle local in the Imperial Valley near the Mexican border. Local 419 members were able to maintain an organizing presence among farm workers in the citrus-growing region east of Los Angeles, and harvest Wobblies out of Brawley and Holtville worked for several years among melon pickers and other field laborers. But it was not until the formation of Fresno Local 66 that the Wobblies possessed a dynamic organizing center for migrant farm labor. Local 66, though, had to pass through a free-speech fight before it could rid itself of local law enforcement harassment and begin to organize migrant farm laborers.[34]

Fresno, like Spokane, acted as a magnet for casual labor. Farm, construction, and railroad workers featured prominently in the floating labor population that frequented the "slave market." Fresno Wobblies held numerous street meetings, handing out IWW literature to the migrant workers who flocked to these open-air gatherings. The Wobblies met with some success by organizing a contingent of Mexican construction workers and leading a strike against the Santa Fe railroad's electrical power plant. Frank H. Little, a miner by trade and original founding member of Fresno Local 66, returned in April 1910 from organizing activity in the Northwest to continue these street meetings. He hoped in this way to gain a foothold among the migrant farm labor population that passed through Fresno. Soon, however, Fresno police were able to force Little and the few other local Wobblies to curtail their street organizing efforts.[35]

Little, a veteran of the Spokane free-speech fight and one of the best IWW agitators, had a firm commitment to street speaking as an organizing strategy. He and other members of Local 66 believed in using any means necessary to reach migrant farm laborers. The Fresno free-speech fight began in late summer and early fall with Frank Little's arrest for violating ordinances against street speaking. In October, a full-blown campaign to force municipal officials to allow Wobblies to speak freely on city streets was underway. Wobblies from around the West descended on Fresno, mounted the proverbial soapbox, and risked arrest. As many as two hundred Wobblies experienced arrest, jail time, and severe treatment at the hands of the police during that fall and into the following spring. Eventually, Fresno's reputation and treasury began to suffer, and a compromise between city officials and jailed Wobblies ensued. The IWW ultimately secured its right to maintain its local and to continue street speaking, though with some constraints.

The ostensible goal of the free-speech fight—to ensure for Wobblies the right to bring their message to migrant laborers, specifically those in agriculture—did not lead to widespread organizing among this group. The free-speech fight seemed to be the extent of the Fresno Wobbly organizing strategy. So it is not surprising that no harvest committee or other coordinated farm labor unionizing effort emerged from Fresno for the upcoming summer harvest season, such as that which followed the Spokane fight.[36]

During the harvest seasons of 1911, 1912, and 1913, the IWW mounted no centrally supervised organizing effort in either California or Washington comparable to that in eastern Washington in 1910. Recruiting agricultural workers into the union continued at a very modest pace in these states and in the Great Plains, particularly in the Dakotas. This work fell to mixed locals that made transient farm workers feel welcome in the union hall, to a handful of determined IWW organizers in the field, and to a few more free-speech fights. None of these efforts resulted in organizing large numbers of migrant harvest workers.

Three distinct problems hindered IWW migrant and seasonal farm labor organizing. First, many Wobblies considered a public, street appeal for union membership an actual organizing strategy. With most migrant harvest workers spending at least a portion of their quest for employment in a town, Wobblies reasoned that a public appeal was the best means to reach these workers. The free-speech fights that followed suppression of these street campaigns, though, may have earned publicity for the IWW and helped advance the cause of free speech in the United States, but did not lead to substantive organizing. The second problem facing the IWW was that the mixed locals, whose existence free-speech fights defended, lacked a cohesive organizing focus. Many of the locals served more as a club for area Wobblies or a place for Wobblies traveling through a given region to flop than as a viable center for union organizing drives among area workers.

The third problem for the IWW was that it was at a difficult point in its own development. The membership was small, especially in the West, and a series of disagreements among the IWW leadership had serious consequences for the morale of the union. For example, the General Executive Board (GEB) of the IWW unanimously voted to relieve Walker C. Smith of his post as editor of the *Industrial Worker* because of his insistence on advocating sabotage by workers and his attacks on union leadership decisions in column after column of the newspaper. For the GEB, Walker was a destabilizing force in the union, despite the fact that he had many western rank-and-file supporters. In addition, a contentious decentralist-versus-centralist debate gripped the union, with the decentralists, many of whom supported Smith, dominant in the West. Decentralists feared a loss of their autonomy to IWW headquarters, and wanted to maintain absolute control over their locals. Though more centralist-minded Wobblies did not want to control western mixed locals outright, they argued that without a coordinated and centrally directed series of organizing campaigns in the West's industries, the union could fall apart. These more centralist-oriented Wobblies believed that the locals had to adhere to some common standards and practices of organization for the union not only to survive but also to prosper.[37]

As bleak as the situation for the union as a whole may have been, the IWW continued to maintain a presence in eastern Washington's wheat country. Hundreds of Wobblies harvested and threshed wheat in the region during the summers of 1911, 1912, and 1913. Due to the agitation during the 1910 summer harvest season, L. C. Crow of the Inland Farmers' Union agreed to channel harvest workers out of Spokane IWW locals to area wheat fields, particularly to those in the Palouse country, and to refrain from using employment agencies. Maintaining the Wobbly rate of $3 a day and attracting more members appear to have been the primary goals of the union's work in the harvest. And by all indications, the Wobblies realized these goals, at least in 1911. The *Industrial Worker* noted the success of several strike actions, particularly in Pomeroy, where the presence of large numbers of harvest Wobblies persuaded farmers to pay the Wobbly wage rate. Wobblies moved through other wheat towns, decorating buildings with stickers. In Lacrosse, Washington, one popular sticker read, "I won't work more than eight hours after May 1, 1912. How about you?" (Unfortunately for the Wobblies, in later years this slogan was used against them with the comment that IWW stood for, "I won't work.") Finally, another round of street speaking actions in summer 1911 in Walla Walla and North Yakima simply fizzled out, landing several Wobblies in jail and curtailing migrant labor organization in these towns.[38]

By summer 1912, concerns about soapbox organizing led to a significant shift away from such tactics, particularly as the pragmatic efforts in eastern Washington bore some fruit. The fact that migrant workers did not flock to IWW locals during and after free-speech fights made it abundantly clear that street speaking and the protection of the right to speak on a city street were not useful organizing tools. W. I. Fisher, a West Coast Wobbly organizer and co-founder of Fresno Local 66, writing in an early June 1912 issue of the *Industrial Worker*, explained that not only did soapbox organizing fail to bring in large numbers of new union members, it reached only a small percentage of the workforce, and especially failed to reach the homeguard agricultural workforce, who did not hang around the downtowns of agricultural communities. Fisher argued that Wobblies must expand the delegate- and professional-organizer system by going into the camps, fields, jungles, and residential areas and spreading the IWW message. In the same issue, J. S. Biscay, a thoughtful and prolific Wobbly writer, amplified Fisher's remarks with a call for Wobbly agitators to seek out foreign-born workers and make them their equals. It was important for Wobblies not to give the recent immigrant worker the impression that Wobblies held the same prejudices as other Americans. Organizing immigrant workers was only possible if they felt respected as workers and believed that IWW members acknowledged their problems and aspirations. Both Fisher and Biscay wanted harvest organizers to broaden the scope of their recruiting efforts beyond white migrant workers.[39]

Fighting for Ford and Suhr

For Wobblies outside of California, the events at Wheatland in 1913 demonstrated the direction that organizing should take. Unfortunately, California harvest Wobblies failed to capitalize on their support among farm workers, focusing primarily on releasing Ford and Suhr soon after their conviction. Their efforts kept the IWW connected to the cause of agricultural laborers, but it would take subsequent organizing efforts in the Great Plains to point the way for the future of harvest Wobbly union activity. In California, the IWW devoted more attention to freeing Ford and Suhr than to the difficult and creative work of developing a viable multiracial and multiethnic agricultural workers' union. Any farm labor organizing took place through mixed locals rather than as a statewide, coordinated effort like the 1910 harvest in eastern Washington. One practical reason for harvest Wobblies to focus on the release of Ford and Suhr was California's severe economic slowdown in 1914. High unemployment, especially among migrant workers, may have convinced organizers that forcing the release of Ford and Suhr might be more achievable than mounting a statewide organizing drive during a recession. Moreover, if the IWW could free the two prisoners, their stature as a militant labor organization that was devoted to its members would only rise.[40]

The IWW had a two-part strategy to free Ford and Suhr. With legal support, they made use of the appeals process. Simultaneously, the California IWW Hop Pickers General Strike Committee inaugurated a campaign to boycott the picking of hops until state authorities released Ford and Suhr and until there were substantial improvements in wages and working conditions in the hop fields. Wobblies reasoned that the hop growers had the political power to pressure the state for the release of the imprisoned men. They set the date for their general strike for 1 August 1914.

Several months before the proposed strike, stickers and fliers explaining the IWW's goals appeared throughout the state (fig. 14). As the deadline drew near, hop growers gave in to some of the Wobbly demands for improvements in working and living conditions. Yet they also appealed to Governor Johnson for help. Johnson, though, believed that only by significantly changing working and living conditions would hop growers protect themselves from IWW agitation. After reading the first annual report issued by the CCIH in 1914, Johnson was convinced that worker discontent resulted from exploitation by employers more

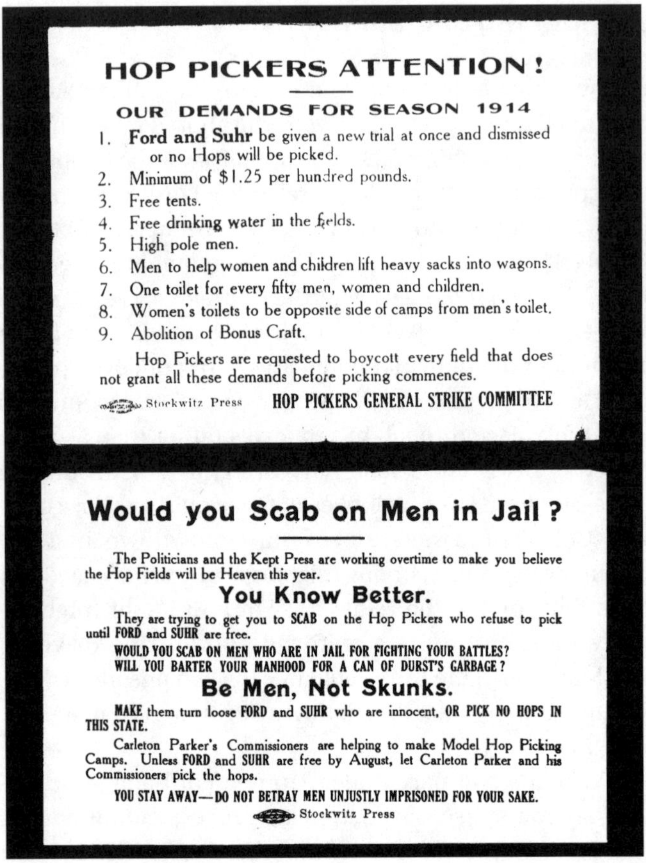

HOP PICKERS ATTENTION !

OUR DEMANDS FOR SEASON 1914

1. **Ford and Suhr** be given a new trial at once and dismissed or no Hops will be picked.
2. Minimum of $1.25 per hundred pounds.
3. Free tents.
4. Free drinking water in the fields.
5. High pole men.
6. Men to help women and children lift heavy sacks into wagons.
7. One toilet for every fifty men, women and children.
8. Women's toilets to be opposite side of camps from men's toilet.
9. Abolition of Bonus Craft.

Hop Pickers are requested to boycott every field that does not grant all these demands before picking commences.

Stockwitz Press **HOP PICKERS GENERAL STRIKE COMMITTEE**

Would you Scab on Men in Jail ?

The Politicians and the Kept Press are working overtime to make you believe the Hop Fields will be Heaven this year.

You Know Better.

They are trying to get you to SCAB on the Hop Pickers who refuse to pick until FORD and SUHR are free.

WOULD YOU SCAB ON MEN WHO ARE IN JAIL FOR FIGHTING YOUR BATTLES? WILL YOU BARTER YOUR MANHOOD FOR A CAN OF DURST'S GARBAGE?

Be Men, Not Skunks.

MAKE them turn loose FORD and SUHR who are innocent, OR PICK NO HOPS IN THIS STATE.

Carleton Parker's Commissioners are helping to make Model Hop Picking Camps. Unless FORD and SUHR are free by August, let Carleton Parker and his Commissioners pick the hops.

YOU STAY AWAY—DO NOT BETRAY MEN UNJUSTLY IMPRISONED FOR YOUR SAKE.

Stockwitz Press

Figure 14. Using stickers such as these, harvest Wobblies spread their views among the large migrant western labor force. (Courtesy, Bancroft Library, University of California, Berkeley)

than from the rhetoric of Wobblies. The governor urged the hop growers to follow the recommendations of the Commission's president, Simon Lubin, and its chief field agent, Carleton Parker, to raise wages, provide ample and clean toilet facilities, create sanitary camp sites, and make plenty of water available in the fields for workers.[41]

When the 1 August deadline passed without the release of Ford and Suhr, the IWW boycott and picket lines against the California hop industry began. Harvest Wobblies focused much of their economic harassment at the wealthiest hop-growers in the state, those who resided in Yuba County, which included Wheatland and Marysville. Distributing leaflets to hop-pickers and other migrant farm laborers and encouraging workers to respect Wobbly picket lines at the larger hop ranches of the Sacramento River Valley had an impact on the hop industry in California. The IWW estimated that the financial damage to the $5 million hop crop came to half a million dollars. Though Wobblies probably exaggerated the cost to growers, the boycott did cut into the profits of hop ranchers. But it failed to gain the release of Ford and Suhr, demonstrating that IWW leaders in California did not grasp the nature of the state's legal system. It should have been obvious that their tactics would not win the release of their fellow Wobblies and that they were squandering an opportunity to organize workers.[42]

Building a Foundation in the Great Plains

In the Great Plains, harvest Wobblies slowly built a presence in the wheat belt that began with the creation of the union. Many of the first IWW members in the West were migrant laborers who found ample summer employment shocking and threshing wheat. According to Joe Burdell, a veteran migrant farm laborer and wheat belt harvester, thousands of Wobblies inhabited the jungles and harvest fields of wheat belt states such as North Dakota by 1910.[43] The problems of organizing on a large scale, though, remained familiar ones. Mixed locals and free-speech fights were the basis of organizational efforts, and these generally proved inadequate. But by the end of 1914, the IWW finally moved to a regionwide unionization strategy among the West's migrant agricultural laborers.

In the summer of 1913, Wobblies attempted to reach migrant laborers in North Dakota with street-speaking propaganda. The state needed large numbers of harvest workers and threshermen, but the going rate for harvest work, such as that in the eastern North Dakota wheat town of Devil's Lake, was an abysmal $1.50 a day. Two veteran speakers and organizers, Jack Law (see fig. 17, page 105) and Jack Allen, brought the Wobbly message, while other Wobblies sold literature to migrants. A report to the *Industrial Worker* claimed that in one August week the IWW gained thirty new members in the Devil's Lake area. Law and Allen traveled west to Minot, North Dakota, where they tried their hand at organizing day laborers in construction. They met with immediate success, and soon began to broaden their appeal to migrants by holding downtown street meetings. Police, city officials, newspaper editors, and other members of the community grew alarmed at the crowds the Wobblies drew, leading the press to launch an assault upon the IWW.

Editorialists, in an unusually vicious manner, singled Law out for abuse. A *Minot Daily Reporter* editorial asked, "Ever see the visible part of a mule going north? Looks like Law. No difference at all. Wouldn't wonder if they were brothers."

City leaders quickly moved to silence the IWW by passing an ordinance banning street speaking, and Law and several other Wobblies were arrested. These events triggered the Minot free-speech fight of 1913, which became one of the bloodiest free-speech fights in Wobbly history.[44] Police officers and vigilantes beat, tortured, and imprisoned Wobblies, local socialists, and migrant workers caught up in the struggle. The IWW locals in Minneapolis and Duluth sent enough reinforcements to fill the jails of Minot. Jack Miller, a Canadian socialist and migrant laborer, had his first experience with the Wobblies in Minot. He had just arrived in North Dakota looking for work, as the Canadian wheat harvest was a poor one that year. Miller received a terrible beating at the hands of police as they tried to break up the crowds that gathered in support of the Wobblies' efforts to hold open-air meetings. Miller became a Wobbly after that beating, though he did not become a dues-paying member for some time. He later vividly described being escorted to the train depot to be thrown out of town, only to be met by a group of women challenging the right of the authorities to treat the free-speech advocates in this manner. In the end, over one hundred and fifty people were arrested and jailed during the fight. Some of the wounded suffered permanent physical injuries as a result of their treatment.[45]

Law, Allen, and their legal representative, North Dakota lawyer Arthur Le Sueur, worked out an agreement with city commissioners for the release of the jailed free-speech fighters. But the Minot free-speech fight did not achieve substantial results in migrant labor organizing.[46] It did, however, rejuvenate the IWW local in Minneapolis, which had a preponderance of migrant and seasonal laborers attached to it; the city was the entry point for thousands of farm laborers looking for work during each harvest season. Peter Johnson, the Minneapolis local's secretary, made a special effort to supply delegate credentials and literature to Wobblies ready to organize the 1914 wheat belt harvest.

In Enid, Oklahoma, a harvest committee formed to set wage and hour demands for the area's agricultural laborers. In addition, P. A. Sullivan, a well-traveled Wobbly in the wheat belt country, reported that he and several Wobblies led a small campaign around several Kansas wheat towns to force the going wage from $2.50 a day for ten hours' work to $3.00 a day. It was not an easy effort, as a number of jungle inhabitants refused to participate or even to work. He and his associates had better luck in Sioux City, Iowa. Here they sold many IWW songbooks and other literature and had at least one sympathetic townsman offer a donation to begin a local. During his travels that season, Sullivan, along with Mat K. Fox and several other Wobblies, launched a free-speech fight in the southeastern South Dakota town of Yankton, which led to their arrest and expulsion from the town. In Aberdeen, South Dakota, a larger free-speech fight took place, with the usual consequences, when Wobblies tried to conduct outdoor meetings that attracted as many as fifteen hundred people.[47]

Despite the energetic work by the West's mixed locals to organize the harvest laborers of the 1914 season and to raise the going wage to $3 for a ten-hour day, they achieved little of substance. J. Gabriel Soltis, writing in *Solidarity* at the close of the season, offered the sober conclusion that without the coordination of Wobbly locals, organization could not take place. Soltis was reiterating a point that seemed to have been lost on many Wobblies: the mixed local and the soapbox organizing tactics of the union had to be changed. A rising call for on-the-job organizing, an end to soapbox organizing, and the creation of more permanent locals, especially industry-specific locals, gradually found more adherents. At the IWW's Eighth Annual Convention in Chicago in September 1913, executive board members asserted that recruiting the workforces of a variety of industries was essential for the survival of the union. Board members criticized the decentralization and lack of coherence of the mixed-local strategy in the West. Industrial union locals needed to take precedence; otherwise, the IWW would never be able to organize workers in the region.[48]

In 1914, Minneapolis Local 64 became a model for farm labor organizing in the way that Spokane locals had several years earlier. The Minneapolis local benefited greatly from the poor quality of the Canadian harvest and the northern plains harvest in the U.S. Large numbers of migrant laborers and farmers from the Canadian prairies, Montana, and North Dakota came to Minneapolis in search of work during the summer of 1914. In Local 64's spacious hall, Wobblies, socialists, and Scandinavian groups offered many public meetings and lectures to welcome the city's unemployed, itinerant population. Over the course of the fall, members of the local established strong relationships with the migrant harvesters, out of which grew new methods of reaching migrant farm labor that would avoid the problems of the past. IWW members concluded that a centrally coordinated effort

Figure 15. Bill Haywood with his companion, Mimmie Wymann, 8 September 1918. Haywood was instrumental in backing a harvest worker organization effort, but was also an influential force in keeping harvest Wobblies firmly within the IWW (Courtesy, Walter P. Reuther Library, Wayne State University)

among locals in the wheat belt would be the only effective way to organize migrant and seasonal farm labor. At the Ninth Annual IWW Convention, they proposed a resolution that the upcoming 1915 harvest season was an opportunity to attempt such a coordinated drive. The influential GEB member Frank Little seconded the resolution, which the delegates then passed.[49]

Bill Haywood, general organizer of the IWW, and the GEB took the next step, authorizing the creation of a Bureau of Migratory Workers (fig. 15). The purpose of the new bureau was to coordinate united action among the different locals, whether in towns or jungles, in "the Grain Belts, Fruit Sections, Lumber Districts and Cotton Zone." The bureau would "gather and compile information as to crop conditions, the time the harvests begin, the probable number of men needed in each locality, [and] the railroad connections." Bureau officials would distribute this information through a bulletin that would counter "the lies of the newspapers and Commercial clubs [according to the IWW, local newspapers, and those local business associations, a precursor of the chamber of commerce]" that lured workers to the harvests by promising high wages and plenty of work but then forced them to compete against one another, driving down wages and employment opportunities. In conjunction with the bureau, Haywood and the GEB called for a conference of harvesters to meet on 15 April 1915 in Kansas City, Missouri. At this mass meeting, according to Haywood, "wages and hours will be determined, also arrangements made for camp delegates or district secretaries so that a line of communication can be established between harvest crews and different districts."[50]

From the close of 1914 through the spring and summer of 1915, a new and much more effective phase in the development of IWW organization among farm workers began. The union now had a presence in the agricultural regions of California, the Pacific Northwest, and the Great Plains. Yet, with the exception of Wheatland, harvest Wobblies had most of their success operating within the unity of migrant white male laborers. As of 1914, the majority of seasonal farm laborers in the West fit this description. So, it should not be surprising that the conference of agricultural laborers was to take place in Kansas City, the gateway to the socially homogeneous Great Plains. And it was here that the center of IWW organizing in agriculture would begin its shift from the Far West to the plains. Of course, the participants did not know that this shift would take place, nor did they know that by continuing to build a foundation among white male migrant workers in the Great Plains they would create a worklife cultural gap between themselves and the dynamic farm labor force in the West: Hispanics, Asians, and harvester families. But these developments were in the future. In 1914, harvest Wobblies were on the threshold of the union's most vibrant period.

Chapter Three

A Bumper Crop of
Harvest Wobblies

⌘⌘⌘

The first annual harvest workers' conference, scheduled to meet in Kansas City, Missouri, 15 April 1915, generated some much-needed enthusiasm within the ranks of the IWW. In 1913, the union had fewer than fifteen thousand members, although Vincent St. John, former general secretary-treasurer, estimated the membership to be approximately thirty thousand in the spring of 1914. Even if St. John was correct, the IWW membership was far less than many of the craft unions that it was trying to replace. Moreover, the union had failed to capitalize on its success among textile workers in Lawrence, Kansas, from the year before, and in many industries where the union had a foothold, no dynamic growth was taking place. In the West, the IWW was in a chronic state of fragmented localism and internal conflict. The *Industrial Worker* suspended publication due to clashes among editors and staff writers over issues such as decentralization of the union and the use of sabotage. One of the few bright spots for the union was migrant labor organizing in the agricultural regions of the Great Plains and Far West. From the Wobbly point of view, these migrant workers epitomized the revolutionary potential of the working class. The upcoming conference stimulated a number of suggestions in *Solidarity* regarding a new industrial union structure for migratory workers. Eventually, through this discussion and the subsequent conference, the IWW would create the most successful farm workers' union up to that time.[1]

As Wobblies discussed how to bring agricultural laborers into their union in large numbers, employers of farm labor instigated another effort to control the supply and distribution of these workers. Farmers and state officials in Midwest and Great Plains states formed the National Farm Labor Exchange for the 1915 harvest season. This organization was a more effective version of a multi-state labor exchange that wheat belt states had tried to create ten years earlier that had failed due to weak state government support. State employment and agricultural department representatives from Montana, Colorado, North and South Dakota, Wyoming, Nebraska, Kansas, Minnesota, Iowa, Missouri, Oklahoma, and

Texas decided that the Labor Exchange would arrange and coordinate the labor needed for the expected bumper-crop harvest. Efficiency of labor distribution was the chief concern of the Labor Exchange, which proposed three distribution centers—Kansas City, Sioux City, and Minneapolis—to act as headquarters for their surrounding regions and to relay information regarding labor needs. Railroad company officials and the federal government's Department of Agriculture and Commission on Industrial Relations sought representation on the Labor Exchange and pledged their support for the effort. Organizers of the Labor Exchange hoped to eventually include representatives from all states and to coordinate labor distribution for all the crops that required seasonal harvest labor.[2]

Creating an Agricultural Workers' Industrial Union

Wobblies were aware of this large-scale effort to control farm labor, which only added immediacy to the goal of organizing this largely unorganized cohort of workers. In late winter and early spring 1915, Wobblies in Minnesota, Iowa, and Kansas flooded *Solidarity* with suggestions for the creation of an industrial union structure during the harvest workers' conference. Like many IWW organizing strategies, ideas percolated as much from the bottom up as from the top down. Most of these suggestions for creating an agricultural workers' organization recognized the unique worklife culture of migrant and seasonal laborers, taking into consideration their mobility, lack of adequate income, and wageworker status. For example, Charles Gray of Minneapolis Local 64, chairman of a special meeting on "harvest agitation," offered a proposal that bore some similarity to the Labor Exchange. He proposed that several existing locals in the wheat and corn belts act as organizing centers for the agricultural industry, dividing the regions into zones. Because the summer and fall harvest workforce was so mobile, he suggested that Wobblies create temporary locals in towns that drew numbers of migrant laborers during the harvest and threshing season. The initiation fee and dues for the new industrial union were to be kept low to encourage a high level of membership among low-paid farm workers. Gray suggested a uniform one-dollar initiation fee.

E. W. Latchem, an experienced migratory worker, also had suggestions for organizing his fellow migrants. He had joined the union as a young man in 1912 and soon became an insightful organizing strategist. Writing from Kansas, he encouraged Wobblies to seek delegate credentials for themselves rather than following the custom of requesting a camp delegate from a local in the area. Latchem wanted to make organizing farm workers as efficient and quick as possible, so he too suggested that Wobblies establish floating locals that would follow the harvest. His vision of delegates, representatives of the union in the workplace, proved prescient, because such delegates would become industrial union or job delegates in later years. Up to this point in the West, camp delegates, men who lived with other Wobblies in jungle camps, acted as the union's delegates outside the local union hall. Yet Latchem and others, like former IWW officer Vincent St. John, thought it would be a mistake to create a national organization of agricultural workers. St. John wrote that such an organization would be "a waste of time, money, and energy." He believed that no national organization should be attempted until union locals had "membership numerous enough to finance [a] National Union administration so that it [could] function properly." Latchem, although initially concurring with St. John, eventually became a prominent and influential harvest Wobbly and remained, unlike St. John, a long-term member of the IWW.[3]

R. Reese, another Minneapolis Wobbly, urged the creation of an organization of agricultural workers that would make use of existing mixed locals to coordinate unionizing activity on the job but with a decidedly national rather than local or regional focus. He thought that because mixed locals were overwhelmingly agricultural anyway, they should seek industrial union status, eliminating their catchall quality. Out of these agricultural locals, harvest Wobblies could establish a national organization. However, others were concerned that relying on mixed locals, whether primarily made up of migrant farm workers or not, would not solve the serious organizational problems that stemmed from competition among mixed locals and hit-and-miss activity. For example, Latchem reminded the readers of *Solidarity* that in the 1914 harvest season, delegates from the mixed locals of Kansas City, Minneapolis, and Vancouver, B.C., and delegates from Missoula's lumber workers' local, all worked as organizers in the Dakota harvest. These delegates caused confusion among workers, as they presented different initiation fees, and experienced frustration amongst themselves when their locals did not pay for propaganda materials supplied by Minneapolis Local 64 that were used in the organizing drive.[4]

Three Wobblies writing from Kansas City, Ed Doree, S. St. John, and G. J. Bourg, published an article in *Solidarity* arguing that an organization of harvest workers must be independent of the mixed locals, possess its own administrative staff, and provide useful information for the upcoming harvest to migrant and seasonal workers. Doree had agricultural organizing experience in Walla Walla, as well as in other agricultural and extractive industrial sectors in the West and South. Having organized out of the mixed locals of the West, Doree understood firsthand the problems associated with them. Doree, St. John, and Bourg also understood that migrant workers needed a union that had their interests at heart, as opposed to the Labor Exchange, which put farmers' needs first.

Further amplifying the suggestions of Doree and his fellow Wobblies, harvest Wobblies from Des Moines, Fred Wenger and James Phillips, argued that IWW members should create a "National Industrial Union of Agricultural Workers" with a small general executive board consisting of members familiar with harvesting, a secretary-treasurer, and a general organizer to supervise and coordinate field organizers. Consequently, no local would dominate farm labor organizing, such as Minneapolis Local 64, which had a large number of migrant workers already attached to it. A formal appeal from Des Moines Local 577's Press Committee seconded this more centralized approach in the pages of *Solidarity*. Their proposal included a national structure that was firmly associated with the national headquarters of the IWW. In the end, the centralization advocated by harvest Wobblies from Des Moines carried the day, but to satisfy the independence of the rank and file and the libertarian nature of migrant and seasonal workers, agricultural locals would retain a considerable amount of influence over the IWW's new national industrial union of farm workers.[5]

In spring 1915, it was clear that the IWW would seek to organize farm workers into a new, centralized agricultural workers' industrial union. But what of the small farmers, especially those who rented or share-cropped? Would they be eligible for membership in such a union? This issue had been part of an ongoing debate in the pages of *Solidarity* and the *Industrial Worker* for several years. A number of farmers wrote letters to the Wobbly newspapers in favor of allowing small farmers and tenant farmers membership in the union. Some agricultural laborers echoed this suggestion. Their basic argument was that these farmers were on the same side as industrial workers in the class war. They were just as exploited as the migrant farm worker, and had to sell their farm products at prices set by a marketplace over which they had no control. Advocates for tenant farmers explained that money from the sale of their agricultural commodities went mostly to pay rent on their property, leaving them with little income. Those farmers of most interest to Wobblies resided in the South. Southern tenant farmers, both black and white, relied primarily upon their own labor and that of their families during harvest seasons. Many of these farmers worked as wageworkers in the timber industry or other fields requiring semiskilled or unskilled labor to supplement their meager farm income.[6]

One of the most articulate and impassioned advocates for including tenant farmers into the IWW was the Southern poet and Wobbly, Covington Hall. Hall had a substantial reputation among Wobblies. He was one of the most effective leaders of the biracial but short-lived Brotherhood of Timber Workers, and had been instrumental in bringing together black and white timber workers who also worked as tenant farmers or farmhands. According to Hall, plantation owners and lumber barons oppressed Louisiana tenant farmers by exacting exorbitant rents and by enforcing the many restrictions on buying and selling their produce. Hall's experience with these agricultural workers, black and white, who were intimately tied together through economic interests and kinship, convinced him that they had a revolutionary character that precluded them from the typical desire to be a landowner expressed by Northern and Western farmers. He believed that Southern tenant farmers were interested only in making a living wage, and that they would welcome a collective form of farm ownership that would mesh well with the Wobbly call for a cooperative commonwealth of all industry.[7]

Despite the arguments of Hall and others, the overall sentiment in the Wobbly press was against bringing farmers into the union. Though IWW members had sympathy for southern black farmers and small farmers in the Great Plains, they believed that their aspirations were those of capitalists. Most tenant farmers, Wobblies argued, wanted to own land, and when they could, they too would employ farm labor for the lowest possible wage. The dividing line in the class war was simple for most Wobblies. If you owned or aspired to own the means of production and you hired labor to work your land—or your factory—then you were part of the employing class, one whose interests were in opposition to the wageworker or the employed class. Wobblies, such as Forrest Edwards, who would become secretary-treasurer of the Agricultural Workers' Industrial Union, reasoned that the IWW was a wageworkers' union. In fact, this was a major difference between the IWW and the only other significantly inclusive labor organization in U.S. history up to that time, the Knights of Labor, which had invited whites and blacks, recent European immigrants, men and women, and all skill levels into a great house of labor. The Knights had welcomed farmers and members of the middle class, but the Wobblies argued that because wageworkers and non-wageworkers did not have the same interests, including the latter would only cause internal conflict in the union. IWW members also wanted to distinguish themselves from the Socialist Party, which accepted workers, farmers, members of the middle class, and anyone else into their party on the strength of their belief in socialism, regardless of the person's class position. Wobblies wanted neither to repeat the mistakes of the Knights nor to become non-revolutionary like the Socialist Party, which preferred to bring socialism to power through the electoral process.

One significant factor that made the inclusion of farmers into the union—and for that matter members of the middle class and small business owners—a moot point was that many IWW members embraced a Marxist analysis of the agricultural economy. In the pages of *Solidarity* and the *Industrial Worker,* Wobblies argued that concentration of the means of production and pauperization of the labor force were already at work in agriculture. Farmers would diminish in number as they were forced into the ranks of the agricultural industrial proletariat. The farming industry itself would eventually fall under the control of fewer and fewer individuals and become exclusively corporate farming or agribusiness. The primary task at hand for Wobblies, then, was to create an industrial union in agriculture so that workers could eventually run the industry themselves. Ultimately, their brand of industrial unionism or homegrown syndicalism in agriculture was part of the overall Wobbly goal of building the new revolutionary society within the corrupt shell of the old.[8]

Founding the Agricultural Workers' Organization

The IWW members who arrived as delegates to the Kansas City convention represented locals in Fresno, Portland, Des Moines, Kansas City, Salt Lake City, San Francisco, Minneapolis, and Denver. Together they established the framework for the Agricultural Workers' Organization (AWO) and set the direction that the organization would take in the field; the AWO, they determined, would be more industrial unionist than revolutionary in its goals. Many of these Wobbly delegates came from backgrounds similar those of the workers they hoped to bring into the AWO. Jack Law, a delegate from San Francisco, was a veteran organizer and street speaker who had organized oil workers out of Tulsa, Oklahoma, in 1914, and western construction workers. He had also been prominent in the free-speech fight of 1913 in Minot, North Dakota. Henry E. McGucken was a delegate from Fresno who began his life as a worker as a bobbin boy. At a very young age he left his home in Paterson,

New Jersey and headed west. He worked a variety of day labor jobs that eventually led him to Seattle. There, after listening to a Wobbly soapbox speech in early 1912, he joined the union at the age of eighteen. Within a year McGuckin worked for the union among lumberjacks in British Columbia and eventually organized workers in the East and West, especially in the San Francisco Bay area. He, Law, and another Wobbly, Ted Fraser, left California together in an empty freight train boxcar bound for Kansas City.[9]

The conference delegates reached a number of conclusions. One was to focus the new organization's unionizing efforts not only on agricultural laborers in the U.S. but also in Canada. In addition, they passed a motion to ban street speaking in harvest towns as a propaganda strategy and as an organizing tool. The delegates wanted their new association to organize workers above all else. They crafted the AWO mission to organize, primarily on the job, but also in the jungles and on the rails. The initiation fee for the AWO would be $2 instead of $1, with dues of fifty cents a month. Though this fee was comparatively high, a majority of the delegates concluded that it would give the organization greater financial strength and would require greater commitment on the part of new members when they joined. The delegates elected a general secretary-treasurer along with a five-member general executive board.[10]

Walter T. Nef was chosen as the AWO's first secretary-treasurer. Nef had earned a reputation as a fine organizer, and when elected he was working out of the Philadelphia local. He proved to be an effective leader of the AWO (see fig. 12, page 66). Originally from Switzerland, he had arrived in New York City in 1901 in his late teens. His work experience typified that of most Wobblies. He was an itinerant laborer who had worked on the waterfront, as a timber worker, in construction, and in agriculture. According to labor historian Peter Cole, Nef, like McGuckin, joined the IWW after listening to a Wobbly give a talk on the power of industrial unionism. The speech Nef heard had been delivered by George Speed on the San Francisco waterfront in 1909; afterwards, Nef plunged himself into IWW organizing, eventually participating in the 1909-1910 Spokane free speech fight. He organized timber workers in the Northwest and in the Great Lakes region, longshoremen in Philadelphia, and agricultural laborers in the West. He knew the limits of street corner propaganda and the possibilities of what could be achieved by stable industrial unions under the umbrella of the IWW. Nef devoted himself to building a durable, pragmatic institution of harvest laborers. Under his leadership, the AWO would quickly become one of the largest branches of the IWW.[11]

The AWO, designated Local 400 in a mocking reference to the four hundred families who allegedly controlled the bulk of American wealth, received a national union charter from the IWW within a few days of the conference. As a national union, the AWO was free from the control of any mixed locals. Secretary Nef issued dues books and dues stamps to job delegates elected from locals throughout the country. Along with the secretary-treasurer and executive committee, an organization committee would help coordinate unionizing efforts on the job. The eventual success of the AWO's elected administrative bodies and the leadership's flexibility in relation to rank-and-file members made this national industrial union system the model for all of the IWW's industrial unions. The enhanced centralization of organizing farm workers would now begin.[12]

The AWO's First Harvest Season

The earliest harvest areas of the wheat belt were in the southern plains, so that is where the AWO's first harvest season began. Some of the delegates who journeyed there later rose to prominence within the union, including Mat Fox, E. W. Latchem, Forrest Edwards, Ted Fraser, Charles W. Anderson, Charles Gray, R. Reese, G. J. Bourg, H. E. McGuckin, and Jack Law.

Arriving in the southern plains town of Enid, Oklahoma, these delegates and other harvest Wobblies found that the harvest had been delayed by rain. They had to wait in camps with hundreds of other workers until the harvest began. To feed themselves and the other independent harvesters that they hoped to bring into the AWO, Wobblies had to work with city officials, but conflict over the distribution of food led to the arrest of Jack Law and another Wobbly by police. Despite this inauspicious beginning, harvest Wobblies forged ahead with their organizing drive.

In Kansas City, Missouri, hundreds of harvest Wobblies arrived to partake in the wheat harvest. Perhaps due to their numbers, the excitement caused by a new harvesters' union, and the anticipated high prices Great Plains farmers expected for their wheat, harvest Wobblies made some rather unrealistic demands on local farmers, such as asking for $5 a day for six hours of work. The AWO leadership decided that it had to provide some viable and uniform goals for harvest work. Their official demands included a minimum wage of $3 for ten hours' work with fifty cents an hour for overtime, decent food, a clean place to sleep with access to blankets, and "no discrimination against union men

(I.W.W.)." The AWO encouraged Wobblies in the southern plains to hold to these demands and called on all harvest workers to make these their essential goals throughout the Great Plains wheat belt. If these demands were not acceptable to farmers, the AWO leadership urged Wobblies to work for whatever they could get. It was important for Wobblies to work because if they found themselves unemployed, they would lose the opportunity to spread the IWW message on the job site and to sign up new members. Unemployment was also an excuse for town and county law enforcement to arrest AWO members on the charge of vagrancy. In mid-June, for example police in Beloit, Kansas arrested twelve harvest Wobblies, presumably on that charge. The AWO's Agitation Committee called for their members to keep a low profile. They even recommended tearing up union cards in front of an employer if that was necessary to get work.[13]

The 1915 southern plains harvest was a learning experience for the AWO. Walter Nef summed up the organizing effort in the region in an article published in *Solidarity*. He noted that the practice of traveling in large groups through the wheat belt had led to trouble, and recommended that Wobblies break up into clusters of twos or threes once the harvest began because of the difficulty of getting hired as a large group of IWW members.

Large groups had their uses, however. They could intimidate a freight train crew, thereby securing nearly unlimited free transportation for themselves and other harvest workers; Wobblies felt this was justified because they believed that they and all harvesters were essential to agriculture. A large number of Wobblies could prevent extortion payments for the ride and put a stop to beatings by brakemen when they tried to force harvesters off the train. They could also thwart train crew efforts to dump workers off on sidetracks, areas away from harvest fields and towns.[14] Another factor helps explain why harvest Wobblies continued to travel together in packs: they now shared a union structure that formalized solidarity in the face of hostile employers, townspeople, and law enforcement. There was not only safety in numbers, there was also camaraderie. For these reasons, Nef's suggestion went largely unheeded, as did subsequent appeals by succeeding AWO leaders.

As members of the AWO, harvest Wobblies immediately experienced hostility. Nef reported that police and sheriff's deputies arrested approximately one hundred Wobblies in Kansas and Oklahoma, though local courts released them within a matter of days or weeks. Nef did not enumerate the charges, but vagrancy was more than likely the official reason for their arrest. Nevertheless, some Wobblies faced more serious charges, including assault and murder. Arlington, Kansas, residents found harvest Wobbly V. J. Bradley, from Portland, Oregon, beaten to death within the city limits in late June. Nef believed that the murderers were probably brakemen, as Bradley had been one of many IWW men assaulted by brakemen who were trying to remove harvesters from empty boxcars. Police arrested four Wobblies and charged them with the murder, but later had to release them for lack of evidence.

Much of the hostility directed at harvest Wobblies stemmed from their efforts to raise the going wage, efforts that were perceived as threatening because they could exploit the frustrations of independent harvesters. For example, the U.S. Federal Labor Bureau, the Farmers Union in Kansas, and the Labor Exchange restricted harvesters' wages to between $2.00 and $3.00, forced them to pay railroad fares, and flooded the labor market with harvesters. According to Nef, once independent harvesters learned that AWO workers earned $3.50 on the job and refused to pay for train transportation, they "lent a willing ear to the A.W.O. of the I.W.W." Nef did not note whether this "willing ear" translated into new members.[15]

On the first of August, as the harvest moved north, AWO delegates held a meeting to set wage rates. The delegates wanted harvest Wobblies in South Dakota to demand a minimum of $3.00 for harvesting and $3.50 for threshing. In North Dakota, the AWO leadership directed members to demand 50 cents more, presumably because North Dakota required more migrant labor than its sister state. The same month, Nef and the executive board moved the AWO from Kansas City to Minneapolis, establishing a permanent headquarters. From Minneapolis, over one hundred delegates fanned out across the north plains, gaining one hundred new recruits a week, mostly in North Dakota. Arrests continued as the harvest progressed north. Again, most were for vagrancy. Individuals identified as IWWs or engaged in signing up new members were most vulnerable to arrest, possibly because of farmers' concerns over the high wages demanded by the AWO. High wheat prices, which many had expected due to the European war and demand for American wheat, did not materialize during the 1915 harvest season. Prices peaked at $1.40 a bushel in May and declined through the summer. For farmers, paying $2.50 a day for temporary labor was as high as they wanted to go, given the declining price for their wheat.[16]

Organizing efforts during the northern plains harvest—mainly in South Dakota, North Dakota, and Minnesota—went well for the new

AWO. Not all farmers resisted hiring self-identified AWO members. For example, North Dakota was home to a number of socialist farmers who preferred to employ IWW crews for harvesting and threshing because Wobblies had a reputation for working diligently and dependably when their demands were met. With the large presence of Wobblies in the region, wages for harvesters tended to hover between $3.50 and $4.00 a day. Labor scarcity, particularly north of Minot, bad weather, and the presence of hi-jacks, or holdup men, were also factors contributing to higher wages in the northern plains. The problem of hi-jacks dogged harvest Wobblies and other migrant harvesters. These armed robbers drove many workers away from the harvest, causing a labor shortage. Editors and contributing writers in *Solidarity* urged harvest Wobblies to protect themselves by carrying as little cash as possible when in the fields and jungles, and on the rails. If they wished, Wobblies could send some of their money to Nef in Minneapolis or to Bill Haywood's office in Chicago for safekeeping.[17]

Despite threats by wealthy farmers and municipal officials in the plains states to bring in African American harvest hands and to utilize equipment that would reduce the need for harvest workers, the 1915 harvest ended on an upbeat note for the AWO. Though Wobblies could do little about mechanization, they welcomed the opportunity to organize African American farm laborers from the South. Over the course of the AWO's first season in the Great Plains, between two thousand and three thousand harvesters joined the IWW. At a mass AWO meeting in November, harvest Wobblies reflected on the success of the organizing effort and determined which cities in the wheat belt had enough Wobblies working in agriculture to support AWO locals. They also set their sights on expanding the AWO to California, as they recently had done in the corn belt regions of Illinois, Iowa, Missouri, and Nebraska, and as they planned to do in Northwest lumber camps later that winter. In fact, by the end of the year, lumberjacks in Minnesota and Washington moved to join the AWO, increasing the number of AWO members and adding to the treasury.[18]

During the November Minneapolis meeting, the AWO put on a smoker, a fundraiser with vaudeville entertainment. Harvest Wobblies and other members of the IWW, displaying greater and lesser degrees of talent, performed for the audience. The program's first act was a blackface comedy, which J. A. McDonald, the soon-to-be editor of the revived *Industrial Worker*, considered "extremely clever and largely original." Musical performances followed. One singing group was the

"Russian quintette," which sang "international revolutionary songs." The best act, according to McDonald, was a tableau, "Master and Slave" and the "Advancing Proletariat." Out of all of the performances, this was the only one to feature a female performer, Olga Lingreen, who played one of the wage slaves with an infant in her arms. A Scotch patter ended the first half of the show. This witty chatter between two Wobblies espousing the virtues of the AWO received a "roar of laughter" and applause. Following intermission, which featured a Charlie Chaplin impersonator, music, food, soda, and cigars, Wobblies presented a "jungle drama" written by Charles Ashleigh. Ashleigh, an English immigrant who joined the IWW a year after his arrival in the U.S. in 1910, was already a beloved poet and writer (see fig. 17, page 105). The play was a comedy, set in the fictional town of Hoosierville, North Dakota. The all-male cast included the part of a "farcical woman's role," an English lord played by Ashleigh, a sheriff, unorganized harvesters, a job delegate named Line-em-up played by Ted Fraser, and several harvest Wobblies. Other performances followed this well-received play, including a ventriloquist act, which McDonald thought "reached the verge of defamation of character." More music, an auction, and another comedy performance finished off the program. [19]

The smoker demonstrated that Wobblies knew how to have a good time. Music, comedy, and plays were the mainstays of Wobbly entertainment from the inception of the union. However, the smoker also reflected the AWO's nearly all-white, all-male constituency. The blackface comedy would not have gone over well with the IWW's Marine Transportation Workers' Local 8 in Philadelphia, which had a substantial number of African American members. Furthermore, Ashleigh's play evoked the largely male world of Great Plains harvesting. Set in the exclusively male living space of the jungle and in the conflict between male workers and male employers, the play reflected the worklife of harvest Wobblies in the wheat belt. It provides sharp contrast to the multiethnic, male and female participants in John Reed's Pageant for the Paterson silk workers' strike of 1913.[20] Finally, the risqué nature of the comedy performances further suggests that the smoker reflected the Wobblies' male constituency in the Great Plains. The real test of this new agricultural laborers' union was whether it could successfully branch out of the wheat belt and adapt to the worklife world of Hispanics, Asians, women, and children in other agricultural sectors, especially California.

The Struggle to Build the AWO in California

While the 1915 harvest season in the Great Plains wheat belt proved to be a turning point for the IWW among migrant farm labor there, California Wobblies continued to obsess over the release of Ford and Suhr, who still languished in prison for their role in the Wheatland affair. This myopic behavior on the part of the IWW in California resulted in a lost opportunity to begin building a viable farm-labor organization in the state. Though seeking the release of these innocent men was a laudable goal, the strategy that California Wobblies eventually employed only insured that Ford and Suhr would remain in prison. Wobbly unionizing activity among agricultural workers was sporadic, becoming a concerted effort only at the end of the year with the AWO California conference in December. At the conference, over fifty delegates met in Sacramento to establish a harvest workers' union with branch locals in the central valleys of the state. Yet California harvest Wobblies still failed to practice on-the-job organizing, so that in 1916, they missed another opportunity to build a union for the state's thousands of migrant and seasonal farm workers.[21]

In early 1915, Ford and Suhr's cause had a great deal of support beyond that of the IWW. The California State Federation of Labor and numerous other labor, church, and women's civic groups throughout the United States pressed Governor Hiram Johnson for the release of the imprisoned Wobblies. Efforts by attorneys representing the State Federation resulted in a March pardon hearing for the two. During the hearing, according to historian Cletus Daniel, an onslaught of appeals from a variety of individuals and organizations supported a pardon. Some of the most influential members of this informal coalition had contributed to Johnson's political fortunes and to those of the Progressive Party in the state. Remarkably, even several individuals who had helped convict Ford and Suhr, including E. Clemens Horst, whose corporation controlled twenty percent of the hop industry in the state, and W. H. Carlin, a prosecutor at the Marysville trial, voiced their support for a pardon. Johnson found enough evidence concerning improprieties in Ford and Suhr's trial in Marysville that he promised to review the case, and if warranted, issue a pardon. At the very least, he concluded that the men's sentences should probably be reduced.[22]

California Wobblies, however, did not wait patiently for an outcome, as other more mainstream labor groups and supporters were willing to do. In the early months of 1915, they vowed to wage an international boycott of California agricultural produce. Some Wobblies in the state, such as Charles L. Lambert, an IWW organizer based in Sacramento and secretary of the Ford and Suhr Defense Committee, wanted to initiate a concomitant sabotage campaign to force the release of the prisoners. The boycott centered primarily on California's hop industry, fruit canneries, and ranching. Hundreds of thousands of stickers announcing the boycott and Wobbly demands in red ink were distributed by union members in California, throughout the United States, and overseas to Australia, New Zealand, and Great Britain. Other stickers issued by the IWW announced wage demands and calls for limits on the workday for agricultural laborers. Some stickers contained veiled threats of sabotage. For example, "Don't stick copper nails or tacks in Fruit Trees or Grape vines IT HURTS THEM" was ostensibly an attempt to prevent sympathetic farm workers and harvest Wobblies from destroying property in the effort to free Ford and Suhr, but in the public mind such stickers only linked the IWW with violence and destruction of property.

Adding to the IWW's reputation for extremism was the effort by the state's newspapers to blame fires in the California countryside on the IWW. Summer fires in the arid, sun-drenched valleys of the state were common, and no court ever convicted a Wobbly of arson, yet the press pinned any fire of suspicious origin on the IWW. Wobblies did not always disassociate themselves from these fires. For example, as Charles Lambert wrote in a telegram to Bill Haywood, with a hint of glee, "[T]he wheat fields are all on fire about fifty miles from here, damage so far is about $250,000." Lambert wanted harvest Wobblies to engage in some form of sabotage at the point of production, but he realized that they did not have the numbers to be effective. Whether he wanted his fellow Wobblies to set fires or merely to strike on the job is not clear. Regardless, federal officials would use Lambert's statements and correspondence against him, as well as against Haywood and many other Wobblies, during the mass trials of Wobblies that took place between 1917 and 1919 (fig. 16).[23]

The boycott and veiled appeals to sabotage reflected the lack of pragmatism exhibited by harvest Wobblies in California in comparison to their counterparts the plains. But such appeals also reflected the weakness of the IWW in California agriculture. In testimony before the Commission on Industrial Relations in 1914, George Speed, a founding member of the IWW and an influential organizer among itinerant workers, noted that between ten and twelve thousand laborers passed through the IWW in the state over nearly an eight-year period. Yet he acknowledged that few remained in the union, as "they necessarily drift here and there." Carleton Parker, whose work with the California

Commission of Immigration and Housing (CCIH) placed him in close contact with the IWW, estimated the union's membership in the state at only a few thousand that same year. Despite the IWW's inability to build a stable membership base, most observers in and out of the union considered it to be very influential among migrant farm laborers in 1914 and 1915. F. C. Mills, an agent for the CCIH, spent the summer of 1914 with migrant laborers in central California. He found that many itinerant workers considered the IWW the only organization that truly represented their interests.[24]

Lambert, though given to incendiary rhetoric, had to acknowledge that the IWW did not have the resources to maintain a picket line to prevent the harvest of California hops, nor could harvest Wobblies protect themselves from the danger posed by the ranchers' hired gunmen. Therefore, he argued that Wobblies had to rely on the boycott of California agricultural products, although he urged them to stay on the job, continue to organize, and spread the message of support for Ford and Suhr among California's agricultural workers.

In response to Lambert, the publicity committee of Fresno Local 66 announced a call for camp delegates to take out credentials and become job delegates of the AWO. The goal was to have delegates sign up new members in every town in the San Joaquin Valley. In Southern California's

Figure 16. Charles Lambert, along with hundreds of other IWW members, faced arrest, trial, conviction, and imprisonment for Wobbly activities. (Courtesy, Walter P. Reuther Library, Wayne State University)

Imperial Valley, however, the IWW was fighting just to maintain its presence, let alone gain new members or work for Ford and Suhr's release. When an unknown assailant killed a city policeman in May in the Imperial Valley town of Brawley, police used the killing as a pretext to arrest several local Wobblies. They did not charge the workers with murder, but with lesser crimes, and sentenced them to sixty days on a chain gang. The Wobblies had the option to leave town rather than serve the sentence, and some chose to do so. According to Herman Kubow, secretary of Brawley's Local 439, county newspapers also tried to pin haystack and cantaloupe-shed fires on IWW members. Kubow was convinced that this was designed to force the IWW out of the valley before the cantaloupe harvest began, thereby preventing harvest Wobblies from organizing melon pickers.[25]

The inflammatory rhetoric of some California Wobblies, unsubstantiated reports of Wobbly arson in the press, and the conflict that followed IWW organizing efforts made Governor Johnson's decision not to pardon Ford and Suhr a politically safe one. It would have been very difficult for him to pardon members of such a radical organization without risking political injury. Johnson's declaration stated that, "So long as, in behalf of these men, the threats of injury and sabotage continue, so long as the preachment exists in their behalf in the State of California, so long as incendiarism is attempted, I will neither listen to appeals for executive clemency, in behalf of Ford and Suhr, nor in any fashion consider the shortening of their terms of imprisonment."

Despite Johnson's self-righteous tone, evidence suggests that the governor never believed the arson reports. It was likely that he simply took political advantage of Wobbly rhetoric and anti-Wobbly hysteria in the media. He appears to have been successful, for California's mainstream labor leaders, though they still supported a pardon for Ford and Suhr, publicly acknowledged that Johnson could not appear to bow to Wobbly violence. Nevertheless, other labor movement leaders in the state, such as Tom Mooney of the Alameda Building Trades, who was secretary-treasurer of the International Workers' Defense League, pointed out that the governor had recognized earlier that the men's sentences should be reduced. Mooney charged that failing to reduce the sentences because of alleged Wobbly misbehavior was unconscionable. He went on to urge AFL unions to work with the IWW in putting economic pressure on the agricultural industry to secure Ford and Suhr's release.[26]

The Wobbly-initiated boycott, while it did not achieve its primary goal, ate into the profits of the state's hop industry. Hop growers made their situation worse by taking on the expense of hiring gunmen to prevent IWW strike actions and pickets. By the end of 1915, hop growers complained that they were losing money; some claimed that they were losing as much as ten thousand dollars a year. As of 1917, California officials and farmers estimated that the IWW's campaign to support Ford and Suhr had cost the state's agricultural industry as much as $20 million. Governor Johnson and several other western state governors called on the federal government to suppress the IWW, but at the time, unless use of the mails was part of alleged IWW criminal activity, there was little the federal government could do. Yet Western agribusiness and politicians would not have to wait long until the federal government had the legal means to launch an attack against the IWW.[27]

Harvest Wobblies in California proved that they could, even with only a small number of organized workers and supporters, significantly disrupt the agricultural industry in the state. But building a robust farm-labor union was a different matter. The California section of the AWO had begun with great fanfare in the Wobbly press. The December 1915 Sacramento conference had a large turnout. Reports in *Solidarity* noted that the delegates there identified important areas for organization, particularly the orange industry of Southern California, and that they had an eye toward year-round opportunities for harvesting work and therefore for organizing. In a subsequent article in March, AWO camp delegate Alex D. Fraser urged his fellow California harvest Wobblies to refrain from time-wasting philosophizing and to get on the job, for there were thousands of migrant agricultural laborers whom he considered ripe for the IWW message. Fraser's pleas seemed to have fallen on deaf ears, however, as the California AWO made few strides toward building a pragmatic union for harvest workers.[28]

Without a doubt the problem stemmed from the revolutionary intransigency of many California Wobblies, and their concern that the Minneapolis headquarters of the AWO would infringe on their independence. These factors, more than any repressive act by California law enforcement, presented serious obstacles to building a stable farm-labor union. Cletus Daniel offers a convincing argument that California Wobblies did not want to trade their street corner propaganda, free-speech fights, boycott campaigns, and sabotage for on-the-job organizing. Instead, they continued to create propaganda leagues, which were open to anyone interested in furthering the cause of the IWW, and more mixed recruiting locals, even as such activities declined in other states. From the beginning of AWO activity in California, Wobblies were suspicious of the national organization. For example, Lambert declared that they already knew how to organize and did not need the help of the AWO. Perhaps if organizers such as McGuckin had returned to California after the 1915 convention, a more effective campaign would have emerged. Instead, Bill Haywood and the IWW executive committee preferred to use McGuckin, Jack Law, George Speed, and other capable organizers to expand the AWO in other areas or to assist in essential strike actions in other industries. Consequently, at the end of 1915, the IWW had to issue the decentralist Californians a separate union charter of the Agricultural Workers Industrial Organization of California No. 444, which elected J. T. Doran its secretary-treasurer. The independent AWIO lasted for only a few months. The vast majority of AWO members in California actually joined the union elsewhere before they even reached California. By the end of 1916, Sacramento, Fresno, and Los Angeles locals sought AWO charters, finally bringing California into the orbit of the AWO. To underscore the anemic nature of agricultural organizing in the state, only Local 66's assistance to striking female fig workers in Fresno can be noted as a meaningful unionizing effort that year.[29]

The Emerging Viability of the AWO

With the advent of the 1916 harvest season, the locus of activity would again occur in the Great Plains wheat belt with less activity in the Far West. Out of the three major extractive industries IWW organizers sought to penetrate during these years—agriculture, mining, and logging—agriculture would prove to be the most successful over the long term. Though some observers of the labor movement had written off the IWW by 1916, Paul F. Brissenden, one of the first scholars to take the IWW seriously as a labor organization, wrote a piece in *The New Republic* critical of those who dismissed the IWW as moribund. He pointed out that the Wobblies were making their presence felt in the harvest fields as well as in the mining industry. And he was right. With the growth of the IWW in harvest organizing, the AWO could contribute substantial financial and personnel support to other industrial organizing efforts and strikes. One of the most important financial contributions the AWO made was for the Mesabi Range miners' strike in the spring of 1916.[30]

Early that year, the AWO began the first nationwide effort to organize timber workers. Logging was part of many migrant workers' annual labor cycle. Scores of men worked in the harvest fields during the summer and worked as loggers in the fall and spring. Secretary-Treasurer Nef thought that only by maintaining an AWO presence among key seasonal labor jobs could the organization prosper. In February, the Spokane Lumber

Workers' Local made its affiliation with the AWO official. The recently sparse treasury of the local received much-needed funds from the AWO to continue its work in the Inland Northwest logging region of eastern Washington, northern Idaho, and western Montana. The strength of the AWO was such that it also assumed leadership of two newly established unions, Local 490 of the Metal and Mine Workers Union and Local 573, a general construction workers' union. Nef was the ostensible administrative head of these unions. He used his position to increase organizing efforts not only among construction workers and miners but also among the loggers of Minnesota and Wisconsin who customarily worked in the mines during part of the year. The AWO's power was demonstrably on the rise early in 1916, as membership continued to grow and more delegates made their way into industries other than agriculture.[31]

Nef had high expectations for organizing the harvest stiffs in the Great Plains that summer. Along with the AWO leadership, he continued the pragmatic strategy of placing improvements in the worklife of migrant agricultural laborers above revolutionary aspirations. The 1916 harvest organizing drive in the wheat belt would be a fine demonstration of the AWO's emphasis on building a following among migrant workers. The harvest Wobblies understood the worklife culture of their fellow agricultural workers in the Great Plains and sought to address their needs. In late May, Nef wrote a brief report in *Solidarity* describing the recent AWO business meeting. AWO delegates had re-elected Nef as secretary-treasurer and had chosen a new executive board for the upcoming wheat harvest season. Approximately three hundred delegates were already in the field with recruiting supplies and credentials, some acting as delegates for the first time. Nef hoped to gain twenty thousand members into the AWO by the end of the year, and if IWW estimates are correct, that number was nearly achieved. According to labor historian Philip Foner, the AWO made up one-third of the total IWW membership at the close of 1916. For that year's season, $4.00 for a ten-hour day was the AWO demand for harvest work in Kansas. Nef noted that the AWO would announce demands for other harvest regions over the course of the summer. For example, the AWO released a flier later in 1916 that was specifically for North Dakota. Here the AWO demanded $3.50 for ten hours of work with an additional fifty cents per hour for overtime, along with improvements in living conditions while on the job. The two living condition demands in the flier were "good clean board" and "clean places to sleep in—with plenty of clean bedding." Nef, whose name and title appears at the bottom of the sheet, pointed out to farmers in the flier that "harvest work is seasonable and unsteady, and must receive consideration. Common laborers are paid in many places 35 to 40 cents an hour on steady employment, and $3.50 a day and board is only 35 cents an hour, not a cent too much." He also promised that if farmers complied with wage and living condition demands, they could count on "satisfactory work."[32]

Although substantial resistance rose to meet the AWO in the southern plains, with vagrancy arrests and other forms of intimidation by local law enforcement, the organization's membership grew by the thousands in the harvest fields. One contributing factor was a disappointing wheat harvest. National and state agricultural experts had predicted a bumper crop, and consequently migrant farm laborers flooded the region. Wheat yields, however, fell far short of expectations. The poor wages and less-than-plentiful work drove many laborers to join the AWO in the hope that the union could force wages up. The going wage rates did climb in Oklahoma and Kansas, with some areas reaching $5 a day, although farmers argued that this increase was not due to the AWO's influence, but to the high price that Europeans were willing to pay for American grain because of the war. Another factor leading to increase AWO membership was that large numbers of IWW workers traveling together on freight trains meant that transportation for Wobblies was free. Though Nef had cautioned harvest Wobblies against moving through the wheat belt in large groups, they continued to do so anyway because they could in effect commandeer freight trains and persuade or force independent harvesters to sign up as AWO members. Ultimately, the little red union card became a ticket on area rail systems.[33]

Unfortunately, the little red union card could not protect Wobblies or other migrants from the dangers of freight train travel. In South Dakota at the peak of the late summer harvest, which turned out to be terribly poor throughout the northern plains, a train loaded with men in boxcars and on top of boxcars—about two hundred of them Wobblies—lost control and jumped the tracks, hurling hundreds of men into the air. Three men died and almost thirty were injured. Most of the IWW members were on top of the boxcars and two of the dead were Wobblies.[34]

Job delegates, immersed in a population of migrant laborers, now had a unique opportunity to build AWO membership. They could try to sign up members on the rails, in the jungles, and on the job. Yet the process of bringing new members into the AWO had its problems. Because a job delegate received fifty cents for every new member he signed up, Wobblies looking only to the commission inevitably signed up workers who had no serious interest in IWW principles. These "hijacks, bootleggers and professional gamblers who infest the harvest fields," wrote E. N. Osborne in *Solidarity*, use the union "as a shield for their dirty work." Purging the growing organization of nefarious individuals became a primary goal of the AWO, for they alienated workers who in good faith joined the union only to find themselves in the company of men who fleeced or robbed them.[35]

Nevertheless, the worst aspect of open recruiting in the field was the practice of coercing people to join before they were allowed to work in the harvest or ride the rails. It was one thing to have enough Wobblies on a job site to induce other workers to join the union. Particularly in North Dakota, Wobblies had control over numerous harvest crews and threshing machine outfits. The non-union worker could always move on to find other employment, but being forced to join the union as a prerequisite to riding the rails deprived these workers of the sometimes free transportation that was common at the time. A $2.00 initiation fee and first month's dues of fifty cents meant that a train ride now cost $2.50. Many workers rejected this fee and IWW membership and principles generally, although an outright rejection of AWO membership could be dangerous. If an independent worker refused to join the organization while riding in a boxcar, it was not uncommon for an AWO organizer and nearby harvest Wobblies to throw him off the moving train. Organizers such as Forrest Edwards supported these rough tactics. He envisioned an AWO picket line stretching across the Great Plains to prevent non-union laborers from working the harvest. For Edwards, this was class war, and war engendered casualties.[36]

The IWW's growing reputation for strong-armed tactics provoked violence between Wobblies and independent harvesters. Redfield, a wheat town in eastern South Dakota, was the scene of a shoot-out between roughly three hundred IWW men and two hundred independents, according to the *New York Times*. A force of one hundred and fifty deputy sheriffs had to intervene to quell the violence. The *Times* went on to note that "harvest hands outside the I.W.W. organization have declared war upon the organization. And these were the aggressors in today's fight." Those who carried concealed weapons, Wobblies and independents alike, were the ones arrested after the fight. Law enforcement officials threw both factions out of town. In another incident in South Dakota, harvest Wobblies threw two African American migrants, who allegedly had refused to join the AWO, off a freight train. The independent harvesters subsequently found a passenger train that transported them to their destination, Tulare, just south of Redfield.

There, harvest Wobblies attacked them. Police arrested the migrants and some of the IWW members for carrying concealed weapons. The Wobblies justified their attack, alleging that these were hi-jacks who had held up a Wobbly in Tulare the previous week.[37]

Farmers, like independent harvesters, had mixed reactions to AWO members; some had no problem hiring them, for others, hiring AWO members largely depended on the availability of non-union labor. The violence that farmers associated with the IWW, though, stimulated a powerful reaction in some areas of the wheat belt. In Mott, a small wheat town in southwestern North Dakota, an IWW member shot Louis Larson, an area farmer, in the heat of an argument. Local law enforcement officials incarcerated the accused man, but they had to move him from the Mott jail to another town out of fear that local townspeople would lynch him. In other North Dakota counties, law enforcement had a no-tolerance policy regarding the presence of IWW members. Sheriff's deputies periodically raided jungles, the primary living place for harvesters, in an effort to purge them of Wobblies. Some wheat farmers, in towns such as Minot, North Dakota, simply refused to hire any IWWs. Two North Dakota farmers wrote letters to the *Industrial Worker* insisting that it was impossible for them to meet the wage demands of the AWO. They would rather let their crop rot on the ground than pay $3.50 to $4.00 a day to a union harvester.[38]

Regardless of these varying levels of resistance to harvest Wobblies, the AWO successfully established itself among the mobile agricultural workforce in the Great Plains over the consecutive harvest seasons of 1915 and 1916. AWO organizers and harvest Wobblies swam among the wheat belt's migrant laborers, experiencing the same worklife culture and seeking to represent the interests of harvest workers. The key to Wobbly success in the region was the focus on organizing in the countryside. The huge and sparsely populated wheat belt of the Great Plains proved ideal for organizing workers who had to travel great distances by rail for employment and had to live in jungles along the way. Organizing in smaller agricultural regions or towns presented a different picture altogether, because townspeople and farmers could combine into a formidable block of opposition. The AWO's efforts to break out of the plains and organize in Washington revealed the problems associated with organizing in such areas.

The AWO in Washington

With each passing year, grain and fruit farmers in eastern and south-central Washington became more and more dependent on migrant and seasonal agricultural labor. Thousands of independent harvesters and hundreds of harvest Wobblies made the state part of their annual labor cycle. In the summer of 1916, AWO organizers made a concerted effort to firmly establish their organization in the state. In North Yakima, known for its heavy reliance on seasonal fruit- and hop-pickers, harvest Wobblies circulated IWW literature over the course of the summer. Organizers rented rooms on Front Street in the city's downtown, or lived in local jungles. The largest concentrations of Wobblies were in area orchards and on nearby construction sites. On 16 September, city police arrested eleven Wobblies at their rented rooms. The arresting officers brought the men before Judge R. B. Milroy, who informed them that North Yakima had no place for the Industrial Workers of the World. Apparently, area fruit-ranch owners, who believed that the distribution of Wobbly literature among pickers impeded recruitment of labor, had filed complaints against the local IWW, particularly against Wesley Brown, an IWW organizer who was among those arrested. Judge Milroy told the Wobblies, whom a *Yakima Morning Herald* reporter described as working men who had seen their fair share of manual labor, that they could bring any grievances that they might have to the state's labor commissioner through proper channels. It was clear that neither city officials nor employers would tolerate the distribution of literature that called for higher wages and better working conditions among fruit pickers. After giving his lecture, Judge Milroy released the Wobblies.[39]

An editorial in the *Yakima Morning Herald* concluded that these Wobblies were a threat to the region's major industry, agriculture. The editorial thought that the IWW needed to be disabused of the notion that all farmers were rich. He assured readers that North Yakima farmers were not wealthy, and that they could not afford to pay the wages Wobblies demanded. The editorial played up the alleged Wobbly penchant for violence as well as the Wobbly tactic of accepting any wage offered by a farmer until reaching the field and then demanding a higher wage. Finally, the editorial noted that agriculture had dramatically changed in recent years, necessitating thousands of migrants for the harvest season. Wobbly agitation among seasonal farm workers would only disrupt the harvest and the livelihood of North Yakima farmers.[40]

The campaign to rid the city of Wobblies involved the familiar strategy of law enforcement harassment and arrest on charges of vagrancy. After a group of Wobblies urged the unemployed of the city not to use the federal employment office but to use a union hall to find work, Chief of Police B. F. McCurdy raided the Wobbly hall on South Front Street. He determined that the Wobblies had no intention of working and ordered the hall closed. During his search of the premises, he found a letter addressed to William Wilson, a local Wobbly organizer, from Richard Brazier, head of the "agricultural division" of the IWW in Spokane. Brazier was notifying Wilson that the IWW would not open a local in Wenatchee, another major fruit-producing center just north of Yakima, but would instead provide a stationary delegate and several job delegates in the surrounding area. Stationary delegates and job delegates did not need a local in which to organize area workers. They could rent a room in a town and work in their own trade, or work full-time signing up new members, as organizers were doing in North Yakima.[41]

Arrests followed the raid. On 21 September, three Wobblies were arrested for vagrancy. A letter found on one of them, requesting that thousands of Wobblies descend on North Yakima from Montana, Idaho, and parts of Washington to compel their release, assured the severity of their sentences. Judge Milroy fined Frank Riley $30 or fifteen days in jail for waiting for "good employment" to come his way. Nels Turnquist, also charged with vagrancy, claimed that he had a job lined up, so the court permitted him to either get to his job "or leave the city immediately." J. A. Doll, who refused to pick hops because the wage was too low, faced a $20 fine for vagrancy. During the sentencing, Wobbly organizer William Wilson laughed openly in the courtroom at these charges and sentences, calling them a joke. Judge Milroy held him in contempt and sentenced him to forty days in jail. As the bailiff led their organizer away, Judge Milroy told the fifty or so Wobblies witnessing the proceedings that those who wanted work would receive help in finding it. Those who chose not to work would risk arrest for vagrancy.[42]

The arrests continued. W. J. Appleby, W. C. Moody, and twelve other suspected Wobblies were arrested for vagrancy on September 24 and 25. A rancher using a police escort in town while searching for farm workers found Appleby urging workers not to accept the rancher's wage offer, which he had also refused. Patrolmen Kauffman and Lizee promptly arrested Appleby for vagrancy. Meanwhile, Chief McCurdy arrested Moody on the same charge. It is likely that McCurdy suspected him of being an IWW organizer, as he had a great number of IWW stickers in his possession when arrested. Townspeople and police officers found similar stickers plastered on telegraph poles and mailboxes all over town. They read, "More wages, shorter hours, better food or sabotage," "Abolition of the wage system," and "Good pay or bum work."[43]

As more Wobblies came into town, the arrests mounted. On the evening of 25 September, a large street meeting convened under the auspices of the local IWW. The meeting focused on the need of migrant farm workers to receive a better wage from area farmers. Also during the meeting, Wobblies voiced their indignation over their treatment at the hands of Police Chief McCurdy, sang Wobbly songs, and mounted a soapbox to address the crowd. At this point, the arrests began. First, officers arrested the speakers; then, when the crowd failed to disperse after being ordered to do so by McCurdy, Wobblies found themselves under arrest left and right. In all, police arrested forty-six IWW men that evening. The city jail now overflowed with Wobblies.[44]

Mayor J. F. Barton called for a public meeting to discuss the community's response to the IWW. While the citizens of North Yakima held their discussion, the Wobblies planned a jailbreak. But the escape was unsuccessful, and a riot broke out instead. The men began to destroy the interior of their cells and sang such popular IWW songs as "Tramp, Tramp, Tramp" and "Solidarity Forever." The authorities could not dampen their rioting and singing, even after spraying them with a fire hose. The next morning, after a meeting at the city's commercial club rooms, two hundred "businessmen . . . armed themselves with pick and ax handles" and headed to the county jail, accompanied by one thousand other citizens. The mob herded the Wobblies out of the jail and marched them to the train depot, forcing them into "two iced refrigerator cars." The railroad workers, though, refused to take them out of town, so the townspeople had to turn around and march the Wobblies back to the county jail.[45]

Following the violence, tempers began to cool. Major Jay Lynch, who had attended the earlier commercial club meeting, went to visit the prisoners. C. W. Ryan, acting as spokesman for the group of jailed Wobblies, assured Lynch that his fellow workers had no intention of destroying farmers' crops, as that was their source of employment. Ryan considered it in the best interests of farmers to pay a living wage to workers to ensure good work. The jailed Wobblies subsequently sent word to Judge Milroy that they would be peaceful if allowed to organize. Milroy replied that "the city was opposed to organization" and would not back down on that point. Milroy, however, sentenced only eleven Wobblies for various misdemeanors, releasing the rest in small numbers and encouraging them to leave town. Finally, the jailed men received their first food in twenty-four hours.[46]

The Wobblies continued to insist on their right to organize despite arrests and hostile public opinion, some of which emanated from newspaper editorials condemning their unionizing efforts. The *Yakima Daily Republic* reminded its readers yet again that area farmers were neither Rockefellers nor avaricious capitalists, but men "whose lot is as hard in its way as the laborer's." Nonetheless, the next day, the editors of the paper noted that they had received an anonymous letter, which they did not publish, indicating that some among the thousand who watched the mob of citizens try to throw the Wobblies out of town contended that the IWW men had had their constitutional rights violated. The paper's editors refuted this contention, claiming that the Wobblies got what they deserved. Defying such sentiments, another open-air meeting was held in downtown North Yakima under the leadership of the local IWW to bring attention to the plight of migrant farm laborers in the area. The arrests that followed were clearly a means of attacking the IWW, for police released anyone who was not a union member. The arrested Wobblies received sentences ranging from fifteen to thirty days in the county jail.[47]

On the following day, Richard Brazier of Spokane arrived in the city to force the issue of organizing rights (fig. 17). He told Judge Milroy that the IWW would not give up on its fight to organize in North Yakima. After

Figure 17. IWW prisoners before surrendering at the Federal Penitentiary in Leavenworth, Kansas. Back, far left: Ralph Chaplin; third from left: Walter Nef; second from right: E. F. Doree; far right: Richard Brazier. Front, far left: Jack Walsh; fourth from left: Jack Law; fifth from left: Charles Ashleigh; second from right: Ben Fletcher. (Courtesy, Walter P. Reuther Library, Wayne State University)

this discussion, according to the *Yakima Daily Republic*, "city officials, members of the citizens' committee, labor union representatives and two leaders of the I.W.W.—Richard Brazier of Spokane and Mr. Brown, who started the organizing work here"—held a conference. The outcome was that the IWW would be allowed to organize. Edward Maurer, a representative of the state's labor council, may have been a decisive voice in favor of IWW activity in the city. He argued that if this labor union were prevented from organizing, then other unions could face the same prohibition. He urged those at the conference not to infringe on workers' right to form unions. On the question of sabotage, which concerned many in attendance, Brazier explained that sabotage did not mean the destruction of property, but the withdrawal of efficiency—in other words, a work slowdown. Even though Milroy and others continued to argue vehemently against IWW activity in the city, Mayor Barton and city officials agreed to allow a Wobbly presence. City leaders would permit an IWW union hall and the right to organize, as long as there was "no preaching of sabotage, no disrespect shown to the flag nor to con-stitutional authority and no distribution of seditious literature." City officials warned Wobblies, though, that the police would strictly enforce vagrancy laws as well as laws against street demonstrations.[48]

This compromise seemed to satisfy most of the parties involved. But one issue remained unresolved. The North Yakima Wobblies wanted their fifty or so fellow workers who were still in jail to be released. Milroy eventually allowed the release of prisoners in small numbers, provided that they pledged to find work or leave town rather than congregate at their union hall. Wobblies continued to agitate for the release of their comrades, and on 6 October, Mayor Barton decided to release all remaining Wobblies from jail without conditions.[49]

In subsequent weeks, the IWW union hall thrived with regular meetings, while North Yakima Wobblies tried to assuage the fears of townspeople by refraining from street meetings or distributing literature on the street. Also, as a conciliatory gesture, organizer Wilson left town. Yet organizing work continued out of the hall. Hop growers complained that Wobblies encouraged hop-pickers to leave the fields for better wages at other sites. The IWW led a strike in neighboring Zillah among seventy to eighty fruit-warehouse workers later in October. Wobblies demanded a wage increase from the going rate of $3 a day to $4. However, they could not persuade female workers from replacing the striking men and accepting the going rate. Although the Wobblies did not attain any organizational control of area industries, they established a presence in the city and surrounding valley that was tolerated by local citizens, at least for the time being. In that spirit, the *Yakima Morning Herald* published the Thanksgiving menu of the downtown IWW union hall:

Solidarity Restaurant

We cater exclusively to rebels.
Local 400, Prop. Hawkeye Brown, Chef
Given to commemorate our victories and to hasten the dawn of emancipation.

Savory Solidarity Specials
Wobbly Roast Turkey
Direct Action Duck
Chicken a la Sabotage

Vegetables
A.W.O. Mashed Potatoes
I.W.W. Sweet Potatoes
O.B.U. Celery
Wooden Shoe Sweet Corn
Rebel Cranberries
Red Ball Apple Salad

Pies and Cakes
400 Squash Pie. Sab. Cat Mince Pie
W.O.T.W.D. Fruit Cake

Drinks
As Only Rebels Make
Jungle Java. CO-OP Milk
Liber-Tea

Ode to Everett
Hither let many a Wobbly's step be bent,
To save our Comrades from imprisonment.[50]

Reining in the AWO

Harvest Wobblies were rapidly becoming a force to be reckoned with in many of the West's most important agricultural sectors. They also developed into a significant influence within the IWW itself. One thousand AWO members and interested townspeople assembled in Minneapolis on 30 October 1916 for a five-day semi-annual meeting that closed with a smoker. As AWO members began to arrive in the city in small groups towards the end of October, according to Ted Fraser in *Solidarity*, "some [were] fairly well dressed, and others almost in rags.

Their faces were tanned by many suns, and there was a determination stamped on every face." Newspaper reporters, photographers, police, and city officials understood the significance of this meeting. Fraser, a newly elected member of the Organization Committee, reported that the AWO had eighteen thousand members and influenced the wage and working conditions of at least fifty thousand more migrant and seasonal laborers.

Conference business included allocating thousands of dollars to support organizing in other industries; strike funds; the IWW's Spanish-language newspaper, imprisoned IWW members in San Francisco, Everett, and Duluth; and families of prisoners. One of the most important issues before the conference, involved the question of whether the AWO should remain a national industrial union or not. At first a majority supported national union status, but the subsequent debate moved the convention to support the view presented by Bill Haywood in an impassioned speech to the conference. Haywood, recognizing the growing strength of the AWO, reminded the harvest Wobblies that the AWO was only a part of the IWW. In fact, he and other Wobblies feared that as the AWO brought more than agricultural workers into its ranks, it could break away from the IWW and become a separate "one big union" of migrant and seasonal workers. The resolution supporting national status failed. Nef resigned as secretary-treasurer, and the AWO members elected Forrest Edwards to take his place.[51]

At the IWW general convention later that month in Chicago, the AWO controlled 252 out of 335 possible votes on the convention floor. Nef was there as a convention delegate for the AWO. It was abundantly clear to the IWW executive board that something needed to be done to keep the AWO from usurping control of the greater union or becoming in-dependent. So the Ways and Means Committee eliminated the terms "local" and "national" from the union's constitution and replaced them with the term "industrial unions." Haywood and the executive board had the support of the convention delegates to centralize the IWW, with the AWO and other industrial unions falling under the leadership of the IWW headquarters in Chicago.

These steps did not fully resolve the matter, however. In December the executive board of the IWW called a special meeting in which they created several industrial unions before the workers in these trades called for them. For example, the executive board created a separate Lumber Workers' Industrial Union and appointed Nef temporarily as its secretary-treasurer. Their intention was to remove two thousand lumber workers from the AWO and put them into their own industrial union.

This restructuring from above outraged Nef, yet he went along with it and later in the month accepted the position of secretary-treasurer of the Marine Transport Workers' Industrial Union (MTW) in Philadelphia. The final move to contain the AWO took place at a special IWW convention in March 1917. Here delegates formally re-chartered the AWO into the Agricultural Workers' Industrial Union No. 400 (AWIU) and restricted it to organizing agricultural laborers only.[52]

Why would AWO members, who had such voting strength and who represented agricultural, lumber, construction, and other workers, not resist the division of the AWO into separate industrial unions? According to E. Workman, an in-house IWW historian, the AWO best represented the mission of the IWW to organize "ALL workers into One union." Despite the power and success of the AWO, Workman believed that most Wobblies accepted the notion that a variety of industrial unions could represent the "one big union" concept as affiliates of the IWW. Nef all along accepted this structure, but wanted rank-and-file control. He and other Wobblies had concerns about the power of general secretary-treasurer Haywood and the General Executive Board. Yet there is no evidence that a rebellion in the ranks took place. Perhaps the logic of this structure won the day, and the potential power that these industrial unions could attain dampened dissent. For instance, the MTW, under the leadership of Nef, Ed Doree, and Ben Fletcher (fig. 17, page 105), rapidly grew in strength on the Philadelphia waterfront. The Lumber Workers' Industrial Union, after its March convention in Spokane, represented six thousand Wobblies. It soon had the strength to lead of one of the most important lumber and mill workers' strikes in the history of the Pacific Northwest. Thousands of harvest Wobblies remained attached to the new AWIU, and its future looked promising for the upcoming harvest season. Though Nef, Doree, and other AWO founders were gone, the new leadership had seasoned harvest Wobblies like Fraser, Edwards, and many others who could ably lead the AWIU.[53]

Articulating Harvest Wobbly Worklife Culture

In early 1917, harvest Wobblies had established an effective, pragmatic, industrial union that could organize thousands of migrant and seasonal farm workers in the western countryside. Inextricably tied to this union was a worklife culture, which provided identity and cohesion for its members. Their worklife culture embodied the virtues of manual labor, worker solidarity, masculinity, rebellion, tenacity, independence, mobility, camaraderie, song, and humor. It was also a significant aspect of their appeal to other agricultural laborers that went beyond demands for higher wages and better working conditions. Together, harvest Wobblies and their job delegates acted as emissaries, spreading the goals of industrial unionism within the context of this attractive culture.

During the 1916 harvest season, several hundred job delegates and thousands of harvest Wobblies traveled and worked throughout the Great Plains wheat belt. The job delegate carried in his bindle his belongings and the tools of his trade: membership cards, dues stamps, IWW literature and buttons, copies of *Solidarity*, and "silent agitators" (stickers) to be plastered on any surface where workers could read of harvest Wobbly demands for higher wages and better working conditions. The job delegate lived with the workers in the jungle camps or rented rooms in agricultural towns so as to be near farm workers. The organization he represented was flexible as well as mobile. The union leadership always urged members to take a job if they could not get the wage that they demanded. Nef and subsequent secretary-treasurers even suggested that destroying one's union membership card in order to get a job had its merits. Nevertheless, harvest Wobblies proved independent of any central authority. Although union leadership encouraged members to take a job even when their wage demands were not met, if Wobblies chose to risk arrest and jail time by staying out of the fields and by urging other workers to join them to force an employer to improve the wage, there was no central authority or inflexible AWO policy to challenge their right to do so.

As harvest Wobblies moved through the wheat belt and among independent harvesters during the harvest and threshing season, they demonstrated a masculine, fighting spirit. As noted earlier, persuading or forcing independent harvesters to join the union was a practice of Wobblies in the countryside. Shoot-outs were not uncommon, nor were fistfights between union and non-union men. When riding the rails, Wobblies by their sheer numbers prevented freight train crews from evicting them as they traveled to the next harvest site. The Wobblies made this defiance into a militant act even though harvesters had used this same strategy for decades by the time the IWW appeared. In past years, railroad company officials had looked the other way when harvesters used freight trains because they knew that it was necessary to their own economic interests for crops to be harvested. Still, it was common for engineers, brakemen, and conductors to extort payment from harvesters because it was technically illegal for anyone to ride in or on top of the boxcars.

The Wobblies demanded free transportation to work sites because they believed that they and all harvesters were essential to agriculture. If their numbers alone did not intimidate railroad crews, they would use physical violence to force them to provide transportation to the next harvest site. Jack Miller, who actually became an AWO job delegate before he became a member, fought it out with a few train crews. In one instance, he and a number of harvest Wobblies battled brakemen on a flat car outside of Council Bluffs, Iowa, before they were able to win a ride on a freight train. The 120-pound Miller badly beat the head brakeman, which endeared him to some of the railroad crew. Miller's exploits reached his destination, the jungle outside of Mitchell, in southeastern South Dakota, before he and his band of Wobblies arrived. There approximately two hundred jungle residents passed a resolution that Miller and his group stay on and work at organizing railroad workers rather than continue following the harvest. Although Miller only had agricultural literature and knew nothing of "the roundhouse lingo," he felt that he had to bow to the will of the majority. Similarly, in summer 1915, McGuckin remembered fighting off an armed group of brakemen who barged into his boxcar demanding payment for the freight train ride. McGuckin, with the able assistance of the AWO's Jack Law and Ted Fraser, disarmed one of the brakemen who brandished a pistol and threatened to "beat the hell out of" the others if they did not back off. The brakemen retreated and the Wobblies made it to their destination, Pocatello, Idaho, free of charge.[54]

But harvest Wobblies were more than just fighting members of a labor union with revolutionary aspirations. They had much in common culturally with independent harvesters, and sought to appeal to them on a variety of levels. Music was one of their tools. In fact, one of the distinguishing qualities of the IWW was a rich collection of songs, songs that helped make the union attractive to Wobbly and non-Wobbly alike. The Wobblies were not necessarily unique in their use of song, either in articulating their dreams, entertaining themselves, or trying to attract other workers to their cause, They were just very good at it. The humor and solidarity of harvest Wobblies were evident in the IWW songbooks, which went through many editions over the years.

West Coast organizer J. H. Walsh, an Alaskan and member of the Socialist Party, was instrumental in spearheading the creation of a songbook. At his urging, a committee formed out of Spokane's IWW locals. In 1909, the committee compiled new songs and existing songs that had been printed only on cards or leaflets into the IWW's first songbook. Those who submitted songs or served on the committee, such as Harry McClintock and Richard Brazier, tended to be migrant rather than homeguard workers, so the first songbook had a decidedly migratory bent. This reflected the early membership and organizational strategies of the IWW in the West. For example, Walsh was a committed advocate of street speaking as a recruiting strategy, McClintock was an itinerant entertainer, and British-born Brazier was a construction worker who had recently migrated from British Columbia. The songbook included some rebel standards, but the majority of the songs in it were written by Spokane Wobblies. In many instances, the songs spoke to the issues that most concerned migrants, such as living on the road, searching for work, and having to deal with employment agencies that charged the worker a fee for finding a temporary job.[55]

A later edition of the songbook, *Songs of the Workers: On the Road, in the Jungles and the Shops*, also published in Spokane, continued in the tradition of the first, celebrating the masculine worklife culture of Wobblies on the road. Songs such as "Meet Me in the Jungles, Louie," by Brazier and "Hallelujah!" by McClintock reflected the largely all-male and casual labor environment of Wobblies and others forced to migrate throughout the West in search of work. The hoboes of "Meet Me in the Jungles, Louie" always helped feed each other when money for food was scarce. In "Hallelujah!" Wobblies offered their contempt for the meager wages offered to workers in the countryside with the stanzas

> *O, why don't you save*
> *All the money you earn?*
> *If I did not eat*
> *I'd have money to burn.*
>
> *I can't buy a job,*
> *For I ain't got the dough,*
> *So I ride in a boxcar,*
> *For I'm a hobo.*[56]

In later editions of the IWW songbook, as the AWO and then the AWIU became an important part of the IWW general organizing program, harvest work featured more prominently. In *I.W.W. Songs: To Fan the Flames of Discontent*, a 1917 edition, the "Harvest War Song" made its first appearance. As in many Wobbly songs, new lyrics were set to a popular melody. Pat Brennan, a Wobbly songwriter, set lyrics about the exploitation of the harvest worker at the hands of the farmer to the tune of "Tipperary":

You've paid the going wages,
that's what kept us on the bum,
You say you've done your duty,
you chin-whiskered son of a gun.
We have sent your kids to college,
but still you must rave and shout,
And call us tramps and hoboes,
and pesky go-abouts.

In the same songbook, some of the history of Wobbly organizing in agriculture made its way into song with "Overalls and Snuff":

One day as I was walking along the railroad track,
I met a man in Wheatland with his blankets on his back,
He was an old-time hop picker, I'd seen his face before,
I knew he was a wobbly by the button that he wore. ...

He took his blanket off his back and sat down on the rail
And told us some sad stories 'bout the workers down in jail.
He said the way they treat them there, he never saw the like,
For they're putting men in prison just for going out on strike....

Now we've got to stick together boys, and strive with all our
   might,
We must free Ford and Suhr, boys, we've got to win this fight.

With songs such as these, which placed the harvest worker's interests against the farmer and the court system, Wobblies could celebrate their defiance of law enforcement and justify their militant actions. In "The Tramp," written by the IWW martyr Joe Hill, the migrant worker's risk of arrest for vagrancy found its way into Wobbly music:

Tramp, tramp, tramp, keep on a tramping,
Nothing doing here for you;
If I catch you 'round again,
You will wear the ball and chain,
Keep on tramping, that's the best thing you can do.

Moreover, "The Tramp" spoke to non-Wobbly workers by emphasizing the commonalities of worklife experience shared by all itinerant laborers. Whether at the strike in Wheatland among a majority of non-Wobbly workers, or in jail with them, IWW members had songs that helped bring workers together.[57]

Figure 18. Mr. Block's search for work reflects the economically exploited and socially marginalized situation for the migrant harvester. (Courtesy, Charles H. Kerr Publishing Company, Chicago, 1998)

Other IWW songs written about the lives of harvest Wobblies reflected a migrant worker's frustrations with long hours and poor pay, and the individual actions a harvester might take to address his working conditions. While sabotage was not unique to harvest Wobblies or to Wobblies in general, these light-hearted musical allusions to destruction of property would have serious repercussions when the federal government moved to suppress the IWW in late 1917. A very popular song, "Ta-Ra-Ra Boom De-Ay," written by Joe Hill, is a case in point:

> *I had a job once threshing wheat, worked sixteen hours with*
>   *hands and feet.*
> *And when the moon was shining bright, they kept me working*
>   *all the night.*
> *One moonlight night, I hate to tell, I "accidentally" slipped and*
>   *fell.*
> *My pitchfork went right in between some cogwheels of that*
>   *threshing machine.*
>
>> *Ta-ra-ra-boom-de-ay!*
>> *It made a noise that way,*
>> *And wheels and bolts and hay,*
>> *Went flying every way.*
>> *That stingy rube said, "Well!*
>> *A thousand gone to hell."*
>> *But I did sleep that night,*
>> *I needed it all right.*

Such sabotage, in the form of destroying agricultural equipment, was actually an uncommon strategy on the part of harvest Wobblies. Their real work was to advance the cause of the union by trying to bring more members into it. For example, the 1918 edition of *I.W.W. Songs* contained "When You Wear that Button," written by Brazier. Here he set his lyrics to a popular song of the day, "When You Wore a Tulip." The opening stanza makes clear the role of the class-conscious harvest Wobbly in the Great Plains countryside:

> *I met him in Dakota when the harvesting was o'er*
> *A "Wob" he was, I saw by the button that he wore.*
> *He was talking to a bunch of slaves in the jungles near the*
>   *tracks;*
> *He said, "You guys whose homes are on your backs;*
> *Why don't you stick together with the 'Wobblies' in one band*
> *And fight to change conditions for the workers of this land."*[58]

Figure 19. Mr. Block, as a harvest worker in North Dakota, can either
work for the going wage and hours or go to jail for vagrancy.
(Courtesy, Charles H. Kerr Publishing Company, Chicago, 1998)

Figure 20. The power of the AWO speaks loud and clear. (Courtesy, Charles H. Kerr Publishing Company, Chicago, 1998)

Figure 21. With the great success of the AWO in summer 1916, harvest Wobblies appeared unstoppable as a force in western agriculture. (Courtesy, Charles H. Kerr Publishing Company, Chicago, 1998)

Through the vehicle of these easily remembered songs, workers could be informed about the goals and history of the union. The same was true of IWW cartoons and illustrations. These drawings reached a wide audience, as they were published in the union's two widely circulated English-language newspapers, *Industrial Worker* and *Solidarity*, and in the non-English-language IWW newspapers.

Ernest Riebe, who developed the Mr. Block series during the 1910s, drew some of the most memorable IWW cartoons. Mr. Block was an unskilled worker who never seemed to understand that the IWW was there for his benefit and that the employer was always out to exploit him. Riebe placed Mr. Block in many situations familiar to workers. For example, "Mr. Block; He Goes Harvesting" illustrated the way that harvest workers were seduced to go West with promises of high wages and plenty of employment only to discover low wages and no jobs. On his way West, Mr. Block refuses to listen to a Wobbly in the boxcar in which he is traveling. When Mr. Block is forced to leave town after discovering there are no jobs available, he is not only smacked on the head by a policeman, but is also asked why he did not ride the boxcar's bumpers if all the boxcars were full (fig. 18). This last point was a serious one, in that riding on the thin iron platform on top of a boxcar bumper was a very dangerous activity. In "Mr. Block; He Goes to the Dakota Harvest," Riebe portrayed a situation faced by many workers in the wheat belt (fig. 19).

As the growing industrial union of harvest Wobblies helped rejuvenate the IWW in late 1916 and early 1917, Ralph Chaplin ("Bingo"), the popular IWW songwriter, illustrator, and editor of *Solidarity*, penned drawings that expressed the spirit of union workers (see fig. 17, page 105). One depicts the straightforward, practical goals of the AWO, though tinged with a threat of sabotage (fig. 20). In another, empowered by membership in the AWO and by the black cat of sabotage, a harvest Wobbly walks in his sabots (wooden shoes) toward the emancipation of his class and the industrial freedom of a new era (fig. 21). As illustrated by Chaplin, harvest Wobblies had a pragmatic organizing strategy, with revolutionary aspirations, to offer agricultural laborers. They also had a worklife culture that embraced the largely all-male, white, and mobile harvest and threshing work crews of the Great Plains. But strategies that had drawn mobile white male workers to the AWIU would soon prove ineffective for the multicultural agricultural laborers in California. Yet that and other challenges lay ahead for harvest Wobblies. Their most immediate concern was the United States' entry into the Great War, which threatened the very survival of the IWW.

Chapter Four

War and Persecution

⌘⌘⌘

The declaration of war on Germany by Congress in April 1917 unleashed waves of patriotic fervor that sometimes took the form of antiradicalism. As intolerance for those who did not openly support the war against Germany grew, the U.S. war effort gave patriotic cover to those who always had been hostile to the IWW and other radical movements. With passage of the Espionage and Sedition Acts, Wobblies and thousands of other Americans and resident aliens experienced intense repression at the hands of the federal government and frequent violations of their civil rights. Wobblies, especially harvest Wobblies, turned to each other, to the goals of their union and, most important, to their worklife culture for survival. By turning to what had worked for them in the past, harvest Wobblies persevered in the western countryside, particularly in areas where they had established a strong foothold before the U.S. entered the war.

The IWW, like other leftist and pacifist groups, did not endorse the Entente powers in their fight against Germany and its allies. Since the outbreak of war in 1914, Wobblies had urged workers to fight the class war at home, arguing that the war in Europe was a war between imperialist, capitalist powers with neither side having any merit. Though the IWW leadership never articulated an explicit antiwar policy, it was clear to anyone who read their literature or listened to a Wobbly speech that the union did not support U.S. involvement. Those committed to American participation in the war on the side of Great Britain and France, as well as patriotic groups that formed soon after the declaration of war, like the American Protective League (APL), saw Wobblies, socialists, and anarchists as threats to the war effort and deemed them domestic enemies.

The Department of Justice, with the assistance of the APL, which had two hundred fifty thousand members by 1918, monitored the patriotism of Americans and the mobilization for war. Newspaper editors, government officials, and citizens' organizations charged that those who did not enthusiastically support the Allied cause were pro-German, a menace to the war effort, and possibly saboteurs. Members of the IWW, leaders of the Socialist Party, prominent anarchists such as Emma

Goldman and Alexander Berkman, and others who did not endorse the war or were outright antiwar activists were the object of bitter criticism in the nation's press. Many of these radicals suffered at the hands of mob actions and eventually found themselves under arrest for violating wartime statutes. Supporters of U.S. intervention on the Allied side and government officials violated the civil rights of Americans, whether native-born or immigrant, who supported Germany in the war, took a neutral position, or were pacifists. Thousands of these ordinary citizens were subject to legal harassment for simply making a comment that an APL member or a deputy sheriff found treasonous.[1]

Because of its activities in 1916 and early 1917, the IWW was singled out as a dangerous, unpatriotic menace to wartime industrial production by business interests and the federal government. With ample assistance from state governments and economic interests that had long wanted help in suppressing Wobbly organizing, the federal government moved to immobilize the IWW as a union and as a revolutionary organization.[2] Government agencies attempted to mitigate a projected shortage of farm labor due to the wartime draft with a coordinated effort to recruit and distribute labor to the country's agricultural sectors. Federal, state, and local law enforcement had no qualms about arresting harvest Wobblies on the pretext of protecting the nation's food supply.

Under the authority of the Espionage Act and other congressional acts that proscribed any interference in wartime industrial production and recruitment of the armed forces, Department of Justice agents, with help from regional law enforcement and APL members, arrested hundreds of IWW members and confiscated the union's property for use in the mass trials of 1918. The AWIU was especially hard hit, with its highest ranking leaders jailed and most of its regional locals as well as its headquarters ransacked and property confiscated. With the AWIU advocating strike actions and sabotage to further its organizational goals among farm workers, the industrial union experienced special scrutiny by the federal government. Federal authorities declared agricultural production central to the war effort, and they made interference with U.S. production efforts a federal offense. Though the AWIU survived this crackdown, the industrial union suffered considerably in the 1917 and 1918 harvest seasons.

Flirting with Success

Prior to these events, the future had looked bright for harvest Wobblies in late 1916 and early 1917. Agricultural laborers by the thousands joined the AWO in 1916, along with timber workers, miners, and oil and construction workers. W. C. King, a frequent writer for *Solidarity,* noted in a January 1917 issue that the AWO was instrumental in establishing $4 for ten hours of work in the harvest fields as the standard for North Dakota. Though he went on to exaggerate IWW job control in many areas of the Great Plains wheat belt, he was on target in his comments about the effectiveness of six hundred job delegates and organizers in the fields and jungles, and on the rails in the region. Furthermore, the AWO harvest organizing drive of 1916 netted a measure of success unlike anything that had ever taken place in American agricultural labor up to this time. In 1917, the AWO justifiably claimed twenty thousand harvest Wobbly members, a substantial segment of the IWW's hundred thousand or more members. The AWO was in a very strong position to create a viable and permanent farm labor union.[3]

Even during the slow winter months of 1916-1917, the AWO continued to increase in membership and initiate farm labor organizing drives. Secretary-treasurer Forrest Edwards reported that the AWO—soon to be renamed the AWIU—gained 1,456 new members in February alone. Also during that month harvest Wobblies led two thousand vineyard workers, many of whom were Italian Wobblies, out on strike near Fresno. It was only a matter of days before grape growers accepted the strikers' demands for higher wages and an eight-hour day. Unfortunately, the IWW failed to enlist the support of Japanese pruners, represented by the Japanese Association of Fresno, until the strike had already commenced. When the pruners refused to honor the strike, as they already had an eight-hour day and a satisfactory wage, Wobblies unleashed a torrent of criticism. Despite Wobbly rhetoric of class solidarity, the union demonstrated yet again its chronic inability to secure sympathetic allies among this multicultural labor workforce.[4]

Still, a couple of months later, Wobblies led strikes among Redland-area orange pickers in Southern California. Although the strike failed because of resistance by the powerful association of orange growers, Wobblies disrupted the harvest and closed fruit-packing plants for a few days. Over the course of the spring, IWWs in California focused on the massive melon and fruit harvest of the Imperial Valley and on rejuvenating the Brawley local. Later that summer, the entire San Joaquin and nearby Santa Clara Valleys became centers of AWIU organizing activity.

The small agricultural town of Turlock in the San Joaquin Valley possessed one of the most vibrant IWW union halls, which Wobblies used as a headquarters and a temporary residence. Here they could bathe, clean their clothing, and cook meals while seeking employment. Other San Joaquin Valley towns, including Stockton, Modesto, and Fresno, had bustling IWW union halls with hundreds of harvest Wobblies working in the surrounding agricultural fields and orchards. Wobbly organizers were also sought out by striking non-IWW workers. For example, in Selma, just south of Fresno, two hundred striking female cannery workers requested an IWW organizer during their mid-August strike. Once the owners of the cannery found out about possible Wobbly involvement, they quickly met the strikers' demands. By many accounts, the harvest Wobblies of the AWIU were at their greatest number and at their most constructive level of activity in California during the summer of 1917.[5]

The AWIU conference in late May 1917 in Kansas City convened in an atmosphere of great confidence in California organizing activities and of preparations for the Great Plains wheat belt harvest. Conference participants set $5 for the minimum wage for harvest work and $60 a month for all farm labor jobs. But the most interesting part of the conference was a message read to the delegates from A. C. Townley, president of the Non-Partisan League of North Dakota, a farmers' political organization. Townley proposed that at the upcoming Non-Partisan League convention, representatives from the AWIU meet with representatives from his organization to establish wages and working conditions for the summer harvest and threshing season in that state. Townley also proposed that the League would help harvest Wobblies with transportation from major cities such as Chicago, Omaha, and Kansas City to North Dakota. Addressing the AWIU conference was Arthur Le Sueur, the League's attorney. He assured the harvest Wobblies that any collective bargaining agreement would be conducted in good faith. Furthermore, he suggested that $5 for a ten-hour day could be established as the going rate for North Dakota. Because the Non-Partisan League had tens of thousands of members in the state, the implication of such an agreement was that North Dakota could become a closed shop for the IWW, at least in regard to agricultural labor.[6]

Harvest season, 1917, promised great accomplishments for harvest Wobblies. The *Industrial Worker* noted that farmers who were once receiving sixty cents a bushel for wheat and who paid harvest workers $2.50 a day plus board were now receiving $2.20 per bushel and could afford to pay harvest workers $5.00 a day plus board. For Wobblies, the harvest drive that summer began in the winter wheat country of the southern plains, Oklahoma and Kansas. In an effort to better coordinate the organizing drive, the AWIU divided Kansas into five districts with a district organizer appointed by the AWIU organization Committee to oversee and to help facilitate communication among stationary and field delegates.[7]

Prelude to the Coming Storm

Even as the AWIU developed new organizing strategies for the harvest season, the industrial union had to deal with an escalating level of repression. Attacks initiated by anti-IWW mobs were something that Wobblies knew how to handle; yet violence carried out by patriot extremists and the increasing severity of attacks were new phenomena. The first such attacks were carried out by vigilante groups and mobs of off-duty soldiers. According to Edwards and Ted Fraser, chairman of the Organization Committee, the "Kansas City hall was raided three times in one day by a mob of soldiers." During these raids, Secretary Bourg of the local was thrown down a flight of stairs several times, and soldiers badly beat Wobblies C. E. Lundberg and W. Francik. Kansas City police did little to protect the union hall. In fact, they arrested Francik and fined him $500 for disturbing the peace. As in many such episodes of mob violence initiated against IWWs and their union halls, the attackers injured Wobblies, broke windows, smashed furniture, and destroyed documents and other property. And as in other similar cases reported by the Wobbly press, local police or sheriff's deputies did not arrest anyone for the break-in, destruction, or violence against Wobblies.[8]

In some instances farmers and others in agricultural areas resorted to violence to protect their economic interests and defy AWIU wage and working condition demands. For example, a mob of farmers, law enforcement officials, and their supporters near Turon, Kansas, about fifty miles west of Wichita, went to the local jungle to arrest organizer George Carey, who had encouraged Wobblies, the largest contingent of harvesters in the area, to refuse to work for less than $3.50 a day. After Carey's arrest, the mob instructed the Wobblies to leave the area, which they did. Several miles down the road "the law and order gang" decided that these harvest Wobblies would be of use in the wheat fields. With guns drawn, they ordered the workers back to the fields to labor for $3.00 a day. On the way back to Turon, a vigilante pistol-whipped and shot Wobbly William F. McNeil. Fortunately, McNeil survived the attack, later writing an account of the events for the *Industrial Worker*.[9]

As the harvest season got off to a rocky start in the wheat belt, California harvest Wobblies participated in cannery workers' strikes near San Jose. A new union, the Toilers of the World, emerged in March 1917 in Santa Clara County, committed to organizing men and women of all races and ethnic groups in the area's canning industry. One of the primary organizers of the Toilers was E. B. Mercadier. Mercadier had worked in the print trade, the coal and hay business, and in socialist and progressive party politics. He had the charisma to bring together a truly diverse constituency of workers. The Toilers elected as their president an Italian, San Filippo. Moreover, they generated support from local churches and gained representation in the Central Labor Council, a rural labor association. The new union had some members with little union experience and others with considerable experience, including dissident AFL members and Wobblies. While a number of AFL members joined the Toilers in an effort to distance themselves from conservative AFL policies, Wobblies joined the organization for other reasons. Some joined to avoid the unpatriotic stigma associated with the IWW and thereby to continue organizing in agriculture. Others joined to bring the Toilers under AWIU leadership. Despite the different motives that men and women had for joining the Toilers, the organization quickly became the largest union in the county, with a diverse membership of Italians, Japanese, Chinese, and native-born whites.

In July, over six hundred Toilers went on strike over wages, hours, and recognition of their union. Their strike brought much of the county's canning industry to a grinding halt. Canning industry owners, local business interests, and conservative political leaders would not tolerate this. They combined to defeat the strike with the use of armed strikebreakers who violently attacked the picket lines. Local political leaders pleaded with California Governor William Stephens to send in the state militia to crush the strike, which he refused to do. However, the commanding officer of neighboring Camp Fremont sent federal troops into the fray, ostensibly to secure the county's food supply. Eventually, local citizens and law enforcement relieved the federal troops in the form of homeguard units. The strikers not only faced assaults from such vigilante groups, hired company gunmen, and federal troops, but they also had to contend with insufficient support from the AFL and the AWIU, and with scab labor offered by local civic women's groups.

At the urging of their leadership, the strikers returned to work while the union negotiated an agreement with the cannery owners. Surprisingly, the Toilers won some concessions from their employers, although recognition of their union was not one of them. That goal was achieved later in the year when the union staged another strike, after which they also gained improvements in wages and hours. These strikes represented the first large-scale cannery strikes in the state. They were also innovative in using mass picket lines and demonstrations to win public sympathy. However, to the dismay of the AWIU and the IWW, the Toilers joined the AFL, prompting the once-sympathetic IWW to disown the union and their involvement in the strike. By all indications, though, harvest Wobblies played a key role in the Toilers. Yet their inability to bring the diverse Toilers into the AWIU demonstrates the industrial union's lack of appeal. Once again, the AWIU's inclusive rhetoric did not translate into practical application. Unfortunately for the Toilers, their union collapsed at the end of the decade due to the failure of another major strike under their leadership, to the public's support of government anti-union tactics, and to the abundance of low-cost labor from Mexico.[10]

Another organization that the IWW worked with on an unofficial basis was the Working Class Union (WCU). The relationship between the IWW and the WCU in the summer of 1917, though, only added in the public's mind to the Wobbly's reputation for violence and lack of patriotism. The WCU of eastern Oklahoma consisted primarily of tenant farmers, sharecroppers, and farm laborers, many of whom were African American or Seminole Indian. Its inclusion, according to the IWW, of "doctors, lawyers, merchants and all and every class of people who wish to belong" prevented the IWW from establishing an official connection. In some respects this was another example of the IWW's failure to secure official ties, out of ideological purity, with farm labor organizations that did not have only wageworkers as members or did not have revolutionary goals. The significance of allying with an organization that boasted a substantial number of ethnic or racial minority members was lost on the AWIU leadership.

Just as it had with the Toilers in California, the IWW chose to distance itself officially from the WCU. Yet on an unofficial level, individual Wobblies and members of the AWIU worked with the WCU's twenty-five thousand members throughout the life of this regional organization during the late 1910s. For example, in early August 1917, Wobblies participated in the "Green Corn Rebellion," in which four hundred WCU members, IWWs, and sympathizers offered armed resistance to the draft in parts of Oklahoma. The "Rebellion" was finally suppressed by mid-August. But even on this unofficial level, the relationship further validated in the public mind the disloyal nature of the IWW.[11]

The Hammer Falls in the Pacific Northwest

Ultimately, a coalition of farm owners, business interests, local and state politicians, and the federal government lined up against the IWW in the West's agricultural sectors. These alliances were not directed solely against harvest Wobblies or the IWW; socialists, anarchists, and anyone suspected of antiwar or pro-German sentiment were subject to vigilante and official political repression. In Washington state, which serves as a good example of the phenomenon, the IWW found itself under attack as early as March 1917, when the state's legislature passed a bill that would have made the "teaching of syndicates, sabotage or use of violence in industrial disputes" a felony. With the IWW defined by state lawmakers as an organization that adhered to such policies, members of the organization could now face arrest. Governor Ernest Lister vetoed the bill, fearing that it would violate the right to free speech, but the state legislature overrode his veto in 1919. Despite Lister's concerns, anti-IWW sentiment and activity attained a significant level of legitimacy among most of Washington's politicians and in the pages of the state's newspapers.[12]

Securing farm labor was a national as well as a state or regional issue. Soon after war was declared, the federal departments of Labor and Agriculture began to coordinate their efforts with state, county, and community agents to provide an information network to determine where labor shortages and labor surpluses existed and to recruit agricultural workers for any given locality. The plan stressed the use of local means to deal with the labor supply problem first before turning to higher levels of government services. The federal government's concern with the supply of farm labor actually led some officials to entertain the idea of importing half a million farm laborers from China for the duration of the war to supplement the projected agricultural wartime labor shortage.[13]

Taking action at the state level to deal with the wartime situation, especially regarding the labor supply issue, Governor Lister appointed prominent academic and industrial leaders to a State Council of Defense, as many other governors did during the war. University of Washington President Henry Suzzallo chaired the council, and A. L. Rogers, a public official, took charge of overseeing farm labor issues. The State Council of Defense affiliated with county councils, made up of representatives of such activities as farming, manufacturing, women's work, home defense, transportation, food supply, and labor. According to one historian, these local bodies acted as "centers of patriotic feeling, national loyalty, and war service."[14]

As one of its first orders of business, Washington's State Council of Defense went on record opposing the importation of Asian labor. This decision accomplished the dual purpose of pleasing both farmers and organized labor. The council then addressed the desire of business owners and farmers to thwart the organizing efforts of the IWW, particularly in the central fruit-growing regions of the state. In late June, members of the council, the president of the State Federation of Labor, Washington's labor commissioner, and the federal immigration commissioner all arrived in North Yakima. They listened to the concerns of farmers about the IWW's "unreasonable" wage demands and those of community leaders that Wobblies might "attack" thousands of high school students recruited to assist in the season's fruit harvest. The representatives also listened to tales of Wobbly sabotage, such as the practice of pressing thumbnails into apples when boxed, thereby ruining them. During the session, there was even a serious discussion of the idea of declaring martial law.[15]

Not only were farmers concerned about securing non-Wobbly farm labor, preventing IWW organizing efforts, and protecting the region's food production from sabotage, but they also were worried about the fallout from the Wobbly-led Inland Northwest lumber strike that had recently begun. Within the first two weeks of July, the strike closed down most of the logging and milling operations of eastern Washington, northern Idaho, and western Montana. North Yakima's fruit growers feared the ramifications of this strike because of their reliance upon Cascade Lumber Company, a local producer that supplied half of all the fruit boxes used by area farmers and that itself was supplied by area lumber mills.[16] At the outset of the strike, Spokane's Chamber of Commerce requested that congressional representatives from Washinton and Idaho send federal aid to help lumber company owners, mine owners, and farmers deal with "the Industrial Worker of the World menace" in the Pacific Northwest. Within days of that request, the State Council of Defense report on the Wobbly situation in North Yakima arrived at the governor's office.

On the basis of the report, Governor Lister appealed to the secretary of war, Newton D. Baker, who was also chairman of the National Council of Defense, for federal aid in protecting Washington's vital food-growing regions, particularly in Cle Elum, Ellensburg, and North Yakima. Concurrently, Lister initiated a program to deputize citizens into homeguard units to replace the state militia, if needed, in areas threatened by the IWW. This action also served to deflect a troublesome situation, in that these state-sanctioned homeguard units undermined the legitimacy of vigilante groups sponsored by the Yakima Valley Producers Protective Association in Yakima, Kittitas, and Benton counties.[17]

Despite the growing level of opposition on the state and local levels and congressional passage of the Espionage Act in June 1917, Wobblies appeared fairly confident about their future. The Espionage Act proscribed any interference with military enlistment, its operations, or war-related industrial production, or the use of the mails for treasonous purposes. The IWW, though refusing to endorse the war, did not have an explicit antiwar policy, which made many Wobblies feel safe from federal persecution. Moreover, the AWIU's Forrest Edwards did all he could to discourage Wobbly street speakers from espousing antiwar and antimilitary propaganda.[18]

In central Washington, harvest Wobblies, throughout the spring and early summer, focused on the coming harvest season and continued their organizational work. Outside of the lumber strike, Wobbly activity in the region consisted of a few agricultural strikes in Walla Walla and a construction strike south of North Yakima, which garnered some newspaper attention. The most significant event at the Wobbly hall on Front Street in North Yakima was a well-attended lecture given by James P. Thompson, a longtime member, organizer, and orator of the IWW. Thompson's talk on the nature and goals of the IWW drew a crowd of three hundred, according to the *Yakima Morning Herald*. In regard to the upcoming harvest season, Wobblies expected Yakima Valley farmers to recognize their labor power, as they called for $3.00 to $3.50 a day with board. Yet the *Industrial Worker* noted that the valley needed dozens of AWIU delegates to organize migrants before the "sage hens," regional tenant farmers, secured the temporary harvest labor jobs to supplement their inadequate farm income.[19]

The Wobblies' optimism about the future was misplaced, however. On Monday evening, 9 July 1917, federal troops raided the North Yakima Wobbly hall, arresting twenty-four Wobblies and confiscating literature found there. The men were arrested under "a federal charge . . . of interfering with the production and harvesting of crops," as the *Yakima Morning Herald* described it; in fact, the army probably arrested the Wobblies for violating the Espionage Act. Lieutenant Orville A. Stevens, commander of the troops stationed in North Yakima—who were actually camped opposite the union hall on Front Street—had enticed Wobblies to engage with him in conversation in the hall the night of the raid. He apparently wanted to lure as many Wobblies as he could into the hall before he summoned his soldiers. Once he had a couple of dozen explaining their position on a number of issues, he ordered a soldier who had accompanied him to blow a whistle, summoning a sergeant and thirty to forty soldiers to begin making arrests.[20]

In subsequent days, the troops arrested more Wobblies in North Yakima, and other raids and arrests occurred throughout the state, especially in rural areas. For example, near the small community of Easton on the eastern slope of the Cascade range, federal troops under the command of Captain Shorkly arrested between fifty and sixty Wobblies. These IWW members faced the same charges as those in North Yakima, with the added charge of disrupting logging operations. Easton was situated in hay country, but it was close to the logging and milling operations halted by the Wobbly-led lumber strike.

These actions taken against the IWW in Easton and North Yakima were not merely an attempt to harass Wobblies, but to eliminate the union from the harvest fields and logging camps of the state. They took place in concert with other raids and mass arrests of IWW members in Washington and in other western states, including Montana, Idaho, Arizona, and Oregon. According to many of the nation's newspaper editors and pro-war politicians at the state and national level, the IWW was in the pay of Germany and therefore a domestic enemy. Further-more, once the Department of War accepted the State Council of Defense's recommendations for federal protection of essential agri-cultural production sites, such as those in the Yakima Valley, federal intervention could begin. The Department of War dispatched troops throughout the state "to protect the food supply and industrial plants." In addition, a combination of federal troops, deputy sheriffs, and hired gunmen began a systematic campaign to arrest Wobblies found riding freight trains, particularly those headed east from Seattle to the fruit country. With freight train travel the primary form of transportation for Wobblies, anti-IWW forces thus hampered Wobbly movement about the state.[21]

After a week, approximately seventy-five Wobblies held in Yakima County's jail still had no formal charges brought against them. The authorities were waiting for word on whether they could charge the men with violating the Espionage Act, which forbade interference with tending or harvesting crops. George F. Vanderveer, the principal IWW attorney, thought that habeas corpus proceedings, which would have forced the authorities to produce a law and evidence that the Wobblies had broken it to justify incarceration, were pointless given the anti-IWW mood in the region. With the IWW legal team stymied, more Wobblies were arrested, prompting North Yakima authorities to make use of a state stockade to house all of them. The Wobblies in custody were not all from North Yakima; some were from nearby fruit-growing towns such as Zillah, Sunnyside, and Wapato.[22]

This group of native-born men from other parts of the country and a few Western European immigrants did not sit quietly while military and law enforcement authorities violated their civil rights. First, they tried to break out of the county jail, but this effort failed, ending in a noisy evening of protest. After being stuck in an overcrowded jail for several weeks, the prisoners instigated a violent demonstration when the lights went out on 28 July. They tore up their cell, breaking the toilet and bathtub. They tore apart their iron bunks and used the iron pipes to smash the walls and floor of the jail. The episode ended when a detachment of soldiers arrived, along with Chief of Police B. F. McCurdy. The sergeant in charge of the unit threatened to shoot any prisoner who did not refrain from such destructive behavior. Eventually, the men realized that their protests were to no avail.

As raids and arrests proceeded unabated in Washington, governors and other state officials of several western states moved to coordinate their efforts at suppressing the IWW. As early as 14 July Governor Lister and Governor Moses Alexander of Idaho met in Spokane and pledged to work together to solve the IWW situation. At the same time, sheriffs from Washington and Idaho met in the panhandle town of Moscow, Idaho, to plan coordinated actions against the IWW. Later in the month, Alexander met again with Lister and with the governors of Utah and Oregon to seek ways to suppress the IWW with the assistance of the federal government. Alexander, who took the lead in the regionwide effort, made it clear that he was not opposed to organized labor, nor did he have "ill will toward any set of citizens." Yet it would have been obvious to any critical observer at the time that local, state, and federal government would not tolerate dissent in the workplace. The largest gathering of Western state government officials took place on 11 August in Portland. The governors of Washington, Oregon, Idaho, Montana, Utah, Nevada, and California's representative, Julius Lubin, met to discuss a variety of wartime concerns, including the Wobblies. The representatives agreed to refuse any arbitration or reconciliation with the IWW. Their goal was clear. They would suppress the IWW with whatever means lay at their disposal.[23]

Fear of an IWW menace to agricultural production spread quickly throughout the Pacific Northwest. If state and local authorities could not secure federal troops, they created homeguard units to protect farm areas. The town of Walla Walla assembled one hundred men into such a unit. In Pendleton, a town in northeastern Oregon, a secret organization of farmers and businessmen formed a homeguard unit that eventually received legal sanction to protect the area's large grain crop. In southwestern Oregon's Klamath Falls, local farmers and community leaders blamed arson fires and stock poisoning on the IWW, though an official investigation could find no evidence linking Wobblies to these events. Anti-IWW hysteria continued in Lewiston, Idaho, where residents at a town meeting considered forming homeguard units to protect agriculture, logging, and mining for the entire Inland Empire of eastern Washington and north Idaho.[24]

Along with government repression of the IWW, Washington state's Harvesters League led the way for employers to secure harvest labor in the spring and summer with the "hope to put the IWW out of business." At the league's headquarters in Seattle, city folk were recruited for employment in grain and fruit harvests. Newspapers in the state gave league activities ample coverage that encouraged imitators among local growers who wished to use area labor. In July, Wenatchee agribusiness owners formed the Wenatchee Harvesters' League, which registered hundreds of individuals throughout the Wenatchee Valley for service during the harvest. Patriotic duty and the satisfaction of displacing the IWW in Washington agriculture inspired harvest league proliferation. Not to be outdone by these state and local harvester leagues, the AFL sought to take advantage of the IWW's apparent weakness in agricultural labor organizing. The Federal Labor Union, affiliated with the AFL, set up shop in North Yakima to recruit migrant and temporary workers of all sorts, particularly those who worked in agriculture.[25]

While agribusiness owners and their supporters pressed for the suppression of the IWW on many fronts, the lumber strike in the Pacific Northwest continued to grow by leaps and bounds. Though the IWW led the lumber strike, most of the striking loggers and mill workers were not IWW members, a fact the region's newspapers made clear to their readers. Also, the workers' demand for an eight-hour day and some basic working and living condition improvements gave the strike wide public support in the region. Throughout July and August the strike gathered momentum. The Olympic Peninsula logging camps and lumber mills, particularly those in and around Port Angeles, closed due to the strike. Employment agencies in Seattle pledged not to send men to logging camps or mills that were on strike but only to those companies that had met the strikers' demands. AFL timber workers joined the IWW in calling for a general strike in the industry. By late summer, ninety percent of the lumber industry in western Washington, which included logging camps and mills, closed down. The strike affected the entire Pacific Northwest, including western Oregon, all of Washington, northern Idaho, and western Montana. Striking workers, as many as fifty thousand, shut down as much as seventy-five percent of the industry in the region.[26]

Over the course of August the lumber strike increased in its effectiveness. The same was true for the Wobbly-led copper and zinc strike in Montana that summer. Only in Arizona, during the Bisbee copper miners' strike, did western Wobblies experience an immediate setback. With the use of federal troops, however, the persecution of the IWW in the Pacific Northwest became more effective with time. Hundreds of Wobblies found themselves under arrest throughout Washington, Idaho, Oregon, and Montana. In order to relieve over-crowded jails, officials built more stockades or "bull pens" to house Wobblies. Federal troops, local law enforcement, homeguard units, and vigilante groups made it difficult to participate in a picket line, organize, or attend to union affairs at an IWW local. At what appeared to be the height of the persecution, James Rowan, IWW Spokane district secretary and head of the Lumber Workers' Industrial Union No. 500, called for a 20 August general strike of all workers in Washington, Idaho, Oregon, and Montana to force the release of all "class war prisoners" currently held throughout the Pacific Northwest. Included in the strike demands were an eight-hour day for construction and lumber work and a ten-hour day for harvest work. Fearing the success of such a strike, law enforcement arrested Rowan and more than twenty other Wobblies at the Spokane union hall on 19 August 1917.[27]

Federal and state officials viewed the strike threat with great apprehension. The logging industry, particularly the spruce logging operations in Washington that supplied much-needed lumber for military aircraft, copper mining, and the fruit and grain industries, had national as well as regional importance. The Department of Justice prepared to use force to break up the strike, as did Governor Alexander of Idaho. Harvey Alfred, Idaho's director of the farm markets bureau, claimed that the IWW shipped phosphorous to Idaho in cake form for use in destroying grain fields and storage facilities throughout Idaho, Washington, and Oregon. The cities of Spokane and North Yakima suppressed Wobbly street meetings and street speaking while Spokane's county council sent agents throughout eastern Washington to persuade harvesters not to honor the strike and to do their patriotic duty by refraining from hampering the war effort. In the Yakima Valley, R. B.

Milroy and the chairman of the Yakima Council of Defense chairman urged employers to make note of those who honored the strike. With estimates as high as five thousand Wobblies in the valley and fifty-five thousand in the entire Pacific Northwest, employers prepared for the worst. Homeguard units, local law enforcement, and vigilante groups assembled throughout the region at strategic points and waited for the Monday strike day.[28]

The fears of the authorities were unfounded, however: the general strike failed miserably. The Pacific Northwest did not have fifty-five thousand Wobblies. Many of those who were in the region were already on strike against the logging and mining industries or in a jail or stockade. In the agricultural areas of the Yakima and Wenatchee Valleys and in the Palouse, independent harvest workers seriously outnumbered harvest Wobblies. Moreover, the Harvesters League demonstrated a great deal of success in finding workers for the fruit harvest of Yakima Valley and other nearby growing regions. More workers than jobs typified the wheat country of the Palouse, especially as the area's yield would be only half of a normal harvest. The strike barely made a dent in harvesting or construction work. Only in the Palouse-area town of St. John did a significant number of harvesters, approximately eighty men, refuse to work. North Yakima newspapers claimed that not a single worker heeded the strike call in the valley.[29]

As August drew to a close and September began, the IWW in the Pacific Northwest struggled to maintain a presence in the region. Union halls that were still open tried to conduct their affairs. The lumber strike continued, as did efforts to organize workers in a variety of industries. On the migrant farm labor front, the AWIU's work in the summer of 1917 was not impressive in Washington or in any other Pacific Northwest state. Facing armed and legal repression and being seriously outnumbered by independent harvest workers, the AWIU could not hold its own against the concerted efforts of the region's farmers and their supporters.

Securing Harvest Labor in the Great Plains

The fortunes of harvest Wobblies on the Great Plains that summer proved equally difficult, though not as disastrous. Given the draft, volunteer service, and the attraction of high-paying industrial jobs, many Great Plains state officials and farmers expressed their concern that a labor shortage might occur during the 1917 harvest and threshing season. The wartime draft had had a dramatic effect on the availability of migrant and seasonal harvest laborers; estimates of agricultural labor shortages ran as high as two million men, with America's wheat belt projected to suffer the most from the shortage. The high price of wheat was further motivation for farmers to procure the labor necessary to harvest their entire yield. In 1917, wheat prices were 130 percent higher than they were in 1914, which meant that farmers received more than $2 a bushel. Therefore, securing seasonal farm labor became a top priority for the region.[30]

To an unprecedented degree, the federal government stepped in to aid plains farmers in meeting their labor needs. For example, in a cooperative effort among the U.S. Departments of Labor, Agriculture, and War, forty-five thousand urban workers found employment in Kansas. Furthermore, a rather effective relationship between numerous chambers of commerce in Great Plains states and the Department of Labor spawned the Employment Service, which successfully placed much-needed labor in harvest areas. The federal government also sponsored the Boy's Working Reserve and the Women's Land Armies to address the projected labor shortage. These organizations of boys and young men under draft age, and of girls and young women interested in aiding the war effort and earning summer wages, participated in harvests across the nation. Although the Women's Land Armies made their greatest impact in 1918, the Boy's Working Reserve placed 150,000 urban youth on farms in 1917.[31]

Another means by which farmers attempted to meet their labor needs came from the Non-Partisan League of North Dakota. The state's farmers depended on migrant labor more than any of the other northern plains states, and the wartime labor shortage amplified their concerns. At the NPL's annual convention, delegates elected a small committee to negotiate working conditions, hours, wages, and labor distribution with a committee of AWIU representatives. *The Leader*, the NPL's official newspaper, determined that seventy-five percent of the migrant farm laborers who ventured into North Dakota each harvest and threshing season were Wobblies. It seemed only reasonable, according to *The Leader*, that a healthy relationship develop between agricultural workers and farmers, as they needed each other.[32] Drawing on the spirit of the initial discussion between NPL members and harvest Wobblies at the May AWIU conference, the two committees settled on a tentative harvest and threshing labor agreement for 1917, setting basic wages and work hours at $4 for a ten-hour day with forty cents an hour for overtime, plus a graduated pay increase as wheat prices increased. The agreement included provisions for sleeping accommodations and for "wholesome and plentiful food." NPL members pledged to hire only AWIU members, and the AWIU agreed to be responsible for satisfying labor needs. In addition, the agreement provided a grievance procedure, so that an individual could turn to his organization for support.[33]

The AWIU ratified the agreement in principle by publishing it in *Solidarity* and in an AWIU bulletin. This endorsement gave the membership the opportunity to act on the agreement. To ease Wobbly concern that this was a labor contract, which would violate the IWW constitution, Forrest Edwards and Ted Fraser maintained that the agreement was only a verbal one, and therefore not proscribed. The NPL's ratification process turned out differently. At first, it appeared as if the agreement would meet with unqualified approval. NPL committee representatives, with letters of support for the agreement from railroad companies, and AWIU secretary Edwards met with North Dakota NPL members in a variety of locations for the ratification vote. In Minot, the vote to approve the agreement ended in an overwhelming victory. Bismarck farmers, after listening to NPL's president A. C. Townley's endorsement, approved the measure as well. However, in the eastern North Dakota towns of Valley City and Devils Lake, farmers were divided on the issue. Some thought that the wage demands were too high, especially as the government could not guarantee what they would receive per bushel of wheat. In the end, the agreement was not ratified by a majority of the NPL membership. Western farmers seemed to favor it, while eastern farmers lined up against it. The leadership dropped the proposed agreement out of fear that it would cleave the League in the state into two irreconcilable camps. For the time being, unity among NPL farmers was more important than securing necessary farm labor.[34]

The failure to establish an official agreement between the AWIU and the NPL left many in both organizations disappointed, but the AWIU forged ahead with its effort to attain the wage and working condition improvements outlined in the agreement anyway. The industrial union also persevered in its goal of attaining widespread recruitment into the union, thereby taking the AWIU another step towards gaining control over the harvest and threshing labor supply throughout the Great Plains wheat belt. Nevertheless, some farmers in North Dakota honored the spirit of the tentative agreement. Many harvest Wobblies noted the improvement in wages and working conditions during the summer 1917 harvest. These improvements came with at a steep price, however, as throughout the rest of the Great Plains, the AWIU and Wobblies in other industries experienced an extraordinary degree of persecution and outright repression.[35]

Weathering Repression in the Wheat Belt

The agricultural labor shortage that farmers, newspaper editors, and government officials feared for 1917 turned out not to be as severe as anticipated. The Kansas City Federal Employment Office successfully placed fifteen thousand farm workers in Nebraska, and comparable organizations placed tens of thousands more in virtually every state. Still, workers were not as plentiful as in former years, and the IWW took advantage of the situation through their organizational presence in the plains. Despite fewer independent harvesters in the field and more Wobblies than ever before participating in the harvest, wages remained far below what the AWIU desired. One reason for the failure of harvest Wobblies to force up wages had to do with their uneven distribution. Kansas attracted few Wobblies, probably due to the successful placement of auxiliary labor, while in South Dakota half the migrants were Wobblies. In Kansas, a ten-hour day earned harvesters on average only $3.00. Oklahoma was not much better for the migrant agricultural laborer. In Nebraska and South Dakota wages did not appear to reach above $3.50 a day. Even though large numbers of harvest Wobblies searched for work in South Dakota, the county councils of defense throughout the state successfully pressured farmers to maintain their wage offer to harvesters at $3.00 a day.[36]

Even if the AWIU could not significantly raise wages for its members or for harvest workers in general, the organization continued to grow in membership, with more money flowing into its coffers. In early July, the AWIU occupied its new seven-room headquarters in Minneapolis. Unbeknownst to the members, they were under constant surveillance by Minneapolis agents of the U.S. attorney general's office, who claimed to have the names and addresses of all the harvest Wobblies in the city. Yet the AWIU leadership felt quite strong, and issued a sympathy strike threat that coincided with the Wobbly-led copper miners' strike in Bisbee, Arizona. Newspaper editors and military authorities took this threat seriously, believing that the union had fifty thousand members who would refuse to work. Newspaper reports also alleged that harvest Wobblies planned to burn crops as part of the strike or as part of a sabotage campaign. Of course, no credible evidence existed to support these allegations. Furthermore, military officials in South Dakota claimed that Wobblies possessed maps of major crop districts in the state and were prepared to commit arson.[37]

In the end, no one set fires in the state, and the threatened strike never took place. After the miners in Bisbee were forcibly expelled from Arizona by vigilantes and dumped from railroad cattle cars in the middle of the New Mexico desert, a new strike threat emerged from the general headquarters of the IWW in Chicago. Bill Haywood, general secretary of the IWW, argued that Bisbee municipal officials must allow the expelled miners, most of whom were residents of Bisbee and not migratory IWW members, to return to their homes. If they did not, Haywood threatened, two hundred fifty thousand Wobblies and sympathetic workers, including thousands of harvesters in the Great Plains, would strike throughout the country. But again, the strike was not carried out.[38]

Strike threats such as these unnerved residents of Aberdeen, South Dakota, who already feared loss of their crops due to severe drought conditions and soaring temperatures. The Wobbly union hall in Aberdeen was bristling with activity in late July, as hundreds of harvesters poured off of freight trains into the town in search of work. These conditions moved anti-IWW forces to raid the hall as local businessmen and others savagely beat arriving Wobblies. These acts of violence were justified in local newspapers, according to the Wobbly press. In response, harvest Wobblies led a statewide strike in mid-August, shutting down harvest operations throughout South Dakota. Primary demands of the strikers included the right to organize and the right to maintain their union halls. By the *Industrial Worker*'s estimate, the strike led to rising wages in the state although toward the end of the month economic necessity drove many harvest Wobblies back to work.[39]

The only truly bright spot for the AWIU was in North Dakota. Due to a variety of factors, Wobblies did not face the same degree of persecution as in other states. Elements within the Non-Partisan League of North Dakota and many North Dakota socialist farmers were sympathetic both to the IWW and to migrant agricultural workers. Although ideological friction existed among NPL members, socialists, and Wobblies, they shared a common bond during the war. For example, NPL members and American socialists both faced suspicion of disloyalty, and in some cases outright persecution, to the same degree as IWW members. In North Dakota, leading members of the NPL either took an actively antiwar position or were simply unenthusiastic about the U.S.'s entry into the European war. The Socialist Party of America was one of the few socialist parties in the world that took an antiwar stand. Most important, the state's governor, Lynn J. Frazier, a member of the NPL, set the tone for the government's attitude toward the IWW. He issued a decree in mid-August, aimed at vigilante groups, that proscribed any harassment of migrant laborers or abridgement of the right of farm laborers to hold out for higher wages. Frazier expected his law enforcement officers to abide by his executive order or face dismissal from office. Given these circumstances, plus North Dakota farmers' reliance on migrant farm labor, a less contentious atmosphere existed between farmers and harvest Wobblies within the borders of that state.[40]

IWW harvesters tried a range of methods to achieve favorable employment conditions in North Dakota. In some instances, farmers met Wobblies halfway. In the small northeastern wheat town of Leeds, farmers organized a meeting with the IWW on 11 August to establish an agreement on wages and hours. The one hundred farmers in attendance wanted more than ten hours out of their hired labor for a day's pay, but Wobblies were insistent on no overtime. The *Industrial Worker* reported that the parties eventually agreed to $3.50 for a ten-hour harvest day and $4.00 for a ten-hour day of threshing. In Fargo, farmers hired harvest labor directly from the IWW union hall at $4.00 a day. When farmers tried to hire through commercial clubs as a means to secure labor at no more than $3.00 a day, the large number of Wobblies in the state helped to thwart the effort, as IWW workers took jobs through these clubs and then attempted to raise wages on the job site. Finally, when a majority of workers at a site were IWW, they forced independents to join the union. A threat to leave a site en masse was enough to motivate a worker to join the union for fear of being let go by a farmer who did not want to have to seek out a new, non-union crew.[41]

The Great Effort to Destroy the IWW

From spring to summer 1917, western economic and political interests—whether farmers, lumbermen, mine owners, business leaders, politicians, bureaucrats, or trade union officials—pleaded with the federal government to find some means to act against the IWW. Throughout August, the federal departments of Labor, War, and Justice, worked on a plan to deal with the Wobblies. Motivated perhaps more by the industrial needs of the war effort, fear of disloyalty, and by the need to deport enemy aliens than for the specific concerns of individual capitalist interests in the West, the federal government moved against the IWW leadership on 5 September. In a series of raids conducted throughout the nation, Department of Justice agents arrested Wobblies in their union halls and private homes and confiscated literally tons of IWW literature, photographs, files, and even furniture, office equipment, supplies, and personal items for use by a federal grand jury in Chicago.[42]

Federal agents raided branch offices of the AWIU and other industrial unions in various cities, including the general headquarters of the IWW in Chicago. The AWIU's Minneapolis headquarters experienced a raid, although it was not followed immediately by arrests. According to Charles W. Anderson, the AWIU's shipping clerk, federal investigators examined the contents of every file, cabinet, and drawer in the office, confiscating only a small amount of property. Anderson noted that the investigators appreciated the cooperation of the AWIU office staff, which included secretary-treasurer Edwards, and spoke rather apologetically about the raid, as they found nothing that warranted their actions.[43]

Eventually, over the course of September, federal officials in Minneapolis began to arrest AWIU members. A grand jury, convened to determine whether the IWW leadership had violated the Espionage Act and the Selective Service Act, indicted seven AWIU members. They went on trial in Chicago with over one hundred other Wobblies. Forrest Edwards, Ted Fraser, and Don Buckley faced the same federal charges. Before law enforcement officials transported them to Chicago, owners of the Kasota Building, which served as the AWIU's headquarters and union hall, charged the men with breaking Minnesota's criminal syndicalism statute. In that building, as in most IWW union hall libraries, Wobblies could read books and pamphlets espousing revolutionary ideas. Minnesota's criminal syndicalism law, passed in April 1917, outlawed industrial sabotage and destruction of property as a means of achieving labor union goals. [44]

Despite the able defense mounted by the AWIU's attorney George L. Siegel, Judge C. L. Smith found the defendants guilty based on confiscated union hall literature that allegedly advocated sabotage in industrial disputes. The convictions of Edwards, Fraser, and Buckley did not lead to jail time, but the AWIU had to vacate its Kasota Building offices. Before the union had a chance to move, two more raids took place at the headquarters, with agents confiscating any file they could find. Anderson, who witnessed the final raid, remarked that "this [third] raid completely cleaned our office of records."[45]

The federal crackdown against the IWW targeted rank-and-file members as well as elected officials. Local police and sheriffs helped federal law enforcement by arresting IWW members who neglected draft registration requirements or who failed to report to military training camps. Foreign-born Wobblies were especially at risk of arrest and deportation as enemy aliens. Union halls could not protect Wobblies, for they were routinely raided by federal troops, Department of Justice agents, and local law enforcement officers. Municipal governments proved very effective at closing IWW halls through legal harassment and prosecution. To this end, arrests on vagrancy charges skyrocketed across the country during fall 1917. In one small Kansas County, three to four hundred vagrancy arrests took place in just a few short months. Independent harvesters became bolder in resisting harvest Wobbly pressure to join the union. For example, a shoot-out between independents and Wobblies in Glencoe, Minnesota left several men dead and three others, all Wobblies, arrested. [46]

With ongoing raids, arrests, and the threat of mass trials, the AWIU's fall convention opened under ominous conditions. The one hundred and fifty members present did not work out much of a strategy for the next harvest season. Most of the business at the meeting centered on electing a new secretary-treasurer and a new Organization Committee, as several of the current AWIU officeholders were in Chicago awaiting trial. Wobblies in attendance elected Charles Anderson secretary by unanimous vote, and elected Mat Fox and a number of others to the Organization Committee. Aside from replacing jailed leaders, the convention participants pledged their support for their fellow workers, whom they termed "class war prisoners." The members present voted to appropriate several hundred dollars for the General Defense Committee, a legal defense body formed to aid hundreds of incarcerated Wobblies.[47]

Harvest Wobblies in California experienced the same federal crackdown. In Fresno, federal agents raided the most significant AWIU branch office in California, arresting twenty-five men on the premises. They confiscated IWW literature and records, and seized control of the local's bank account. Raids in San Francisco, Sacramento, Stockton, Los Angeles, and other California cities swelled the ranks of Wobblies under federal indictment. Most of the California Wobblies faced the charge of obstructing the U.S.'s war effort. Arrested IWW members in California faced an additional charge of creating a conspiracy to interfere with employers' right to hire labor throughout the United States. From the Wobbly perspective, this was a perfect example of the federal government's attempt, in conjunction with capitalist interests, to wipe out the union.[48]

Later in the fall, Department of Justice officials, convinced that Omaha, Nebraska, would be the next headquarters of the AWIU, arrested sixty-five Wobblies attending a special conference in that city on 13 November. The arrested men came from Midwest, Great Plains, and Far West states, with a few from Australia and Great Britain. The agents also seized two tons of material, everything from songbooks to business records, in the search for evidence that the union engaged in industrial sabotage.[49]

In 1917, the AWIU also functioned as the parent union for the Oil Workers' Industrial Union (OWIU) in Kansas and Oklahoma. The relationship was a holdover from the period in which the AWO had oil, construction, and timber workers in its ranks. Because the OWIU did not have sufficient funds to operate as an independent local, its relation to the AWIU continued. Frank Gallagher, a primary organizer in the oil fields of the region, sought Anderson's assistance in initiating an organizing drive among oil field workers. Anderson agreed with Gallagher that despite the current wave of federal raids and indictments, the union must continue organizing. In November, just east of Wichita, federal officers raided the Augusta and El Dorado, Kansas, locals of the IWW, the chief organizing centers for the OWIU and the surrounding region. In all, law enforcement officials arrested between two hundred fifty and three hundred fifty Wobblies. Though the courts quickly released most of them, several, including secretary Anderson, were indicted on federal and state charges.[50]

By the end of 1917, the AWIU leadership and the leaders of other industrial unions of the IWW faced federal charges, the most severe of which was violating the Espionage Act. In all, about two hundred members were under indictment at four primary locations: Chicago, Sacramento, Omaha, and Wichita.[51] IWW industrial unions in agriculture, mining, lumber, transportation, and other industries tried to continue organizing efforts, but had to spend most of their energy supporting their jailed fellow workers.

Crippling the AWIU in Washington

While the AWIU leaders awaited trial, harvest Wobblies continued organizing in the fields and orchards as best they could. In Washington, the federal government, in conjunction with local law enforcement, effectively repressed AWIU activity. To keep a better watch on Wobblies, Governor Lister employed a cadre of spies to observe and, if possible, infiltrate the union. He appointed C. B. Reed as the chief of the Washington State Secret Service. These spies fanned out across the state, settling themselves into large and small towns, sending information to Reed, who then reported to Lister. Spies in North Yakima, Wenatchee, and other agricultural-area towns sent in hundreds of such reports. A careful study of these reports reveals that secret service agents successfully undermined the AWIU.[52]

With Wobbly activity at a low ebb, federal troops withdrew from the Yakima Valley by mid-October. Strikes in area orchards were few and far between. The dozen or so active Wobbly delegates spent much of their energy collecting funds for the defense of fellow Wobblies who were either in prison or awaiting trial, particularly those in Chicago. As locally jailed IWW members gained their freedom when charges were dropped or when they had served out their sentences, many left town for the winter. According to the North Yakima-based operatives, IWW members in the city hesitated to reopen their union hall for fear that local law enforcement would raid the hall, confiscate IWW property, and arrest the secretary. Fred H. Bohn, the North Yakima IWW branch secretary, used a shack behind the St. Paul Hotel as both a residence and an underground union hall. Bohn forbade Wobblies to enter with their union cards and stipulated that members conduct their meetings in secret, as he feared that stool pigeons and spies would more easily attend open meetings.[53]

With Wobblies existing in effect as an underground organization in the city, they had to find safe places to congregate. Pool halls, some restaurants, individual Wobbly-rented apartments, and downtown skid row areas sufficed for a time. An unsavory element that existed among the Wobblies may have had something to do with this kind of underworld existence. A group known as the Jamaica Ginger Gang operated out of the downtown pool halls and claimed membership in the IWW. They panhandled in an aggressive manner, expecting Wobblies, workers, and others walking down the city streets to give them money. Another element in the city was the "two-day bums," who also claimed IWW membership. They typically worked a short period of time on a ranch and then quit, using their earnings for alcohol and a flophouse bed. The AWIU leadership found that both elements had a detrimental effect on the IWW in the city and among area harvesters whom Wobblies desperately needed to bring into the union. By January 1918, the Organization Committee of the AWIU initiated a program to purge them from the IWW. Because of a policy of open recruiting and no screening process when new members signed up, however, the struggle to remove troublesome or dangerous groups from the union remained an ongoing problem.[54]

In early 1918, two events took place in Yakima—North Yakima citizens shortened the city's name about this time—that demonstrated the weakness of the IWW in the face of state and federal authorities' efforts to destroy the union. D. F. Costello, better known as Operative 43 in his reports to Chief Reed, had gained the trust of Secretary Bohn. Suspecting that a raid was imminent, Bohn sent his credentials and other IWW records to Spokane for safekeeping. Costello believed that someone sympathetic to the IWW in the mayor's office had leaked word of the impending raid to Bohn. Costello had called for a law enforcement search of the IWW shack primarily because he suspected Bohn of plotting to use germ warfare. Bohn owned a microscope, books on chemistry and water analysis, and photographs of area flumes, canals, factories, and agricultural growing areas. Bohn's explanation to Costello—that he and fellow Wobbly J. H. Bowling studied together as a kind of hobby and that photographs of the region aided them in their organizing work—did not satisfy Costello. The agent's reasoning convinced him that Bohn's devotion to the IWW meant that he would resort to germ warfare to avenge the suppression that the IWW was experiencing in the valley. Costello suspected that Bohn and Bowling would spread typhoid or diphtheria through the water or milk supply, acquiring the "germs" they needed at a laboratory owned by the city's health department.[55]

On 29 January, secret service agents, federal officials, and local police raided the underground Wobbly hall. They confiscated material and arrested Bohn, Bowling, and Costello. The *Yakima Daily Republic* told its readers that the captured Wobblies might have wanted to spread poisons among the orchards in the valley. In its pages, the newspaper convicted the men of pro-German sentiment, of having pockets filled with gold of suspicious origin, and of having plans to poison Yakima citizens. Costello successfully maintained his cover through his arrest. The IWW attorney for the three men, W. J. Costello (no relation to D. F. Costello), arranged to have Operative 43 released, but law enforcement officials kept Bohn and Bowling incarcerated for a possible grand jury hearing with the other IWW members in Chicago. Costello continued to operate as a spy under the cover of being a freelance photographer and a seasoned Wobbly. He developed a good relationship with local IWW members in that he never took sides with one faction or another and made his small apartment available for union meetings.[56]

The other event that further weakened the IWW in Yakima took place in March. IWW headquarters in Spokane had sent an organizer, Frank S. Meyers, to the city. In a secret meeting held on the outskirts of town, a small group of Yakima Wobblies elected Meyers secretary of the struggling local, thereby alienating him from perhaps one hundred and fifty Wobblies in Yakima. Some did not consider Meyers fit for the job, as his only leadership experience was as a job delegate. Others believed that supporting a local in Yakima was a misuse of funds as long as no union hall could remain open in town and hundreds of jailed Wobblies required legal defense funds. Meyers' unpopularity caused serious problems for the city's Wobblies in maintaining solidarity in the face of extraordinary repression. He was supposed to act as the conduit between the two most prominent industrial unions and their members in town. The AWIU recognized Meyers immediately, but the Construction Workers' Industrial Union only grudgingly certified him as their primary representative. Such discontent only made coordinated action difficult.[57]

Wobbly activity began to increase at the end of February, as work on ranches, both for day laborers and ranch hands, opened up. Harvest Wobblies began arriving on Northern Pacific freight trains in significant numbers, using their red cards to acquire free passage. According to Costello, Wobblies consider this a "soft ride," for some train crews sympathized with the Wobblies and slowed down their freight trains to pick Wobblies up in jungle camps along the rail lines. In central Washington, IWW members found work on farms and sheep ranches, but also on major construction projects such as the Tieton Canal Works, where Wobblies made up a substantial number of the workers at the Rimrock construction camps. Some IWWs rented rooms in Yakima and surrounding towns or lived at the work site. Given winter temperatures, the jungles were largely uninhabitable, though they provided a relatively safe place for groups of Wobblies to meet and discuss union affairs. On several occasions a larger venue was useful, as Costello's rented room could hold no more than twenty-five people.

With several hundred Wobblies now in the region, the AWIU leadership supplied job delegates to central Washington in the hope of organizing independent harvesters and other agricultural workers. The union wanted to bring the area's sheepherders, lambers, and shearmen into the fold. A significant number of the sheep workers were Mexicans and Spaniards, though the majority were native-born whites. Their ethnic diversity hindered united action, as the immigrants considered the native-born to be prejudiced against them, and the whites considered the immigrants too willing to work for low wages. Nevertheless, in February, the sheep workers contemplated a strike to increase their wages. They believed that owners benefited greatly from wartime profits in wool and therefore could afford to increase their monthly wage to $100. Several of the sheep workers were Wobblies, but most belonged to the AFL-affiliated Sheep Shearers' Union. The primary AWIU organizer sent to try to recruit the sheep workers was George Constantine, a Greek immigrant. Another Washington secret service agent, F. L. B., tried to prevent AWIU affiliation and the strike by working with Yakima police to frighten Constantine into breaking off his efforts by threatening him with jail time. They had more luck in intimidating Domingo Villanenta, a Spanish strike proponent. F. L. B. and the assistant chief of police accosted Villanenta at the Brunswick Bar in downtown Yakima. They threatened him with deportation, persuading him to take the next freight train out of town. Nonetheless, the strike took place anyway, although the sheep workers chose to remain with the less-controversial AFL even after appeals by Meyers and other AWIU members.[58]

In early March 1918 the federal government launched another series of raids and arrests directed against the IWW. The official justification for this wave of federal prosecution was to crack down on "enemy aliens." Yet it was no coincidence that the federal action took place primarily in the Pacific Northwest a day after the last holdouts in the lumber industry capitulated to striking workers' demand for an eight-hour day.[59]

In this atmosphere of legal persecution, Yakima civic leaders and businessmen felt confident to take measures into their own hands against the IWW. Late in the evening of 18 March, between thirty and fifty "unmasked men" abducted Secretary Meyers from his downtown room. They drove him out into the countryside and pretended that they were about to lynch him, stopping at large trees and asking each other if this or that tree would do the job. According to Costello's report, Meyers pleaded for his life and claimed that he was forced into the union. Tar and feathers, rather than hanging, awaited Meyers. The mob stripped the Wobbly and applied the tar to every part of his body, and then covered him with feathers. He was handed his clothes and told to leave town and never to return. According to Costello, half the Wobblies in Yakima left town the following day.[60]

Meyers got help in Wapato, a small town south of Yakima. His injuries were not severe, and he eventually made his way back to Spokane to continue his service to the AWIU. Almost immediately the AWIU sent another delegate to Yakima. Secret service agent F. L. B. expected the arrival of the twenty-year-old from Seattle, Charles Koler, and had the police arrest him. The courts held Koler for the grand jury, and, since he could not pay the $1000 bail, kept him in jail. Meanwhile, Tom Elliott, one of the most active AWIU delegates in the area, did all he could to find the culprits in the Meyers case. He had help from B. M. Williams, the secretary of the Building Trades Council of Yakima. Even though Williams received numerous letters and phone calls warning him that he would get the same treatment as Meyers if he did not let the matter go, he remained undeterred in his search for the perpetrators' identities. Other Wobblies and AFL-affiliated union members worked with him. It turned out that those involved in the mob action were among the most prominent civic and business leaders in the city. Although the *Yakima*

Daily Republic admonished the vigilante mob for their behavior, the paper did not identify the culprits by name, nor did the police arrest anyone for the crime.[61]

The anti-IWW environment notwithstanding, Wobblies arrived in the Yakima Valley daily for a variety of springtime work in agriculture and construction. Despite this influx and suspicions on the part of secret service operatives in Yakima that the mayor and some city council members were sympathetic to the IWW, Wobbly activity in the city never recovered. In fact, throughout Washington, Idaho, Oregon, and Montana, the IWW was in a holding pattern as a result of arrests, trials, and raids. In most respects, it can be said that the union began its decline in the Pacific Northwest, particularly among harvesters.[62]

As the 1918 harvest season approached in the Yakima Valley and other agricultural areas of the state, labor was plentiful. Boys, girls, and women supplemented the pool of experienced local and migrant male agricultural laborers. The Federal Employment Service, the Washington State Harvesters' League, and the State Council of Defense channeled workers to needy areas. The most salient example of the paucity of Wobbly organization in the area was the creation of the Fruit Workers' Union of Yakima (FWUY). The FWUY began in early September, and by late October had almost one thousand paid-up members. From the outset the union affiliated with the AFL, and soon worked to establish a wage scale for fruit pickers in the valley for a variety of picking and packing jobs. In some instances, the FWUY proposed to raise wages by as much as fifty percent, but usually the workers called for between $3.50 to $4.50 for an eight-hour day plus paid transportation to the job site.[63]

In mid-October, the union sent employers their proposed wage scale. Almost every employer in the valley refused to meet it, precipitating a strike on 15 October. Even though the union had hundreds of members honoring the walkout, the ample pool of non-union labor in the valley prevented the strike from affecting any but a few harvesting or packing operations. After surveying the situation, A. R. Garden, an AFL organizer, advised the FWUY strike committee to call off the strike. On 24 October, the strike ended, and many frustrated workers returned to work. In disgust, some workers refused to work at the old scale and worked other jobs in Yakima or returned to their hometowns.[64]

One of the notable features of this strike action, and of the FWUY generally, was the absence of IWW involvement, indicating that the AWIU had reached a low point in its organizational effectiveness. A second significant aspect was that the workers failed to hold out against employers and attain the wages and hours that they considered fair. Even the AFL, which had no antiwar baggage or taint of disloyalty, could not help the workers. Clearly, the farmers had complete control over the work lives of their laborers. As long as the labor supply was sufficient, their united action kept wages low and work hours long during the harvest season.

Holding the AWIU Together in the Plains

In the Great Plains and in California, from fall 1917 to the end of 1918, the AWIU did not fare much better than in the Yakima Valley. Trials in Chicago, Sacramento, and Wichita, and the cause of those in prison in Omaha awaiting trial, took up much of the AWIU's time. To raise legal defense funds, members were urged to buy defense or assessment stamps for their membership books. Nonetheless, harvest Wobblies tried to make their presence felt in the areas where they had made strides in the past. California proved to be extraordinarily difficult in this regard. The raid on and subsequent arrests of Fresno Wobblies eliminated the leadership of the AWIU in the state. Though harvest Wobblies continued to work in California agriculture, they no longer had a role to play in shaping the direction taken by organized farm labor. The combined efforts of business organizations and federal, state, and local law enforcement made IWW unionizing efforts in agriculture almost impossible. Police and sheriff's deputies arrested any Wobblies found carrying membership cards, though most were soon released because the courts filed no charges or because they had served out their vagrancy convictions. The effect of these arrests was demoralizing. In addition, the state's abundant farm labor supply, particularly Mexicans and Asians, helped thwart Wobbly organizing, because the union had never made the necessary inroads among these prominent laborers in California agriculture. Given these challenges, IWW organizing did not surface again until late 1918.[65]

For the harvest season of 1918, the situation of the AWIU in the Great Plains was not much better than in Washington and California. A major problem faced by harvest Wobblies there, beyond legal and vigilante persecution, was the huge influx of auxiliary agricultural labor. With another shortage of labor for the 1918 wheat harvest projected by government officials, the campaign to flood the wheat belt with seasonal workers proved more successful than in 1917. Furthermore, the Department of War exempted farm workers of draft age as long as they remained actively engaged in agricultural work. But the most important conduit for seasonal labor into the harvest was the specialized activity of the Farm Service Division of the U.S. Employment Service. The Department of Labor's decision to provide a more focused approach to agricultural labor culminated in the placement of over one hundred thousand farm workers. Also, the United States Boys Working Reserve, which drew upon young men between the ages of sixteen and twenty-one, placed 250,000 boys in farm labor jobs. Finally, college and university students and many women found employment opportunities during the harvest season.[66]

Remarkably, during this inflamed antiradical period, there were some individuals who argued that the AWIU was a fine source of agricultural labor. Thorstein Veblen, working as a special investigator for the Food Administration, and his assistant, Isador Lubin, researched the IWW's agricultural branch in the northern plains and prairie counties of the Midwest. In a spring 1918 memorandum, Veblen contended that the AWIU's members were not the lazy, pro-German saboteurs that the press and politicians made them out to be. He considered them hard-working migrant or resident farm workers who had some very reasonable wage and working condition demands. Through his contacts with the AWIU's secretary and other harvest Wobblies, he concluded that their demands for employment consisted of the following: "(a) freedom from illegal restraint; (b) proper boarding and lodgings; (c) a 10-hour day; (d) a standard wage of $4 for the harvest season; and (e) tentatively, free transportation in answering any call from a considerable distance." Veblen reasoned that if farmers met these demands, they could count on a contingent of experienced harvesters, possibly fifty thousand, to harvest a substantial portion of the nation's wheat crop. Finally, Veblen discovered in his research that the biggest problem that the Wobblies faced was not from farmers, especially if one examined the relationship between North Dakota farmers and harvest Wobblies. It was the commercial clubs, main-street business interests, local law enforcement, and temporary organizations such as the state councils of defense, protective associations, and the like that fanned the flames of hysterical anti-IWW sentiment.[67]

Seconding his findings was a report by Robert W. Bruere, a writer for the *New York Evening Post*. Bruere's research took place primarily at the AWIU headquarters in Minneapolis before the great raids of 5 September 1917. There he met with Edwards, who was still secretary of the industrial union. Bruere was amazed by the welcoming atmosphere of the headquarters, even after making it clear to the Wobblies present that he was not an IWW member but a writer on assignment. Bruere wrote that he had a very candid meeting with Edwards, who opened his office and records to inspection. Bruere, who was also aware of the amicable relationship that many harvest Wobblies had with Non-Partisan League farmers of North Dakota, stressed in his article the symbiotic relationship that could exist between farmers and harvest Wobblies throughout the wheat belt if the public would put away their irrational fears of the IWW and cease their legal and vigilante persecution.[68]

Such reasonable evaluations were strictly in the minority; the fortunes of the AWIU would not improve in 1918. Neither government officials, community leaders, nor farmers' associations acted on the recommendations of Veblen or Bruere. Ironically, compounding the AWIU's problems was the increase in wages paid by many wheat belt farmers in reaction to the labor shortage and the high market price of wheat. Of course, harvest Wobblies welcomed the higher wages, but the large and rather patriotic auxiliary workforce in the Great Plains had little interest in IWW organizing. These neophyte harvest workers had no knowledge of the struggles of workers in the past to gain adequate wages, and did not recognize the temporary nature of the wage increase. Consequently, the AWIU's harvest drive for 1918 in the Great Plains had the worst results since the creation of an IWW-led farm labor association.[69] Despite a claim made by the secretary-treasurer that there were four hundred AWIU delegates in the field, most of them in the wheat belt, harvest Wobblies did not significantly increase in number or gain job control in many areas outside of North Dakota.

The AWIU tried to continue functioning, even though the industrial union now bordered on collapse. It maintained regular union meetings, electing secretaries and members of the Organization Committee. Participants at the AWIU convention elected M. G. Bresnan secretary-treasurer after Charles Anderson found himself under indictment in Wichita. Bresnan, assisted by James Rohn, chair of the Organization Committee, pressed on with legal defense work and with publishing job news in the *Defense News Bulletin*. Due to raids, arrests, and censorship of the mails by federal agents, the *Industrial Worker* and *Solidarity* could only publish and circulate sporadically, but the *Defense News Bulletin* was not hampered in this way. As its title makes clear, the primary focus of the newspaper was the defense of jailed Wobblies, although it also included many reports by industrial union secretaries, which were very useful for Wobblies, especially agricultural migrants who needed to know where they could find employment.[70]

In early 1918, AWIU members worked to cut costs, function more efficiently, and simultaneously maintain a presence in the wheat belt. To save money and find more secure office space, the union leadership moved the headquarters to Chicago. For similar reasons, the most important AWIU local in the Far West moved to Portland from Spokane. The Minneapolis branch and other Great Plains and Midwestern AWIU offices did everything that they could to recover from raids and arrests. Consistent with the pragmatic strategy of many harvest Wobblies, Secretary Bresnan made a serious effort to present the AWIU's demands for the 1918 harvest season to the Department of Agriculture. He tried to argue that more than thirty thousand Wobblies would be available to harvest every kernel of grain if AWIU members could be protected from local persecution, earn fifty cents an hour for general agricultural labor, and receive free transportation to job sites. Of course, the federal government ignored his offer. Nonetheless, the union managed to regroup and weathered the storm of repression. By the end of the year, Mat Fox assumed the secretary-treasury position of the AWIU and instituted a streamlined plan to increase the number of field delegates for 1919. Fox was a noteworthy choice for secretary. He had ample experience as a harvest worker, and was one of the original AWO job delegates who had worked the plains wheat belt harvest in 1915. His experience and dedication to harvest Wobblies would help the AWIU survive this trial by fire.[71]

Surviving Federal Prosecution

The mass federal trials of the IWW leadership, including many AWIU members, brought to light some of the less-than-noble tactics of harvest Wobblies. The practice of sabotage, which Wobblies claimed meant only the conscious withdrawal of efficient labor, did in some instances involve the destruction of property, particularly in the West's agricultural fields. From the prosecutors' perspective, both sabotage and the union's organizing tactics directly related to the charges brought against the Wobblies in federal court in Chicago, Sacramento, Wichita, and Omaha. Yet according to Melvyn Dubofsky in *We Shall Be All* and to William Preston Jr. in *Aliens and Dissenters*, the prosecutors also wanted to perpetuate the anti-IWW atmosphere that permeated the entire trial period because they knew that lurid accounts of bullying behavior and property damage by Wobblies could only help their case.[72]

The charges brought against IWW members in Chicago involved what Preston considered industrial and wartime crimes. The industrial charges focused on seditious conspiracy to thwart "the execution of certain specified legislation that provided for the production and transportation of war supplies." The other industrial count included indictments that related to a conspiracy to prevent producers and manufacturers from their right to honor government contracts. Both of these umbrella charges dealt with the production of agricultural goods along with other wartime materials. As to wartime crimes, prosecutors charged the IWW with conspiracy to impede the Selective Service Act and transgress the Espionage Act. These two charges directly suggested that the IWW had chosen to take an active antiwar stand with the goal of hampering the U.S. war effort. These were just the primary charges; Dubofsky estimates that each of the 113 Wobblies who eventually came to trial in Chicago faced four hundred counts, amounting to nearly ten thousand charges in all.[73]

Although the trial covered an enormous range of Wobbly activity, the harvest Wobblies drew special attention. The prosecutors brought forth witnesses who testified that Wobblies had forced them to join the union before allowing them to work at a particular harvest site, and if they did not join they would be prevented from working in the area or be beaten by IWW members. However, this kind of testimony appears to have been used to paint a picture of the IWW as a gangster organization to excite the prejudices of the jury rather than to provide evidence of a conspiracy. More important allegations brought by witnesses for the prosecution concerned the issue of sabotage.[74]

Destruction of crops and destruction of farm equipment were the two primary charges directed at the IWW regarding sabotage. Two witnesses testified that they had heard James Rowan, head of the union in Spokane, give a speech in summer 1917 in which he called for the use of the "five -finger disease" against farmers who refused to honor Wobbly wage and working-condition demands. This "disease" consisted of apple pickers or packers pressing their fingernails into the fruit, thereby ruining them for market. With Rowan among those on trial, this was damaging testimony.[75] But even more damaging allegations came from witnesses from the Palouse and from North Dakota. Individuals such as Joe Burdell and Jesse N. Banks, both migrant harvesters, and William Cole, a deputy sheriff from Whitman County, Washington, testified to Wobbly involvement in setting threshing machines on fire or destroying the machines' interior mechanisms by throwing foreign objects into them. Though these witnesses could not point to a specific Wobbly in the courtroom who engaged in this behavior, nor in most cases identify a specific Wobbly with whom they had worked in the fields, the testimony proved quite damning to the defense. It also corroborated the testimony of Frank E. Wermke, a harvest Wobbly who testified that he engaged in an assortment of sabotage, particularly in destroying threshing machines, as a means to further the goals of the IWW.[76]

Under unusually difficult circumstances, the IWW's outstanding defense attorney George Vanderveer brought a number of individuals to the stand who could describe positive experiences with Wobblies in the harvest fields. Unfortunately, Vanderveer had to face government restrictions on the union's use of the federal mail system. Censors had the legal right to search any mail sent to or from the union headquarters or defense team. This made contacting sympathetic witnesses and those interested in funding the defense team problematic. According to Preston in *Aliens and Dissenters*, "the loss of letters, newspapers, appeals, and circulars that were declared nonmailable was, of course, a crippling blow to the defense." And this was only one small part of the case. In regard to conspiracies in other industries and to violation of the Espionage Act and the Selective Service Act, Vanderveer experienced many of the same problems. Yet, according to most of the historians who have written about the IWW, especially on the Chicago trial, Vanderveer's courtroom performance should have been devastating to the prosecution. He was able to make cogent arguments that ripped apart the conspiracy charges. But the atmosphere of the trial, the harsh courtroom rulings of Judge Kenesaw Landis, the lack of an adequate means of legal defense, and a prejudiced jury made the outcome of the trial a foregone conclusion. After four months of trial proceedings, the jury deliberated for one hour on all ten thousand "crimes" and came back with a verdict of guilty for all the defendants.[77]

Though some received minor sentences, Judge Landis handed out substantial prison terms for a significant number of Wobblies. The top fifteen leaders of the union, which included Bill Haywood and the first two secretary-treasurers of the AWIU, Walter Nef and Forrest Edwards, received twenty-year prison sentences. The prosecution used Nef's and Edwards's correspondence, and publications that referred to their leadership of the AWIU, against them, regardless of the fact that the prosecution could link neither Nef nor Edwards to sabotage. Nevertheless, they presided over a union with alleged saboteurs in its ranks, thereby making them conspirators to sabotage. Vanderveer argued that neither Nef nor Edwards, nor any other AWIU or IWW leader, had control over the behavior of union members. He also challenged the prosecution to deliver hard evidence that the men on trial instructed anyone to perform an act of sabotage. But justice was not in the cards. Eliminating a wartime domestic enemy was the purpose of the trial.[78]

Unlike the Chicago trial in which agricultural sabotage and conspiracy made up a small part of the prosecution's case, the Sacramento trial focused heavily on alleged Wobbly havoc in California's agricultural industry. The first federal arrests in California in September 1917 netted a number of Wobblies, many of whom were AWIU members. Over the next several weeks, federal officials released some prisoners but retained others, as they built up their case against the IWW. Following the 17 December bombing of the governor's residence in Sacramento, a new wave of arrests swept the state. Federal and state officials, along with the news media, attributed the bombing to the IWW. Only much later would the truth be known; the bombing was the work of a district attorney seeking a re-election issue.[79]

In February 1918, Sacramento's federal grand jury indicted fifty-four men and one woman, Theodora Pollok, on the same charges as those in the Chicago trial. While they waited for the trial to begin, the prisoners endured terrible living conditions. Like the rest of the nation, they experienced the influenza epidemic. With inadequate food and insufficient heat in the damp jail cells, five of the prisoners died before the December trial. As the prisoners languished in jail, federal agents of the Bureau of Investigation gathered evidence against them, including letters, union documents, Wobbly newspaper articles, and other IWW literature seized in a number of raids on both locals and private dwellings. The prosecution also had the help of two paid informants.[80]

By the time the trial began, the federal court had released several defendants for lack of evidence. The unique feature of this trial is that forty-three of the forty-six defendants refused counsel. According to Mortimer Downing, spokesman for the group that refused legal representation, "[W]e decided upon the silent defense because we despair of justice for the working men being achieved through the court." With the constant raids on offices and dwellings of Wobblies and their supporters, arrests of the same, and censorship of IWW literature and correspondence by the postal service, Downing had good reason to suspect that a fair trial was impossible. Furthermore, the entire union was on trial in Sacramento. Prosecuting attorneys introduced evidence of a conspiracy that began with the union's formation in 1905. In fact, much of the evidence entered into the prosecution's case pre-dated the U.S. declaration of war, and focused on events surrounding the Wheatland affair and subsequent Wobbly boycotts and strikes in the hop industry.[81]

The evidence introduced to prove a conspiracy in California was even flimsier than that in Chicago. Two men arrested in raids on the IWW, Elbert Coutts and Jack Dymond, turned state's evidence, thereby gaining their release. In the Sacramento trial, Coutts and Dymond began a career as professional witnesses against the IWW. There they testified that they, along with other Wobblies, conspired to obstruct the U.S. war effort, largely through sabotage. Coutts and Dymond explained how they traveled the San Joaquin Valley setting haystacks on fire. They characterized defendants Elmer Anderson, Caesar Tabib, Edward Quigley, Harry Brewer, Robert Connellan, and Edward Goetz as part of an "arson gang" within the IWW in California. The "gang" was alleged to have used phosphorous and other materials to wreak havoc on California farms to further the goals of revolution or to redress grievances against particular farmers. Witnesses emerged from other parts of the state who testified that arson had been used to destroy haystacks, barns, canneries, and other agricultural sites. Though the witnesses alleged that the IWW members on trial were responsible, they could produce no proof.[82]

At the conclusion of the trial on 16 January 1919, Judge Frank H. Rudkin instructed the jury to remember that mere membership in the union did not constitute conspiracy and that the jury needed to consider each defendant on an individual basis. According to Hyman Weintraub, in his thorough history of the IWW in California, Judge Rudkin practically called for the jury to return with a verdict of "not guilty." Within one hour of deliberation, however, the jury had found the defendants guilty on all counts. Judge Rudkin sentenced the silent defendants to prison terms of from one to ten years, while the three who retained counsel, which included Pollok, received lesser sentences.[83]

After being held for many months, thirty-four Wobblies in Wichita were indicted by federal prosecutors on 14 March 1918 for violating the Espionage Act, the Food and Fuel Control Act, and other wartime legislation. The prosecutors argued that the IWW conspired "to violate the Food and Fuel Control Act by urging strikers to cut off or decrease the production and supply of foods, feeds, and fuel necessary to the armed forces." When the case eventually came to trial on 1 December 1918, only twenty-seven defendants remained under indictment, the court having released others for lack of evidence.[84]

Despite the different venue, the legal process proceeded along the same lines as the other federal cases against the IWW. Frank E. Wermke again appeared with his allegations that Wobblies in Kansas and Oklahoma engaged in acts of sabotage on the region's farms. IWW attorney Fred H. Moore, who had assistance from Vanderveer, and others sympathetic to the IWW's plight, such as the National Civil Liberties Bureau, argued persuasively that conspiracy just did not emerge from the prosecution's evidence, but prejudice and federal harassment of the defense team produced the same outcome as in the Chicago and Sacramento trials. The jury found all of the defendants guilty. The men received prison terms from one to nine years, with Charles Anderson, the third convicted AWIU secretary-treasurer, receiving the only nine-year sentence.[85]

The case of the Omaha defendants proved quite different from those in Chicago, Sacramento, and Wichita. The fifty-one men indicted by a federal grand jury after being arrested in a series of raids did not stand trial in 1918. The federal government, knowing that its evidence was weak, did not want to jeopardize its case against the first-tier IWW leadership in Chicago with a legal setback in Omaha. Federal agents who interrogated the prisoners learned little more than that the men tended to be laborers, mostly in agriculture, who joined the IWW to better their working conditions, and that they never resorted to property damage to further their goals.[86]

By spring 1919, the prosecution's case against the incarcerated men did not improve. None of those in Omaha were major figures in the AWIU, nor were they influential members in the IWW. What evidence the federal government did possess pertained, albeit marginally, to leaders, not to the rank-and-file men in custody. Also, as Dubofsky argues, federal officials began to experience "pangs of conscience about the propriety of sentencing another large group of probably innocent men to prison." In any case, prosecutors dropped their charges against the Omaha Wobblies in April 1919. The men had been in prison for a year and a half.[87]

The trials, raids, and arrests took a great toll on the IWW as a whole. In fact, Dubofsky argues in his study of the IWW that the union went into steep decline beginning in 1919. He suggests that the IWW had transformed itself into a legal defense organization, battling for appeals and amnesty for those in federal prison and fighting arrests of members on criminal syndicalism charges. Yet, despite a serious drop in membership during the war years, the union did not fall apart. For the Wobblies who chose to remain in the IWW, their persecution only made their devotion to the union stronger. Few labor historians have given the postwar IWW the attention that it deserves, even though it was in those years that the union rebounded, with the AWIU a significant element of the organization's resurgence.[88]

Chapter Five

Perseverance Amid Change

⌘ ⌘ ⌘

Before the AWIU, or the IWW as a whole, could rebound from federal wartime persecution, Wobblies had to endure a second wave of attacks by law enforcement. This wave came largely at the hands of state governments in the form of criminal syndicalism statutes. California was the most aggressive state in using these laws to repress harvest Wobblies, though other states in the Far West and the Great Plains used the same tactic for similar effect.

Legal repression, however, was only one problem the AWIU faced. Another was a dramatic change, especially in California, in the characteristics of the farm labor workforce from one that was made up predominantly of white males to one made up of Hispanics, Asians, and white families. Furthermore, the workforce throughout the West changed from packs of mobile, single white men traveling by freight train to men and families traveling by car and truck. First in California, and somewhat later in Washington, the dual effects of legal repression and accelerating sociocultural change essentially ended AWIU activities in the Far West and limited the industrial union geographically. Workforce demographics began to change in the Great Plains region as well, but did not yet affect the union to the same degree as in the Far West. For harvest Wobblies, 1919 and 1920 were indeed years of perseverance amid change. They continued to work in the fields and orchards, institute organizing campaigns, and attend to AWIU affairs. The industrial union would survive, but it also had to restructure itself into an organization poised to emerge anew as a significant force in the Great Plains wheat belt.

Outlawing the IWW

Beginning in 1917 and continuing through 1920, twenty-one states and two territories enacted criminal syndicalism legislation. According to Eldridge Dowell in his definitive *A History of Criminal Syndicalism Legislation in the United States*, legislatures, such as those in California, defined criminal syndicalism as a labor movement strategy that employed sabotage, violence, and advocacy of crimes to achieve ends beneficial to labor in the industrial or political sphere. Some states went even further. For example, Washington, which used the same core definition of criminal syndicalism as California, also included teaching and aiding such unlawful acts on the list of criminal activities. The most sweeping statute, according to Dowell, was Idaho's, which made illegal the withdrawal of efficiency on the job, the one definition of industrial sabotage that most Wobblies accepted.[1]

These state laws all had a common origin in legislation enacted by the federal government. In June 1917, Congress passed the Espionage Act, which made hampering wartime industrial production, military operations, and recruitment in the armed forces illegal. In 1918, Congress enacted the Sedition Act, which expanded the scope of the Espionage Act. Now it became illegal to express "any disloyal, profane, scurrilous, or abusive language" concerning the United States government, the Constitution, the flag, or any armed services uniform. As it had done before—in the 1790s and the 1860s—the federal government sanctioned antiradical hysteria and exaggerated fears of disloyalty, resulting in the abrogation of citizens' civil rights. As noted, federal officials jailed antiwar activists and those they considered a hindrance to the war effort. The postwar repression of radicals, undertaken by many states, continued and extended this trend of suppressing dissent. One key difference, though, was that the focus shifted from concerns about pro-German sentiment and impediments to recruitment to concerns about pro-Bolshevik sympathies, communist agitation, and revolution.[2]

Those concerns came to the fore following the Bolshevik Revolution in Russia in 1917 and the announcement of the formation of the Third, or Communist, International ("the Comintern") there in 1919. These events raised the specter of a worldwide communist threat, giving many Americans a sense that a new enemy, foreign and domestic, required confrontation. In fact, in several large American cities, communists began to organize in 1919. Nationwide, the numerous strikes of that year took on ominous meaning in an atmosphere of potent antiradicalism. For example, Seattle experienced a general strike that closed the city down for several days in February. Although a coalition of AFL trade unions led the strike, rather than the nascent American communist movement, some newspapers portrayed the strike as a precursor to a Bolshevik-style revolution in the United States. Moreover, newspaper reporters and editorial writers conflated labor organizers, including the AWIU and its parent organization, the IWW, with actual communists; both became simply "Reds": radicals bent upon destroying American institutions and values. Never mind that the IWW had serious ideological differences with the Bolsheviks in Russia and with communists in America. Nonetheless, anticommunists painted Wobblies with the same brush as those advocating Bolshevik-style communism.[3]

In this climate of antiradicalism, and drawing upon the example of federal legislation, state legislatures drafted legislation to stymie union organizing and to prevent "Reds" from interfering with "business prosperity." Business and agricultural interests, both in and out of government, were clearly the principal supporters of criminal syndicalism legislation. And with the IWW still the largest and most prominent leftist organization in the country, Wobblies experienced the brunt of these repressive laws. In the estimation of a diverse group of labor historians, criminal syndicalism legislation was aimed squarely at making membership in the IWW illegal.[4]

Harvest Wobbly Perseverance

It was in this context that the AWIU fought to reassert itself in agriculture. The harvest drive of 1919 would demonstrate the perseverance of the AWIU in the face of state repression, but it would also reveal its problems in organizing a changing farm workforce in the Far West. Certainly, in early 1919, few West Coast Wobblies knew that California and Washington would be lost causes for the AWIU. In December 1918, young male and female agricultural-industry Wobbly job delegates from Los Angeles worked among southern California orange pickers in the San Gabriel Valley. While they worked, they brought the message of the IWW, using fliers written in English, Spanish, and Japanese. They had plenty of membership dues books and stamps handy to sign up new members. During the war years, much of the predominant farm labor cohort, white men, had left the region for better-paying urban industrial jobs or to serve in the armed forces. Mexican workers, many of whom had been recruited in Mexico by citrus growers, supplied the necessary labor in that industry. At first growers did all they could to make orange picking and packing attractive to these Hispanic workers out of fear that a labor shortage would destroy their industry. Yet by the end of the war, it became apparent that there would be no labor shortage in the foreseeable future because of the ever-growing influx of Mexican agricultural laborers from across the border. Consequently, with no pressure to attract workers to the industry, the working and living conditions of the largely Hispanic and Japanese workforce deteriorated dramatically.[5]

Over the course of several weeks in December, Wobbly delegates successfully organized Mexican and Japanese pickers in the region. In late January 1919, a committee of workers brought several demands to representatives of area orange growers, including a dollar-a-day wage increase and a one-hour reduction in the workday, amounting to $4 for an eight-hour day. When the growers' representatives rejected these demands, the more militant segment of the region's orange pickers called for a strike throughout the citrus industry. Hundreds of male and female workers honored the strike, and soon packinghouses began to close for lack of oranges from the valley's orchards.

As the strike picked up momentum in the ensuing weeks, the *Los Angeles Times* carried stories that suggested a Bolshevik revolutionary conspiracy lay behind it. [6] The *Los Angeles Times*, a newspaper well known for its anti-labor and antiradical editorials, featured the headline "I.W.W. Plot To Spread Bolshevism Among Orange Pickers Of Valley Bared" over one of its stories on the strike. The consequence of such hysterical anticommunist rhetoric was the development of a substantial and diverse anti-strike confederation. Local law enforcement, vigilante groups, state and federal officials, a docile scab workforce of adults and children, and even the Los Angeles-based Mexican Consul worked to break the strike. After suffering for weeks from law enforcement and vigilante attacks, the strikers' resolve began to weaken. The final straw came when law enforcement officers arrested strikers and kidnapped a number of strike leaders operating out of what Southern California newspapers called a "Russian House." The press vilified the strike leaders, describing them as Russian Bolsheviks, bohemians, and men and women of low moral character. Led by local law enforcement, several hundred citrus growers and their supporters took the kidnapped strike leaders to Los Angeles, depositing them in the Russian immigrant neighborhood of Boyle Heights. The strike leaders, though they were white, were neither Russian nor of Russian heritage. This bewildering attempt to link them with a Bolshevik scheme undoubtedly left them confused, but relieved that they had escaped physical violence. After this incident, the strike quickly fell apart. Even AWIU secretary-treasurer Mat Fox's call for more organizers to the area could not save the strike, which collapsed in March.[7]

With the AWIU, and the IWW as a whole, at a postwar nadir, the AWIU's semi-annual national convention was an important event. Harvest Wobbly delegates chose Sioux City, Iowa, as the location for the 21 April convention, probably because it was a major distribution center for migrant agricultural labor and because the IWW's presence in the city dated back to at least 1915. Although harvest Wobblies had experienced harassment at the hands of Sioux City law enforcement, the AWO and later the AWIU did not suffer the same degree of repression that they did in other agricultural communities. In fact, Mayor Wallace Short, who was a Congregational minister when the IWW made its first appearance, had welcomed the aid that the IWW, in conjunction with the city's socialists, gave to the hundreds of unemployed and hungry men of the city in 1915.[8]

Mayor Short was an unusually progressive city official. He won his election in 1918 with the strong support of labor. Although Short tried to reach out beyond the labor movement and working-class residents to local business interests and area farmers, his overtures were only reciprocated by workers, socialists, and certain segments of the progressive middle class. His testimony for the defense at the Chicago IWW trial in 1918 further weakened his support in the community. The local press quickly condemned him as a Wobbly supporter. Eventually, a coalition of outraged conservatives in the city proposed recalling him. Despite all of this, Mayor Short planned to honor a Wobbly invitation to make a speech opening the AWIU convention in April.[9]

As the convention date neared, Wobblies from across the United States and from Canada and Mexico arrived in Sioux City. The newspapers featured stories about an invasion of Wobblies and the "violence" that they would bring into the city. Yet Mayor Short assured the townspeople that the police department could handle any problems that might arise. He also appeared before a town meeting convened by concerned citizens whose leadership preferred to remain anonymous. Mayor Short challenged those who had organized the meeting to show themselves. When no one stepped forward, the mayor began to read the Constitution of the United States to the crowd, particularly the passages regarding freedom of speech and assembly. After the mayor and a few resident Wobblies left the meeting, the county sheriff and several Commercial Club members stepped up to urge the formation of a citizens' committee to recall Short and to drive the IWW out of town.[10]

As scheduled, harvest Wobblies held their convention, and as planned, anti-Wobbly forces tried to oust them from the city. To the alarm of the conservatives, Bill Haywood made an appearance. He was out on bail after his Chicago trial and had come to give a pre-convention speech. The following day, harvest Wobbly delegates convened as scheduled to hear Mayor Short's opening address. Along with the Wobbly delegates sat a Department of Justice agent sent to take notes on the proceedings. The delegates passed a motion allowing the agent to remain, though some Wobblies objected to his presence. The first two days of the meeting went well, with delegates deliberating on a variety of union matters. They especially focused on issues regarding AWIU prisoners in Wichita.

While the convention continued, a Commercial Club assembly met at the West Hotel, and there a citizens' committee formed. On 22 April, the Wobbly meeting adjourned for two hours while the resolutions committee formulated proposals for changes in the organizational efforts of the union. During the recess, approximately two hundred Sioux City men armed with revolvers and shotguns and led by the local sheriff raided the convention hall. No one was arrested, but the sheriff, his deputies, and supporters confiscated all the records, IWW literature, and supplies found in the hall. The sheriff then closed the hall and padlocked the door, claiming that he was only trying to prevent bloodshed. Without missing a beat, the Wobbly delegates, finding their convention abruptly terminated, resolved to hold the remainder of the convention proceedings on the city streets the next day.[11]

The delegates completed their convention affairs and subsequently returned to their home districts, preparing for the upcoming harvest season. According to the Assistant Secretary of Agriculture, Clarence Ousley, agricultural experts expected a bumper crop of wheat in the southern Great Plains that summer, and Kansas alone would need one hundred thousand harvesters. Southern plains farmers began meeting before the harvest began to devise plans to assure an adequate labor supply. Kansas farmers from thirty-five western counties set wages and hours for harvest workers at fifty cents an hour for a ten-hour day. In other areas of the southern plains, farmers agreed on even higher wages. With competitive wages and decent hours, farmers hoped to give migrant workers an incentive to remain in a given area until they completed the harvest. For the AWIU, the goal was to get as many delegates in the fields as possible. The union leadership reasoned that the call for thousands of harvest workers would, as usual, result in a glut of labor and a subsequent reduction in pay. These discouraged workers could make ready recruits for the union. The AWIU chose not to set a standard wage in the wheat belt. Mat Fox and the AWIU's Organization Committee urged harvest Wobblies to accept any job at any wage or hours and push for better conditions if they had strength in numbers on a particular job site.[12]

Late spring and early summer seemed promising for the AWIU in the Great Plains and the Far West. Fox and the Organization Committee encouraged members to take out credentials so that they could become job delegates and sign up new members in the field. Hundreds took up the call. In California, fifty new delegates entered the agricultural areas of the Sacramento and San Joaquin Valleys in June alone. Moreover, California harvest Wobblies and construction workers called a joint mass convention for late June in Stockton, just south of Sacramento. Here the AWIU planned to reassert itself as a leader in farm labor and general migrant labor organizing. Wenatchee and Yakima were also areas of revival for the AWIU as delegates made their way to these Washington cites with the hope that several hundred would be on hand when fruit harvesting got underway.[13]

Regardless of this enthusiasm, the summer 1919 harvest season required perseverance, as state and local officials worked in tandem to suppress harvest Wobbly activity with criminal syndicalism statutes and the tried and true legal hammer of vagrancy laws. In Kansas, state and federal officials geared up to prevent union organizing efforts among farm workers and to suppress the revolutionary presence of harvest Wobblies. They coordinated their efforts to thwart the IWW on a number of fronts. Surveillance agents monitored as many trains traveling into and out of the state as possible. Agents arrested Wobblies on trains and in wheat towns waiting for work. State and federal law enforcement targeted job delegates above all other Wobblies, and officials not only apprehended them but also confiscated all of their supplies and literature. By mid-June, Kansas authorities had arrested one hundred IWW job delegates. In Oklahoma, a similarly coordinated effort resulted in the incarceration of numerous union members. In contrast to the staggering number of arrests and long prison sentences during the war years, AWIU members this time around spent little time in jails. Some were held only for a matter of days before being released. Others had their charges dropped after Fred Moore defended them at pre-trial hearings. Though there were fewer arrests and less violence, the effect on organizing proved just as debilitating. Job delegates could not stay in the field, ride the rails, or organize in towns without risking arrest. Once released, they would have to move on to catch up with the harvest and then would again risk a similar fate in the next town or county. In the end, legal and law enforcement harassment prevented any continuity in organizing in the southern plains.[14]

Another serious problem for wheat belt organizers was the presence of large numbers of college students and ex-servicemen. Though many of these workers had little experience in harvesting, the unusually high wages—sometimes reaching eighty cents an hour in some counties—

attracted workers who were fiercely anti-union and anti-Wobbly. With the labor market saturated, wages competitive with non-agricultural labor, and surprisingly few unemployed workers in the region, harvest Wobblies had a difficult time attracting prospective members. In addition, the legal open season on AWIU members discouraged migrants from becoming embroiled in conflicts with area business owners or farmers. Independent harvesters wished only to earn their wages and move on.[15]

Despite the repression that AWIU delegates faced in the wheat belt, they managed to sign up new members for the union. The thirteen hundred new members who came on board in July did not bring the overall membership up to the levels of previous years, though it was far better than the eighty members recruited in 1918. As harvest Wobblies and their delegates moved north with the ripening wheat, they became more successful at recruiting. In addition, the repression that Wobblies confronted in the southern plains abated as they moved north. For example, during a brief lull in the harvest, northbound AWIU members put on a mid-July picnic with a dance band and a speech by one of the IWW's best orators, Abner E. Woodruff, in Sioux City. Moreover, freight-train travel from Nebraska to Iowa to the Dakotas proved as accessible and free as in past harvest seasons.[16]

August and September brought the AWIU several thousand more members, mostly in the Dakotas, and substantial funds into its coffers. By the onset of the threshing season in late summer, the AWIU had five hundred job delegates in the field, most of them in the Dakotas. While in the southern plains wages were unusually high, with a ten-hour workday as the standard, northern plains farmers offered workers between fifty and seventy cents an hour with a twelve-hour workday. This probably contributed to the AWIU's recruitment in the region. Fox, the Organization Committee, and other AWIU leaders encouraged harvest Wobblies to continue accepting whatever wage farmers offered. Yet they now urged members to restrict their workday to ten hours. From Fox's point of view, and from the perspective of D. N. Simpson, the AWIU's General Organization Committee chairman, the shorter the workday, the greater likelihood of full employment. The one chronic problem that harvesters in general faced in the Dakotas was the presence of hi-jacks, men who made their living robbing migrant workers. Again the Wobbly leadership advised harvesters to send any extra cash to the AWIU headquarters for safekeeping. This sort of support that a union could offer a migrant harvester was a strong selling point emphasized by job delegates in the fields of the northern plains.[17]

The Beginning of the End of the AWIU in the Far West

Though the AWIU's experiences in the Great Plains wheat belt posed serious challenges for the industrial union, the 1919 harvest season in California and Washington proved disastrous for harvest Wobblies and their job delegates. Law enforcement officials raided the late-June joint convention of Wobbly agriculture and construction workers in Stockton, arresting all of the members present and charging them with criminal syndicalism. With many of the AWIU's most dedicated members and job delegates jailed, agricultural organizing came to a near standstill. Harvest Wobblies had to maintain a low profile, as mere membership in the organization became illegal under California's 1919 criminal syndicalism statute. Furthermore, beginning in fall 1919, mobs of soldiers, sailors, and vigilante groups periodically attacked Wobbly union halls through-out the state, largely with impunity. By the end of the year, the first criminal syndicalism court cases against IWW members in California began to unfold.

To the north, Washington AWIU organizing never even got off the ground during the harvest season, despite continued calls for delegates to make their way to the Wenatchee and Yakima Valleys. Many of the AWIU delegates that did try to organize workers in the fruit-growing region of Washington ended up arrested and jailed by local law enforcement. In many instances, they were charged under Washington's 1919 criminal syndicalism law.[18]

California and Washington enacted some of the most stringent anti-IWW legal tools in the United States. Their criminal syndicalism statutes—largely pushed through the state legislatures by coalitions of agricultural, timber, mining, and manufacturing interests—made it very difficult for the IWW to function. For example, in Spokane, city police arrested Wobblies for doing nothing more than wearing IWW buttons on their clothes. Though not all arrested Wobblies were charged with criminal syndicalism, those who were spent weeks in jail awaiting trial, and if convicted faced years in prison. California would lead the nation in the enforcement of its criminal syndicalism laws by prosecuting over five hundred Wobblies between 1919 and 1924. Washington, Oregon, and Idaho would follow, with hundreds arrested and prosecuted in these states between 1919 and 1921.[19]

Though harvest Wobblies could weather this legal onslaught, as they had demonstrated over the years, changes in the fruit and vegetable harvest workforce proved a greater challenge to the union. In California, the workforce of single white males continued to decline in proportion to the number of Hispanic and Asian workers and families of harvest workers who traveled by automobile. Leaders of the AWIU, as they had for years, urged harvest Wobbly job delegates to reach out to Hispanic and Asian workers in the fields of California, but to no avail. Like Asian workers in earlier years, Hispanic workers began to form their own self-help associations within their communities as their population in the region grew dramatically between the late 1910s and early 1920s. Within their associations and segregated residential areas, religion, culture, language, and family ties acted as support networks. In addition, they formed mutual-aid societies, the one type of organization common to most immigrant California farm laborers. These self-help groups assisted members in finding employment, housing, and food. They could also offer protection to members, which was largely unavailable in white-controlled municipal institutions. Mexicans also used mutual-aid associations to maintain strong ties to their homeland; these voluntary associations were Mexican in culture and Spanish in language. They met the needs of most Hispanic workers in ways that an AWIU union hall and IWW revolutionary message could not.[20]

At the same time, families of harvesters traveling in second-hand automobiles became a substantial feature of the farm labor workforce. These workers, white, Asian, and Hispanic, did not live in jungles, ride the rails, or frequent Wobbly union halls. When working a particular harvest site, they usually lived in work camps created by their employers. Once the harvest ended, they packed up and moved on to the next work site and camp. Many of these families were so poor that children as young as five years old had to work alongside their parents. Another characteristic of these harvest families was that they were too fearful of violent repercussions to contemplate joining a union or participating in a strike to ameliorate their difficult working and living conditions. Other harvest families were not in desperate circumstances at all and viewed their participation in farm work as a temporary rather than as permanent feature of their lives. The appeal of a farm labor union was lost on them. In the case of Hispanic harvest families, many of whom were Mexican nationals, deportation was a real consequence for challenging the power of an agricultural employer. For all these reasons, harvest families were impervious to the IWW message of direct action in the workplace, unionization, or revolution.[21]

As the number of Hispanic workers increased in California, so did the number of Filipino, Japanese, Chinese, and American Indian workers in Washington's fruit, sugar beet, and hop harvests. By 1919, paralleling farm labor changes in California, they were joined by families of white harvesters who traveled to work sites by automobile, especially in the Yakima Valley. This cohort of migrant workers was by far the largest segment of the migrant labor workforce, rivaling the number of local seasonal laborers. Astute newspaper reporters predicted that such families would become the new and permanent migrant farm labor workforce in Washington. Again, as in California, the AWIU found it difficult to reach these workers.

Ironically, the anti-union movement in central Washington cooled somewhat in the 1919 season. When the Fruit Pickers' Union of Yakima, an AFL affiliate largely comprising white resident harvest workers, proposed a wage scale that called for an increase in wages for every facet of the picking and boxing process, area employers did not reject the proposition outright. The high profits and readily available markets for their produce motivated farmers and packers to meet many of the wage demands of organized workers. The Pickers' Union even appeared to become a full member of the labor union community of Yakima, even as it participated in the late summer Labor Day parade in downtown Yakima.[22]

The prosperity of the region began to attract corporate interests and to stimulate greater agricultural development. For example, the American Fruit Growers, Inc. purchased one thousand acres of Yakima orchard land in July 1919, bringing their total holdings to over two thousand acres. This corporate buying trend was a slow development, as the 1920s witnessed a period of growth of intensive small farming operations. As the Yakima and Wenatchee Valley growing areas expanded, with more and more farms in operation, ever-larger numbers of workers were required for harvesting the labor-intensive crops under cultivation. Still, the agricultural economy of the region maintained a boom-and-bust quality through the 1920s and 1930s, making both farmers and agricultural laborers economically insecure. Though in 1919 farmers appeared to accept the presence of a pickers' union, most agricultural employers, possibly due to the volatile nature of the industry, maintained an anti-union posture in subsequent decades.[23]

During the 1920s and 1930s, the farmers' need for temporary labor only increased. The living and working conditions of the migrants remained substandard, at least according to Wobblies working in the region. But the IWW found the challenge of organizing harvest families, non-white workers, and the few AFL fruit union workers almost impossible. Part of the problem stemmed from the union's inability to appeal to the social and cultural attributes of the workforce. Harvest Wobblies remained overwhelmingly male, traveled by freight train, and lived in jungles, a very different way of life from automobile-traveling harvest families. Most of these workers did not consider themselves permanent migrant laborers, while most harvest Wobblies did. Further hampering their ability to appeal to these new workers was the continuing problem of repression at the hands of police and sheriff's deputies. In 1919, law enforcement officials arrested Wobblies practically on sight. Whether they were caught stealing a ride on a freight train or merely frequenting a downtown soda shop, Wobblies were never safe from arrest in the south-central agricultural regions of Washington.[24]

An incident in Centralia, Washington, between local Wobblies and American Legionnaires on Armistice Day, 11 November 1919, damaged an already weakened IWW in that state. After months of harassment and raids against their southwestern Washington union hall, and knowing that another raid against their Centralia headquarters was imminent, local Wobblies, most of whom were area loggers, armed themselves and prepared to repulse an attack. The assault came as expected when the participants in the town's Armistice Day parade drew near the union hall. A contingent of Legionnaires in full uniform rushed the union headquarters. Well-positioned Wobblies met them with a volley of gunfire, claiming the lives of several ex-servicemen. The raiders regrouped, and now thoroughly armed, attacked and overtook the hall. Wesley Everest, one of the Wobblies in the hall and a veteran of the war in Europe, escaped into the surrounding woods with a pistol. Before pursuing Legionnaires overpowered him and took him to jail, he shot and killed one. Later that evening, a lynching party arrived at the jail and took Everest away without any resistance from law enforcement. They hanged him from a bridge over the Chehalis River outside of town. Police and sheriff's deputies arrested more than twenty Centralia Wobblies in the following days. Eventually, several were tried and given long prison sentences for murder.[25]

The incident at Centralia triggered a massive crackdown on the IWW that spilled over from Washington into northwest Oregon, especially Portland, but also to that state's logging communities, which had a strong Wobbly presence. Police and sheriff's deputies brought in IWW members in the logging industry, maritime sectors, and mining areas in a general roundup. In Spokane, a major distribution hub for agriculture and timber workers, police arrested seventy-four Wobblies. Local law enforcement and American Legionnaires in the central agricultural regions of Washington rounded up Wobblies in such cities as Kennewick, Leavenworth, Cashmere, and Wenatchee. By the end of that year and into 1920, dozens of Wobblies were on trial for criminal syndicalism.[26]

Continuing Postwar Struggles

Despite the heavy-handed legal repression in the Far West and the failure to bring Hispanics, Asians, and migrant farm families into the AWIU, union leaders and delegates nevertheless prepared for the upcoming fall 1919 convention in Sioux City, Iowa. These two issues were a high priority as the convention date neared. In such tense times, even finding a venue for the convention proved difficult. Commercial Club members in Sioux City tried to prevent the AWIU from holding its convention in their city. Mayor Short, who survived a recall election by a wide margin, attempted to assuage the concerns of citizens about the harvest Wobbly presence in the city by placing the militia on alert.[27]

The AWIU convention took place as scheduled, although accommodations for the delegates were less than satisfactory. Bill Haywood's speech to the assembled members had to be delivered from the second-story window of the union hall while harvest Wobblies stood in the streets below. For five days the convention proceeded, and by the end of the gathering the AWIU had substantially reorganized itself. One of the most important outcomes of the reorganization process was the establishment of three semi-independent AWIU branches as districts for each of the major regions of the industrial union. The convention participants also resolved that these new Midwest, California, and Northwest districts would each have its own convention to nominate candidates for secretary-treasurer and General Organization Committee members. Delegates hoped that regional conventions would reduce the hardship members from Washington and California experienced trying to attend AWIU conventions, which were held in areas where members tended to be most numerous, that is, in the central part of the United States. Breaking the AWIU down into districts also gave harvest Wobblies and job delegates the opportunity to work on organizing strategies that would be most useful for their own region's distinctive needs and stimulate greater participation of the membership in convention affairs.

In an effort to make the AWIU a truly worker-led union, the convention passed a resolution requiring elected officials to work in a harvest for one season before they could be eligible for another term in the same office. The members passed other resolutions requiring both the secretary-treasurer and the chairman of the General Organization Committee to supervise the union's funds. These changes reflected a decentralization of the AWIU and an attempt to make it more responsive to its members' needs. At the same time, the union was taking a scholarly approach to the work done by IWW members: it published Abner

Woodruff's *Evolution of American Agriculture*, the first of many efforts by the AWIU to analyze the development of the agricultural industry and the role played in it by migrant farm labor and the AWIU.[28]

As 1919 came to a close, so did one of the most turbulent years in American labor and radical history. Many of the year's major strikes engendered an unprecedented level of retaliatory violence. Probably in response to federal suppression of foreign-born radicals, the year saw a number of bombings aimed at prominent businessmen and government officials, most notably Attorney General A. Mitchell Palmer, which stimulated another wave of federal persecution. The antiradical atmosphere of the period peaked in January 1920 with a series of Department of Justice raids in conjunction with the nascent Bureau of Investigation and its General Intelligence Division, the precursor to the Federal Bureau of Investigation. Attorney General Palmer and his federal law enforcement agents arrested ten thousand individuals, especially communists, Communist Labor Party members, and alien radicals. However, this federal action abrogated the basic civil rights of so many individuals that a serious backlash occurred among the public and within the federal government itself. Secretary of Labor William B. Wilson and his assistant secretary, Louis Post, proved instrumental in leading the fight against the heavy-handed antiradicalism of the Department of Justice, for the Department of Labor oversaw federal immigration policy. It was also obvious to officials in Labor and other branches of government that most of the victims of the raids turned out to be workers and intellectuals who had no relationship to communist or anarchist groups.[29]

For many men and women of the American Left, including Wobblies, the postwar years were a time of revolutionary fervor. The new communist state in Russia, the burgeoning international communist movement, the substantial growth in unionization among American workers, and the intense strike activity in the United States and throughout the world suggested to many American radicals that a new socialist world was just around the corner. The federal and state repression that many radicals had to endure in the United States only made their commitment to transforming American society, and that of the world, stronger. Harvest Wobblies were no exception to this trend. The AWIU leadership was convinced, especially as exhibited in the pages of the IWW's newspapers and its news magazine, the *One Big Union Monthly*, that it was on a difficult but historic mission to organize American agricultural workers into a revolutionary union. Furthermore, the growth of agricultural organizing movements in Australia and

Argentina strengthened the AWIU's conviction that an international association of revolutionary workers, including those who labored in agriculture, could eventually overthrow the global capitalist system.[30]

Despite revolutionary rhetoric, though, in early 1920 the AWIU remained primarily committed to developing a cohesive and flexible industrial union of harvest workers. Not long after the fall 1919 convention, the AWIU convened a special meeting to formulate a means by which the Far West districts could participate in the spring 1920 convention and thereby have a voice in coordinating overall AWIU union activity. Already the restructuring of the AWIU was put into doubt by the anemic quality of the union in the Far West. During this special Omaha meeting on 8 February, AWIU officials suggested a fifty-cent raise in monthly dues to replenish a seriously depleted treasury, a proposal that the overall AWIU membership eventually approved. But the more substantial changes in the AWIU took place at the April convention in Sioux City, when members approved a resolution to hold conventions through delegate representatives. In addition, the AWIU's number designation changed from 400 to 110, as the IWW overhauled its industrial union organizational structure. At the convention, delegates also elected a new secretary-treasurer, Fred Fisher, and a new chairman of the Organization Committee, C. L. Johnson. This ended what was to be the last mass convention of the AWIU. Now members turned towards the upcoming harvest season, which would test the union's ability to continue its organizational efforts amidst very difficult circumstances.[31]

In many respects the 1920 harvest season resembled that of 1919. Again farmers feared a labor shortage, and again large numbers of workers answered the call for harvesters. Wages rose to an all-time high throughout much of the wheat belt during the season. With many of their agricultural industries still suffering from the destruction wrought by war and revolution, Europeans paid top dollar for much-needed North American wheat. In some counties in Kansas, farmers paid almost $9 a day. Even the notoriously low harvesting wages of Nebraska reached the $7 mark. Along with the high wages came an increasingly efficient federal and state effort to distribute agricultural labor. The United States Employment Service cooperated with Great Plains and Midwestern state employment services to guide tens of thousands of workers in the central United States to work sites. For the AWIU, which relied on under-employment, poor wages, and poor working conditions among harvesters to motivate laborers to join the union, the ease with which many workers could find secure and well-paid seasonal employment meant that the union fared poorly.[32]

Criminal Syndicalism and the Collapse of the AWIU in the Far West

Another similarity to the 1919 harvest season was the serious effort throughout the West to repress the IWW with criminal syndicalism laws. Even the publication of the General Executive Board's 1918 resolution prohibiting the destruction of private property or any form of violence to achieve "industrial reform" did not deter state persecution. The IWW leadership "reaffirmed" the resolution in December 1919, and IWW publications communicated it to the membership beginning in April 1920. But it was to no avail: in 1920, there were more Wobblies and other radicals behind bars in the United States than ever before. According to Bill Haywood, now the secretary of the General Defense Committee, over two thousand Wobblies were in jail on a variety of charges, primarily stemming from the Espionage and Sedition Acts and from the many state criminal syndicalism codes.[33]

During 1920, harvests Wobblies in the Great Plains, Washington, and California were especially hard hit with criminal syndicalism arrests and convictions. Kansas's fire marshal, L. T. Hussey, who convinced himself on little evidence that the IWW planned to burn that year's wheat crop, claimed that he extinguished the IWW "fire menace" by arresting scores of Wobblies, in lieu of a statute banning the union from the state. Municipal officials in Eldorado, Kansas, went as far as to procure a court injunction against IWW organizing, though this temporary writ did not end IWW activities in the city or surrounding county. Eventually, the pressure to establish a criminal syndicalism statute in Kansas became too great for a majority of legislators to resist. Yet despite Kansas's criminal syndicalism law, Wobblies still tried to organize in the state's wheat and oil fields.[34]

In enacting a criminal syndicalism law, the Kansas legislature was joining other major wheat-growing states—Oklahoma, Nebraska, South Dakota, Montana, and Minnesota. Yet in the Great Plains states, harvest Wobblies could endure in a way that was not possible in Washington or California. The union was able to hold on in the wheat belt during the 1920 harvest and threshing season, despite the arrest and jailing of many of its members. On the other hand, the AWIU in the Far West virtually collapsed as an effective organizing force in agricultural labor. As early as January 1920, many AWIU members in California were under arrest on criminal syndicalism charges, as were the most important AWIU job delegates in Washington.[35]

One of the key reasons the AWIU survived in the Great Plains and not in the Far West was sheer numbers. While Wobbly membership had been relatively high in California and Washington in the prewar years—George Speed, one of the most important West Coast IWW organizers, estimated that the IWW had thousands of members at work in California agriculture in 1915—wartime repression, criminal syndicalism statutes, and changes in the demographics of the farm labor force took their toll on the union in the Pacific coast states. By 1919, AWIU membership in Washington fell to just a few hundred.

During the postwar years in California, AWIU members probably never numbered more than two thousand out of a total IWW membership of five thousand in the state. Though they would never attain the same levels as they had in 1916 and 1917, AWIU membership in the Great Plains during this period ran well into the thousands. Even during the very difficult year of 1919, when the AWIU met constant frustration trying to reassert itself, it could boast of over eight thousand members by the fall. Because most AWIU members were in the Great Plains wheat belt, harvest Wobblies could absorb the loss of members and job delegates and still maintain a strong presence as long as that region required such high levels of young white male harvest laborers. It continued to do so in the early 1920s.[36]

By spring 1920, Washington and Oregon had over three hundred Wobblies in prison, according to John Engdahl, the chairman of the Northwest District Defense Committee. The vast majority of them were in Washington, mainly in the logging, agriculture, and construction industries. The arrests that began after the Centralia affair continued through 1920. It was not safe for Wobblies to meet, as their meetings ended in arrest for those in attendance. Harvest Wobblies suspected of sabotage were on trial in Spokane, Yakima, and Wenatchee. Whether suspected of destroying farmers' property over employment disputes, or of simply being members of the IWW, most Wobblies on trial were convicted in 1920 and 1921.

In the case of several IWW members on trial in Wenatchee in January 1920, a jury of farmers and ranchers listened as the prosecution put the entire organization on trial, using Wobbly literature and songs. It took the jury only five minutes to find the defendants guilty of violating the state's criminal syndicalism law. Sentences for the convicted men could be as short as two years but some were as long as ten years in the state penitentiary. On rare occasions during the height of the anti-IWW hysteria, juries found some Wobblies, such as John Grady, an IWW defense fund secretary, innocent of criminal syndicalism. With the state prepared to prosecute Wobblies, and with ample farm labor receiving comparatively high wages, AWIU organizing ground to a halt in the Wenatchee and Yakima Valleys and in the Palouse in 1920. Though Wobblies continued to work in Washington agricultural sectors for many years to come, they would make little headway in AWIU harvest organizing drives.[37]

In California, little agricultural organizing took place in 1920 beyond a few scattered work stoppages involving very few AWIU members. This would be the last year that any notable AWIU organizing activity occurred; by the end of the year, the AWIU could only maintain a small presence in central and southern California vegetable and fruit-growing regions. According to agricultural labor historian Stuart Jamieson, "[N]o strikes or collective bargaining were reported as carried out officially by representatives of the I.W.W. in California after 1920." Strikes that took place in fruit picking and packing plants in subsequent years tended to be spontaneous events, though it is conceivable that harvest Wobblies participated in these actions because they continued to work in California agriculture for the next two decades. Any organized action by workers during the 1920s, however, was the result of independent agricultural unions or AFL activity, especially in the canning industry.[38]

As in Washington, California state officials went to great lengths to prosecute Wobblies, sparing no expense. For example, the case of N. Steelik, a longtime Wobbly and migrant worker, went all the way to the California Supreme Court, which ruled against him. During his 1920-1921 trial, the prosecution's case rested on evidence that went back many years. Prosecutors accused Steelik of participating in arson campaigns in 1917 against San Joaquin Valley farms, advocating the violent overthrow of the United States government, acting as a job delegate for the IWW, a "criminal" organization, and committing a variety of other transgressions. His conviction landed him in San Quentin prison with a growing number of other California Wobblies.[39]

More than legal persecution, the rapidly changing nature of the California farm labor force reduced the viability of the AWIU in the state. The IWW, and the AWIU in particular, continued to appeal more to young white male migrant workers, but this social group of laborers in Pacific coast agriculture was diminishing rapidly. Farmers in California, through employment agencies and labor contractors, sought Mexican, Filipino, Japanese, and other Asian labor to work in their fields and spent less time seeking migrant white male labor on downtown streets or at railroad depots. These non-white workers accepted the low wages and long hours that farmers demanded. White workers, of course, had many more employment options than did non-white workers. Discriminatory hiring practices restricted Mexican and other Hispanic workers, as well as Asian workers, to the most menial employment opportunities in the state; farm work thus remained their primary employment option. Moreover, through newspaper advertisements, farmers sought families of harvesters to meet their seasonal agricultural needs. Whether these families arrived in their automobiles from urban or rural areas, they tended to be isolated from one another. The phenomenon of large numbers of white male workers traveling together on freight trains and living in jungles throughout California had faded dramatically by 1920. When the AWIU's California branch met at a Sacramento conference in February 1925, only twenty-one members attended.[40]

The AWIU Retools for the Future

In the Great Plains, the white male harvest worker still predominated. As the 1920 harvest season drew to a close and the threshing season proceeded in full swing in the northern wheat belt, the tenth semiannual AWIU convention commenced in New Rockford, North Dakota. The Midwest district of the AWIU wanted to make sure that a substantial number of workers could attend this fall meeting. Because a significant portion of AWIU members were in the region at the time, primarily working on threshing rigs, attendance was good. On the opening day of the conference, Bill Haywood gave an afternoon speech to the assembled workers, and many of the surrounding threshing operators took the day off to hear him speak. The AWIU wanted the meeting to be as peaceful as possible, for North Dakota was the one state where harvest Wobblies could find ample work and freedom from mass arrests. For this reason, the union urged its members to make a good impression on the townspeople of New Rockford, many of whom turned out to hear Haywood.[41]

Convention leaders presided over an organization that refused to die. They showed their confidence in the organization by their willingness to allow the Oil Workers' Industrial Union (OWIU) to separate permanently from the AWIU. A number of agricultural workers in Kansas and Oklahoma had found permanent employment in the oil fields of the southern plains, so it made sense to AWIU members to separate the two industries. They pledged fifteen hundred dollars to help the OWIU get on its feet.[42] Furthermore, the AWIU passed several resolutions aimed at helping their own union grow. They approved a measure raising the commission rate to one dollar for every person a job delegate could bring into the union, thereby encouraging more members to become delegates. After several years of raids and legal persecution, the work of stationary delegates took on added importance as an organizing tool for the industrial union. They could serve the same functions as a local without drawing the negative attention that an actual union local would attract. A stationary delegate could rent a room in a downtown hotel and conduct union affairs there, or on the street, in a nearby jungle camp, or at area job sites. Through resolutions, stationary delegates gained the power to provide credentials and to procure supplies for prospective job delegates in their area without having to go through a local or AWIU headquarters.

Another resolution with ramifications for the future of the union involved improved communications. If workers gained "job control" at a harvest or threshing site—meaning seven or more Wobblies at a given site—the members agreed that a job steward would be elected there. The job steward's primary function was to facilitate communication between that site and AWIU work crews at other sites. But the position also had the potential to become a basis for a series of "industrial district councils" that would preside over delegate elections to upcoming AWIU conventions and conferences. With the collapse of the AWIU districts in the Far West, the delegates had found it necessary to "fall back on the mass convention." Its unwieldy nature, though, required devising some means to make the convention process better suited to a large, mobile, industrial union workforce like the AWIU.

Other convention resolutions involved the length of the workday. Though participants set no wage minimum, they resolved that members should adhere to a ten-hour day in the harvest fields and on threshing rigs "wherever the workers had the moral courage to force the issue." Those members who violated the ten-hour maximum, once established at a job site, risked expulsion from the union.[43]

Many of these resolutions could be found in the new bylaws that the participants approved during the convention. The 1920 bylaws were more fully developed than those of 1917. When the industrial union was still young, instructions to job delegates, found in the 1917 bylaws, focused more on promptness of paperwork, legible writing, and following basic organizational rules in order to be productive. These bylaws also explained the organizational structure of the AWIU so job delegates and branch secretaries could describe their union to prospective and current members.

The 1920 bylaws had much of the same information as the earlier version, but updated to correspond to changes in the structure of the organization. The AWIU leadership made this new booklet available to all union members. It was most specific on the conduct of job delegates in the field, the most important organizing arm of the AWIU. Not only did the bylaws instruct delegates on how to initiate new members, approach an unorganized work crew, and communicate with the unemployed, but also on the delegate's personal behavior. Job delegates could not drink to intoxication or gamble without risking expulsion from their posts. Overall, the AWIU bylaws reflected a desire to establish a professional, responsible, and efficient job-delegate and branch-secretary structure for the union. Members recognized that their union had to function in a way that inspired confidence that the AWIU was here to stay, and that workers could count on it to meet their needs.[44]

To underscore the AWIU's role in the creation of a new society built on the interests and needs of workers, E. W. Latchem, a seasoned veteran of the AWIU, later closed his account of the fall 1920 AWIU convention in *One Big Union Monthly* with the following story about the precarious nature of the migrant farm worker's life. After the convention, a few harvest workers left New Rockford for a free ride on a stock train headed east. They hoped to find work at a potato harvest site. When the train stopped at Hannaford, North Dakota, a special agent working for the Great Northern railroad commanded the harvesters to get off the train. They did so, but then the agent immediately ordered them at gunpoint to put up their hands. Again they did so, offering no resistance to the agent. Without any provocation, he opened fire on the workers. He later said that he wanted to teach the harvesters a lesson about stealing a train ride. Joe Bagley, one of the harvesters, was hit by a bullet that pierced his lungs. He was taken to a hospital in Fargo, although he eventually died from his wounds. A clear photograph of Bagley's corpse accompanied Latchem's convention report and account of the killing. Even though wages were temporarily high for wheat harvest workers in 1920, Latchem wanted his readers to remain focused on the reality of their conditions as farm laborers. He reminded them that they could not afford to pay fares to travel to job sites, stay in hotels on the road, or procure sufficient food during the harvest season because of their inadequate earnings. Furthermore, the only protection they had on the road was what they could provide for themselves as organized workers. Ultimately, Latchem believed that only through worker organization and through the fundamental transformation of American society would harvest workers be free of violence and economic hardship. The historic mission of the AWIU, then, was to help create this future.[45]

Chapter Six

The Resurgence of Harvest Wobblies

⌘⌘⌘

The AWIU persevered through the immediate postwar years of criminal syndicalism persecution, and its members reorganized themselves into an agricultural union that was more responsive to the needs of its members. In the short term, the AWIU emerged in 1921 with renewed strength, assisting the IWW in achieving several years of resurgence as a militant labor organization. Though it was not yet evident, the long-term prospects of the AWIU would, after the mid-1920s, be cut short by changes in wheat-harvest worker transportation and the worklife culture of Great Plains farm laborers, and by major technological innovations in agriculture. Yet before these historic transformations occurred, harvest Wobblies would bring the AWIU to full maturity. They would develop a literary and theoretical justification for their existence as organized workers that was filled with socioeconomic insight, humor, and collective cultural identity.

As the years immediately following the war came to a close and the wartime economic boom ended, the IWW and some of its constituent industrial unions experienced a level of growth and development that rivaled the union's glory days of the prewar years. With a depression in American agriculture and with new and improved organizational tools, the AWIU prospered in membership and in financial dividends. It exemplified the sophisticated and pragmatic nature of the IWW in the early 1920s. AWIU organizers, officials, and activists combined their traditional organizational tactics with a focus on education. They wanted farm workers to understand the significant role that they played in agriculture and why it was necessary for this group of workers to hold AWIU membership. Based on a unique blend of Marxist and industrial union theory, harvest Wobblies brought a series of theoretical tracts, pamphlets, and leaflets to the West's farm workers. This commitment to education was coupled with an elaborate communication network, drawn from the experiences of harvest Wobblies in the fields and orchards of the West, that made the AWIU a truly rank-and-file-controlled industrial union.

Crafting an Ideological Appeal

Although only a few of the thousands of people who joined the AWIU left behind a written record of their beliefs, their IWW membership does indicate that the masses of harvest Wobblies accepted at least part of the union's distinctive ideology. That belief system was a unique blend of Marxism, libertarian socialism, industrial unionism, and direct action at the point of production. They reasoned that only through democratically controlled industrial unions could they establish a new society within the shell of the old. During the early 1920s, the majority of IWW members considered their path toward social and economic democracy superior to the dynamic communist movement that offered its own theory of revolution. In fact, one motivation for Wobblies to articulate a theoretical justification for their organization and a vision of the future could be found in their competition with communists for recruits among the American working class. Working-class Wobbly intellectuals argued that nonviolence, workplace democracy, and individual liberty would work in the American context, but Marxist-Leninist theories of armed insurrection, following the leadership of a vanguard communist party and establishing a dictatorship, had little hope of attracting workers in the United States. Furthermore, the IWW had always placed its faith in an educated mass of organized workers who would use the industrial union structure to bring an end to the capitalist system and to manage the new cooperative society. For Wobblies, the worker and the workplace were the focus, not political parties and the state, as communists and other socialists seemed to believe. And it was here that the Wobblies distinguished themselves as radicals and as revolutionaries, for they believed that it was ultimately up to the workers themselves to achieve their own emancipation from the capitalist system and to create a new society. Wobblies acted on this idea in the early 1920s with an impressive educational campaign that permeated their entire organizational network. The AWIU of this period offers a fine example of how education and organization worked in tandem to create a pragmatic and effective industrial union of workers.

Both Paul F. Brissenden in his book *The I.W.W.: A Study of American Syndicalism* and Thomas H. McEnroe in his dissertation, "The Industrial Workers of the World: Theories, Organizational Problems, and Appeals, As Revealed Principally in the *Industrial Worker*," emphasize that the union relied on its own publications to educate and direct IWW members and non-members alike. At different points in the history of the union, one could find a dozen or more Wobbly newspapers and periodicals in twenty different languages circulating around the country and other parts of the world. Although many of these publications survived only briefly, the *Industrial Worker, Solidarity*, and several non-English language newspapers had long runs (the *Industrial Worker* is still published today). Other formats proved durable as well. *One Big Union Monthly*, and its successor magazine, *Industrial Pioneer*, were forums for discussion and education on a variety of topics. Along with these serials, the IWW, and especially the AWIU, turned out leaflets and stickers designed to reach workers at the job site. Although primarily directed at harvest workers, the content of these leaflets often found their way into IWW newspapers.[1]

In the past, Wobblies had used stickers with slogans printed on them to communicate a variety of messages to workers, such as demands for pay increases, improvements in working conditions, and boycott announcements. Just as important as the actual message, the stickers announced the presence of the IWW in the area. In the prewar days, leaflets or fliers had the same function for the union, especially for the AWO. Fliers had the advantage that they could convey more information and give a better justification for a particular Wobbly position. Walter Nef's 1916 AWO message to wheat harvest workers and Great Plains farmers, cited in chapter 3, is a good example of this kind of broadly distributed leaflet.[2]

During the postwar years, AWIU leaflets conveyed more complex messages. These new leaflets, with titles like *You Need Industrial Unionism; The Two Triple Alliances; Vegetable and Fruit Workers!; Harvest Time Is Honey Time; Dare to Be Different; Agriculture, the Mother Industry;* and *He Was Not a Ten Hour Man in 1922*, had varying themes but all sought to explain the essential role that harvest workers played in American agriculture and gave workers strategies on how to improve their working conditions. For the IWW, these propaganda sheets were designed to stimulate a collective class-consciousness among harvest workers by identifying their common cultural experience as workers, thereby focusing workers' attention on a future society that would meet their needs.

During the early 1920s, leaflets flew off the IWW presses at an unprecedented rate. Whether it was at the beginning of the fruit harvest or the wheat harvest, AWIU leaders tried to have a pertinent leaflet available at Wobbly union halls and in the field, distributed by harvest Wobblies and job delegates. AWIU members revised some of these tracts from earlier editions, and they targeted some at specific regions. For example, in April 1922, the AWIU issued a revised *Vegetable and Fruit*

Workers! leaflet for West Coast migratory workers. In it, the AWIU urged workers to evaluate their working conditions, hours, and pay in proportion to the prosperity of California, Oregon, and Washington farms, thus encouraging them to recognize their indispensable role in the production of agricultural wealth. This particular leaflet still focused on the white male migrant worker.

Another leaflet, written by Seattle Wobblies and published in the *Industrial Worker*, had a more expansive view of the demographic make-up of seasonal farm laborers.[3] In *You Need Industrial Unionism*, harvest Wobblies offered harvest workers a theory of civilization that placed agriculture at the foundation of all industry and of society itself. The leaflet explained to farm laborers that "the agricultural workers are the most important members of society," for they made all other industry possible. The union then asked the reader why workers lived and worked in such miserable conditions if they were so central to civilization. The answer, of course, was that capitalism required their exploitation. "Waste no time in worry over the woes of those who are hungry for rent, interest and profit," the leaflet advised. The farmer, the banker, and the factory owner, whether large or small, were not of the same class as the harvest worker, and it was with one's class that workers needed to create and maintain solidarity. For example, the tract noted that "Not only must your union take in the Negro, the Japanese, the Mexican, the foreign-born worker, the woman and the child, as well as the adult citizen, but it must make common cause with the rest of the workers."

You Need Industrial Unionism went on to explain how the AWIU met the special needs of farm laborers. The universal transfer system, which was unique to the IWW, made it possible for workers to move from industry to industry without having to pay a new initiation fee as a worker would have to do in AFL unions. This was important to migrant agricultural workers, who tended to work in more than one industry over the course of a given year. The initiation fee for the AWIU was only $2 and monthly dues only fifty cents. In addition, the IWW union hall could hold a worker's mail while the worker was on the road, as well as keep AWIU bulletins on hand for workers to read. These bulletins contained job announcements for agricultural work throughout the United States, but especially west of the Mississippi River, where migrant labor remained a vital part of the West's agricultural industry. They also contained listings of workers' pay and hours at numerous job sites, news about the harvest season such as what kinds of crops were due to ripen that particular week, and tracts on economic history and the current needs of imprisoned workers. From the AWIU's perspective, these bulletins gave farm workers information that was not available in newspapers or from employment recruiting stations.[4]

Fostering a sense of community among harvest workers by articulating a common worklife culture was another significant goal of these leaflets and bulletins. Most of the fliers in circulation during the early 1920s, as well as the weekly bulletins put out by the AWIU, addressed their messages to the white male migrant worker. This approach proved very useful in acquiring members for the AWIU, even during the worst periods of state and federal persecution of the union. Fliers such as *Harvest Time is Honey Time* and *The Two Triple Alliances* appealed to wheat belt migrants who resided in jungle camps, had to make a stake to survive the winter, and had to fight not only the boss, his lawyers, and the bankers, but also gamblers, bootleggers, and hi-jacks who preyed upon them. These themes were consistent with those of the prewar days when harvest Wobblies were just getting their start as an organized force in western agricultural labor.[5]

Moreover, writings that placed migrant farm laborers within the larger context of the agricultural industry and the American capitalist system were a means of valuing the humanity of farm workers. The male migrant agricultural worker still tended to be underskilled and underemployed. During the postwar agricultural depression years, wages for seasonal labor fell to a near all-time low. In the Far West, where the seasonal workforce was increasingly made up of Mexicans and families of farm laborers, wages and working conditions continued to deteriorate. The AWIU tried to instill among these workers a sense of common humanity that could translate into collective direct action at the job site and improve their working and living conditions.[6]

In the end, the AWIU was a do-it-yourself union whose worklife culture was interpreted less by the leadership than by the rank and file, which largely accounts for the union's white male migrant orientation. Though the secretary-treasurer and the chairman of the General Organization Committee (GOC) wrote the weekly bulletins and issued them to all members and union halls, much of the information in the bulletins was contributed by AWIU members. Even the AWIU Education Bureau, an early-1920s creation, relied on the help of members. In February 1922, Tom Doyle and Tom Connors, the secretary and GOC chairman, respectively, called for members to play a role in the creation of AWIU leaflets "because they know the agricultural industry and its workers, their wages, hours, and conditions, better than anyone else."[7] In addition, Doyle and Connors solicited members' help in writing a series of economic studies in serial form for publication in *Solidarity*.[8]

Adapting an Organizational Structure to the Migrant Way of Life

The AWIU bulletins, which in many respects were the descendants of bulletins published in *Solidarity* and the *Industrial Worker* during the prewar years, proved to be a significant communication device for harvest Wobbly organization and education. Moreover, for a historian, they reveal essential information about the rank-and-file nature of the industrial union and its workers.

Using the blank "Job Report" form in many of the AWIU bulletins, harvest Wobblies could convey information to the entire membership regarding pay, working conditions, and types of crops at specific sites across the nation. A worker simply had to fill out the form and mail it to the AWIU headquarters in Chicago. Doyle and Connors, or their successors, would then publish the report along with others in the "Job News" section of each bulletin. Even though by the early 1920s harvest Wobblies were found primarily in the wheat belt of the country's midsection, "Job News" reports came in from all over the nation. For example, in May 1922, a group of sixteen harvest Wobblies reported that they had held a general membership meeting in Horatio, a village in southwest Arkansas, where they had found employment in berry picking. Here they initiated seven new members into the union. More common, however, were reports from areas that had a traditional union presence, such as Enid, Oklahoma, where harvest Wobblies, during the same harvest season, held a meeting of fifty-two AWIU members. These bulletin reports about meetings of harvest Wobblies, whether from Arizona, Michigan, or Montana, reveal how widespread the AWIU was during the early 1920s.[9]

One of the primary characteristics of these geographically dispersed harvest Wobblies, as revealed in the bulletins, was that they tended to be migrant as opposed to locally based workers. The AWIU devised a means to reach as many of these migrant workers as possible. Bulletins were posted at all Wobbly union halls, distributed by AWIU job delegates in the field, published in IWW newspapers, or mailed to them at post office boxes that they used during the harvest season.

The industrial union did grow in membership during the early 1920s, but it had trouble reaching workers through stationary delegates and branch offices. Continued repression of the IWW made increasing the number of union halls difficult. But as of August 1923, there were branches and stationary delegates in Fargo, North Dakota; Sioux City, Iowa; Minneapolis, Minnesota; Omaha, Nebraska; Modesto, Marysville,

and Fresno, California; Spokane, Washington; amd the AWIU's headquarters in Chicago.

Official AWIU contact points were few and far between in the
immense western landscape. Still, harvest Wobblies were expected to
vote in AWIU elections. This could be a troublesome process. First, they
needed to find an AWIU job delegate, a stationary delegate, or an
industrial union branch to procure a ballot. Second, they needed
information about the issues on the ballot and the individuals running
for office; this could be found in bulletins and Wobbly newspapers. For
these reasons, even though harvest Wobblies made up a substantial
percentage of the IWW's 1923 membership of fifty-eight thousand, their
migratory nature tended to reduce their participation in elections. For
example, according to published reports in AWIU bulletins, the union's
1923 summer elections drew only eight hundred forty-nine ballots out
of a possible twenty thousand. In addition, despite a substantial increase
in the number of job delegates in the field in 1922, over a hundred of
them were delinquent for many months in filing reports with AWIU
headquarters. The mobility of the union's members and the large
geographic area that the AWIU administered made such basic organizational functions difficult. These organizational problems were not
unique to the AWIU. Other industrial unions in the West, such as those
representing logging and construction workers, experienced similar
problems among their far-flung memberships.[10]

The AWIU's migrant worklife culture posed serious problems for the
union beyond the lack of voter participation and the delinquency of job
delegate reports. Maintaining the membership was a chronic headache
for the organization. In fact, critics of the AWIU argued that the industrial
union was far better at selling membership cards than actually
organizing workers. To address this problem, the AWIU issued a leaflet,
Hang on to Your Life Belt, in July 1922. The main thrust of the tract was
to encourage members to maintain their membership after the harvest
ended. The turnover rate for the IWW overall was extraordinarily high,
and the AWIU was no exception. One explanation for this turnover is that
workers joined the AWIU or another IWW industrial union for short-term
gains. It is important to remember that the IWW had an overwhelming
number of itinerant laborers who worked many jobs over the course of
a year. Being a member of the AWIU entitled one to ride free on freight
trains, gain higher wages at AWIU-controlled work sites, and experience
the camaraderie of Wobblies on the road and in the jungles. However,
after completing the harvest season and going on to winter in San
Francisco or work as a day laborer, continued IWW membership offered

no immediate gains. The union's universal transfer system allowed harvest Wobblies who finished their harvest work in October and moved on to work in the logging industry, for example, to maintain membership in the IWW by transferring to the Lumber Workers' Industrial Union No. 120. When the Wobblies were ready to go back to the harvest the following season, they could transfer back to the AWIU. *Hang on to Your Life Belt* was intended to explain to harvest Wobblies that the IWW needed them in order to achieve the goal of building the new society within the shell of the old through the mass organization of the U.S. workforce. Unfortunately for the AWIU, and for the IWW as a whole, many who joined the union expected to have their needs met on a continual basis in order to maintain membership. This problem reflects the breakdown between IWW ideology and harvest Wobbly culture. For most of those who joined the AWIU, immediate gains and cultural appeal overrode ideology.[11]

Though the AWIU had its problems with the migrant nature of its membership, the life experience of these workers received ample understanding and downright praise in Wobbly literature and song. The lonely and sometimes dangerous life on the road still motivated harvest Wobblies to seek out each other's company. In the early 1920s, the migrant worklife culture that the IWW had recognized as a revolutionary force in the 1910s remained a union focus. It was here that the AWIU found its core support, so the union and in many ways fostered this type of life.[12]

History and Theory According to the AWIU

The most significant AWIU theoretical literature concerning the American agricultural economy highlighted the role of migrant farm labor. Beginning with Abner E. Woodruff's 1919 study, the AWIU postulated that the contemporary migrant farm laborer was the logical product of the development of the capitalist system. In his *Evolution of American Agriculture,* Woodruff took his reader from the beginnings of agricultural development in the Americas to its origins in the United States, giving special consideration to the western expansion of the country's farm systems after the Civil War. It was here that the migrant farm laborer, particularly in the wheat belt, became predominant. Mechanization of agriculture in the prairie and Great Plains states, with a drive to specialize in one crop, spawned an agricultural proletariat analogous to African American farm laborers in the South. Whether free or slave labor, blacks in the South were tied to the land as farm tenants and sharecroppers by white landowners. In the Midwest, Great Plains, and Far West, the farmhand apprentice system collapsed around 1900, according to Woodruff, as homestead opportunities faded. The farmhand, who once had the chance to apprentice himself to a farmer, save his earnings, and purchase a farm, had given way to the seasonal or migrant farm worker who would never earn enough money to purchase a farm. Therefore, during the first few decades of the twentieth century, farm laborers in the South, Midwest, and West become a permanent feature of the U.S. agricultural economy. Woodruff's study not only analyzed American agricultural history, but it justified the AWIU as the only existing organization that could meet the needs of agricultural laborers. He closed his comprehensive study with a call for the farm workers of the country to join the AWIU.[13]

A second piece of scholarly writing concerning American agricultural development was the IWW's Bureau of Industrial Research's *Agriculture: The World's Basic Industry and Its Workers*. This study involved a history of agriculture throughout the world, from its origins, through the ancient world, to Europe and finally to the Americas. Like Woodruff's, this study included an explanation of the contemporary agricultural situation with its system of migrant farm labor. The authors of *Agriculture* encouraged cooperation between small farmers and agricultural laborers, as they were both exploited by the capitalist system. Once capitalist farmers were overthrown in the coming revolution, agricultural laborers would be free to organize agricultural production through the industrial union structure of the IWW. Small farmers would be free to join the IWW, if they gave up their individual claims to the land. If they chose to live on land that they could farm by their own labor without employing a wage-worker, then they would be free to do so. *Agriculture* ended with a call for migrant workers to join the AWIU, just as Woodruff's book did. However, the writers of *Agriculture* explained in greater detail why migrant workers only had the AWIU to turn to for assistance in ameliorating their poor working and living conditions. For example, migrant workers, due to their homelessness, could not vote, and even if they could, those politicians who tried to help them would be thwarted by capitalists who controlled the state and federal political machinery.[14]

Reshaping Harvest Wobbly Worklife Culture

These ideas that circulated in a variety of IWW literature were also the subjects of Wobbly songs. The 1923 edition of the IWW songbook, a continuing part of Wobbly worklife and literary culture, still contained Pat Brennan's "Harvest War Song" and other songs relating to agricultural work and migrant life, such as "We Have Fed You All For A Thousand Years," "When You Wear That Button," and "The Tramp," along with newer songs on the same themes.[15]

Harvest Wobblies in the jungles probably spent more time singing songs out of the Wobbly songbook than discussing the merits of a political essay published in a leaflet or in the *Industrial Worker*. Singing about their experiences helped to create an atmosphere that made their lives more bearable. Harvest Wobblies in the 1920s were still plagued by the problems of the previous decade: railroad agents who tried to eject them from trains, their primary form of transportation, and sheriff's deputies who tried to run them out of the jungle camps, their primary living quarters when on the road. Jungle life had not changed much since the prewar years, except for one key difference—it was now more common for Wobblies, by their sheer numbers within the ranks of wheat belt harvest workers, to be in control of jungle camps or freight trains bound for a harvest work site.[16]

During the early 1920s, the AWIU seemed to be of two minds about the migrant worklife culture of its membership. On the one hand, Wobbly literature celebrated the migrant harvest worker's life on the road. On the other hand, harvest Wobblies were encouraged to break free of the jungle life. For example, the May 1922 AWIU leaflet *Dare to Be Different* argued that the Wobbly life of the jungle was a very primitive way to live and work. The leaflet offered the standard Wobbly line that workers could only emancipate themselves from these conditions through industrial union organization, the kind found within the IWW. But the leaflet also included a call to "eliminate the jungle and the jungle standard." Moreover, the tract called on homeguard workers, who did not travel in search of work, to unite with migrants to end an economic system that made every homeguard worker a potential migrant worker because of the insecurity of employment.[17]

It was not that the IWW had ever considered jungle life an adequate existence for workers in the past. To the contrary, the IWW and the AWIU had always contended that migrant life was a difficult existence for the individuals forced by economic circumstances to live that way. What was new in the 1920s was the emphasis on the capitalist system as the cause of the migrants' situation, the argument that workers were the only force in society that could end this exploitation, and the conviction that having a steady job, wife, and family was what all itinerant workers really wanted. Again, educating workers by offering them an interpretation of their worklife was a major means by which the AWIU hoped to recruit them into the union. Yet, in this instance it is also clear that the target group was still the single white male migrant laborer, and not the families of harvesters, especially Hispanics, whose numbers were growing dramatically in the Far West. Despite this narrow viewpoint, the AWIU's Education Bureau produced a number of intellectually complex leaflets and theoretical works on agriculture. The Bureau also produced two important pamphlets during the early 1920s: *An Economic Interpretation of the Job* and *What is the I.W.W. Preamble?: A Dialogue.* These works gave job delegates and harvest Wobbly activists more recruiting tools.

The AWIU's Education Bureau had grown out of the IWW's effort to create a scholarly inquiry into socioeconomic problems in history and contemporary society. In 1920, participants at the IWW's general convention also commissioned a Bureau of Industrial Research. The Bureau's function was to examine government-sponsored studies of economic and social issues as well as academic projects in the same areas. The Bureau conducted its own research and analysis, producing books, pamphlets, and articles in the *Industrial Worker, Solidarity,* and Wobbly magazines. In 1921, the AWIU's Education Bureau replaced the Bureau of Industrial Research. With twenty-five thousand members, the AWIU could afford to take on the financial responsibility of such a project. Furthermore, in 1922 the AWIU merged its own Department of Education with the Educational Bureau of the IWW's general head-quarters. The AWIU maintained an extraordinary degree of influence over the IWW's educational work through its financial contributions to the union. Without question, the educational efforts directed at harvest Wobblies verged on surpassing those of other industrial unions within the IWW.[18]

The AWIU's Education Bureau also published studies on a variety of topics of concern to the IWW membership at large. These studies surfaced in the major organs of the union and spawned a number of leaflets. In 1922 alone, the Education Bureau printed one hundred ninety thousand copies of eleven different tracts.

A deep commitment to the development of its members characterized the AWIU's Education Bureau. In its fall 1921 convention, the AWIU commissioned a course of study for members "in the Social Sciences and Literature, Economics, Marxism, Psychology, (and) Sociology." Scholarships would be available for members who did not have the means to take these courses. The AWIU was also a major financial supporter and advocate of the Work People's College in Duluth, Minnesota. Tom Wallace, the secretary-treasurer, and Albert Hanson, the chairman for the GOC, thought the Work People's College should be a place that harvest Wobblies consider spending their winter off-time, as the following passage from an AWIU bulletin of December 1923 suggests:

> *The Work People's College, for example, educates men and women along lines that enable them to understand the workings of capitalist society and how these operate to the disadvantage of the wage workers. . . . Moreover, it teaches them to understand the evolutionary historical process that brought about capitalism, which is destined to be superseded by the kind of industrial society for which the I.W.W. is striving. In its mathematical and bookkeeping classes it is enabling [students] to qualify in positions where they will be capable of serving their class. . . And the tuition fee is only $8.00 per month, while clean, steam-heated rooms, with abundant well cooked board, is only $31.00 per month. Board, room, schooling, gymnasium, and laundry for $39.00 per month. The College evidently is not run for profit. It is cheaper to put the winter there than to 'shack up'.*[19]

Educating laborers in the field, however, remained the primary way that harvest Wobblies worked to "enlighten" non-Wobblies. For example, both *An Economic Interpretation of the Job* and *What is the I.W.W. Preamble?: A Dialogue* were efforts to bring the IWW message to migrant as well as homeguard workers. These publications could be found at Wobbly union halls or purchased through the *Industrial Worker* or *Solidarity*. *An Economic Interpretation of the Job* followed a basic Marxist theory of capitalist development, the role of the workers, and their place in industry. Each chapter—whether it examined labor as a commodity, class struggle, origins of capital, or market forces—closed with a series of study questions. Aimed at the non-Wobbly worker, the pamphlet *What is the I.W.W. Preamble?: A Dialogue* was more of a one-act play than an instructional booklet, though a very didactic play. Set in a pastoral landscape in summer 1922, the play consists of a conversation between a Wobbly technical engineer and his boyhood friend, a common laborer who has lost his job and plans to hop a freight train to search for work in the wheat belt harvest. Over the course of their conversation, Wobbly Henry Tichenor convinces his skeptical friend, Bob Hammond, that the capitalist system expanded through the exploitation of the working class.

Tichenor has to dissuade Hammond of his preconceived notions about the Wobblies and capitalism before he can convince him to join the union and to help emancipate his class.[20]

One of the interesting features of both of these AWIU publications is that they were decidedly Marxist in their interpretation of the contemporary economic situation and determined to link the migrant worker with the coming collapse of the capitalist system. The basic economic equation for the Wobblies was that increased mechanization displaced homeguard urban industrial workers, so that migrant workers increased in number. But the most notable feature of these two tracts is their concern with creating an educated, class-conscious, independent-minded laborer who would join a rank-and-file union. Yet their focus on the white male worker continued to isolate the AWIU from the fastest-growing sectors of the farm labor workforce, but during the early 1920s, this did not significantly affect their organizing effort in the Great Plains wheat belt, for in that region, the workforce was still overwhelmingly white and male. The Wobblies' theories on agricultural development go a long way towards explaining why they did not see any urgency in recruiting the masses of harvest workers who were Hispanic, Asian, or worked as families.

The Problem with Theory

The economic analysis found in the literature of the AWIU was only partly correct. Following the economic boom years of 1916-1920 came the depression of 1920-1922, in which millions of men and women were thrown out of work, particularly in the manufacturing, transportation, construction, and mining industries. Some of these displaced workers made their way to the agricultural harvest areas of the central and western states, as the AWIU leaders claimed they would. And, as Wobblies predicted, machines displaced some of these workers in a variety of industries when the economy rebounded in 1923. According to the historian Irving Bernstein in *The Lean Years*, the 1920s were characterized by advances in technology and a tremendous increase in mechanization. He notes that over the course of the decade, "machines displaced 3,272,000 men, of whom 2,269,000 were reabsorbed and 1,003,000 remained unemployed."[21]

Integral to the postwar depression was an agricultural depression that AWIU economic theorists believed would bring an end to the independent small farmer. Prices for farm products declined dramatically in 1920. The high wages that agricultural laborers enjoyed that year plummeted the following. In 1922, market prices for grains, fruits, vegetables, and other farm products rose again, so that farm labor wages began to increase in 1923. But farm prices would "weaken and falter" by mid-decade. For example, wheat prices, in the economist Daniel J. Ahearn, Jr.'s estimation, began "a long descent to the abyss of 1932." Most other major farm commodities declined in price during the decade as well. Farm wages, on the other hand, remained stable from 1924 to 1929. The attraction of better wages, working conditions, and shorter hours that urban employment offered probably led farmers to hold wages steady to attract workers. In fact, from 1920 to 1929, approximately twenty million people left the country's agricultural sectors for urban employment. Many of those who left the countryside were white male laborers who had given up on the idea that they could ever climb the agricultural ladder to farm ownership. They were also drawn to the possibility of a family life in urban areas. Manufacturing or office employment could offer the economic stability and possible advancement that rural labor could not. AWIU theorists got the migration direction wrong. Workers were leaving rural areas for urban employment, not the other way around.[22]

AWIU economic theory did point to real problems in American agriculture, but it proved substantially faulty in the long run. During the early 1920s, an imminent economic collapse seemed plausible. But with the economic recovery that began in 1922, most industries demonstrated unprecedented levels of productivity for the balance of the decade. Mechanization did not lead to a substantial increase in migrant agricultural labor and an increasingly impoverished working class. The restrictive federal legislation of the mid-1920s slowed foreign immigration to a trickle, which helped to stabilize the urban workforce and made it possible for urban areas to absorb an influx of rural Americans. While it was true that workers did not enjoy the economic prosperity of the 1920s to the same extent as the middle and upper classes did, most urban workers did have steady employment.[23]

Urban workers and resident rural workers without steady employment made up eighty percent of the seasonal farm labor supply in the wheat belt during the early 1920s. Yet these workers did not become permanent migratory workers. They eventually returned to their urban trades or local year-round rural employment. By this point, the professional migratory agricultural worker in the wheat fields had already declined as a factor in the region's farm workforce. Again, Wobbly agricultural theory did not pan out as expected. Small farmers were *not* forced into the ranks of migrant agricultural laborers. Industrial agricultural development did *not* lead to small numbers of individuals owning most U.S. farmland. Through the 1920s, a combination of small, medium, and large farm operations continued to define American agriculture.[24]

The owners of these farms faced difficult times in the early 1920s. Some farmers lost their land due to the economic downturn. The trend towards concentration in ownership of land and an increase in farm tenancy was taking place across the nation, but it moved slowly during the decade. In the wheat belt, for example, there was little change in the number or size of farms during the 1920s. There was no substantial increased need for farm labor during this period, which was what harvest Wobblies had expected to occur. Nevertheless, debate broke out in the IWW press, especially in the *Industrial Worker*, over perceived changes in the agricultural industry. The focus of this debate was the relationship between the IWW and farmers, and whether to recruit them into the union.[25]

Harvest Wobbly Strategies for Dealing with Farmers

As farm prices collapsed in the postwar period, Wobblies contributed a number of ideas on how farmers could deal with the hard times. One writer suggested that the IWW establish a farmers' auxiliary. Here farmers could organize for their own interests but work in tandem with the IWW. Together wageworkers and farmers could mobilize against a common enemy, namely the capitalist system. The writer argued that farmers and workers had both become alienated from the product of their own labor. Other Wobbly writers concurred, arguing that because of the mechanization of industry, factory jobs reduced workers to low-skill labor. Workers did not make a finished product, only a small part of a finished product. Farmers, too, had become alienated from their work, according to Wobbly reasoning. They tended to grow only one crop that they did not process, so most had to buy their food just as workers did. Farmers were no longer self-sufficient agrarians, but the most exploited of businessmen, tied to a market system over which they had no control. According to the Wobbly delegate P. C., the industrialization of American agriculture would eventually eliminate the small and medium-size American farm and those who owned them.

A ranking AWIU member and experienced farmhand, Albert Hanson, concluded that most farmers would not raise a hand to stop a social revolution when the collapse of the capitalist system occurred. Hanson believed that the IWW would have ample time to win farmers over to a

Figure 22. In an issue of *Solidarity*, 30 June 1923, common cause is made between the farmer and the harvest Wobbly. The "true" foes of the two producers are downtown business and its servant law enforcement. (Courtesy, Walter P. Reuther Library, Wayne State University)

cooperative structure for the agricultural industry, because as long as farmers had a market for their produce they would be indifferent to a social revolution. The harvest Wobbly E. D. Banner believed that the 1921 harvest season was an extraordinary opportunity to educate American farmers. The harvest Wobblies who were distributed across the countryside could explain to farmers that it was hopeless to expect the capitalist system to fully reward them for their own labor and produce, that they needed to prepare themselves for their eventual inclusion among the growing American proletarian class, and that the economic system as a whole was doomed to collapse. Yet writers such as a Wobbly by the name of Stumpy were more realistic. They had no confidence that farmers would understand the IWW program or that they would remain neutral during a social revolution. Stumpy argued that Wobblies needed to take their message to harvest workers, tenant farmers, and share-croppers. The latter two groups would be far more amenable to the Wobbly message than would landowning farmers. Overall, harvest Wobblies were largely wrong in terms of their Marxist analysis of impending changes in American agriculture, and wrong, too, in predicting a social revolution in the United States. But most important for the harvest drives of 1921, '22, and '23, farmers tended to be just as unfriendly to Wobbly organizing and just as hostile to their presence in the wheat belt as they had been in previous years.[26]

The farmers' opposition to AWIU organizing, and to harvest Wobblies in general, was reflected in IWW literature. For example, an illustration in the June 1922 issue of *Solidarity* depicted a Great Plains sheriff walking in a wheat field, and to his exasperation the heads of the wheat are Wobbly job delegates. In another illustration in *Solidarity* the following year, a wheat farmer jumps up and down exclaiming that he cannot get the help he needs to harvest his crop, and rain is on its way. A calm, hearty-looking IWW wheat shocker explains to the farmer that he could get "lots of help John, if you make the hours and wages right." Not all Wobbly cartoons were anti-farmer, however, for the practical reality was not lost on harvest Wobblies that farmers and the AWIU could attain a symbiotic relationship (fig. 22).[27]

A Mature AWIU Takes to the Fields

With the postwar depression in full swing in 1921, the AWIU considered the migrant white male worker of America's trans-Mississippi West ripe for organizing. The AWIU, armed with a commitment to educating farm workers and using a mixture of new and traditional organizing tools, was confident that it could recruit large numbers of workers in the fields of western agriculture. In fact, 1920 and 1921 witnessed an unusually high number of urban workers from the automobile, tire, and other manufacturing industries searching for harvest work on the Great Plains. In addition, some farmers who had lost their land during the early 1920s depression turned to agricultural labor for their livelihood as well.[28]

Harvest Wobblies knew that this harvest was extremely important for the AWIU. It was not enough for the union merely to exist: it had to expand in order to be effective. At a February business meeting at the AWIU headquarters in Chicago, representatives passed a resolution authorizing "that we send a traveling delegate to the fruit districts of the East during the fruit season." The union also articulated some basic rules for the rank and file to nurture unity among harvest Wobblies. Representatives at the business meeting went "on record as being opposed to any member of 110 shocking by the acre or threshing by the bushel." Piece rate work was simply not ging to be tolerated. Expanding the scope of AWIU organizing and maintaining a standard work day and wage were crucial goals for the union.[29]

These sentiments were echoed by members at the spring convention of the AWIU, held in Sioux City, Iowa, who incorporated the resolutions into the convention proceedings. Some harvest Wobblies arrived in Sioux City broke and unable to pay for food or lodging. Their fellow workers who had the means made sure that all AWIU members in attendance at the convention had a place to sleep and plenty to eat. Despite the hardships that harvest Wobblies faced due to poverty, joblessness, and prison time, they exhibited an unusual level of confidence at their convention. Perhaps the presence of a federal agent seated in the back of the convention hall throughout the proceedings inspired them to put on their best faces.[30]

The AWIU members engaged in a variety of union business with an orderliness that surprised seasoned convention participants. Members issued telegrams to their fellow Wobblies in prison, pledging their support, and a telegram to President Warren G. Harding demanding a pardon for all "the political prisoners in this country." The participants agreed to maintain the ten-hour day in the harvest field with "time starting and ending at (the) barn." A permanent AWIU hall in Kansas City, Missouri, finally received its needed funding. But one of the most important convention acts that demonstrated the union's confidence was a resolution stating that future conventions would be based on a delegate system rather than on a mass convention basis. Over the past several years it had been impossible for the AWIU to organize a delegate convention due to repression of harvest Wobblies by federal, state, and local authorities. However, harvest Wobblies agreed not only that mass conventions haphazardly pulled workers from the job site but also that the resolutions enacted at such conventions were rarely implemented in a systematic manner in the countryside. Delegates who returned to their work areas after the convention could better direct the organizing work of AWIU members. With these considerations in mind, the participants worked out a system by which members on jobs would elect a representative to a field conference, and these representatives would in turn elect a delegate to the next AWIU convention. (This decision was reversed at the fall 1922 convention, because the intensely mobile nature of harvest work made it impossible to elect a sufficient number of delegates from all of the harvest Wobbly work sites.) The spring 1921 convention closed with a call for members to remember 1915 when the Agricultural Workers' Organization had been instrumental in breathing new life into the IWW. Now, with the union recovering from its worst period of federal and state repression, it urged members to view 1921 as a critical year for all Wobblies.[31]

In June as the harvest season began in Kansas and Oklahoma, Albert Anz and R. S. Morgan, the secretary-treasurer and chairman of the GOC of the AWIU, respectively, urged all Wobblies irrespective of their industrial union status to come to the wheat harvest if they were in need of employment. Anz and Morgan did not want unemployed urban Wobblies to wait for the economy to rebound in their particular industry. They wanted Wobblies to take whatever work they could in order to expand the AWIU, force up wages, and improve working conditions for all harvest workers.[32]

In Kansas, officials prepared to charge every harvest Wobbly with the state's 1920 criminal syndicalism law. But the Kansas Supreme Court ruled that this law did not bar members of the IWW from entering the state, so there was no legal justification for arresting Wobblies on sight as they came into Kansas. Wobblies were, as usual, migrating to Kansas to participate in the harvest. And it was in that state that AWIU fortunes took a turn for the better in the harvest season of 1921. In a series of meetings, Kansas farmers tried to hold wages to $4.50 a day. But the sheer number of laborers who were harvest Wobblies pushed the wage up to $5.00 or more, according to the editors of *Solidarity*. Part of the success of harvest Wobblies in Kansas stemmed from the strategy of staying clear of large towns and concentrating on harvest job sites in the countryside. This strategy made arrest and harassment by law enforcement less of a concern for workers. With many unemployed workers from industrial urban areas who lacked experience in agricultural work turning to the countryside for jobs, experienced harvest workers were in high demand. Perhaps due to the fact that Kansas's farmers needed all the experienced help they could get in this particular harvest season, no mass repression of harvest Wobblies took place. Not even the murder, by an unknown assailant, of a young prosecutor, Arthur C. Banta, who had been "active in the prosecution of (the) I.W.W.," could spawn a wave of anti-Wobbly actions.[33]

As the wheat harvest progressed northward from the southern plains, it became clear to harvest Wobblies that this would be a resurgent year for their industrial union. The call that had gone out to invoke the spirit of 1915 changed to a call to invoke the spirit of 1916. In 1915, the Agricultural Workers' Organization formed and began to craft an organizational strategy that was the first of its kind in American agricultural history. In 1916, harvest Wobblies implemented their first coordinated organizational drive in the wheat belt and successfully acquired thousands of new members for the IWW. In July 1921, Anz claimed that the AWIU was in the midst of its largest recruitment drive since 1916. Wobblies throughout the union were heartened by the resurgence of their fellow members in the fields of the Great Plains. Ralph Winstead, a frequent writer for *Solidarity*, advised harvest Wobblies that now was the time to establish the agricultural organizational structure that would replace the independent farmer. Winstead reasoned that the IWW's industrial union strategy would bring American agriculture fully into a scientifically managed arrangement, with agricultural workers controlling all facets of the industry.[34]

Of course, the AWIU was in no position to "take over" American agriculture. Still, the industrial union did acquire more members over the summer, and it distributed tens of thousands of AWIU and IWW leaflets, pamphlets, and newspapers to the thousands of workers, Wobbly and non-Wobbly, who made their way through the Great Plains wheat harvest. Nevertheless, repression was always on the horizon. As the migrants made their way north, South Dakota farmers and North Dakota American Legionnaires prepared to meet the Wobbly "menace." The former planned to hold to a $3 a day maximum wage. In North Dakota, American Legionnaires planned to enforce that wage on behalf of farmers. With the market price of a bushel of wheat half what it was the previous year, north plains farmers decided that they had no choice but to cut their labor costs. According to the editors of *Solidarity*, however, harvest Wobblies, by their numeric strength in the field, were able to break the wage limits by a dollar or more a day.[35]

AWIU members had reason to be proud in the summer of 1921. The entire wheat belt had a sizable Wobbly presence, and individual Wobblies reported to the AWIU headquarters that when they had the numbers they could force up wages. In addition, Wobblies on a number of freight train lines had control over who could ride and who could not. This meant that on these particular lines a harvest worker who wanted a ride had to have a red card. If he had no card, he was given a choice: join the union or be thrown from the train.

Harvest Wobblies, though, did have a number of problems with law enforcement officials during the harvest season. Sheriff's deputies and police arrested several members of the AWIU in Oklahoma, and five Mexican harvest Wobblies were deported after they were arrested in the state. The Oklahoma arrestees remained in jail until August.

In Nebraska, South Dakota, and North Dakota, farmers, Legionnaires, and local political and law enforcement officials grew increasingly alarmed by the massive numbers of harvest Wobblies traveling to work sites in the region. The *New York Times*, which frequently covered news in the wheat belt during the harvest season, pinned the deaths of four harvesters on the IWW. The men either died after falling from a moving freight train or they were shot. The newspaper contended that IWW members had killed them because they refused to join the union. Another case in point was that of harvest Wobbly Frank Daring. Prosecutors accused Daring of killing W. D. Henderson on a Milwaukee train around Wolsey, South Dakota. The Wobbly press suggested that Daring was defending himself from Henderson, a hi-jack. The *New York Times*, on the other hand, accused Daring of shooting Henderson because he refused to join the AWIU despite the fact that three hundred harvest Wobblies were on that particular freight train.[36] The *Times* also accused AWIU members of dozens of beatings of independent harvesters who would not join the union. Though none of these accusations resulted in arrests or convictions of Wobblies, it is probable that the migrants used heavy-handed tactics when riding the rails. However, it is unlikely that IWW members participated in outright murder. With all of the accusations concerning Wobbly violence over the years, few Wobblies were ever arrested for murder, let alone convicted. It is more likely that hi-jacks killed the men.[37]

When a huge influx of Wobblies came into Aberdeen, South Dakota, the local sheriff was quick to arrest the first job delegate he could find, an IWW organizer by the name of Casey. Casey had arrived in Aberdeen just after several hundred Wobblies had left the harvest fields in protest over the maximum pay of $3. He encouraged the workers to stay out of the wheat fields until the wage went up, and he also began to initiate new members into the union, particularly those men who had left the fields with the Wobblies over the low wages. Within a matter of hours, the local sheriff arrested Casey. Approximately five hundred harvest Wobblies contemplated marching on the jail to free him, but cooler heads prevailed, and a committee was elected to approach the sheriff to demand the release of their job delegate. While the Wobblies waited for Casey's hearing, American Legionnaires and sheriff's deputies prepared to run them out of town. The following morning, prosecutors raised the charge against Casey from "obstructing the streets" to criminal syndicalism. Before the Wobblies could organize a protest of some sort, they were expelled from the town.[38]

By August, most harvest Wobblies congregated in the northern plains, especially in North Dakota, where migrant farm labor continued to be essential for the wheat harvest. Although farmers needed temporary labor, they were sensitive to their labor costs as the price of wheat remained low. Despite numbers of AWIU members reaching into the thousands, and the recent history of tolerance for harvest Wobblies in the state, some townspeople sought to drive the migrants out because they disrupted an affordable labor supply. Harvest Wobblies continued their customary practice of staying out of the fields if the wage was substandard. Most galling to farmers and townspeople, Wobblies would stay in town and try to persuade independent harvesters not to go into the fields either, but to join the union and hold out for a higher wage. In addition, Wobblies gained control of freight train travel throughout the north plains, ejecting those workers who did not hold a Wobbly red membership card and refused to join the industrial union. AWIU members did not question the merits of either practice, but considered such actions essential to their organizational work.

Their success with these tactics invoked a powerful anti-Wobbly response in several communities. In the eastern North Dakota towns of Fairmount, Hoople, Valley City, and Fargo harvest Wobblies endured either mob attacks or arrests. Mob actions directed at Wobblies usually consisted of a coalition of local businessmen, independent harvesters, and law enforcement officers. Farmers, dispersed throughout the countryside, rarely participated in such actions. When they had strength in numbers, anti-Wobbly citizens could drive Wobblies out of town, most often at gunpoint. Harvest Wobbly delegates had their share of arrests in these towns as well. Since North Dakota did not have a criminal syndicalism law, the tried and true charge of vagrancy accounted for most of the arrests. Yet police also used other laws to harass harvest Wobblies. For example, police arrested Tom Doyle, who presided over a Wobbly street meeting in Fargo, for "speaking without a permit."

In most cases the Wobblies responded in two ways. One was to instigate a boycott against a hostile community. If they could persuade Wobblies and independent migrants from frequenting downtown businesses, they could put economic pressure on law enforcement to lighten up on their treatment of IWW members. This tactic was only effective during the height of the harvest season when migrant laborers moved though wheat belt towns by the hundreds or the thousands. Second, if a member languished in jail, harvest Wobblies tried to maintain a presence in the town. They would organize street demonstrations, demanding their fellow unionist's release from jail. If they had a job delegate with them, they might also try to organize migrant laborers in town.[39]

Trials and Tribulations of the AWIU in the Far West

Once the AWIU membership had passed the ten-thousand mark, it was clear that 1921 could be the biggest year in the industrial union's history. Though in the past, AWIU headquarters had admonished harvest Wobblies for congregating in large groups as they moved through the wheat harvest, this season they found encouragement in *Solidarity* to travel this way. Commentators in *Solidarity* believed that by acting in large numbers, harvest Wobblies could persuade independents to join the union, continue the present growth in membership, and force up wages.

With the bulk of harvest Wobblies in North Dakota by mid-August and the threshing season about to begin in the northern plains, the AWIU leadership encouraged members who did not plan to find threshing jobs to head west or to other regions in need of migrant laborers. But it was especially to the fruit-growing regions of Washington that the Wobbly press urged harvest workers to make their way, even though there was a high probability that great opposition would meet a harvest drive in Wenatchee and Yakima. The Wobbly press may have believed that the success in recruiting new members in the Great Plains could be duplicated among fruit workers.[40]

Wobblies did make their way to the Wenatchee and Yakima Valleys to participate in the fruit and hop harvests, as well as to western Oregon. Sheriffs, their deputies, and city police prepared for the influx, which local newspapers referred to as an "invasion." Sheriffs and their deputies in both valleys raided jungle camps and makeshift AWIU headquarters in the countryside and arrested anyone with a red card. By October several dozen Wobblies were in jail. Even though Yakima's prosecuting attorney decided to drop charges against four Wobblies after they had served twenty-two months in the local jail, other Wobblies experienced arrest and prosecution. Those who were not subsequently released after serving time for vagrancy were charged with criminal syndicalism. Four Wobblies were so charged in Wenatchee.[41]

The Wenatchee criminal syndicalism case was significant for the AWIU because the jury found the defendants not guilty. The attorney for the prosecution used IWW literature to convince the jury that the men on trial believed in sabotage as a means of reforming harvest working conditions. Prosecutor Frank Lebeck introduced the "Harvest War Song" from the Wobbly songbook as evidence. One of the stanzas read: "Up goes machine or wages, and the hours must go down!" But Lebeck's allusions to sabotage were answered by IWW attorney George F.

Vandeveer. He was able to convince the jury that the prosecution could produce no witnesses that linked the men on trial to any acts of violence or destruction of property. It was only a matter of hours after closing arguments in the trial in late January 1922 that the court released the Wobblies. Largely owing to a series of expensive criminal syndicalism cases being thrown out or decisions falling in favor of the defense, as in the Wenatchee case, Washington's criminal syndicalism law became, for all intents and purposes, a dead letter.[42]

However, newspaper editors and law enforcement officials were not the most significant challenges facing IWW members in Washington. Harvest Wobblies, accustomed to working alongside other single, itinerant men or local temporary male workers, now found themselves working side by side with itinerant families of harvesters who had arrived in the valleys not by freight train but by their own automobiles. In 1921, such families made up a substantial portion of the migrant workforce. Surprisingly, one Wobbly job delegate, writing in the *Industrial Worker* from Hood River, Oregon, noted that many of the harvest families who picked apples in that area were members of the IWW. But his observation was an anomaly. Wobbly writers dubbed these farm labor migrants "automobile tramps." The job delegate and his wife, who also belonged to the AWIU, were automobile tramps too. Harvest Wobbly Fred Koffee, who encountered these workers in the packing warehouses of the Yakima Valley, wrote in the *Industrial Worker* of the low pay, poor working conditions, and makeshift housing for harvest family workers on the road. He found them to be a wretched and impoverished lot whose primary concern was finding work. According to Koffee, union organization was far from their thinking.[43]

In fall 1921, some harvest Wobblies had also made their way to California for the fruit and vegetable harvests. Yet because the more successful use of criminal syndicalism legislation there made arrest a more likely proposition, few made the trip. Also the handful of AWIU job delegates in the state operated only in the central growing regions. Nothing came of the union's effort to revive organizing in California. Rarely did job news appear in the Wobbly press or in AWIU bulletins from that state in 1921, which indicates that few AWIU members there were doing more than working and maintaining a low profile. Whatever members there were in California, they did not send a delegate to the October AWIU convention.[44]

The Limits of Resurgence

In August, harvest Wobblies began to elect their delegate representatives to the October AWIU convention. With the majority of AWIU members in the northern plains and Pacific Northwest at that time, all of the convention delegates came from North Dakota, Nebraska, or Washington. If the industrial union had hoped to keep most of its members on the job site rather than traveling to a mass convention, they got their wish, because only eleven delegates from these states attended this first annual delegate convention of the AWIU. The delegates, who claimed to represent twenty-five thousand AWIU members, made some notable decisions, though it was unlikely that they actually represented much of the membership. With the substantial funds that the AWIU headquarters possessed, the delegates allocated money for the legal defense of imprisoned members, foreign-language Wobbly newspapers, the Wobbly press in general, famine relief in Soviet Russia, and the Education Department and educational programs for AWIU members. But most important, the delegates worked out some basic strategic policies for harvest Wobblies to adhere to when on a job site. For example, they agreed that wages should be less of an issue for workers than lodging and shorter hours. The delegates wanted harvest Wobblies to enforce a ten-hour day, as they understood that wages fluctuated with farm prices and region, and they also knew that shorter hours meant that more workers could be employed. As to living conditions, the delegates determined that harvest Wobblies should force employers at threshing sites to do away "with the present poorly ventilated, vermin-infested bunk cars" and "build sanitary bunk houses with sanitary beds." Furthermore, they wanted AWIU harvest workers to end the practice of carrying one's bedding from one harvest work site to another. They argued that harvest workers, who far outnumbered threshing workers, should at least be able to count on a clean blanket when sleeping in a farmer's barn.[45]

Even though few harvest Wobblies attended the convention, the AWIU had high hopes of implementing these policies with the harvest drives of 1922 and 1923. While revolutionary goals remained a rhetorical part of the AWIU message, pragmatic organizational goals proved to be the key to harvest Wobbly success over the course of the early 1920s.

During 1922 and 1923, Wobblies tried to move the AWIU membership to seek out and organize families of harvesters. Making harvesters aware of the plight of harvest families was one means of achieving this. For example, a steady stream of articles in both the *Industrial Worker* and

Solidarity reported on the plight of migrant farm families, especially the exploitation of children. The sugar beet harvests from Michigan to Colorado fell under the scrutiny of Wobbly writers. Using state and federal reports and their own investigations, Wobbly writers reported on the health problems and lack of educational opportunities for children of farm families whose poverty forced them to work the sugar beet harvests. For Wobblies, the growing presence of harvest family labor was a logical consequence of the industrialization of American agriculture. Labor was only a commodity to farmers, reasoned Wobblies, especially those engaged in large-scale agricultural operations such as the sugar beet industry.[46]

Yet despite these calls to extend organizing efforts to new areas, the Great Plains wheat belt remained the area to which most harvest Wobblies flocked. This harvest still required thousands of migrant workers each year, and wages for farm work remained relatively stable. The IWW membership card still provided freight train transportation from large urban areas and adjacent rural areas. Moreover, by the early 1920s, harvest Wobblies had been working the wheat harvest for many years, and the work, travel, and regional culture were familiar to them.[47] Perhaps equally significant were the AWIU roots in the region. By 1923, harvest Wobblies could boast of AWIU branches in such cities as Sioux City, Minneapolis, Omaha, and Fargo, each having had a harvest Wobbly presence for almost ten years. Even cities that did not have official branches, such as Kansas City, Missouri, and Enid, Oklahoma, had a continuous Wobbly presence for the same period in the form of stationary delegates or resident Wobblies. These cities were jumping-off points for harvest workers in the Great Plains or prairie states, giving the Wobblies a crack at organizing thousands of migrant workers in the wheat, corn, and potato harvests of the West every year.[48]

Only through a consistently maintained organizational structure with a committed cadre of job delegates could the AWIU continue to survive in the still hostile anti-union environment that typified American agriculture. One measure adopted at the spring 1923 AWIU convention to make becoming a job delegate more attractive to AWIU members was to increase the commission paid for each new initiation made in the field to one dollar. This cash incentive inspired hundreds of harvest Wobblies to take out credentials. Another inducement for members to become job delegates that was ratified during the spring convention was to offer the delegate who secured the most subscriptions to IWW publications tuition for a three-month-long course at the Work People's College. To protect job delegates and AWIU members in general from criminal syndicalism prosecution, the fall AWIU convention participants adopted a "pledge against violence" that all prospective members of the industrial union had to sign before becoming members. The anti-violence pledge proscribed destruction of property as well as harming individuals as a means of achieving Wobbly goals. In most respects, the resolution was a reiteration of the IWW postwar stance on violence. But it exemplified the industrial union's effort to promote pragmatic organizing and to steer clear of revolutionary acts that clearly did not bring the union any success.[49]

Nevertheless, conflict, violence, and arrests haunted the lives of harvest Wobblies on the Great Plains and in other agricultural sectors that they frequented. Whether in Enid, Oklahoma, or Yakima, Washington, law enforcement officials continued to arrest Wobblies simply for being members of the IWW. If a worker had little or no Wobbly support in a community, he would have to serve his sentence like the job delegate Frank La Vera, who was arrested in Yakima in May 1923 while "selling I.W.W. buttons and literature." He had to serve an eighty-day sentence. Wobblies who were struggling to raise the wheat-shocking wage to $6.00 a day in Enid had a different experience. In June 1922, county sheriff deputies arrested fifty-six Wobblies outside of town after a raid on their jungle camp. Prosecutors charged them with vagrancy. The men appeared in court with AWIU attorneys from Chicago and one hundred fellow Wobblies in the courtroom to witness the proceedings. The court quickly dropped all charges against the men. The large number of Wobblies in the courtroom, their determined defense team, and the substantial number of harvest Wobblies in the area's agricultural workforce probably motivated the judge to throw out the case to avoid an AWIU harvest strike call.[50]

Harvest Wobblies also took steps to rid the migrant worker's life of the hi-jack, although they could pay with their lives for this effort. Paul Bednarcek, a World War I veteran and IWW member in good standing, was shot to death by a hi-jack during an effort to purge the man and his gang from a jungle camp in the southern plains in spring 1922. But most of the violence that harvest Wobblies faced originated at the hands of law enforcement and vigilante groups. In the northeast corner of North Dakota, near Aberdeen, harvest Wobblies and independent harvesters worked the area's wheat fields and caught the many freight trains that frequented this railroad junction site. In August 1922, Aberdeen police arrested Harry Arthur, an IWW member, and held him in jail without charge. Two days later, plainclothes policemen released Arthur and drove him to a remote location where they beat him severely before leaving him outside of town. The Ku Klux Klan was a threat as well. In Oklahoma, Klansmen attacked and beat AWIU members on several occasions. Klan members took it upon themselves to rid the region of union organizers, by which they meant IWW members.[51]

But by and large during the early 1920s, harvest Wobblies more often faced arrest than physical violence. Vagrancy charges were still the primary means by which local law enforcement, business interests, and farmers tried to suppress AWIU organizing. In Kansas, the vagrancy law held a maximum twelve-month sentence. The most serious charge that Wobblies faced as union members or organizers during the early 1920s continued to be criminal syndicalism. In some instances, law enforcement officials held workers on a vagrancy charge while prosecutors tried to determine whether they could make a successful criminal syndicalism case. When IWW workers faced trial on the charge of criminal syndicalism, the union's legal defense committee went into action and attorneys for the defense were usually available. Long and expensive trials were probably the reason that most criminal syndicalism cases never made it to court.[52]

In Oklahoma, the law had not been used as often as in other states. According to Negal Sellars in *Oil, Wheat & Wobblies*, many Oklahoma farmers had socialist and populist sympathies. Yet when Klan membership dramatically increased in 1922 and 1923, the judicial system, just like other institutions in the state, experienced a wave of Klan infiltration. Consequently, the judicial system sought to prosecute Wobblies, especially those in the oil industry, with renewed vigor. In Kansas, a criminal syndicalism law continued to be used against Wobblies until the mid-1920s.[53]

In the Far West, criminal syndicalism legislation continued to thwart Wobbly activity, particularly in California. Renewed activity of harvest Wobblies in Washington's Palouse country inaugurated a new series of criminal syndicalism cases, although very few led to trials, let alone convictions. In California, renewed Wobbly involvement in the construction, marine transportation, and agricultural industries led to an increase in arrests that precipitated a boycott of all California products and helped to generate a general strike call to release all political prisoners in the United States.[54]

At the IWW's fourteenth convention in fall 1922, the delegates passed a resolution authorizing a general strike to free all "class-war prisoners." This included Wobblies in prison for violation of the Espionage and Sedition Acts, as well as for those convicted of criminal syndicalism in California and elsewhere. Over the next several months, the *Industrial*

Worker explained to its readers how to strike both on and off the job. The general strike was planned for late April 1923. Although the IWW had returned from the brink of collapse by 1923 with substantial industrial union organization in construction, logging, marine transportation, and agriculture, the union as a whole was in no position to close down any industries in the United States. Most of the strike actions took place in the Far West, with the notable exception of the Marine Transport Workers of New Orleans. The Marine Transport Workers in California successfully tied up shipping in San Pedro and San Francisco. IWW lumber workers in the Northwest also struck. The union claimed that fifteen thousand out of a workforce of forty thousand had honored the strike call. In each of these cases, the strikers called for the release of federal political prisoners or state criminal syndicalism prisoners, and for improvements in local wage and working conditions. The general strike lasted only a matter of days, though, and then devolved into piecemeal and intermittent actions.[55] At the AWIU's May 1923 convention, participants resolved to renew the general strike after it had collapsed in the Far West. But in the end, a general strike and intermittent strike actions were left up to the General Organization Committee in conjunction with individual AWIU branches and groups of harvest Wobblies in the field.[56]

No strikes in agriculture took place until mid-summer, when harvest Wobblies assembled for union meetings in Fargo, North Dakota; Sioux City, Iowa; Groton, South Dakota, and elsewhere to plan. North Dakota farmers and business interests, as well as the U.S. Department of Agriculture and Department of Justice, grew concerned over the impact a strike would have in a state that relied so heavily on migrant farm labor, especially migrant labor organized by the AWIU. But the poor crop of 1923 motivated the AWIU in North Dakota and eastern Montana to refrain from calling a strike. Other strike actions in the Great Plains wheat belt were merely brief labor stoppages calling for the release of political prisoners and improvements in wages and working conditions for harvesters. Only in the Palouse country of Washington did harvest Wobblies working the wheat crop pull off a substantial and sustained strike.[57]

In Washington, Wobblies continued to maintain a strong presence in the lumber and marine-transport industries. Wobbly loggers in the Northwest overall still numbered in the hundreds, if not thousands. Harvest Wobblies, with support from the Lumber Workers Industrial Union of the IWW, tried to resurrect organizing efforts in the state's central and southeastern agricultural regions. They continued to work in the grain and fruit harvests of the state as they had for many years, and by 1923 had reestablished an AWIU branch in Spokane. In 1922 and 1923, Wobblies numbered several hundred during the peak of the fruit-picking season in the Wenatchee and Yakima Valleys. During these years, AWIU job delegates, both traveling and stationary, sought to sign up new members, and had some luck in doing so. However, it was the bumper Palouse wheat crop of 1923 and an accompanying heavy influx of migrant farm labor that inspired harvest Wobblies and their job delegates to flock to Whitman County. Here they launched their last major strike action.[58]

Surprisingly, California was the scene of the most prolonged and determined IWW strike actions throughout the year. Though the union had few members at work in agriculture, it continued to have several thousand members in other industries. In fact, before the general strike in April collapsed, the IWW's Oakland Joint Branch called for a boycott of the California film industry and of the state's canned fruit and other agricultural products. The boycott was taken up by the AWIU and other industrial unions of the IWW, and lasted for several years. Release of federal and state prisoners and an end to prosecution of IWW members in the state were the primary goals of the boycott. The AWIU in California tried to instigate strikes in harvest work by passing a resolution at their conference in Stockton in September, but the ten members who attended symbolized the weakness of the AWIU in the state. In comparison to the thousands of California Wobblies in construction, logging, and, most important, marine transportation, California harvest Wobblies were not numerous enough to carry out strike actions. However, the power of IWW members in these other industries motivated California law enforcement officials to arrest hundreds of Wobblies throughout the state in 1922 and 1923, and to convict dozens of criminal syndicalism, for which they faced years of imprisonment.[59]

Therefore, despite President Calvin Coolidge's decision to release all remaining IWW federal prisoners on 15 December 1923, the IWW still had many members in California's state prison system serving sentences for criminal syndicalism convictions and others awaiting trial on similar charges. The IWW sought to challenge the legitimacy of the state's anti-Wobbly legislation through legal means. Yet it also tried to maintain its activism through strikes, boycotts, and continued organizing activity. In one last effort, California AWIU members joined Wobblies in marine transportation, logging, and construction in a statewide effort to organize their respective industries into the IWW. AWIU members embarked on an ambitious organizing drive in the San Joaquin Valley and the orange belt in Southern California. Harvest Wobblies opened new AWIU branch offices and established a series of stationary delegates to begin a farm-worker membership drive that would again make the IWW a factor in California agriculture.[60]

With the close of 1923, the AWIU had firmly established itself in the Great Plains and had created a vibrant organizational structure that seemed capable of growing and developing among many of the West's agricultural laborers. Harvest Wobblies proved that they could survive federal repression and endure continued state prosecutions. The red IWW membership card was a ticket for freight-train travel throughout much of the West. Harvest Wobblies had control over many jungle camps, and they demonstrated their ability to force up wages in the agricultural areas where they congregated. The organizational structure of the AWIU made it possible for harvest Wobblies to communicate over great distances and to coordinate strike actions. Moreover, harvest Wobblies appeared to have finally created a successful rank-and-file industrial union of harvest hands.

Accompanying the organizational structure of the industrial union was an educational focus that demonstrated harvest Wobbly commitment to worker self-emancipation. An educated, class-conscious workforce had been always a primary goal of the IWW. The working-class intellectuals of the AWIU took great strides in achieving that goal by offering their unique brand of worklife culture, organization, and theory to agricultural workers. The large volume of literature that the AWIU produced demonstrated an understanding of the necessity to organize all farm workers. Yet it maintained a disproportionate appeal to single white male migrant workers in its educational and organizational efforts. Nevertheless, for harvest Wobblies, particularly in the Great Plains, the year 1924 looked very promising.

Chapter Seven

The Road to Oblivion

⌘ ⌘ ⌘

Contrary to what many historians have argued, particularly labor historians, the IWW was not in a state of wholesale decline during the early 1920s. Melvyn Dubofsky, Patrick Renshaw, Robert L. Tyler, and others have contended that after 1919, the IWW was primarily concerned with education, propaganda, publishing, and legal defense rather than with organizing. It is true that the union was not as dynamic or vibrant as it was in 1916 and 1917, and that it struggled to maintain itself between late 1917 and 1920 as it weathered federal and state repression. Furthermore, during the early 1920s the union had serious financial problems and a variety of internal disputes. Nevertheless, by 1921 the union was growing in membership again and engaged in a number of organizing drives in agriculture, construction, marine transportation, and logging. The early 1920s was a period of resurgence for the union, albeit a brief one. Scholars such as Nigel Sellars, Peter Cole, and John Gambs support this interpretation of the IWW in their work. A split in union ranks in 1924 eventually led to its general decline, as the IWW's in-house historian Fred Thompson and the sociologist Leland W. Robinson maintain. From this point on, the IWW would never recover from its organizational crisis.[1]

Harvest Wobblies and the IWW's Organizational Crisis

Though the issues that led to the split in 1924 are complex, it is important to investigate them because of the prominent role that the AWIU played in the IWW at the time and its role in the actual split. As of 1924, the AWIU provided half of the IWW's treasury and perhaps as much as one-third of overall Wobbly membership; the AWIU also contributed more than most of the IWW's other industrial unions towards paying off the bond debt that the IWW incurred when several of its most prominent leaders, among them Bill Haywood, jumped bail and left the country to avoid long prison terms. In addition, AWIU men rose to high elective office in the IWW. In 1924, Tom Doyle, a long-term member of the AWIU and former AWIU secretary-treasurer, served as the secretary-treasurer of the IWW. Joe Fisher, another AWIU member and veteran harvest

Wobbly organizer, served as the IWW's general organizer. These were the most powerful elected administrative positions within the union.[2]

The power of the AWIU within the larger organization was one of the most important reasons for the split in which a segment of the IWW broke away and set up its own version of the IWW. The AWIU represented the substantial faction that argued for the One Big Union structure of the prewar period. This concept stressed a strong, centralized organizational structure in which the IWW coordinated the actions of constituent industrial unions. Some of the industrial union rank and file, such as the powerful Lumber Workers Industrial Union (LWIU) No. 120, under the leadership of James Rowan, favored a more decentralized structure for the IWW, giving greater autonomy to industrial unions, their locals, and leaders. Also, critics of the AWIU held it responsible for emphasizing the organization of migrant workers over homeguard workers. The result of this focus, according to these critics, was to alienate potential members of the homeguard, the non-migratory and family-oriented workers, from the union. Though decentralizers and other critics of the AWIU did not always join forces, they did share concerns over the influence of the AWIU on the future of the IWW.[3]

The centralization-versus-decentralization issue, however, was a complicated one, as is exemplified by a conflict involving the Philadelphia branch of the Marine Transport Workers (MTW) of the IWW. The very successful Philadelphia branch, which had several thousand members, many of whom were African Americans, assessed a $15, and eventually a $25, initiation fee to join. Ironically, the very men who feared the influence of the AWIU and the One Big Union concept challenged the MTW's right to charge such a high initiation fee. The AWIU advocated a sliding scale that allowed each industrial union the freedom to impose an initiation fee—with some limits—that its members voted to impose on new members. AWIU delegates at their fall 1923 convention reasoned that the MTW workers had a unique problem that other Wobbly locals did not face. They needed to fund union halls in as many large port towns as possible, which required expenses that few other IWW union halls required. As the IWW traditionally and constitutionally advocated a small initiation fee in order to appeal to the unskilled and semiskilled worker, James Rowan and other members of the LWIU advocated expelling the Philadelphia branch because of its high initiation fee. Tom Doyle and Joe Fisher supported the Philadelphia branch's decision to have a high initiation fee if that is what its members had decided. This supports Dubofsky's observation in *We Shall Be All* that the decentralization-versus-centralization debate was more a matter of organizational tactics and administrative policies than a power struggle between IWW headquarters and industrial union leadership.[4]

Another issue that divided IWW members was the presence of communists in the union. From 1920 to 1922, communists, both inside the IWW and outside, tried to move the union to affiliate with the Third International, or Comintern, short for Communist International. According to Russian, American, and Wobbly communists, the IWW needed to be a part of the revolutionary current that was sweeping across Europe and, soon, the world. For most Wobblies, however, leadership by an elite vanguard party of communists and a focus on state control of society ran counter to their commitment to rank-and-file industrial unionism and to their libertarian socialist sensibility. Though Wobblies were sympathetic to the Russian Revolution and the new Soviet state, they rejected affiliation with the Third International by a referendum vote in December 1920. The membership also rejected affiliation with the Red International of Labor Unions (RILU) at the union's annual convention in 1922. Most Wobblies, along with most European syndicalists, viewed the RILU as a communist front organization bent on breaking the independence of militant leftist unions. The contentious debates that surrounded the issue of communist affiliation left a residue of deep divisions within the union.[5]

Still other contentious issues led up to the split. Individual clemency was one of them. Individual clemency meant that individual Wobblies could gain early release from federal prison if they agreed to abide by federally mandated restrictions after their release. In the minds of some members, this option flew in the face of worker solidarity. Other concerns included the lack of revolutionary rhetoric in the IWW press, the ownership of private property by the union, the spending habits of the union's headquarters, whether to organize migrant workers or homeguard workers, personal animosities, and the lack of freedom of expression in the IWW press. Not all of these matters neatly divided AWIU members and LWIU members into opposing camps. Eventually, in late summer 1924, AWIU and LWIU members on the General Executive Board (GEB) of the IWW divided into two factions over some of these issues, and each faction drew allegiance from other industrial unions represented on the GEB. The dissenting group, led by Rowan and Mick Radock, a GEB member and a leader of an anti-communist movement within the IWW, challenged the administrative actions of Doyle and Fisher and their supporters. Rowan and Radock accused Doyle and Fisher of violating the IWW constitution over a number of matters, including the Philadelphia MTW situation, plans to buy a building for IWW headquarters, and failure to expel members who sought individual clemency from federal prison sentences.[6]

The dispute came to a head in late summer when the Rowan-Radock faction and the Doyle-Fisher faction, meeting in different rooms of the IWW headquarters, expelled each other from the union. Each group sought to establish itself as the official representatives of the IWW. The Rowan-Radock faction went so far as to draw up an Emergency Program that called for the abolition of the GEB and for a redirection of most administrative power to each industrial union of the IWW. The Emergency Program would eliminate any oversight of the Wobbly press by the GEB and basically end the One Big Union structure, establishing a federation of independent revolutionary industrial unions that would certainly not own any private property such as a building for their headquarters. Furthermore, the Rowan-Radock faction called on the IWW membership at large to repudiate the actions of the AWIU dominated 1923 IWW general convention. The Doyle-Fisher group, for its part, physically evicted the Rowan-Radock wing from union headquarters with the help of a contingent of Chicago Wobblies.[7]

Had the Rowan-Radock faction simply appealed to the IWW membership at large for support at the upcoming fall IWW general convention in Chicago, it probably would have met with great success. The Doyle-Fisher faction was certainly out of line in expelling the Rowan-Radock group from union headquarters, but more important, during their term in office Doyle and Fisher had acted on their own without union sanction in a number of instances. Also, the IWW's general treasury was almost empty, a problem for which Doyle and Fisher shared some blame. Unfortunately for Rowan and Radock, they made a serious tactical error. They sought a court injunction to remove the Doyle-Fisher faction from union headquarters, which a district court judge granted, putting IWW union headquarters under lock and key. This "bourgeois" behavior of appealing to a "capitalist" legal system by a self-proclaimed revolutionary wing of the IWW significantly reduced any support that it would have received from the IWW membership.[8]

To further complicate matters, the two factions presented the October 1924 IWW general convention delegates with two convention sites in Chicago. When the vast majority of IWW delegates ignored the two groups, Doyle, Fisher, and their supporters immediately submitted to the democratic authority of the general convention. On the other hand, Rowan, Radock, and their supporters clung to their own convention site. The majority of delegates called on Doyle, Fisher, Rowan, Radock, and each group's administrative supporters to plead their case before the convention. All of the Doyle-Fisher faction complied, but only one member of the rival group did so. The delegates decided to remove them from office for their transgressions, but not to expel them from the union. Convention participants then voted to expel Rowan, Radock, and the others who had failed to appear. In addition, the 1924 convention delegates ejected several locals of four industrial unions that supported the Rowan-Radock faction.[9]

Rowan and his group, known as the EPers for the Emergency Program, set up a rival IWW in the Pacific Northwest, made up mostly of LWIU members, though the majority of that industrial union did not join. Despite the fact that they had a headquarters in Portland, Oregon, and their own newspaper, the *Industrial Unionist*, the EPers failed to persuade many IWW members to come over to their organization. The newspaper folded in 1926 for lack of support. In a matter of several years, the EPers shrank to a few hundred members, and by the early 1930s disappeared as an organization.[10]

Why a Collapse in the Wake of the Split?

Fallout from the split had serious consequences for the IWW. A small number of Wobblies sided with the EPers, but a larger number stayed loyal to the original IWW. According to Fred Thompson, a Wobbly at the time and subsequent historian for the union, "most members dropped out the middle." He estimated that perhaps seven to eight thousand members left the union immediately after the split. Robinson's study of the IWW during its declining years suggests that the 1924 split had a disillusioning effect on active members. His study reveals that the most talented organizers, leaders, writers, and other activists of the union remained loyal members, but over the next several years, the split caused many of them to become inactive and eventually to leave the union. The main problem was that the issues that led to the split remained unresolved and the opposing sides on most of these matters were still in the original IWW. Therefore, many of these conflicts continued to haunt the union for the rest of the decade, making it an unattractive organization to join, as it could not resolve its own financial and organizational problems. Reflecting the misfortunes of the IWW, membership went into steep decline after 1924. Robinson estimates that the union's average dues-paying membership went from a high of thirty-five thousand in 1923 to approximately seventeen thousand in 1925. In 1926, the union's average dues-paying membership was a little over seven thousand. The union would never rise above ten thousand dues-paying members again. In fact, after 1930, it would not even rise above three thousand members in good standing, that is, Wobblies who did not let their dues payments fall into arrears.[11]

The near-disintegration of the IWW after 1924 stemmed from more than internal wrangling over union policies, organizational problems, and financial difficulties. Even the general decline of unionization and the intolerance for radicalism that typified the 1920s that historian Irving Bernstein examines in *The Lean Years* does not adequately explain why the IWW essentially collapsed by the end of the decade. The core of the IWW's problems lay in the failure of its constituent industrial unions to organize large numbers of workers. For a variety of reasons, Wobblies could not persuade non-union workers or workers belonging to trade unions to accept the IWW's vision of a new society within the shell of the old. The collapse of the AWIU, one of the IWW's most successful industrial unions, provides some insight into this failure.

Most AWIU members did not support the Emergency Program nor did they join the EPers' alternative IWW. EPers could not convince harvest Wobblies to give up on the organization that had served them so well in recent years. The AWIU maintained a strong position in the IWW, and harvest Wobblies found no compelling reasons to abandon it. In addition, the men under attack by the EPers were former AWIU men. Harvest Wobblies who chose to support the Emergency Program, such as those in California, went on record at a special Sacramento conference allying themselves with the Northwest EPers in April 1925. Participants at the AWIU's spring 1925 conference in Omaha, on the other hand, expelled harvest Wobbly supporters of the EPers, went on record supporting the original IWW, and repudiated the Emergency Program. Although there was some concern that a number of "fraudulent" job delegates would confuse that summer's harvest drive by signing up new members with the Emergency Program Wobblies, such a problem did not occur.[12]

Despite the serious ramifications of the split, the AWIU needed to prepare for the harvest of 1925. The drive ended up being very similar to that of 1924. During each, AWIU bulletins and editorials and reports in *Industrial Worker* and *Industrial Solidarity* urged harvest Wobblies and their job delegates to begin the harvest drive in the southern plains, move on to the northern plains, and move from there to the prairies of Canada or to the Far West states of Washington and California for more wheat or fruit harvesting. In fact, the Wobbly press exhorted their harvest workers, especially job delegates, to work in agriculture year round in order to bring the AWIU to all wage-working farm laborers. Wobbly writers made sure to explain to their readers the nature of farm worker exploitation and the need for harvest Wobblies and to urge their job delegates to get into the struggle for better wages and working conditions by organizing the unorganized. This effort included the Wobbly press's focus on the lives of women and child farm workers along with its usual stories about the plight of the migrant male worker. Also as in previous harvest drives, job delegates brought the *Industrial Worker, Solidarity*, and other AWIU and IWW literature with them to distribute to independent harvest workers.[13]

The Wobbly harvest drives of the Great Plains met with mild success. For the 1924 harvest-organizing cycle that ran from October 1923 to September 1924, the AWIU initiated almost ten thousand new members. This figure was down from the preceding harvest drive that netted over fifteen thousand new initiates. Part of the reason that the AWIU did not make as good a showing might have been the unusually long harvest season in late summer 1924. Northern Great Plains farmers had the opportunity to shock much of their own crop, thereby reducing the need for laborers. The 1925 harvest-drive cycle netted only 8,500 new initiations. The 1925 wheat crop in the southern plains, especially in Kansas, was a poor one, and farmers did not need as many workers. Still, such a modest membership gain was not cause for great alarm for the AWIU, given the precarious nature of the industry.[14]

In California, the harvest drive was a bust. The promise of a revived AWIU in California never materialized. Despite a number of stationary delegates and an AWIU branch, the union there could not solve its organization problems nor protect its members from arrest for criminal syndicalism violations, which diminished enthusiasm for working in the state. For example, police arrested Fred Thompson in spring 1923 in Marysville for selling IWW literature and for being a member of the union. His conviction landed him in a California prison with over a hundred other Wobblies. He spent the next four years there.

Repression was not the defining reason for the decline of the AWIU in California. The failure of the industrial union was due to its inability to organize Hispanic and family harvesters. Harvest Wobblies could not or would not break free of their own worklife culture to articulate a meaningful message to these workers. Ironically, the IWW met with some success in organizing Hispanic day laborers and construction workers in California as early as 1910, and Hispanics in the marine transportation industry in the early 1920s. In these cases, IWW organizers were homeguard workers, just like those they were organizing, and showed a willingness to provide a union hall environment and social gatherings amenable to both Hispanic and white families. Harvest Wobblies, with their stubborn adherence to a migrant worklife culture, could not bridge the cultural gap between themselves and those they needed to organize to remain viable as an agricultural industrial union. Moreover, the 1924 split severely destabilized all recruitment efforts in the state, and the IWW slowly disintegrated in California in the second half of the 1920s and over the course of the next decade. In regard to AWIU organizing in California, the AWIU 1924 fall convention participants recommended that "the G.O.C. [General Organization Committee] man in California function there during the winter months and spring months, and then proceed to Washington for the harvest, as there is very little to be accomplished in the agricultural industry of California during the summer, as all the members leave the state during that period."

Even though the AWIU appeared unable to generate enthusiasm for organizing in California, it continued to fund efforts there in the hope that something good would come from an AWIU branch in the state. Harvest Wobblies would maintain a presence in the state for years, but without serious organizational gains.[15]

In Washington, on the other hand, the organizational work of harvest Wobblies in 1922 and 1923 did bear some fruit. The AWIU secured an office branch in Spokane and established several stationary delegates in the state. Spokane even hosted a Northwest Agricultural Workers' Industrial Union conference in spring 1924 and the annual AWIU convention in fall 1926. But organizing workers in the wheat country or in the fruit-growing valleys proved as difficult as ever for harvest Wobblies. By the middle 1920s, there is no evidence of Wobbly organizing in the state's wheat fields. Some harvest Wobblies still shocked and threshed eastern Washington's wheat harvest, especially that of the Palouse, but the AWIU's presence was minimal in the region.[16]

In the Wenatchee and Yakima Valleys, the union's fortunes were not much different. The AWIU's problem there sheds light on the difficulty of recruiting new members in the Palouse. By one AWIU member's own estimate, the Wenatchee Valley required four thousand migrant workers to harvest its fruit crop. This member, who identified himself only by his job delegate number, AG-1351, pointed out that three thousand of these migrant workers arrived in their own cars. It is reasonable to assume that in the nearby wheat country a considerable number of harvest workers had traveled there by tin lizzie as well. U.S. government studies of the region during the mid-1920s corroborated AG-1351's observations concerning the fruit country's migrant labor workforce. In fact, in the

Wenatchee Valley, migrants performed seventy-five percent of the packing and ninety percent of the picking. Those who arrived by car or truck and lived in camps established by employers were overwhelmingly families of harvesters, with women being a substantial part of this workforce. In fact, some single women arrived for the harvest and packing season and resided in dormitories provided by employers. Most of these transient workers still had to pitch a tent wherever they could find space in the valley.

These fruit workers of the Northwest did not live in traditional jungle camps like the bulk of AWIU membership, or use freight trains for transportation. Most were not transient laborers by trade, but men and women, some bringing their children, who worked the summer harvest to supplement their annual income. Upon completion of the harvest they returned to their hometowns and to their primary trade. The industrial union message and revolutionary goals of the harvest Wobbly did not appeal to them. Those Wobblies who attempted to organize these workers met with complete rejection. But the union's failure started at the cultural divide. For example, wholesale arrests of harvest Wobblies on vagrancy charges continued to be commonplace. The jailing of a family of farm workers was highly unlikely, as many of them secured, or at least tried to secure, employment through state or independent agencies. Because of their different relationships with employers and law enforcement, along with lifestyle differences, families of harvesters and harvest Wobblies did not share some significant experiences. In one instance in summer 1926, fifty to sixty Wobblies attempted to orchestrate a strike among Wenatchee's apple packers. None of the workers that they sought to organize lived at the all-male jungle camp. There is no evidence that any of the apple packers, many of them women, supported the harvest Wobbly-led strike call. Wenatchee police arrested all of the harvest Wobblies at their jungle camp. Those who refused to work were convicted of vagrancy. Others, because of their impoverished situation, accepted the going wage, and the rest were forced to buy train tickets taking them out of town.[17]

Canadian Harvest Wobblies

The only bright spot for the AWIU in the mid-1920s was the industrial union's organizational work and increase in membership among Canadian harvest workers, a cohort very similar to the Great Plains harvester. The success of AWIU work in Canada culminated in the first-ever AWIU conference outside of the United States. In late November

1925, Canadian AWIU members met in Calgary, Alberta, to establish a strategy for the next year's harvest. The one hundred harvest Wobblies present resolved to break the Canadian prairie wheat harvest and threshing season into two districts, with traveling delegates, stationary delegates, and a centrally located General Organization Committee (GOC) person to disseminate job news and other information necessary to coordinate a harvest drive. That same year, the AWIU had a job branch or stationary delegate in Calgary and Edmonton, Alberta; Moose Jaw and Saskatoon, Saskatchewan; and Winnipeg, Manitoba.[18]

The IWW was in Canada before the war, with most of its members working in the extractive industries of logging, mining, and wheat harvesting in the western provinces. In 1911, the union could claim 47,183 members in Canada. Once Canada became embroiled in the European conflict, however, law enforcement officials moved to suppress the radical, antiwar IWW. By 1918, it was illegal in Canada to be a member of the union, though this ban was lifted in 1925. Regardless of their legal status, IWW members continued to organize in the country, and harvest workers from the United States continued to cross the border into the Canadian prairies, as they had done before the war. In fact, a floating workforce in the thousands regularly crossed back and forth across the border from sometime in the 1870s to the 1920s, with most of these workers laboring in the extractive and construction industries of the American and Canadian West. From 1921 to 1926, the IWW did well in the Dominion, particularly with AWIU activity in the prairie provinces of Alberta, Saskatchewan, and Manitoba. As in wheat belt organizing in the U.S., the 1924 split did not immediately affect unionization efforts in Canada by the AWIU.[19]

Like wheat farmers in the Great Plains, Canadian prairie farmers needed thousands of harvest and threshing workers in the summer months to harvest and process their crops. Cecilia Danysk, in her study of Canadian prairie agriculture, *Hired Hands*, argues that the agricultural ladder of central Canada broke down after World War I. It became increasingly difficult for farmhands to serve as apprentices, save their wages, and purchase their own farms after 1918. According to Danysk, Canadian farm help became proletarianized during this period. In fact, it appears that what took place in the American West's grain belt well before World War I occurred in Canada after the war. The socioeconomic consequences of this change gave the AWIU a large pool of dissatisfied itinerant workers to organize.[20]

And organize they did. In 1923, business was brisk for the AWIU, with Canadian and American job delegates signing up more members with each passing year. By 1925, the team of Sam Scarlett and John A. MacDonald led the organizing effort out of an expanding AWIU branch in Calgary. Scarlett, a veteran of the Chicago trial and years in federal prison, was a tireless orator for the AWIU, appearing in town halls and theaters in the villages and cities of central and western Canada. The enthusiasm he generated helped to create a new AWIU hall in Winnipeg. MacDonald wrote a series of articles in the *Industrial Worker* and *Solidarity* on the organizing work of Canadian and American AWIU job delegates in the country. He was instrumental in probing the problems that harvest Wobblies and their job delegates faced on the plains and prairies. In addition, he tried to educate his readers on the development of agriculture within a global capitalist system, serving as a propagandist for the industrial union's work in Canada. MacDonald, as a GOC member of the AWIU and special Canadian harvest organizer, was not interested in revolutionary rhetoric but only in the job of union organizing.[21]

The AWIU, however, experienced some problems in organizing migrant and seasonal farm labor in Canada that it did not face in the United States. Wobblies traditionally organized harvest workers on the rails, in the jungles, and on the job. But in Canada, agricultural laborers did not hop freight trains to the same degree that harvest workers did in the states, nor did they have the same tradition of living in jungles between harvest and threshing jobs. Provincial governments subsidized travel costs, and Canadian railroad companies offered reduced rates to harvest workers. Most workers who left the Canadian cities of the East for the West's prairie jobs rode trains as paid passengers. In Canada, the red membership card was not required as a train ticket to the harvest, making it impossible for groups of Wobblies on trains to prevent independent harvest workers from traveling to job sites.[22]

Also, there was not the same tradition of workers living in jungle camps between jobs because the Canadian government played a considerable role in recruiting and distributing needed harvest labor directly to farmers. Canadian farm laborers did not have to roam the countryside in a hit-and-miss search for work as they did in the United States; provincial farm labor hiring halls were a common feature. Here a worker could hire out to a local farm, or an employer could find workers by visiting the hall. The U.S. agencies that had hiring halls or information bureaus at different times in the 1910s and 1920s lacked the organization, efficiency, and continuity of the Canadian system. Canadian government officials and railroad companies even went as far as to recruit agricultural laborers in Europe, especially the British Isles, for work on the prairies. Canadian railroad company agents participated in the enterprise by offering reduced fares to these workers even before they left Europe. According to Danysk, this coordinated recruitment campaign resulted in a flood of cheap, docile, foreign labor into the region. Thus, AWIU job delegates found another important element of their organizational strategy thwarted by the different agricultural labor system to the north.[23]

Canadian harvest workers did resist long hours and poor pay by "job hopping," that is, leaving a job that a worker did not like for another with better pay or conditions. This strategy did not work for foreign labor because much of it was contracted, and the penalties for breaking labor contracts could be as severe as deportation back to Europe. Canadian government officials and farmers also had other legal methods of forcing workers to work. The Masters and Servants Act made it illegal for a harvest worker to end his employment with a farmer without the farmer's permission. From the Wobbly perspective, this law made it illegal to strike for a higher wage. Therefore, harvest Wobblies found themselves with a serious problem when organizing on the job because their spontaneous strike technique could easily involve the Canadian Mounted Police, whose job it was to enforce the Masters and Servants Act.[24]

Wobblies in Canada found themselves under the close watch of Canadian law enforcement. As in the U.S., large numbers of job delegates and harvest Wobblies faced arrest on vagrancy charges and other "crimes" in a concerted attempt to suppress the union. In addition, under a broad interpretation of the nation's Immigration Act, American Wobblies could be arrested and deported for organizing workers. Most American Wobblies had to hide their union cards because of the diligent efforts of provincial police to bar members of the IWW from entering the country. Yet despite these obstacles, the AWIU managed to mount harvest drive campaigns in 1924 and 1925. Many Wobblies ended up being arrested, fined, jailed, deported, and in some instances beaten by enraged farmers and townspeople in summer and fall 1925. But the industrial union persisted. In some cases, organized workers reduced the normal twelve-hour Canadian agricultural workday to ten hours and raised the wages by a dollar. Nonetheless, in 1926 the AWIU collapsed on the prairies. Part of its demise in Canada was the result of government repression that closed many of the union's halls. Also, harvest Wobblies and their job delegates had a difficult time dealing with the Canadian agricultural labor system. Ultimately, though, the AWIU's fall in Canada was caused by the same factors that led to the industrial union's collapse in the United States.[25]

The Demise of the AWIU in the North American Wheat Belt

After years of organizing in the Great Plains, the AWIU continued to face efforts by farmers to set wages as low as they could. To insure low-wage labor, county agents under the auspices of the U.S. Department of Agriculture tried to persuade farmers to hire harvest labor through their offices. The AWIU in 1924 and 1925 could obstruct these efforts by controlling who could travel on freight trains that moved through the wheat belt, especially trains bound for the northern plains. Perhaps if railroad companies that instituted limited reduced rates during the early 1920s for harvest laborers had reduced them further, they would have attracted more riders. In the end, most migrant harvest workers still arrived by freight train to harvest work sites because they could not afford even the reduced rate. On these trains rode job delegates and hundreds of harvest Wobblies who had the power to persuade or force independent harvesters to join the AWIU. With strength in numbers they could then push for high wages from farmers and insist on a maximum ten-hour day.[26]

Public response to the IWW in the northern plains was as mixed as ever. At the opening of the fall 1924 AWIU convention in the wheat town of Kenmare, in northwest North Dakota near the Canadian border, the mayor of the city officially welcomed the one hundred seventeen harvest Wobblies in attendance. During his Sunday-morning speech, the mayor explicitly noted that the city's municipal officials, downtown business owners, and farmers were well aware of the importance that the migratory harvester played in Kenmare's prosperity, and that of North Dakota as a whole. The mayor concluded his speech with a donation of fifty dollars, on behalf of the town's business community, for the AWIU convention participants to use in any fashion that they desired. The Wobblies approved a special resolution thanking the mayor and the citizens of Kenmare, and put the money toward feeding the convention participants who were short on cash.[27]

But harvest Wobblies still could just as easily face mass arrest and mob actions. In mid-August 1925, railroad agents arrested twenty-two harvest Wobblies as they got off their freight train in Fargo, North Dakota, on charges of trespassing on railroad property. Yet the arrests did not stop there. Within a few days, police arrested nineteen more Wobblies after they circulated a petition calling for the release of their fellow workers. These nineteen faced vagrancy charges. Over the next several days, Fargo police, Cass County law enforcement, and a citizens' committee continued to arrest dozens of harvest Wobblies on vagrancy charges. By the end of the month over one hundred harvest Wobblies were in jail for vagrancy and trespassing, including the AWIU Fargo branch secretary and staff, which effectively shut down the industrial union's hall.[28]

While protesting their confinement and the "unsanitary conditions" of the jail, the men loudly sang Wobbly songs, refusing to accept individual release until the court released all members simultaneously. The sheriff's deputies' response to these protests was to turn fire hoses on the men. The county prosecutor wanted to hold three Wobblies for prosecution, but was willing to accept the county commissioner's decision that the rest of the prisoners be released. The harvest Wobbly response was to boycott Fargo, an action that had a serious impact on a business community that depended on agricultural-worker patronage during the harvest season.[29]

The judge in the case of the harvest Wobblies, Leigh J. Monson, along with Assistant State Attorney V. R. Lovell and Sheriff Ross, decided to drop the charges against the IWW men in Fargo. Unfortunately, that was not the end of the prisoners' ordeal. A mob of angry business owners, ex-servicemen wearing their Legionnaire buttons, sheriff's deputies, and other townspeople gathered on the night of 24 August in front of the county jail and waited for the deputies to release the men. As the harvest Wobblies exited the county jail, the heavily armed mob ordered them to head quickly out of Fargo across the city's bridge to the neighboring town of Moorehead, Minnesota. For extra emphasis, the mob attacked the Wobblies as they departed, creating a gauntlet of sorts that workers had to endure. The good citizens of Fargo beat the harvest workers unmercifully as they fled to Moorehead.[30]

The Wobblies' reception in Moorehead was in stark contrast to Fargo. Here the townspeople gave them sanctuary. The AWIU members immediately opened a new branch headquarters. City officials publicly announced that local citizens and law enforcement would not accost harvest Wobblies in any manner while they were in the town. The AWIU filed civil suits against officials in Fargo. But tempers in the North Dakota town quickly cooled, and Wobblies were able to reopen their industrial union hall. The harvest was moving north into Canada anyway, which meant that most Wobblies would go in that direction to try to break the anti-Wobbly "blockade" at the border. Many succeeded, allowing union workers to flood into the prairie wheat belt of the Dominion.[31]

If all AWIU members had needed to do was confront intermittent episodes of repression, periodic efforts by farmers and their supporters to fix wages, and frustrating internal union problems, the AWIU would

Year	New A.W.I.U. initiations
1919	7,920
1920	*
1921	11,674
1922	14,459
1923	15,217
1924	9,219
1925	8,507
1926	1,538
1927	783
1928	1,051
1929	639

Figure 23. This chart reveals the growing success of the AWIU in the early 1920s, though insufficient data exist for new members in 1920. However, the chart also reflects the dramatic drop in new members after 1925 and the lack of recovery. (Numbers are based on AWIU reports printed in *One Big Union Monthly* and in AWIU convention minutes.)

probably have continued to function in the Great Plains and the prairies of Canada for many more years. But serious changes in the worklife culture of Great Plains harvesters and substantial changes in wheat and other grain harvest and threshing technology dealt the fatal blow to the industrial union.

The most straightforward indicator of the union's decline was the inability of job delegates to sign up new members. The 1925 harvest drive, as noted earlier, only recruited a modest eighty-five hundred new members. The 1926 harvest drive that ran from October 1925 through September 1926 netted only fifteen hundred new members. The 1927 effort during the same series of months gained less than a thousand new members. These numbers would not improve to any great degree over the succeeding years (fig. 23).[32]

The most immediate reason for the decline in new recruits into the AWIU was the changes in the worklife culture of the workers that the industrial union depended on for its survival. In the second half of the 1920s, many migrant and seasonal wheat belt harvest workers turned from train travel to the secondhand automobile, know as "flivvers" or "tin lizzies." By 1926, the AWIU was fully aware of the problems that these workers posed for the industrial union's job delegates. For years, job delegates found migrant fruit workers, particularly in Washington, impervious to AWIU membership appeals. Soon the same would be true for harvest and threshing workers in the wheat belt. The fact that the automobile tramp of the wheat belt no longer needed a Wobbly red card for train travel removed a key means by which job delegates and harvest Wobblies could persuade or coerce new members into the union. Workers who traveled by car or truck to work sites tended to avoid jungle camps because they could drive directly to job sites and, with camping gear stowed in their vehicle, camp there. They did not have to wait in a jungle camp for the harvest in that location to begin. They could always journey elsewhere for work and return when the harvest or threshing operation was ready. These workers did not have to rely on farmers to seek them out at a jungle camp or a downtown street corner; they could find out about employment opportunities at a local employment bureau and head to a work site from there, or they could go directly to area farmers and ask for work. Thus Wobblies lost another opportunity to interpose themselves between independent workers and farmers.[33]

Other problems in recruitment also plagued job delegates. Harvesters who traveled by car or truck were dependent on their vehicles' needs such as gas, oil, and maintenance. Although the vehicles themselves were cheap to buy, if used—some could be purchased for as little as five dollars—they still required financial upkeep. The extra expense of an automobile tended to make auto tramps more conservative with their meager funds. Additionally, driving alone or in small numbers through the wheat belt isolated harvest workers from each other. The AWIU appeal, which had a very strong cultural and social component based on sharing the freight train ride, lacked meaning to these more isolated harvesters. Finally, many of the harvesters who traveled in flivvers were the sons of farmers from the corn and dairy states, college students, and poor young men from the southern plains who had little interest in militant industrial unionism. Most of the better-off workers had no intention of becoming permanent migrant farm laborers.

It was only this class of permanent migrant farm workers that the AWIU was able to recruit, although even these harvesters dreamed of eventually owning a farm or finding a permanent job in agriculture or in some other industry. The less well-off auto tramps, many of whom pooled their financial resources to purchase their car or truck, proved uninterested in the expense or message that IWW membership entailed. In many respects, the migrant class of agricultural workers in the Great Plains of several years earlier had nothing to lose and something to gain by becoming AWIU members. This new generation of young harvest workers had little to gain and at least a secondhand car to lose by becoming a harvest Wobbly and striking for higher wages or better working conditions. In fact, these workers did not have to engage in a strike. In their tin lizzies, they could easily move on to find more amenable employment down the road. Also, due to their mobility—as long as they had gas money—they did not have to fear vagrancy laws or confrontations with local police or sheriffs. In the end, the camaraderie and shared experiences that typified harvest workers moving through the wheat belt ended with the automobile. The worklife cultural appeal that harvest Wobblies used so successfully among white male migrant harvest workers no longer had any drawing power.[34]

Dancing Around the Problem of the Auto Tramp

The immediate effect of "flivver harvesters" on the AWIU was a steep drop in new members in 1926. During that year, a U.S. Department of Labor study concluded that 65 percent of wheat belt migrant workers traveled to work sites in their own automobiles. In 1928, 90 percent of migrant labor in Kansas traveled in the same manner. As early as 1923, the AWIU had struggled to come up with a means to organize the auto tramp. During the fall 1923 AWIU convention, participants resolved to entice harvest Wobblies "who own automobiles to take out credentials and literature to educate and line up the workers who travel from place to place in automobiles." This was not much of a strategy, and the fall 1925 AWIU convention's call to harvest Wobblies "to devise ways and means of organizing this class of workers next summer" came to nothing.

Harvest Wobblies at the 1925 and 1926 conventions could only dance around the issue that was proving fatal to their industrial union. Participants at the 1925 convention actually voted to dispose of automobiles owned by the AWIU for GOC members and traveling delegates because of their expense. But the vote was close, and a minority contingent attempted, but failed narrowly, to rescind the motion. At the 1926 convention, participants debated the purpose that an AWIU automobile should have in organizational work, but still no strategy emerged from these discussions. The issues debated in subsequent conventions tended to focus on financial concerns, such as what the initiation and dues should be or the spending habits of AWIU headquarters or whether AWIU branches should remain open year round. Another topic of convention debate concerned devising a better way to organize job delegates in the harvest drive, especially their accountability to headquarters. In short, the innovation that typified earlier conventions regarding organizing was no longer in evidence as the 1920s wore on.[35]

It was only when harvest Wobblies fully understood that the homeguard agricultural worker rather than the migrant worker was the future of the AWIU that the industrial union resolved its internal differences. But this was too little too late. The AWIU had virtually no base of support among resident harvest workers in the Great Plains or in the prairies of Canada. Harvest Wobblies literally had to contradict years of agitation and theory that saw the migrant worker as the core of the union and as the backbone of an American revolutionary proletariat. In 1924, the AWIU Wobbly Mike Doyle wrote with pride: "As far back as history records the nomads have been the pioneers in any progressive movement. The membership of the IWW at present is 90 percent migratory, and understanding the colossal job the IWW has, it is up to them to make an extra effort this year and prove once more their historical mission: that of being the vanguard—the force that makes human advancement."

His comments summarized succinctly years of effort to organize migrant workers, whether in the Far West or on the Great Plains. Occasionally, Wobblies wrote in their newspapers about the importance of homeguard workers. Nonetheless, AWIU leaders, job delegates, and rank-and-file members continually focused on the migrant worker. Even though harvest Wobblies, at the fall 1927 AWIU convention, drafted a resolution that explicitly called for organizing men with families who worked year round in the agricultural industry, especially those who worked on large farms, there is no evidence that the AWIU ever made inroads among these workers over the course of the decade.[36]

Compounding the problem of a severe drop-off in new membership was the attrition of current members, who left the union never to return. The industrial union always had a difficult time retaining its members. Many of the members who had left the AWIU in previous years left the IWW altogether, without bothering to transfer to another industrial union. Still, many signed up again during the subsequent harvest season. This meant that the new recruits each season actually included large numbers of former harvest Wobblies who were simply rejoining. Although this meant that the AWIU's numbers fluctuated over the course of a year, it also meant that the membership was actually rather stable during each harvest season. However, in the second half of the 1920s, just as new harvesters failed to join, so too did former members.[37]

The reasons that veteran harvest Wobblies decided not to rejoin the AWIU were similar to those of the new generation of harvest workers. Despite all of the efforts of AWIU leaders and theorists to provide an ideological rationale for membership, rank-and-file harvest Wobblies appreciated the culture of everyday life and work over ideology. After 1925, as freight trains gave way to automobiles and jungles gave way to camping at the job site, the intimate camaraderie that made migrant harvest work unique broke down and the benefits of AWIU membership disappeared. No longer could large numbers of harvest Wobblies move through the plains controlling transportation routes and jungles and influencing wages and working conditions. Furthermore, with a lack of new recruits came a lack of revenue. The AWIU could no longer support local union halls, job bulletins, and other support systems that made AWIU membership useful to migrant laborers. Finally, the call of city life enticed veteran harvest Wobblies as it did other migrant laborers. The boom in manufacturing jobs and office work may have not paid exceptionally well, but it could be steady and permanent. There is no indication that harvest Wobblies who gave up the itinerant life and chose a more stable form of urban employment maintained their IWW membership. Again, it appears that AWIU membership was based more on cultural bonds and pragmatism than on ideological commitment.

In the end, retaining veteran harvest Wobblies was not as important to the survival of the AWIU as recruiting the new generation of auto harvesters and homeguard agricultural laborers. The simple fact that most veteran harvest Wobblies who remained in the AWIU could not see past the worklife culture that served them so well in years past stifled the union's ability to evolve and adapt to a changing workforce. The only sure way for the continuation of a Wobbly presence in the wheat belt was for the new generation of auto tramps and resident Great Plains agricultural workers to take over the AWIU, molding it to meet their special needs as workers. But such workers found few practical, cultural, or ideological reasons to join the union. The few new members who did join over the course of the 1920s and into the 1930s continued to be migrant laborers by trade and adhered to the IWW's ideology of revolutionary industrial unionism.

The Changing Nature of Grain Harvesting Technology

Another problem greeted harvest Wobblies during the second half of the 1920s. A slow but steady increase in the availability and affordability of tractors, trucks, and combines led to a dramatic decline in the need for migrant farm workers from the southern plains to the Canadian prairies. As farmers purchased these tractors and trucks in ever-greater numbers, horses and the men to drive and tend them became unnecessary. The internal-combustion-engine tractor was readily adaptable to the self-binder, driving the header out of wheat harvesting because of the difficulty of pulling it by tractor. The self-binder bound the wheat into sheaves, while the header required a team of men to do the work of cutting the wheat. Furthermore, tractors could be used to power smaller threshing machines, which came on the market in the mid-1920s. These machines were not as costly as the large steam-powered threshing outfits that farmers formerly used. No longer were large numbers of migrant and seasonal workers necessary to operate the larger equipment; a single farmer could purchase a small threshing machine, or pool his money with several neighboring farmers, to thresh his own crop using just his family or homeguard workers. There was also always the option of a labor exchange among area farmers to thresh the grain themselves.[38]

The greatest laborsaving device to appear on the North American wheat farm in the mid- to late-1920s was the combine. This machine joined cutting and threshing wheat into one operation, dramatically reducing the need for migrant farm labor for both tasks. The one wheat-harvesting job that most migrants could count on in preceding decades, shocking the sheaves, disappeared with the advent of the combine. Although versions of the combine had been in use since the 1880s, the earlier contraptions were extremely expensive and required many horses and men to operate them. However, the postwar combines were true laborsaving devices. Five men could now do the work that previously required three hundred and twenty. And they were available in varying sizes, so even small farmers could afford them. In Kansas, where fifteen thousand combines were in use in 1927, the state's department of agriculture estimated that the need for migrant farm labor that year fell by fifty percent. In Oklahoma, combines reduced farmers' need for temporary labor by the same amount. Correspondingly, Okalahoma's state employment bureaus had fewer and fewer harvest labor jobs to direct migrants and residents towards as the use of combines spread. During the war years, the bureaus found employment for 11,296 harvesters. In 1927, the number of jobs fell to 1,482, and in 1932 the number fell again to 165. By the end of the decade, combines eliminated anywhere from thirty to ninety thousand migrant farm labor jobs in the wheat belt. The Canadian prairies experienced the same trend. Cecilia Danysk goes so far as to argue that reducing or even eliminating labor costs was a primary motive for farmers in Canada to acquire this farm machinery. Given the problems, both real and perceived, that U.S. farmers faced with independent harvesters and harvest Wobblies over the years, it is plausible that American farmers found machinery

Year	Hired labor (in 1,000s)
1909	182
1910	181
1911	180
1912	181
1913	182
1914	182
1915	183
1916	185
1917	182
1918	176
1919	174
1920	178
1921	181
1922	186
1923	188
1924	191
1925	196
1926	203
1927	216
1928	214
1929	210
1930	208
1931	192
1932	176
1933	161
1934	143
1935	148
1936	136

Figure 24. This chart demonstrates that the wheat belt continued to employ tens of thousands of agricultural laborers, peaking in demand for workers as the AWIU disintegrated. (Source, Shaw and Hopkins, *Trends in Employment in Agriculture, 1909-1936*)

preferable to migrant laborers, too. According to one Oklahoma farmer, wheat harvested by temporary laborers cost him thirty-five cents a bushel, while combine harvesting brought the rate down to sixteen cents a bushel.[39]

These profound changes in wheat belt agriculture did not necessarily have to spell doom for the AWIU. Migrant and seasonal farm labor did not disappear overnight from the wheat belt. True, some jobs went into decline, but hired labor remained steady throughout the 1920s and only began to decline overall after 1930 (fig. 24). For example, in 1928, wheat farmers in Kansas still required forty thousand migrant and seasonal workers to help with the harvest and threshing season. In North Dakota, the combine was slow to arrive; as of the late 1930s, only twenty-five percent of that state's wheat farmers used one. In 1938, twenty-five thousand migrant and seasonal farm laborers found work in the state. In short, although the combine, tractors, and trucks had become more affordable farmers still needed to have enough cash to purchase them or a bank willing to lend them the capital. At first, therefore, usually only large wheat farmers had the capital to purchase combines. There were also other forms of resistance to the combine that slowed its spread, including a commitment to tradition, differences in climate, and a lack of understanding of the benefits of the new technology. Because of these factors, it took many years before the combine became common from the south plains of Texas and Oklahoma to the prairies of Canada.[40]

Over the course of the second half of the 1920s, AWIU secretary-treasurers, organization committee members, job delegates, harvest Wobblies, and other IWW members made their familiar call as in previous years to organize on the job, in the jungle, and on the rails. But these calls now had a hollow, antiquated ring. As the wheat belt became increasingly more mechanized, harvest Wobblies seemed able only to lament the decline in the need for migrant harvest and threshing laborers. Despite the fact that these jobs did not suddenly disappear, for thousands of laborers continued to find work on the plains, Wobblies seemed capable only of bemoaning the conservatism of the harvest auto tramp and homeguard worker. They were unable to develop an effective strategy to deal with the social, cultural, and technological changes sweeping the wheat belt [41]

Epilogue

⌘ ⌘ ⌘

In the wheat belt, harvest Wobblies rapidly diminished in number in the latter half of the decade and over the course of the 1930s. With them went AWIU union halls, job delegates, and other traces of the organization. Nevertheless, enough harvest Wobblies maintained their membership and a few men and some women continued to join so that the AWIU could hold periodic conventions and special meetings. These union gatherings took place primarily where the IWW first gained a foothold in western agriculture: Washington, California, and North Dakota. Although harvest Wobblies struggled to make a comeback, the AWIU had difficulty electing officers who had substantial farm labor experience. The industrial union was increasingly acting as a club for Wobblies rather than as an actual union. That is not to say that the members who ran the AWIU were totally inexperienced or incompetent. Older veteran members such as Joe Fisher, W. I. Fisher, Arthur Boose, and Tom Connors and energetic new members such as Charles Velsek tried to deal with changes in the IWW and their industry.[1]

At the annual conventions and special meetings, harvest Wobblies and their leadership tried to focus on migrant farm labor in the wheat belt and Pacific Coast states. Outside of periodic meetings and publication of the occasional flier, the few harvest Wobblies in North Dakota, California, and Washington showed little signs of life. It is noteworthy that Los Angeles Wobblies could boast of acquiring a new Spanish-speaking branch of the union with a couple of dozen Hispanic members in 1928, but there is no indication that the AWIU could gain such members in California agriculture. Out on the north plains, when a spontaneous sugar beet worker strike erupted in Montana and Nebraska, the AWIU was simply too weak to have any impact on organizing these largely Hispanic and white family farm workers. Even a fall 1929 AWIU convention call to find a Spanish-speaking job delegate and to begin organizing these seriously exploited sugar beet workers came to nothing.[2]

Many of the sugar beet workers of Colorado, Montana, and Nebraska were Hispanics, Mexican nationals, and American Indians who also worked in the Colorado coal mining industry. Some of the Hispanic and Mexican workers were sympathetic to the IWW, for many worked with

IWW mineworkers and organizers during the 1927 and 1928 Colorado mineworkers' strikes. In fact, state police killed one Hispanic Wobbly mineworker, Clemente Chavez, in a raid on the Walsenburg, Colorado, IWW union hall. A Hispanic bystander also was killed during the raid, and several miners died during that year's violently suppressed coal miners' strikes. But in the end, neither the coal miners of Colorado nor the sugar beet workers of Montana, Colorado, or Nebraska turned to the IWW for organizing. The Colorado sugar beet workers in particular turned to more powerful AFL unions or tried creating their own independent unions.[3]

Except for one great flurry of activity in the Yakima Valley in 1933, the AWIU accomplished little in farm worker organizing in the United States over the succeeding years. The story of Yakima apple pickers organized by the IWW is ably told by James G. Newbill in "Farmers and Wobblies in the Yakima Valley, 1933" and by Cletus E. Daniel in "Wobblies on the Farm: The IWW in the Yakima Valley." Both historians offer a solid analytical narrative of the brief success of AWIU organizers, and their ultimate suppression by area farmers, local businessmen, and county law enforcement. Because of their efforts to force up wages and improve working conditions, AWIU organizers, members, and supporters faced mass arrests and severe beatings at the hands of the anti-Wobbly coalition. Although some migrant farm laborers were sympathetic to the AWIU message, many were so impoverished due to the ravages of the Great Depression that job delegates had a difficult time organizing many workers. A weak industrial union and meager membership could not sustain itself for long in such a hostile environment. Ultimately, the IWW as a whole and the AWIU in particular did not have the resources to provide adequate aid to the organizing effort.[4]

The AWIU held conventions throughout the 1930s as it had during the late 1920s, and the industrial union continued to prepare for harvest drives each season. Yet its failure to adapt to the changing needs of American workers is indicative of the problems of the IWW in these years. Though the AWIU had a strong track record of placing pragmatic organizing above revolutionary goals, its members were now becoming more rigidly ideological. According to Robinson, in "Social Movement Organizations in Decline," as the membership of the union shrank, only core idealists remained. Therefore, ideologically inspired journalism and meetings, rather than union organizing, dominated Wobbly activity. IWW members, and harvest Wobblies in particular, found themselves marginalized from the American left and the labor movement. The burgeoning communist movement of the 1930s eclipsed the IWW as a progressive, revolutionary path to a new society, and the highly pragmatic organizing of the Congress of Industrial Organizations (CIO) took the concept of industrial unionism to heights that Wobblies could only dream of. With the demise of the AWIU, and the IWW a shadow of its former self, farm workers continued to turn to their own ethnic-oriented labor associations but also to the Communist Party, and later the CIO.[5]

Harvest Wobblies eventually disappeared completely from the West's agricultural industry, but their worklife culture and their industrial union stand as one of the first concerted efforts by thousands of farm workers to resist the dehumanizing nature of industrial agriculture. Harvest Wobblies offered to agricultural laborers a unique and innovative union. Their job delegates were able to organize a highly mobile workforce, which in turn fought for higher wages and better working conditions. Though the creation of a new society was a part of AWO and AWIU literature and free-speech fight rhetoric, harvest-Wobbly job delegates in the field and harvest Wobbly organizational leadership consistently focused on practical and earthbound goals. For harvest Wobblies, improving the immediate work lives of farm workers was their foremost priority.

Nevertheless, the most important problem that harvest Wobblies and the AWIU leadership could not satisfactorily overcome was their worklife culture. This cultural bond that had acted as a powerful draw for migrant agricultural laborers in the 1910s and early 1920s ironically came to be an isolating force, creating a gulf between harvest Wobblies and other workers. Homeguard workers remained impervious to the union's message. Hispanic and Asian farm workers, along with the families of agricultural laborers in the Far West, were not attracted to the culture and message of the AWIU. In the Great Plains, young men had once traveled by rail and lived in jungle camps between jobs and found the worklife culture of harvest Wobblies an empowering force in their lives. But with the appearance of the cheap secondhand car, young harvesters did not find it in their interest to sign up as AWIU members. They did not need a red membership card that could act as a freight-train pass, nor the protection and camaraderie of the AWIU when living in jungle camps. This new generation of harvest workers traveled in small groups in their own cars and trucks and directly solicited work from farmers. They carried their own camping equipment and had no use for the facilities of a jungle. As independent harvesters, they carried their jungle in the trunk of their tin lizzies.

Harvest Wobbly economic theory predicted an increase in white male migrant farm laborers, prompting the AWIU to prepare itself for the concentration of farmland in the hands of the few and the proletarianization of most Great Plains farmers. This did not come to pass in the 1920s. Instead, harvest Wobblies found themselves locked into a worklife culture crafted for the needs and wants of itinerant white men. They either could not or would not break free from this way of life, and missed their opportunity to address the needs of the more dynamic members of the western farm labor workforce. Harvest Wobblies let slip through their fingers the opportunity to organize the migrant and seasonal farm labor population who would labor in the industrial agricultural sectors of the American West for the remainder of the twentieth century.

Notes

⌘ ⌘ ⌘

Introduction

1. *Industrial Worker,* 18 August 1923; *Agricultural Workers Industrial Union No. 110 of the I.W.W. Bulletin No. 37,* 26 September 1923 Box 186, Folder 32 (hereafter *AWIU, bulletin number,* and date), IWW Collection, Archives of Labor and Urban Affairs University Archives, Wayne State University, Detroit, Michigan (hereafter IWW, WS); *Spokesman-Review,* 16 August 1923.

2. *Industrial Worker,* 18 August, 1 September 1923; *Spokesman-Review,* 16-18, 24, 31 August 1923.

3. *Industrial Solidarity,* 15 September 1923; *Industrial Worker,* 6, 19, 22, 26 September, 3, 6 October 1923.

4. William Preston, Jr., *Aliens & Dissenters: Federal Suppression of Radicals, 1903-1933,* 2nd ed. (Urbana: University of Illinois Press, 1994), 265-66; Fred W. Thompson and Patrick Murfin, *The I.W.W.: Its First Seventy Years, 1905-1975* (Chicago: Industrial Workers of the World, 1976), 140-50; Hyman Weintraub, "The I.W.W. in California: 1905-1931" (master's thesis, University of California, Los Angeles, 1947), 199-210.

5. The history of the IWW among migrant farm labor has several notable scholarly treatments. Philip S. Foner's *History of the Labor Movement in the United States,* vol. 4, *The Industrial Workers of the World, 1905-1917* (New York: International Publishers, 1965) offers a solid, though brief, account of Wobbly organizing in the Great Plains and in California among migrant and seasonal farm labor. The IWW's official history of the union, *The I.W.W.,* by Thompson and Murfin, includes a rather incomplete treatment of harvest Wobblies. Melvyn Dubofsky's *We Shall Be All: A History of the Industrial Workers of the World,* 2nd ed. (Urbana: University of Illinois Press, 1988) is the most comprehensive study of the IWW from 1905-1924, but it lacks a full examination of harvest Wobblies. Yet he does identify some of the most serious problems that the AWIU had in maintaining its viability as an agricultural union. The most effective of the local histories of the IWW in agriculture is Nigel Sellars's *Oil, Wheat, & Wobblies: the Industrial Workers of the World in Oklahoma, 1905-1930* (Norman: University of Oklahoma Press, 1998). Sellars's monograph offers an analytical narrative of Wobbly organizing in Oklahoma's oil and wheat-growing industries and covers the postwar era of the IWW that has been generally neglected by labor historians. An equally useful history of harvest Wobblies is Stanley Fast's "The Agricultural Workers' Organization and the Harvest Stiff in the Midwestern Wheat Belt, 1915-1920" (master's thesis, Mankato State College, 1974). Fast's is a monograph-length history of Wobbly organizing in the entire Great Plains wheat belt. As the title suggests, however, his study ends in 1920 before the resurgence of the IWW. Adding to the literature on IWW organizing in western agricultural labor is Cletus Daniel's *Bitter Harvest: A History of California Farm workers, 1870-1941* (Ithaca: Cornell University Press, 1981). Though Daniel gives an account of the union's activity in California, he places IWW agricultural organizing within the context of Progressive-era reform politics and not within the larger history of western agriculture. His study is significant because he establishes the most important themes in the history of the IWW in California agriculture. In "The I.W.W.," Weintraub offers an analysis of Wobblies in agriculture within the framework of the history of the IWW in California. His study is useful in understanding the

successes and failures of the union in California's many industries and the repression that the IWW faced. Gregory Woirol's *In the Floating Army* (Urbana: University of Illinois Press, 1992) is a fascinating study of itinerant life and work in California in the mid-1910s that includes the journal writings of F. C. Mills, an agent for the California Commission of Immigration and Housing, who worked as an itinerant laborer in California's seasonal industries. Mills's goal was to understand the life of itinerant California workers, their attraction to the IWW, and how the commission could work to reform California industries that relied on migrant and temporary workers.

6. Carlos A. Schwantes, "Spokane and the Wageworkers' Frontier: A Labor History to World War I," in *Spokane & The Inland Empire: An Interior Pacific Northwest Anthology*, ed. David H. Stratton (Pullman: Washington State University Press, 1991), 123-41.

7. Some scholars have explored this era of farm labor history. Stuart Jamieson's *Labor Unionism in American Agriculture*, Department of Labor Bulletin No. 836 (1945; rpt., New York: Arno Press, 1976) is the most comprehensive work of its kind, though it is heavily weighted toward the 1930s. However, *Labor Unionism* has numerous passages that explain, in brief, early twentieth century western agricultural labor systems and early union organizing among western farm workers. Daniel's *Bitter Harvest* and Carey McWilliams' *Factories in the Field: The Story of Migratory Farm Labor in California* (Boston: Little, Brown and Company, 1939) offer well-detailed social histories of the multiethnic farm labor workforce of California from the late nineteenth century to the outbreak of World War II. Several sociocultural studies of California farm labor of note are Camille Guerin-Gonzales, *Mexican Workers and American Dreams: Immigration, Reparation, and California Farm Labor, 1900-1939* (New Brunswick, NJ: Rutgers University Press, 1994); Gilbert G. Gonzalez, *Labor and Community: Mexican Citrus Worker Villages in a Southern California County, 1900-1950* (Urbana: University of Illinois Press, 1994); Sucheng Chan, *This Bittersweet Soil: The Chinese in California Agriculture, 1860-1910* (Berkeley: University of California Press, 1986). Each of these monographs explores class, ethnicity, race, and labor within California agribusiness. For the Great Plains wheat belt the best studies of labor of the early years of the twentieth century are those by Donald D. Lescohier. Lescohier, an economist and employee of the U.S. Department of Agriculture, wrote a series of articles in the early 1920s for the Department of Agriculture that took the form of department bulletins. His work is very useful in uncovering a social profile of wheat belt farm labor. Two other significant studies, one academic and the other popular, that offer a comprehensive analysis of migrant and seasonal farm labor, agricultural development, and technological innovations in the Great Plains are Allen G. Applen's "Migratory Harvest Labor in the Midwestern Wheat Belt, 1870-1940" (Ph.D. diss., Kansas State University, 1974) and Thomas D. Isern's *Bull Threshers and Bindlestiffs: Harvesting and Threshing on the North American Plains* (Lawrence: University Press of Kansas, 1990). One other notable history of migrant wheat harvest farm labor during this era is Cecilia Danysk's *Hired Hands: Labour and the Development of Prairie Agriculture, 1880-1930* (Toronto: McClelland & Stewart Inc., 1995). Her focus is the Canadian portion of the North American wheat belt. Danysk's analysis demonstrates concurrent labor themes within the industry on both sides of the border.

8. David E. Schob, *Hired Hands and Plowboys: Farm Labor in the Midwest, 1815-60* (Urbana: University of Illinois Press, 1975), 267-71; Applen, "Migratory Harvest Labor," 1-3; Philip L. Martin, *Harvest of Confusion: Migrant Workers in U.S. Agriculture* (Boulder, CO: Westview Press, 1988), 4-5; Carlos Arnaldo Schwantes, *Hard Traveling: A Portrait of Work Life in the New Northwest* (Lincoln: University of

Nebraska Press, 1994), 28-29; Toby Higbie, "Indispensable Outcasts: Harvest Laborers in the Wheat Belt of the Middle West, 1890-1925" *Labor History* 38 (Fall 1997), 394.

9. William G. Robbins, *Colony & Empire: The Capitalist Transformation of the American West* (Lawrence: University Press of Kansas, 1994), x; Patricia Nelson Limerick, "The Trail to Santa Fe: The Unleashing of the Western Public Intellectual," in *Trails: Toward a New Western History*, eds. Patricia Nelson Limerick, Clyde A. Milner II, and Charles E. Rankin (Lawrence: University Press of Kansas, 1991), 70-71; Donald Worster, *Under Western Skies: Nature and History in the American West* (New York: Oxford University Press, 1992), 23-24.

10. *Proceedings, The Founding Convention of the IWW* (New York: Merit Publishers, 1969), 1-6; Foner, *Labor Movement*, vol. 4, 17-19, 77; Salvatore Salerno, *Red November Black November: Culture and Community in the Industrial Workers of the World* (Albany: State University of New York Press, 1989), 98-99; Dubofsky, *We Shall Be All*, 105-06; *Industrial Worker*, 1 July 1909; for a succinct theory of syndicalism and how closely it resembles the IWW revolutionary industrial unionism and the Wobbly vision of the new society, see Earl C. Ford and William Z. Fosters, *Syndicalism* (1912; rpt. Chicago: Charles H. Kerr Publishing Company, 1990).

11. Richard A. Rajala, "A Dandy Bunch of Wobblies: Pacific Northwest Loggers and the Industrial Workers of the World, 1900-1930" *Labor History* 37 (Spring 1996), 209-212.

One: Working for Wages in the West

1. For a superb analysis of agrarianism within the context of California agriculture see Daniel's *Bitter Harvest*, and for a more thorough definition of agrarianism within the context of American agricultural history see A. Douglas Hurt, *American Agriculture: A Brief History* (Ames: Iowa State University Press, 1994); Schwantes, *Hard Traveling*, 28-29; Robbins, *Colony and Empire*, 150-52; United States Commission on Industrial Relations, *Report of Commission on Industrial Relations*, vol. 5 (Washington, D.C.: GPO, 1916), 4932-36; Higbie, "Indispensable Outcasts," 394.

2. For an outstanding history of farming on the Great Plains during the second half of the nineteenth century, see Gilbert C. Fite, *The Farmers' Frontier, 1865-1900* (1966; rpt., Norman: University of Oklahoma Press, 1986); Fred Shannon, *The Farmer's Last Frontier: Agriculture, 1860-1897* (1945; rpt., New York: Harper Torchbooks, 1968), 292-95; Gilbert C. Fite, *American Agriculture and Farm Policy Since 1900* (New York: Macmillian Company, 1964), 3-15; Wayne D. Rasmussen, ed., *Agriculture in the United States: A Documentary History*, vol. 4 (New York: Random House, 1975), 2646-47, 2658-66; for an accessible overview of this time period in American farming (1900-1932) that features a useful bibliography, see Hurt, *American Agriculture*, 221-279; Daniel, *Bitter Harvest*, 68.

3. Donald Worster, *The Wealth of Nature: Environmental History and The Ecological Imagination* (New York: Oxford University Press, 1993), 60-63; Hiram M. Drache, *The Day of the Bonanza: A History of Bonanza Farming in the Red River Valley of the North* (Fargo: North Dakota Institute for Regional Studies, 1964), 4-6; Fite, *Farmers' Frontier*, 52-53, 101-4; Applen, "Migratory Harvest Labor," 25-26.

4. Fite, *Farmers' Frontier*, 52-53, 97-98, 101-4, 118-19; Applen, "Migratory Harvest Labor," 25-26; Drache, *Day of the Bonanza*, 24-25; Robbins, *Colony and Empire*, 72.

5. Drache, *Day of the Bonanza*, 68-72; Shannon, *Farmer's Last Frontier*, 154-61; Fite, *Farmers' Frontier*, 76-86.

6. Alfred N. Terry, Interview, 17 August 1954, Institute for Regional Studies, North Dakota State University, Fargo (hereafter IRS); Drache, *Day of the Bonanza*, 73,

111-12; Mrs. O. L. Ferguson, Interview, 9 October 1954, IRS; Eldon E. Shaw and John A. Hopkins, *Trends in Employment in Agriculture, 1909-36* (Philadelphia: Works Progress Administration, National Research Project, Report No. A-8, November 1938), 59-63.

7. Robbins, *Colony and Empire*, 75-76; Applen, "Migratory Harvest Labor," 30-31; Nat C. Murray, "The Wheat Crop of 1913-14," *Farmers' Bulletin No. 629* (Washington, D.C.: GPO, 1914), 4-5; Drache, *Day of the Bonanza*, 12-13.

8. Hurt, *American Agriculture*, 144-46; 195-98; Isern, *Bull Threshers and Bindlestiffs*, 8-11, 25-31, 57-59; Fite, *Farmers' Frontier*, 104-6; Shannon, *Farmer's Last Frontier*, 134-36; Jack Spiese, Interview, 27 October 1967, Minnesota State Historical Society, Saint Paul (hereafter Spiese interview, MSHS).

9. Isern, *Bull Threshers and Bindlestiffs*, 71-89; Drache, *Day of the Bonanza*, 115-16, 121-22.

10. Shaw and Hopkins, *Trends in Employment in Agriculture*, 59-63; Paul S. Taylor, *Labor on the Land: Collected Writings 1930-1979* (New York: Arno Press, 1981), 93, 57-63; Jamieson, *Labor Unionism*, 396-97; Mary Wilma M. Hargreaves, *Dry Farming in the North Great Plains, 1900-1925* (Cambridge: Harvard University Press, 1957), 439-53; George K. Holmes, *Supply of Farm Labor* U.S. Department of Agriculture Bureau of Statistics Bulletin 94 (Washington, D.C.: GPO, 1912), 12-17; Tom Connors, "The Industrial Union in Agriculture," in *Twenty-Five Years of Industrial Unionism* (Chicago: Industrial Workers of the World, 1930), 36; Michael Samuel Sideman, "The Agricultural Labor Market and the Organizing Activities of the I.W.W., 1910-1935" (master's thesis, Northwestern University, 1965), 57; Lewis Farr Garey, "Relation of Labor Income to Size and Type of Farming in Madison County, Nebraska" (master's thesis, University of Nebraska, 1915), 44.

11. Donald D. Lescohier, "The Farm Labor Problem," *Journal of Farm Economics* 3 (January 1921), 10-15; Donald D. Lescohier, "With the I.W.W. in the Wheat Lands" *Harper's Magazine* 147 (August 1923), 380; Isern, *Bull Threshers and Bindlestiffs*, 137; Donald D. Lescohier, *Harvest Labor Problems in the Wheat Belt*, U.S. Department of Agriculture Bulletin No. 1020 (Washington D.C.: GPO, 1922), 3-11; T. P. Cooper, F. W. Peck, and Andrew Boss, *Labor Requirements of Crop Production* Bulletin No. 157 (Saint Paul: University of Minnesota Agricultural Experiment Station, 1916), 10-20; 10-11; William Grannat, Testimony, *United States v. William D. Haywood, et al.* Box 111, Folder 5, (hereafter Grannat testimony) IWW, WS; William Casebolt, Testimony, *United States v. William D. Haywood, et al.* Box 111, Folder 5 (hereafter Casebolt testimony) IWW, WS.

12. Donald D. Lescohier, *Conditions Affecting the Demand for Harvest Labor in the Wheat Belt*, U.S. Department of Agriculture Bulletin No. 1230 (Washington, D.C.: GPO, 1924), 5-14; Cooper et al., *Labor Requirements*, 26-28; John A. Hopkins, *Changing Technology and Employment in Agriculture* (1941; rpt., New York: Da Capo Press, 1973), 119-20.

13. Lescohier, *Conditions Affecting*, 21-23; Sideman, "Agricultural Labor Market," 24; Hargreaves, *Dry Farming*, 168, 201; Hopkins, *Changing Technology*, 32.

14. Lescohier, *Conditions Affecting*, 26-30; Cooper et al., *Labor Requirements*, 25.

15. Donald D. Lescohier, "Hands and Tools of the Wheat Harvest," *Survey* 50 (August 1923), 378. The term "bindle stiff" was derived from the bedroll and belongings that migrants carried with them on their rural quest for employment. A harvest stiff was a migrant agricultural laborer. Irving Werstein, *Pie in the Sky; An American Struggle, the Wobblies and Their Times* (New York: Delacorte Press, 1969), 131-32; Holmes, *Supply of Farm Labor*, 30-36; Carleton H. Parker, *The Casual Laborer and Other Essays* (New York: Harcourt, Brace and Howe, 1920), 70; Applen, "Migrant Harvest Labor," 69-70; Isern, *Bull Threshers and Bindlestiffs*, 147; Donald D. Lescohier, *Labor Problems*, 19; Lescohier, *Sources of Supply and Conditions of*

Employment of Harvest Labor in the Wheat Belt, U.S. Department of Agriculture Bulletin No. 1211 (Washington, D.C.: GPO, 1924), 7; Lescohier, "Hands and Tools," 382, 409.

16. Lescohier, "Hands and Tools," 380; Lescohier, *Labor Problems*, 16-17; Lescohier, *Sources of Supply*, 2.

17. Lescohier, "Hands and Tools," 381-82; Lescohier, *Sources of Supply*, 4-5; Grannat testimony, IWW, WS; Casebolt testimony, IWW, WS; Fast, "Agricultural Workers' Organization," 12-13; *Minneapolis Morning Tribune*, 19 July 1915.

18. Lescohier, *Labor Problems*, 17-18; Lescohier, "Harvest Tools," 382; Lescohier, *Sources of Supply*, 4-5; Lescohier, "Harvesters and Hoboes," 486-87; Len De Caux, Interview, 1985, Oral History Program, Research Library, Special Collections, University of California, Los Angeles (hereafter De Caux interview, Oral History, UCLA); Len De Caux, *The Living Spirit of the Wobblies* (New York: International Publishers, 1978), 91-92.

19. Lescohier, *Labor Problems*, 28-29.

20. Lescohier, *Labor Problems*, 24-25; Lescohier, *Sources of Supply*, 10-11; Fast, "Agricultural Workers Organization," 20-22; *Minneapolis Morning Tribune*, 19 July 1915, 12 August 1917; Applen, "Migrant Harvest Labor," 103.

21. Lescohier, *Labor Problems*, 28-29; Lescohier, *Sources of Supply*, 11-12; Fast, "Agricultural Workers' Organization," 22; Joe Murphy, Interview, 23 September 1978, Deborah Shaffer papers, State Historical Society of Wisconsin, Madison (hereafter Murphy interview, Shaffer Papers, SHSW); *Mankato Free Press*, 2 June 1917.

22. Lescohier, *Sources of Supply*, 12-13; Applen, "Migrant Harvest Labor," 112; John L. Miller, Interview, 11 March 1974, John L. Miller Papers, Allen Library, Archives and Manuscripts, University of Washington, Seattle (hereafter Miller interview, Miller Papers, UW); De Caux interview, Oral History, UCLA; Murphy interview, Shaffer Papers, SHSW; *New Solidarity*, 2 & 9 August 1919.

23. Lescohier, *Sources of Supply*, 13-14; Applen, "Migrant Harvest Labor," 118-19.

24. Isern, *Bull Threshers and Bindlestiffs*, 150-52; Lescohier, *Sources of Supply*, 14-15; Applen, "Migrant Harvest Labor," 131-44; *Report of the Industrial Commission on Agriculture*, vol. 10, 846; *Mankato Free Press*, 5 June 1917.

25. Lescohier, *Sources of Supply*, 17-19; Rasmussen, *Agriculture in the United States* vol. 3, 2744-46; Lescohier, "Hands and Tools," 410; Miller interview, Miller Papers, UW; Lescohier, "Harvesters and Hoboes," 484; Lescohier, *Conditions Affecting*, 32-45.

26. Stewart Bird, Dan Georgakas, and Deborah Shaffer, eds., *Solidarity Forever: An Oral History of the IWW* (Chicago: Lake View Press, 1985), 37, 42-43; E. W. Latchem "The Modern Agricultural Slave," *One Big Union Monthly* 7 (August 1920), 54; Fast, "Agricultural Workers' Organization," 25; *Minneapolis Morning Tribune*, 12 August 1917; Bird et al., *Solidarity Forever*, 37; Spiese interview, MHS; ; Nels Petersen, Interview, 23 February 1978, (hereafter Petersen interview) Shaffer Papers, SHSW.

27. Frank E. Wermke, Testimony, *United States v. William D. Haywood, et al.* Box 105, Folder 7 (hereafter Wermke testimony) IWW, WS. Wermke commented during the Chicago trial of Bill Haywood and a number of other Wobblies that as a migrant farm worker he engaged in sabotage partly because specific farmers fed him so poorly during the harvest season. Murphy interview, Shaffer papers, SHSW; Spiese interview, MSH; Sam Krieger, Interview, 24 September 1978, (hereafter Krieger interview) Shaffer Papers, SHSW.

28. Spiese interview, MHS; Grannat testimony, IWW, WS; Casebolt testimony, IWW, WS; Lescohier, "Hands and Tools," 411-12.

29. Nels Anderson, *The American Hobo: An Autobiography* (Leiden, Netherlands: E. J. Brill, 1975), 167-68; Nels Anderson, *The Hobo: The Sociology of the Homeless Man*

(1923; rpt., Chicago: Midway Reprint, 1975), 91-95, 98; Fred Thompson, Interview, 26 May 1973, State Historical Society of Wisconsin (hereafter Thompson interview, SHSW); Bird, et al., *Solidarity Forever*, 45; Applen, "Migrant Harvest Labor," 105-12; Spiese interview, MHS; Grannat testimony, IWW, WS; Petersen interview, Shaffer Papers, SHSW.

30. Thompson interview, SHSW; Anderson, *The Hobo*, 21-26; Anderson, *The American Hobo*, 95-96.

31. Krieger interview, Shaffer papers, SHSW; Miller interview, Miller Papers, UW; Joe Burdell, Testimony, *United States v. William D. Haywood, et al.* (hereafter Burdell testimony) IWW, WS; Spiese interview, MHS.

32. Philip Taft, "I.W.W. in the Grain Belt," *Labor History* 1 (Winter 1960), 57; Applen, "Migrant Harvest Labor," 110-11.

33. McWilliams, *Factories in the Field*, 20; Daniel, *Bitter Harvest*, 17-23; Richard Steven Street, "Tattered Shirts and Ragged Pants: Accommodation, Protest, and the Coarse Culture of California Wheat Harvesters and Threshers, 1866-1900" *Pacific Historical Review* (November 1998), 577.

34. McWilliams, *Factories in the Field*, 59-63; Daniel, *Bitter Harvest*, 33-35; Donald Worster, *Rivers of Empire: Water, Aridity, and the Growth of the American West* (New York: Oxford University Press, 1985), 96-111.

35. Taylor, *Labor on the Land*, 108-18; Harry Schwartz, *Seasonal Farm Labor in the United States, with Special Reference to Hired Workers in Fruit and Vegetable and Sugar-Beet Production* (New York: Columbia University Press, 1945), 18; Hopkins, *Changing Technology*, 132-35; McWilliams, *Factories in the Field*, 87-88, 145; J. Donald Fisher, "A Historical Study of the Migrant in California" (master's thesis, University of Southern California, 1945), 8; Shaw and Hopkins, *Trends in Employment in Agriculture*, 74-75.

36. Daniel, *Bitter Harvest*, 40-46; Fred Krissman, "Californian Agribusiness and Mexican Farm Workers (1942-1992): A Binational Agricultural System of Production/Reproduction" (Ph.D. diss., University of California, Santa Barbara, 1996), 117-19; for a thorough analysis of the white segment of the wheat harvest workforce before 1900, see Street's "Tattered Shirts and Ragged Pants."

37. Taylor, *Labor on the Land*, 118-19; State Board of Control of California, *California and the Oriental* (Sacramento: California State Printing Office, 1920), 101; Schwartz, *Seasonal Farm Labor*, 54; for an analysis of Chinese immigrant truck farming and late nineteenth century farm ownership, see Chan, *This Bitter-Sweet Soil*.

38. Daniel, *Bitter Harvest*, 26-32; Taylor, *Labor on the Land*, 119; *Pacific Rural Press*, 11 February 1888; Varden Fuller, *Hired Hands in California's Farm Fields: Collected Essays on California's Farm Labor History and Policy* (Oakland: Division of Agriculture and Natural Resources, California Agricultural Experiment Station, 1991), 17-20; *Report of the Industrial Commission on Agriculture*, vol. 10, 973; Chris Friday, *Organizing Asian American Labor: The Pacific Coast Canned-Salmon Industry, 1870-1942* (Philadelphia: Temple University Press, 1994), 64-65; for a thorough account of Chinese workers in California agricultural as laborers and as farmers, see Chan, *This Bitter-Sweet Soil*.

39. Taylor, *Labor on the Land*, 118; Fuller, *Hired Hands*, 22-23; *California and the Oriental*, 25-31; Schwartz, *Seasonal Farm Labor*, 54-55.

40. Daniel, *Bitter Harvest*, 73-76; Fuller, *Hired Hands*, 24-31; *California and the Oriental*, 101-104; *Industrial Worker*, 15 July 1909, 23, 25 June 1910; Paul S. Taylor, *Mexican Labor in the United States*, vol. 1 (Berkeley: University of California Press, 1930), 5-6; Schwartz, *Seasonal Farm Labor*, 55-56.

41. Fuller, *Hired Hands*, 33-34; McWilliams, *Factories in the Field*, 116-19; Taylor, *Mexican Labor*, 6; *California and the Oriental*, 101-102; *Report of Commission on*

Industrial Relations, vol. 5, 4924, 4926; R. L. Adams and T. R. Kelly, "A Study of Farm Labor in California," Agricultural Experiment Station, *Circular No. 193* (Berkeley: University of California, 1918), 8.

42. Juan Gomez-Quinones, *Mexican American Labor, 1790-1990* (Albuquerque: University of New Mexico Press, 1994), 129-50.

43. Clark, "Mexican Labor," 466-85; Daniel, *Bitter Harvest*, 66-67; Taylor, *Labor on the Land*, 120-21.

44. McWilliams, *Factories in the Field*, 124-30; Fuller, *Hired Hands*, 45-52; Taylor, *Mexican Labor*, 2-18; Paul S. Taylor, "Mexican Labor in the United States. Migration Statistics II" in *University Publications in Economics*, vol. 12 (Berkeley: University of California Press, 1929), 1-7.

45. Friday, *Organizing Asian American Labor*, 123-28; Taylor, *Mexican Labor*, 7; Taylor, *Labor on the Land*, 120-21; Fuller, *Hired Hands*, 52-54; McWilliams, *Factories in the Field*, 120-24, 130–33; Daniel, *Bitter Harvest*, 67–68; Schwartz, *Seasonal Farm Labor*, 55.

46. *Report of the Industrial Commission*, vol. 10, xxi; *Report of Commission on Industrial Relations*, vol. 5, 4955-56, 4967; Taylor, *Mexican Labor*, 40-45; Parker, *Casual Laborer*, 70.

47. *Report of Commission on Industrial Relations*, vol. 5, 4924-25, 4929, 4955-59, 4967, 4972; *Report of the Industrial Commission*, vol. 10, 972; Parker, *Casual Laborer*, 69-72; Adams and Kelly, "Study of Farm Labor," 6.

48. *Report of Commission on Industrial Relations*, vol. 5, 4955; Woirol, *In the Floating Army*, 57-64, 78-80, 96, 101-2; Schwartz, *Seasonal Farm Labor*, 56-57.

49. Don Mitchell, *The Lie of the Land: Migrant Workers and the California Landscape* (Minneapolis: University of Minnesota Press, 1996), 22-23; Parker, *Casual Laborer*, 69; E. P. Todd to Lubin, 13 January 1915, Box 1, Lubin to Mr. Fels, 17 January 1914, Box 4, J. V. Thompson to George Bell, 28 July 1917, Box 5. Simon Julius Lubin Papers, Bancroft Library, University of California, Berkeley (hereafter Lubin Papers, UCB).

50. Woirol, *In the Floating Army*, 30, 91; *Report of the Industrial Commission*, vol. 10, 955, 972; *Report of Commission on Industrial Relations*, vol. 5, 4918, 4925-29, 4967; Mitchell, *Lie of the Land*, 59; *Fresno Republican*, 25 July 1924.

51. James Foy, "A Migratory Worker's Diary," *Industrial Pioneer* (February 1924), 29; James Foy, "More About the Migratory Worker's Diary," *Industrial Pioneer* (April 1914), 14; David Montgomery, *The Fall of the House of Labor: The Workplace, the State, and American Labor Activism, 1865-1925* (Cambridge: Cambridge University Press, 1987), 136.

52. Carlos A. Schwantes, *The Pacific Northwest: An Interpretive History* (Lincoln: University of Nebraska Press, 1989), 166-71; Robert E. Ficken and Charles P. LeWarne, *Washington: A Centennial History* (Seattle: University of Washington Press, 1988), 60; Fite, *Farmers' Frontier*, 137-48; Shannon, *Farmer's Last Frontier*, 266-67; D. W. Meinig, *The Great Columbia Plain: A Historical Geography, 1805-1910* (Seattle: University of Washington Press, 1968), 241-51.

53. Alexander Campbell McGregor, *Counting Sheep: From Open Range to Agribusiness on the Columbia Plateau* (Seattle: University of Washington Press, 1982), 12-13, 156-57; Edwin Bates, *Commercial Survey of the Pacific Northwest* (Washington, D.C.: GPO, 1932), 265; Ficken and LeWarne, *Washington*, 60-64; William Cole, Testimony, *United States v. William D. Haywood, et al.*, IWW, WS; Fite, *Farmers' Frontier*, 148-53; Meinig, *Columbia Plain*, 251-83.

54. Ficken and LeWarne, *Washington*, 64-67; Agricultural Economics Survey and Studies, 1912-1965, Box 12, folder 129, Washington State University Libraries, Manuscripts, Archives, and Special Collections, Pullman; Wayne D. Rasmussen, "A

Century of Farming in the Inland Empire," in *Spokane & The Inland Empire: An Interior Pacific Northwest Anthology,* ed. David H. Stratton (Pullman: Washington State University Press, 1991), 35; Fite, *Farmers' Frontier,* 153-54; Meinig, *Columbia Plain,* 340-44, 379-81, 472-73; McGregor, *Counting Sheep,* 219-20.

55. Bates, *Commercial Survey,* 15-16, 255, 272-73; McGregor, *Counting Sheep,* 176-77; Fite, *Farmers' Frontier,* 154-55.

56. Cletus Edward Daniel, "Labor Radicalism in Pacific Coast Agriculture" (Ph.D. diss., University of Washington, 1972), 7-8; Paul H. Landis and Melvin S. Brooks, *Farm Labor in the Yakima Valley, Washington* (Pullman: State College of Washington, Agricultural Experiment Station, 1936), 14-15; Bates, *Commercial Survey,* 259.

57. Schwantes, *Hard Traveling,* 1, 28, 31, 35; Daniel, "Labor Radicalism," 11; Landis and Brooks, *Farm Labor,* 40; Jamieson, *Labor Unionism,* 212; Sideman, "Agricultural Labor Market," 82; John C. Schneider, "Tramping Workers, 1890-1920: A Subcultural View," in *Walking to Work: Tramps in America, 1790-1935,* ed. Eric H. Monkkonen (Lincoln: University of Nebraska Press, 1984), 218; Grannat testimony, IWW, WS.

58. *Industrial Worker,* 15 July 1909.

59. E. H. H., "An Ill Wind in the Palouse," *Industrial Pioneer* (October 1921), 43-44; Bates, *Commercial Survey,* 261; Schwartz, *Seasonal Farm Labor,* 30; *Yakima Daily Republic,* 6 January 1911.

Two: Organizing Workers in the Streets and on the Farms

1. United States Department of Agriculture, *Yearbook of the United States Department of Agriculture* 1913 (Washington, D.C.: GPO, 1914), 440; *Report of Commission on Industrial Relations,* vol. 5, 4932-36; California Commission of Immigration and Housing, *First Annual Report* (Sacramento: GPO, 1915), 18. The California Commission of Immigration and Housing, organized in 1913, grew out of Governor Hiram Johnson's and the California state legislature's concerns about immigration and labor problems in the state. The Commission investigated the Wheatland affair and began to inspect the state's farm labor work sites, sending recommendations to Governor Johnson. For a more thorough history of the commission and its early work among migrant farm laborers, see Woirol, *In the Floating Army* and California Commission of Immigration and Housing, *First Annual Report.* Foner, *Labor Movement,* vol. 4, 262-63; Durst flier, Lubin Papers, UBC; Superior Court. County of Yuba. *People v. Richard Ford, et al.,* vol. 4, IWW Seattle Office, Allen Library, Manuscripts and Archives, University of Washington (hereafter *People v. Ford, et al.,* IWW Seattle, UW); *Solidarity,* 30 August, 11 October 1913.

2. Parker, *Casual Laborer,* 63-64; *Report of Commission on Industrial Relations,* vol. 5, 4999-5000; Douglas M. Clark, "The Wheatland Hop Field Riot" (master's thesis, Chico State College, 1963), 12-13; Mortimer Downing, "The Case of the Hop Pickers," *International Socialist Review* 14 (October 1913); Alvin W. James, Testimony, (hereafter James testimony) *The People of the State of California against Richard Ford and H. D. Suhr. Appellants. Volume 2.* Box 2 (hereafter *Cal. against Ford and Suhr*), IWW Seattle, UW.

3. Clark, "Wheatland," 18; Daniel, "Labor Radicalism," 57; Stuart Marshall Jamieson collection of field notes, UBC; Dubofsky, *We Shall Be All,* 295; *Solidarity,* 11 October 1913.

4. Foner, *Labor Movement,* vol. 4, 263; Clark, 19; James testimony, *Cal. against Ford and Suhr,* IWW Seattle, UW; Earl Smith, Testimony, *Cal. against Ford and Suhr,* IWW Seattle, UW; *Solidarity,* 11 October 1913.

5. Foner, *Labor Movement*, vol. 4, 264; Clark, 19-20; Dubofsky, *We Shall Be All*, 296; James testimony, *Cal. against Ford and Suhr*, IWW Seattle, UW; Percy H. James, Testimony, *Cal. against Ford and Suhr*, IWW Seattle, UW; A Jack London article from the San Francisco Bulletin reprinted in *Plotting to Convict Wheatland Hop Pickers* (Oakland: International Press, 1914), 25-26.

6. *Solidarity*, 18 October, 1 November 1913; an extract from a letter sent to Women's Clubs of California by International Workers' Defense League reprinted in *Plotting to Convict*, 7-10; affidavits of R. W. Burton and R. M. Royce concerning Edward Gleaser's kidnapping reprinted in *Plotting to Convict*, 13-18; Foner, *Labor Movement*, vol. 4, 265-67; Clark, "Wheatland," 21-23.

7. Daniel, *Bitter Harvest*, 90-91; Foner, *Labor Movement*, vol. 4, 267-68; Clark, "Wheatland," 24-26; *Solidarity*, 20 December 1913.

8. Daniel, "Labor Radicalism," 59-60; Foner, *Labor Movement*, vol.4, 267-70; *Solidarity*, 13 December 1913, 7 February 1914; Superior Court. County of Yuba. *People vs. Richard Ford, et al.*, IWW Seattle, UW.

9. Daniel, "Labor Radicalism," 60-61; Dubofsky, *We Shall Be All*, 299; Clark, "Wheatland," 30; Woirol, *In the Floating Army*, 116-22; *Solidarity*, 30 May 1914; Foner, *Labor Movement*, vol. 4, 271.

10. Weintraub, "The I.W.W. in California," 16-17; Philip S. Foner, ed., *Fellow Workers and Friends: I.W.W. Free-Speech Fights as Told By Participants* (Westport, CT: Greenwood Press, 1981), 3-22.

11. *Industrial Worker*, 14 May 1910; Edward McDonald, *The Farm Laborer and the City Worker: A Message to Both* (Cleveland: I.W.W. Publishing Bureau, n.d.), 1-13; *Industrial Worker*, 4 June 1910; *Solidarity*, 27 April 1910.

12. *Industrial Worker*, 20 October 1909, 5 February, 30 April 1910; *Solidarity*, 27 April 1910; *Industrial Union Bulletin*, 9 November 1907; Paul F. Brissenden, *The I.W.W.: A Study of American Syndicalism* (New York: Russell and Russell Inc., 1957), 315-16 [first published 1919]; Salerno, *Red November Black November*, 7-8; Daniel, "Labor Radicalism," 42; Donald M. Barnes, "The Ideology of the Industrial Workers of the World: 1905-1921" (Ph.D. diss., Washington State University, 1962), 76-78; Dubofsky, *We Shall Be All*, 144-45.

13. Schwantes, "Spokane and the Wageworkers' Frontier," 125; *Industrial Union Bulletin*, 30 March 1907; *Industrial Worker*, 1, 8, 22 July, 20 October, 17 November 1909, 23 April 1910; *Solidarity*, 2 July 1909, 19 July 1913; E. Workman, *The Agricultural Workers' Organization: A Story of a Class Union in the Making* (New York: One Big Union Club, 1939), 7; Daniel, "Labor Radicalism," 43.

14. Daniel, *Bitter Harvest*, 76-77; Austin Lewis, "The Drift in California" *International Socialist Review* 12 (November 1911), 272-74.

15. Weintraub, "I.W.W. in California," 62-63; Jamieson, *Labor Unionism*, 55-58; Daniel, *Bitter Harvest*, 78-81.

16. *Industrial Union Bulletin*, 16 March 1907, 1 February 1908; Daniel Rosenberg, "The IWW and Organization of Asian Workers in Early 20th Century America" *Labor History* 36 (Winter 1995), 77-87; Yuji Ichioka, *The Issei: The World of the First Generation Japanese Immigrants, 1885-1924* (New York: The Free Press, 1988), 3; *Industrial Worker*, 15 July 1909; *Solidarity*, 27 April 1910.

17. For an insightful examination of IWW organizers using common work experiences to create worker solidarity among black and white Louisiana loggers, see David Roediger, "Gaining a Hearing for Black-White Unity: Covington Hall and the Complexities of Race, Gender and Class" in *Towards the Abolition of Whiteness: Essays on Race, Politics, and Working Class History* (London: Verso, 1994), 127-80; Ichioka, *The Issei*, 110-13; Daniel, "Labor Radicalism," 44; Weintraub, "I.W.W. in California," 49-57; *Industrial Worker*, 22 April, 10 November 1909, 4, 23 June, 16 July, 6 August 1910, 12 December 1912; *Solidarity*, 27 August, 5 November 1910, 3

May 1912, 12 September 1914; J. V. Thompson to George L. Bell 23 July 1917, Lubin Papers, UCB. For a photograph of Chinese IWW members Chinn Poo, Hing Ching, and Sik Sui Dang, see Shaffer Papers, SHSW. Although it is difficult to make judgments about whether all Wobblies accepted the racial and ethnic inclusiveness of the union, one is hard-pressed to find racist or ethnically prejudiced sentiments in IWW newspapers, official publications, or in the oral histories left behind by Wobblies.

18. *Industrial Union Bulletin*, 30 March 1907, 11 January, 30 May, 6 June, 11 July 1908; *Industrial Worker*, 8 July 1909.

19. *Industrial Worker*, 1 May 1912; Foner, *Fellow Workers*, 12-13; Dubofsky, *We Shall Be All*, 173-75.

20. *Industrial Worker*, 25 March 1909; *International Socialist Review* 10 (December 1909), 483-84; Foner, *Fellow Workers*, 29-30; Jonathan David Knight, "The Spokane and Fresno Free-Speech Fights of the Industrial Workers of the World, 1909-1911" (master's thesis, Washington State University, 1991), 57-67; Schwantes, "Spokane and the Wageworkers' Frontier," 134-35.

21. *Spokesman Review*, 6 March, 11 March, 1 December 1909; *Spokane Press*, 3, 6, 10 November 1909; Knight, "Spokane and Fresno Free-Speech Fights," 91-94, 121, 146, 211; Foner, *Fellow Workers*, 30-34, 71-73; Elizabeth Gurley Flynn, *The Rebel Girl: An Autobiography, My First Life (1906-1926)* (1955; rpt., New York: International Publishers, 1994), 106-111.

22. *Industrial Worker*, 25 March, 29 April 1909.

23. *Industrial Worker*, 22, 29 July 1909.

24. United States Department of Agriculture, *Yearbook of the United States Department of Agriculture* 1909 (Washington, D.C.: GPO, 1910), 446-52; *Industrial Worker*, 15, 22, 29 July, 19 August 1909; *Spokesman Review*, 6 August 1909; Werstein, *Pie in the Sky*, 132.

25. *Industrial Worker*, 14 May 1910; Bird et al., 77-81; Schneider, "Tramping Workers," 228.

26. *Industrial Worker*, 28 May 1910; Salerno, *Red November Black November*, 51, 137; Vincent St. John, *The I.W.W.–Its History, Structure and Methods* (Chicago: I.W.W. Publishing Bureau, 1917), 16.

27. *Industrial Worker*, 11, 25 June, 9 July 1910; *Solidarity*, 2 July 1910.

28. *Industrial Worker*, 2 July 1910.

29. Ibid.; *Industrial Worker*, 9 July 1910.

30. *Yakima Daily Republic*, 11, 13, 14, 15, 20, 21 July 1910; *Industrial Worker*, 4 June, 16 July 1910.

31. Peter Cole, "Shaping Up and Shipping Out: The Philadelphia Waterfront During and After the IWW Years, 1913-1940," (Ph. D diss., Georgetown University, 1997), 179-80; *Industrial Worker*, 30 July 1910; Dubofsky, *We Shall Be All*, 216-17, 321.

32. *Industrial Worker*, 6, 20 August 1910; *Spokesman-Review*, 11 August 1910.

33. *Yakima Daily Republic*, 22 August 1910; *Industrial Worker*, 1 October 1910.

34. *Industrial Union Bulletin*, 30 March 1907, 11 January, 1 February, 30 May, 6 June, 11 July 1908, *Industrial Worker*, 22 April, 27 June, 1, 22, 29 July, 20 October, 17 November 1909, 23 April 1910.

35. Foner, *Labor Movement*, vol. 4, 185; Knight, "Spokane and Fresno Free-Speech Fights," 167; Daniel, "Labor Radicalism," 47-49; *Solidarity*, 27 April, 27 August 1910; Dubofsky, *We Shall Be All*, 186-87.

36. Daniel, "Labor Radicalism," 49-56; *Solidarity*, 29 October, 12 November, 13, 17 December 1910; Industrial Worker, 8 October 1910; H. Minderman, "The Fresno Free-Speech Fight," *Fellow Workers and Friends*, 105-22; Knight, "Spokane and Fresno Free-Speech Fights," 201-03.

37. *Industrial Worker*, 30 March 1911, 23 November 1912; Thompson and Murfin, *The I.W.W.*, 50; Ewald Koeltgen, "I.W.W. Convention," *International Socialist Review* 14 (November 1913), 275-76; Dubofsky, *We Shall Be All*, 287-88.

38. *Solidarity*, 12 August 1911; *Spokane Daily Chronicle*, 2, 5 August 1911; *Industrial Worker*, 27 July, 3 August 1911; *Spokesman-Review*, 18, 26 July, 8 August 1911.

39. Daniel, "Labor Radicalism," 54-56; *Industrial Worker*, 6 June 1912.

40. Cletus E. Daniel, "In Defense of the Wheatland Wobblies: A Critical Analysis of the IWW in California," *Labor History* 19 (Fall 1978), 495-96; *Solidarity*, 9 May 1914; *Report of Commission on Industrial Relations*, vol. 5, 4945; Weintraub, "I.W.W. in California," 82-85; *Report of Commission on Industrial Relations*, vol. 2, 1462.

41. Daniel, "Labor Radicalism," 62-64; *Solidarity*, 25 April 1914; Telegram to Hiram W. Johnson from Carleton H. Parker, 10 February 1914, Lubin to R. H. Durst, 11 June 1914, Lubin Papers, UBC; California Commission, *First Annual Report*, 50.

42. Foner, *Labor Movement*, vol. 4, 272-73; Daniel, "Labor Radicalism," 64-65; *Solidarity*, 29 August 1914; *San Francisco Chronicle*, 12 August 1914.

43. Burdell testimony, IWW, WS.

44. *Industrial Worker*, 14, 21 August 1913; Foner, *Fellow Workers and Friends*, 157; Charles James Haug, "The Industrial Workers of the World in North Dakota, 1913-1917," *North Dakota Quarterly* 39 (Winter 1971), 85-89.

45. *Industrial Worker*, 4 September 1913; Miller interview, Miller Papers, UW; Jack Miller, Interview, 21 February 1978, (hereafter Miller interview) Shaffer Papers, SHSW; *Solidarity*, 30 August, 27 September 1913; Haug, "Industrial Workers of the World in North Dakota," 88-89.

46. Haug, "Industrial Workers of the World in North Dakota," 90-92.

47. Fast, "The Agricultural Workers' Organization," 37-38; *Solidarity*, 27 June, 4, 25 July 1914; Foner, *Fellow Workers and Friends*, 173-77.

48. *Solidarity*, 10 October 1914, 25 October, 8 November 1913, 3, 10 January 1914; *Stenographic Report of the Eighth Annual Convention of the Industrial Workers of the World*, Chicago, Illinois, 15-29 September 1913, 33-37, IWW Proceedings microfilm, IWW, WS.

49. Fast, "Agricultural Workers' Organization," 38-40; *Solidarity*, 10, 17 October 1914.

50. *Solidarity*, 28 November 1914.

Three: A Bumper Crop of Harvest Wobblies

1. Unfortunately, no accurate records of the membership exist for the prewar years, as federal agents seized and destroyed most IWW records by court order during the antiradical hysteria of the war and immediate postwar years. Brissenden, *The I.W.W.*, 332-37; *Solidarity*, 13 February 1915; Dubofsky, *We Shall Be All*, 288-90; Thompson and Murfin, *The I.W.W.*, 79; *Report of Commission on Industrial Relations*, vol. 2, 1445; Foner, *Labor Movement*, vol. 4, 107-08, 367-68, 349.

2. *Solidarity*, 6, 20 March 1915; Applen, "Migratory Harvest Labor," 153-54; Sellars, *Oil, Wheat, and Wobblies*, 46-47.

3. E. W. Latchem to Fred Thompson, Frederick W. Thompson Papers, Box 9, Folder 25, Archives of Labor and Urban Affairs University Archives, Wayne State University, Detroit, Michigan (hereafter Thompson Papers, WS); *Solidarity*, 27 February, 3, 10 April 1915.

4. *Solidarity*, 13 March, 3, April 1915.

5. Foner, *Labor Movement*, vol. 4; 118; *Solidarity*, 6, 13, 20 March 1915.

6. *Solidarity*, 6 March 1915; *Industrial Worker*, 6 February, 6 March 1913; Foner, *Labor Movement*, vol. 4, 258-59.

7. *Solidarity*, 27 March 1915; for an analysis of Hall's efforts to build an interracial timber workers' union, see Roediger's "Gaining a Hearing for Black-White Unity: Covington Hall and the Complexities of Race, Gender, and Class."

8. *Industrial Worker*, 16 January, 13 February 1913; *Solidarity*, 22 February, 10 May 1913, 10 April, 20 March, 5 November 1915; Foner, *Labor Movement*, vol. 4, 259; Fast, "The Agricultural Workers' Organization," 33-34.

9. Sellars, *Oil, Wheat, and* Wobblies, 49, 67; Henry E. McGuckin, *Memoirs of a Wobbly*. (Charles H. Kerr Publishing Company, 1987), 7, 35, 42-57.

10. *Solidarity*, 24 April, 5 June 1915; Minutes of the Harvest Workers Conference copied by E. W. Latchem, E. W. Latchem Papers, Minnesota Historical Society (hereafter Latchem Papers, MHS).

11. McGuckin, Memoirs, 69-70; Dubofsky, *We Shall Be All*, 178, 334, 315, Foner, *Labor Movement*, vol. 4, 118, 475; ; Joyce L. Kornbluh *Rebel Voices: An IWW Anthology* (Chicago: Charles H. Kerr Publishing Company, 1988), 99; Cole, "Shaping Up and Shipping Out," 178.

12. Connors, "The Industrial Union in Agriculture," 38; Thompson and Murfin, *I.W.W.*, 94; Foner, *Labor Movement*, vol. 4, 475.

13. *Solidarity*, 12, 26 June, 3, 31 July 1915; Rasmussen, *Agriculture in the United States*, vol. 3, 2665; E. Workman, *History of "400" A.W.O.: The One Big Union Idea in Action* (New York: One Big Union Club, 1939), 13; Foner, *Labor Movement*, vol. 4, 476.

14. *Solidarity*, 31 July 1915.

15. Ibid.; Isern, *Bull Threshers and Bindlestiffs*, 168-69.

16. *Solidarity*, 7, 28 August 1915; Connors, "Industrial Union," 39; Dubofsky, *We Shall Be All*, 315; Rasmussen, *Agriculture in the United States*, vol. 3, 2665.

17. *Solidarity*, 9, 16 October, 18 September, 13 November 1915; C. O. Carlson, Testimony, *United States v. William D. Haywood, et al.*, Box 115, Folder 1 (hereafter Carlson testimony), IWW, WS.

18. *Solidarity*, 16, 30 October, 27 November, 25 December 1915; Connors, "Industrial Union," 39; Dubofsky, *We Shall Be All*, 315-16.

19. *Solidarity*, 25 December 1915; Foner, *Labor Movement*, vol. 4, 477; Donald E. Winters, Jr., *The Soul of the Wobblies: The I.W.W., Religion, and American Culture in the Progressive Era, 1905-1917* (Westport: Greenwood Press, 1985), 101-2.

20. Dubofsky, *We Shall Be All*, 279-81; Foner, *Labor Movement*, vol. 4, 364-67

21. *Solidarity*, 25 December 1915.

22. Daniel, "In Defense of the Wheatland Wobblies" 499-500; Vincent DiGirolamo, "The Women of Wheatland: Female Consciousness and the 1913 Wheatland Hop Strike" *Labor History* 34 (1993), 252-55; Weintraub, "The I.W.W. in California," 79; Daniel, "Labor Radicalism," 66-67; *Report on Commission of Industrial Relations*, vol., 5, 4922-23.

23. Foner, *Labor Movement*, vol. 4, 274-76; Daniel, "In Defense of the Wheatland Wobblies," 500-501; *Solidarity*, 6 March, 5 June, 31 July, 25 September, 2 October 1915; *San Francisco Chronicle*, 12 September 1915; Telegram, C. L. Lambert to Wm. D. Haywood, 10 June 1915, IWW California Office, Manuscripts and Archives, Allen Library, University of Washington, Seattle (hereafter IWW Cal., UW).

24. *Report of Commission on Industrial Relations*, vol. 5, 4936, 4945; Weintraub, "I.W.W. in California," 84-85; Woirol, *In the Floating Army*, 115-16.

25. Foner, *Labor Movement*, vol. 4, 274; *Solidarity*, 24 April, 1, 29 May, 26 June 1915.

26. Daniel, "In Defense of the Wheatland Wobblies," 502-5; *San Francisco Chronicle*, 12, 27 September 1915.

27. Foner, *Labor Movement*, vol. 4, 276-78; Preston, *Aliens and Dissenters*, 59-62; Woodrow C. Whitten, "The Wheatland Episode," *Pacific Historical Review* 17 (February 1948), 36.

28. *Solidarity*, 1 January, 4 March 1916.

29. Weintraub, "I.W.W. in California," 88-90; Workman, *History of "400" A.W.O.*, 17; Daniel, "Labor Radicalism," 75-77; *Solidarity*, 2, 9 September 1916; McGuckin, *Memoirs of a Wobbly*, 73-83; Foner, *Labor Movement*, vol. 4, 376.

30. P. F. Brissenden, "Lively Corpse," *The New Republic* 18 (26 August 1916), 95;
Dubofsky, *We Shall Be All*, 321; Foner, *Labor Movement*, vol. 4, 511.

31. Connors, "Industrial Union," 39-40; Dubofsky, *We Shall Be All*, 336; Fast,
"Agricultural Workers' Organization," 48; Workman, *History of "400" A.W.O.*, 15.

32. *Solidarity* 27 May, 18 November 1916; Foner, *Labor Movement*, vol. 4, 479; AWO
flier, Joseph Labadie Papers, University of Michigan, Ann Arbor, Special
Collections.

33. Fast, "Agricultural Workers' Organization," 52; Sellars, *Oil, Wheat & Wobblies*, 141-
42; James Maloney, Testimony, *United States v. William D. Haywood et al.* Box 112,
Folder 2, (hereafter Maloney testimony) IWW, WS; Forrest Edwards, Testimony,
United States v. William D. Haywood, et al. Box 111, Folder 5 (hereafter Edwards
testimony) IWW, WS.

35. Workman, *History of "400" A.W.O.*, 10; *Solidarity*, 9 September 1916.

36. *Solidarity*, 2 September 1916; Burdell testimony, IWW, WS; Taft, "The I.W.W. in the
Grain Belt," 60-61; Fast, "Agricultural Workers' Organization," 56-57.

37. *New York Times*, 28 July 1916; Fast, "Agricultural Workers' Organization," 53-54.

38. Larry J. Sprunk, "Hugh O'Connor–New Rockford" *North Dakota History* 44 (1977),
46-50; Haug, "The Industrial Workers of the World in North Dakota," 98-100; Fast,
"Agricultural Workers' Organization," 55.

39. Schwantes, *Pacific Northwest*, 160; *Yakima Morning Herald*, 15, 16 September
1916.

40. *Yakima Morning Herald*, 17 September 1916.

41. *Yakima Morning Herald*, 23 September 1916.

42. *Yakima Daily Republic*, 22 September 1916; *Yakima Morning Herald*, 23
September 1916.

43. *Yakima Morning Herald*, 24 September 1916; *Yakima Daily Republic*, 25
September 1916.

44. Ibid.; *Yakima Morning Herald*, 26 September 1916.

45. *Spokesman Review*, 26 September 1916; *Yakima Daily Republic*, 25, 26 September
1916; *Yakima Morning Herald*, 26, 27 September 1916.

46. *Yakima Daily Republic*, 27 September 1916; *Yakima Morning Herald*, 27
September 1916.

47. Ibid.; *Yakima Daily Republic* 28 September 1916; *Yakima Morning Herald* 28
September 1916.

48. *Yakima Daily Republic*, 29, 30 September 1916; *Yakima Morning Herald*, 30
September, 1 October 1916.

49. *Yakima Daily Republic*, 30 September, 4, 6 October 1916; *Yakima Morning Herald*,
5, 6 October 1916.

50. *Yakima Daily Republic*, 6 October 1916; *Yakima Morning Herald*, 6, 20, 22
October, 5 November, 1 December 1916; *Spokesman-Review*, 21 October 1916.

51. *Solidarity*, 11, 18 November 1916; Fast, "Agricultural Workers' Organization," 65-
66; Workman, *History of "400" A.W.O.*, 19-20.

52. Fast, "Agricultural Workers' Organization," 66-67; Connors, "Industrial Union," 40;
Dubofsky, *We Shall Be All*, 344-45; Brissenden, *The I.W.W.*, 337-39; Kornbluh, *Rebel
Voices*, 232; Workman, *History of "400" A.W.O.*, 20-21.

53. Workman, *History of "400" A.W.O.*, 22-23; Dubofsky, *We Shall Be All*, 318, 344-45,
61-65; Cole, "Shaping Up and Shipping Out," 177-79; 40-41; Howard Kimeldorf,
*Battling for American Labor: Wobblies, Craft Workers, and the Making of the Union
Movement* (Berkeley: University of California Press, 1999), 40-41; Thompson and
Murfin, *The I.W.W.*, 109, 115-16.

55. David A. Carter, "The Industrial Workers of the World and the Rhetoric of Song"
The Quarterly Journal of Speech 66 (1980), 365-66; Richard Brazier, "The Story of

the I.W.W.'s 'Little Red Songbook," *Labor History* 9 (Winter 1968), 91-105; Kornbluh, Rebel Voices, 65-66.

56. *Songs of the Workers: On the Road, In the Jungles and In the Shops* (Spokane: Spokane Local of the I.W.W., 1912?), 27, 34; Winters, *The Soul of the Wobblies*, 39-40.

57. *I.W.W. Songs: To Fan the Flames of Discontent* (Chicago: I.W.W. Publishing Bureau, 1917), 7, 27, 12; Winters, *The Soul of the Wobblies*, 50-51.

58. Ibid., 17; Brazier, "Story," 91; *I.W.W. Songs: To Fan the Flames of Discontent*, General Defense Edition (Chicago: I.W.W. Publishing Bureau, 1918), 31.

Four: War and Persecution

1. Nick Salvatore, *Eugene V. Debs: Citizen and Socialist* (Urbana: University of Illinois, 1982), 280-96; Kenneth C. Wenzer, *Anarchists Adrift: Emma Goldman and Alexander Berkman* (St. James, NY: Brandywine Press, 1996), 65-83; Ronald Schaffer, *America in the Great War: The Rise of the War Welfare State* (New York: Oxford University Press, 1991), 13-30. Also see David M. Kennedy, *Over Here: The First World War and American Society* (Oxford: Oxford University Press, 1980).

2. Dubofsky, *We Shall Be All*, 1988), 350-58; M. J. Heale, *American Anticommunism: Combating the Enemy Within, 1830-1970* (Baltimore: Johns Hopkins University Press, 1990), 51-53.

3. *Solidarity*, 6, 13 1917; Dubofsky, *We Shall Be All*, 349-350; Daniel, "Labor Radicalism," 77-79; Miller interview, Shaffer Papers, SHSW; St. John, *The I.W.W.*, 23-24; "Memorandum for the Attorney General," from A. B. Bielaski, 29 November 1917, Melvyn Dubofsky, ed., *Department of Justice Investigation Files. Part I: The Industrial Workers of the World* (Frederick, MD: University Publicans of American, 1989), (hereafter Dubofsky, *DJF*).

4. *Solidarity*, 17 March 1917; Daniel, "Labor Radicalism," 79; Jamieson, *Labor Unionism*, 64.

5. *Solidarity*, 14 April, 2 June 1917; *Industrial Worker*, 19 May 1917; *AWIU No. 400, California District Bulletin #3*, 13 August 1917, IWW Cal., UW; Jamieson, *Labor Unionism*, 65; McWilliams, *Factories in the Field*, 169; Daniel, "Labor Radicalism," 79-80; 23 July 1917 report by J. Vance Thompson and 28 July 1917 report without name, Lubin Papers, UCB.

6. *Industrial Worker*, 9 June 1917; *Solidarity*, 9 June 1917; Dubofsky, *We Shall Be All*, 359; Andrew A. Bruce, *Non-Partisan League* (New York: The Macmillian Company, 1921), 142-43; Noel Sargent, *Non-Partisan League Leaders Work with the I.W.W.* (St. Paul: Minnesota Sound Government Association, 1920?), 1.

7. *Industrial Worker*, 9 June 1917; *Solidarity*, 16 June 1917.

8. *Solidarity*, 23 June 1917; *Industrial Worker*, 21 July 1917; *Yakima Morning Herald*, 10 June 1917.

9. *Industrial Worker*, 21 July 1917.

10. Weintraub, "The I.W.W. in California," 90-91; Jamieson, *Labor Unionism*, 65-66; Daniel, "Labor Radicalism," 80-82; *Solidarity*, 4 August 1917; Elizabeth Reis, "The AFL, the IWW, and Bay Area Italian Cannery Workers" *California History* 64 (Summer 1985), 174-242.

11. *Solidarity*, 9 June 1917; Jamieson, *Labor Unionism*, 263-64; Carey McWilliams, *Ill Fares the Land: Migrants and Migratory Labor in the United States* (Boston: Little, Brown, and Company, 1942), 193; *Yakima Morning Herald*, 4 August 1917; H. C. Peterson and Gilbert C. Fite, *Opponents of War, 1917-1918* (Madison: University of Wisconsin Press, 1957), 40-41; Sellars, *Oil, Wheat, & Wobblies*, 77-92.

12. Heale, *American Anticommunism*, 53; *Spokesman-Review*, 7 March 1917; *Wenatchee Daily World*, 21, 29 March 1917; Eldridge Foster Dowell, *A History of Criminal Syndicalism Legislation in the United States* (Baltimore: Johns Hopkins

Press, 1939), 63-64, 70-71; Robert L. Tyler, *Rebels of the Woods: The I.W.W. in the Pacific Northwest* (Eugene: University of Oregon Books, 1967), 149-50.

13. *Yakima Morning Herald*, 18, 26, May, 6 June 1917.

14. Carl F. Reuss, "The Farm Labor Problem in Washington, 1917-1918," *Pacific Northwest Quarterly* 34 (October 1943), 343-44.

15. Ibid.; *Yakima Morning Herald*, 28 June, 1 July 1917; *Spokesman-Review*, 2 July 1917.

16. Tyler, *Rebels of the Woods*, 92; *Yakima Morning Herald*, 3 July 1917; Memo from F. A. Watt to Office Chief of Staff War College, regarding IWW activities, at Spokane, Wash. 19 June 1917 *U.S. Military Intelligence Reports: Surveillance of Radicals in the United States, 1917-1941* (Frederick, MD: University Publications of America, Inc., 1984), (hereafter *MIR*); Tim Hanson, "Wobblies in the Woods: The 1917 Lumber Strike in the Inland Empire" *Pacific Northwest Forum* 4 (1991), 72.

17. *Yakima Morning Herald*, 30 June, 3 July 1917; *Spokesman-Review*, 2, 3 July 1917.

18. Heale, *American Anticommunism*, 53; Kennedy, *Over Here*, 75-76; John D. Buenker and Edward R. Kantowicz, eds., *Historical Dictionary of the Progressive Era, 1890-1920* (New York: Greenwood Press, 1988), 144-45; Dubofsky, *We Shall Be All*, 406, 354-55; Document entitled "The Defendant Forrest Edwards." n.d., *DJF*.

19. *Spokesman-Review*, 12 April, 11 May 1917; *Yakima Morning Herald*, 1, 3 June, 31 May, 1917; *Industrial Worker*, 23 June 1917.

20. Preston, *Aliens and Dissenters*, 104-6; *Spokesman-Review*, 8 July 1917; *Yakima Daily Republic*, 9 July 1917; *Yakima Morning Herald*, 10 July 1917.

21. *Yakima Morning Herald*, 12 July 1917; *Yakima Daily Republic*, 10, 11 July 1917; *Spokesman-Review*, 10 July 1917.

22. *Yakima Morning Herald*, 18 July 1917; *Spokesman-Review*, 17, 22 July 1917; *Yakima Daily Republic*, 17, 18 July 1917; *Solidarity*, 18 August 1917.

23. *Yakima Daily Republic*, 16, 29 July 1917; *Yakima Morning Herald*, 13 July 1917.

24. *Spokesman-Review*, 1, 2 August 1917; *Yakima Morning Herald*, 14 July, 12 August 1917; *Yakima Daily Republic*, 14, 27, 31 July 1917.

25. *Spokesman-Review*, 8, 14 July 1917; *Yakima Morning Herald*, 11, 17 July 1917.

26. Reuss, "Farm Labor Problem in Washington," 346; *Spokesman-Review*, 10 July 1917; *Yakima Daily Republic*, 7 July 1917; *Yakima Morning Herald*, 31 July 1917.

27. *Spokesman-Review*, 2 August 1917; Tyler, *Rebels of the Woods*, 93-94; Jonathan Dembo, "A History of the Washington State Labor Movement, 1885-1935" (Ph.D. diss., University of Washington, 1978), 162; Bird et al., *Solidarity Forever*, 113; Vernon H. Jensen, *Lumber and Labor* (New York: Farrar & Rinehart, Inc., 1945), 126; Charlotte Todes, *Labor and Lumber* (New York: Arno Press, 1975), 166-67.

28. Dubofsky, *We Shall Be All*, 403, 385-91, 367-69; Report to U.S. Attorney General's Office, no names, 30 July 1917 Dubofsky, *DJF*; Tyler, *Rebels of the Woods*, 133-34; *Spokesman-Review*, 15 August 1917; *Yakima Morning Herald*, 16, 17 August 1917; *Yakima Daily Republic*, 15 August 1917; Hanson, "Wobblies in the Woods," 76-77.

29. *Yakima Daily Republic*, 16, 18 August 1917; *Yakima Morning Herald*, 16, 18 August 1917; *Spokesman-Review*, 2, 12, 16, 18 August 1917.

30. *Spokesman-Review*, 6, 21 August 1917; *Yakima Morning Herald*, 21 August 1917; *Yakima Daily Republic*, 17 July, 21 August 1917; Tyler, *Rebels of the Woods*, 134; Reuss, "Farm Labor Problem in Washington," 345.

31. Kennedy, *Over Here*, 166-67; Schaffer, *America in the Great War*, 176; *New York Times*, 18 July 1917; Daniel J. Ahearn, *The Wages of Farm and Factory Laborers, 1914-1944* (New York: Columbia University Press, 1945), 93, 99; *Minneapolis Morning Tribune*, 12, 26 August 1917.

32. Ahearn, *Wages of Farm and Factory Laborers*, 93; Jamieson, *Labor Unionism*, 403; Schwartz, *Seasonal Farm Labor*, 24; Harry Schwartz, "Agricultural Labor in the First World War," *Journal of Farm Economics* 24 (February 1924), 185.

33. Haug, "Industrial Workers of the World in North Dakota," 101; Bruce, *Non-Partisan League*, 144.

34. *Proposed Tentative Agreement Between the National Nonpartisan League of North Dakota and the Agricultural Workers Industrial Union of the I.W.W. for the Harvest and Threshing Season of 1917*, Box 111, Folder 5, IWW, WS; Edwards testimony, IWW, WS.

35. John Edenstorm, Testimony, *United States v. William D. Haywood, et al.*, Box 111, Folder 1, (hereafter Edenstorn testimony) IWW, WS; Edwards testimony, IWW, WS; *Solidarity*, 21 July 1917; Haug, "Industrial Workers of the World in North Dakota," 102; Fast, "Agricultural Workers' Organization," 73-74; *League Abandons Plan to Import Organized Labor to Harvest N. D. Crops*, 1-6, Arthur Le Sueur Papers, Minnesota Historical Society, St. Paul, Minnesota (hereafter Le Sueur Papers), MHS; Bruce, *Non-Partisan League*, 142; Sargent, *Non-Partisan League Leaders Work with the I.W.W.*, 2.

36. *League Abandons Plan*, Le Sueur Papers, MHS; Dubofsky, *We Shall Be All*, 360.

37. *New York Times*, 18 July 1917; *Solidarity*, 7, 14, 21, 28 July 1917; Jamieson, *Labor Unionism*, 404; Schwartz, "Agricultural Labor," 183.

38. Fast, "Agricultural Workers' Organization," 75; Telegram to U.S. Attorney General Thomas W. Gregory, 26 July 1917, Dubofsky, *DJF*; Dubofsky, *We Shall Be All*, 370-75; Thompson and Murfin, *The I.W.W.*, 118-19; *Yakima Daily Republic*, 3, 6 July 1917; *Yakima Morning Herald*, 7 July 1917; *Spokesman-Review*, 7 July 1917.

39. *Yakima Daily Republic*, 31 July 1917; Dubofsky, *We Shall Be All*, 385-91.

40. *Yakima Morning Herald*, 29 July 1917; *Solidarity*, 4 11 August 1917; *Industrial Worker*, 22 August 1917; Fast, "Agricultural Workers' Organization," 75-76.

41. Frederick W. Thompson to Joel A. Watne, 12 June 1967, Thompson Papers, WS; Peterson and Fite, *Opponents of War*, 65-67; Philip S. Foner, *History of the Labor Movement in the United States*. Vol. 7, *Labor and World War I, 1914-1918* (New York: International Publishers, 1987), 7-8, 24-26; Harry Curran Milbur to U.S. Senator Duncan U. Fetcher, 23 July 1917, Dubofsky, *DJF*; *Solidarity*, 18 August 1917; Hargreaves, *Dry Farming*, 265; William C. Pratt, "Socialism on the Northern Plains, 1900-1924," *South Dakota History* 18 (Spring/Summer 1988), 19-22.

42. *Industrial Worker*, 15, 29 August, 12 September 1917; *Solidarity*, 25 August 1917.

43. Dubofsky, *We Shall Be All*, 398-406; Peterson and Fite, *Opponents of the War*, 62; Selig Perlman and Philip Taft, *History of Labor in the United States, 1896-1932*. vol. 4, *Labor Movements* (New York: The Macmillian Company, 1935), 417-18; *New York Times*, 6 September 1917.

44. Statement of C. W. Anderson on first raid, n.d., Box 99, IWW, WS; Statement of Forrest Edwards on first raid, n.d., Box 99, Folder 10, IWW, WS.

45. Fast, "Agricultural Workers' Organization," 77-78.

46. Ibid., 78-79; Statement of C. W. Anderson on second and third raids, n.d., Box 99, Folder 10, IWW, WS.

47. Fast, "Agricultural Workers' Organization," 79-80; Earl Bruce White, "The United States v. C. W. Anderson et al.: The Wichita Case, 1917-1919," in *At the Point of Production: The Local History of the I.W.W.*, ed. Joseph R. Conlin (Westport, CT: Greenwood Press, 1981), 151; *Defense News Bulletin*, 10 November 1917; *Yakima Morning Herald*, 9 September 1917; *Solidarity*, 22 September 1917.

48. *Solidarity*, 20 October 1917; *Industrial Worker*, 27 October 1917; Fast, "Agricultural Workers' Organization," 80.

49. Weintraub, "I.W.W. in California," 139; Daniel, "Labor Radicalism," 86-87; *San Francisco Chronicle*, 6, 7 September 1917; *Defense News Bulletin*, 10, 17 November 1917.

50. David G. Wagaman, "'Rausch Mit': The I.W.W. in Nebraska During World War I," in *At the Point of Production*, ed. Joseph R. Conlin (Westport, CT: Greenwood Press,

1981), 126-27; *Itemized Inventory of Property Seized From I.W.W. Headquarters, Omaha, Nebr., Nov. 13th, 1917*, Box 99, Folder 10, IWW, WS.

51. White, "United States v. C. W. Anderson et al.," 145-53.

52. Fast, "Agricultural Workers' Organization," 77-78; Daniel, "Labor Radicalism," 86-87; Wagaman, "'Rausch Mit,'" 125-28; Kornbluh, *Rebel Voices*, 318; Dubofsky, *We Shall Be All*, 442-44.

53. See Papers of the Washington State Secret Service in the Governor Ernest Lister Papers, Washington State Archives, Olympia, Washington (hereafter SS Lister Papers, WSA).

54. Report by B., 1 December 1917, Report by J. F. M. and F. L. B., 12-13 October 1917, Report by Op. 43: 14 February 1917, Report by F. L. B., 18 November 1917, Report by J. F. M., 30 October 1917, Report by J. F. M. and B. R., 7 November 1917, SS Lister Papers, WSA.

55. Reports by Op. 43: 29, 30 December 1917, 18 January 1918, SS Lister Papers, WSA.

56. Reports by Op. 43: 11, 14 January 1918, SS Lister Papers, WSA.

57. *Yakima Daily Republic*, 30 January, 23 February 1918; Report by Op. 43, 27 January - 10 February 1918, SS Lister Papers, WSA.

58. Reports by Op. 43: 18, 24, 26 February 1918, SS Lister Papers, WSA.

59. *Yakima Daily Republic*, 1 April 1918; Report by B. R., 25 February, 1, 3-7 March 1918, Report by F. L. B., 1, 2 March 1918, Report by Op. 43, 22, 24,26, February, 1-5 March 1918, SS Lister Papers, WSA.

60. *Yakima Daily Republic*, 2, 4 March 1918; *Seattle Post-Intelligencer*, 1 March 1918.

61. *Yakima Daily Republic*, 19 March 1918 *Yakima Morning Herald*, 19 March 1918; *Industrial Worke*r, 23 March 1918; Report by Op. 43, 18-20 March 1918, SS Lister Papers, WSA.

62. Reports by Op. 43, 18-20, 25, 29, 30 March 1918, Report by F. L. B., 22 March 1918, SS Lister Papers, WSA; *Yakima Daily Republic*, 22 March 1918; Thomas Elliott to Governor Lister, 12 April 1918, SS Lister Papers, WSA.

63. Report by Op. 43: 1, 6 April 1918, SS Lister Papers, WSA; *Yakima Morning Herald*, 22 March 1918; Report by L. M. Hammett, 29 April 1918, C. B. Reed to Governor Lister, 14 May 1918, SS Lister Papers, WSA; *Yakima Daily Republic*, 18 April 1918; *Spokesman-Review*, 4, 5 April, 3 May 1918.

64. *Wenatchee Daily World*, 13 September 1918; *Yakima Morning Herald*, 30 June, 7, 16, 28, 30 July 1918; *Yakima Daily Republic*, 24 April, 16, 25, 30 September, 4, 7 October 1918; Reuss, "Farm Labor Problem in Washington," 346-52.

65. *Yakima Daily Republic*, 11, 15, 16, 18, 24 October 1918; *Spokesman-Review*, 20 October 1918.

66. *Yakima Morning Herald*, 23 March 1918; *Solidarity*, 13 October 1917; *Defense News Bulletin*, 8 December 1917, 19, 26 January 1918; Fast, "Agricultural Workers' Organization," 98; Daniel, "Labor Radicalism," 87-88; Daniel, *Bitter Harvest*, 87; Adams and Kelly, "Study of Farm Labor," 1-4, 9-10, 17-22.

67. Schwartz, "Agricultural Labor," 184-87; Fast, "Agricultural Workers' Organization," 105-8.

68. Thorstein Veblen, "An Unpublished Paper on the I.W.W.," *Journal of Political Economy* 40 (December 1932), 796-807.

69. Robert W. Bruere's article reprinted in *Defense News Bulletin*, 27 April 1918.

70. W. J. Furse to Nebraska State Council of Defense, 8 June 1918, State Council of Defense Papers, Series 3, Nebraska State Historical Society, Lincoln, Nebraska (hereafter NSCD, NSHS); Fast, "Agricultural Workers' Organization," 108.

71. Mat K. Fox, "The Story of No. 400," *One Big Union Monthly* 1 (September 1919), 49; *Defense News Bulletin*, 1 June, 26 January, 23 March, 15 June 1918; Dubofsky, *We Shall Be All*, 429.

72. *Defense News* Bulletin, 15 June, 18 May 1918; Spy reports on the AWIU Minneapolis branch, no author, 1, 14, 31 October, 15 November 1918, Northern Information Bureau Collection, Minnesota Historical Society, St. Paul, Minnesota (hereafter NIBC, MNS); Fast, "Agricultural Workers' Organization," 110.

73. Elizabeth Gurley Flynn, *Sabotage: The Conscious Withdrawal of the Workers' Industrial Efficiency* (Cleveland: I.W.W. Publishing Bureau, 1916), 5; *Yakima Morning Herald*, 30 June 1918; Dubofsky, *We Shall Be All*, 432-33; Preston, *Aliens and Dissenters*, 142-44.

74. Preston, *Aliens and Dissenters*, 119-20; Dubofsky, *We Shall Be All*, 433.

75. Frank B. Gibson, Testimony, *United States v. William D. Haywood, et al.*, Box 106, Folder 1, (hereafter Gibson testimony) IWW, WS; Burdell testimony, IWW, WS.

76. Charles Selby, Testimony, *United States v. William D. Haywood, et al.*, Box 107, Folder 2, (hereafter Selby testimony) IWW, WS; Henry A. Pierce, Testimony, *United States v. William D. Haywood, et al.*, Box 111, Folder 5, (hereafter Pierce testimony) IWW, WS.

77. Burdell testimony, IWW, WS; Jesse N. Banks, Testimony, *United States v. William D. Haywood, et al.*, Box 105, Folder 7, (hereafter Banks testimony) IWW, WS; William Cole, Testimony, *United States v. William D. Haywood, et al*, Box 106, Folder 1, (hereafter Cole testimony) IWW, WS; Wermke testimony, IWW, WS; *Yakima Daily Republic*, 1 June 1918; *Pullman Herald*, 8 February 1918.

78. Carlson testimony, IWW, WS; Maloney testimony, IWW, WS; Dubofsky, *We Shall Be All*, 434-36; Preston, *Aliens and Dissenters*, 146-51; Philip Taft, "The Federal Trials of the IWW," *Labor History* 3 (Winter 1962), 69-76; Foner, *Labor Movement*, vol. 7, 309-10; *New York Times*, 18 August 1918.

79. Fast, "Agricultural Workers' Organization," 101-4; Reports on Forrest Edwards, no name, no date, Dubofsky, *DJF*.

80. Dubofsky, *We Shall Be All*, 438-39; Preston, *Aliens and Dissenters*, 132-35; Taft, "Federal Trials of the IWW," 76-77; Weintraub, "I.W.W. in California," 139-42.

81. Preston, *Aliens and Dissenters*, 119-20; Dubofsky, *We Shall Be All*, 440; Taft, "Federal Trials of the IWW," 77-78; Weintraub, "I.W.W. in California," 143-44.

82. Weintraub, "I.W.W. in California," 143-53; Daniel, "Labor Radicalism," 87; Preston, *Aliens and Dissenters*, 120; Taft, "Federal Trials of the IWW," 78.

83. Dubofsky, *We Shall Be All*, 440; Weintraub, "I.W.W. in California," 155-56; Portions of testimonies of Joseph F. Pfost, D. D. Cornwall, and L. E. Farmer in *United States of America v. Elmer Anderson, et al.*, Dubofsky, *DJF*, 1-10; Summary notes on "Sacramento I.W.W. Defendants," Dubofsky, *DJF*, 8-12, 36-37.

84. Weintraub, "I.W.W. in California," 156-59; Dubofsky, *We Shall Be All*, 440-41; Taft, "Federal Trials of the IWW," 78-79.

85. Taft, "Federal Trials of the IWW, 79-80; Preston, *Aliens and Dissenters*, 119; White, "United States v. C. W. Anderson et al.," 156-57.

86. White, "United States v. C. W. Anderson et al.," 157-59; Taft, "Federal Trials of the IWW," 80; Preston, *Aliens and Dissenters*, 131-32.

87. Wagaman, "'Rausch Mit,'"128-29; Reports by M. Eberstein on C. Bates, 22 November 1917, George Adams, 20 November 1917, William Boyler, 20 November 1917, John Stein, 22 November 1917, and C. G. Baldwin, 20 November 1917, *MIR*.

88. Wagaman, "'Rausch Mit,'" 130-31; Dubofsky, *We Shall Be All*, 442-43; Preston, *Aliens and Dissenters*, 136-38.

89. Kornbluh, *Rebel Voices*, 321; Dubofsky, *We Shall Be All*, 443-44; Preston, *Aliens and Dissenters*, 150-51; Weintraub, "I.W.W. in California," 158-59.

Five: Perseverance Amid Change

1. Kornbluh, *Rebel Voices*, 321; Dowell, *History of Criminal Syndicalism*, 17-18, 91.

2. Buenker and Kantowicz, *Historical Dictionary*, 144-45, 423-33; Dowell, *History of Criminal Syndicalism*, 13-14. For a thorough account of antiradicalism in the United States, see Heale, *American Anticommunism*.

3. McWilliams, *Factories in the Field*, 182; Heale, *American Anticommunism*, 62-63; Harvey O'Connor, *Revolution in Seattle: A Memoir* (New York: Monthly Review Press, 1964), 125-45.

4. Dubofsky, *We Shall Be All*, 381-82; Kornbluh, *Rebel Voices*, 322; Sellars, *Oil, Wheat & Wobblies*, 133-34; Irving Bernstein, *The Lean Years: A History of the American Worker, 1920-1933* (Boston: Houghton Mifflin Company, 1966), 222.

5. Nelson Van Valen, "The Bolsheviki and the Orange Growers," *Pacific Historical Review* 22 (February 1953), 39-41; Guerin-Gonzales, *Mexican Workers*, 60-63.

6. Daniel, "Labor Radicalism," 88; J. A. Stromquist, "California Oranges," *Industrial Pioneer* 1 (March 1921), 23-26.

7. Daniel, "Labor Radicalism," 89; Mat K. Fox, "Agricultural Workers Industrial Union No. 400 I.W.W.," *One Big Union Monthly* 1 (1 March 1919), 58-59; Van Valen, "The Bolsheviki and the Orange Growers," 42-50.

8. Mat K. Fox, "Agricultural Workers' Industrial Union No. 400, I.W.W. Bulletin No. 29," *One Big Union Monthly* 1 (May 1919), 56; Mrs. Wallace M. Short, *Just One American* (n.p.: Mrs. Wallace M. Short, 1943), 79-86.

9. Short, *Just One American*, 93, 101-2, 111.

10. *New Solidarity*, 19 April, 3 May 1919; Short, *Just One American*, 112-13.

11. Fast, "Agricultural Workers' Organization," 111-12; Philip Taft, "Mayor Short and the I.W.W. Agricultural Workers" *Labor History* 7 (1966), 173-77; *New Solidarity*, 3 May 1919; Mat K. Fox, "Agricultural Workers' Industrial Union, No. 400 Bulletin No. 32," *One Big Union Monthly* 1 (June 1919), 56.

12. Fast, Agricultural Workers' Organization," 113; Fox, "Bulletin 32," 57; *New Solidarity*, 24 May 1919.

13. *New Solidarity*, 31 May, 14 June 1919; *Industrial Worker*, 18 June 1919; Mat K. Fox, "Agricultural Workers' Industrial Union No. 400 Bulletin No. 37," *One Big Union Monthly* 1 (July 1919), 57-58.

14. *New York Times*, 15 June 1919; Fast, "Agricultural Workers' Organization," 115; "The Campaign of the Agricultural Workers," *One Big Union Monthly* 1 (August 1919), 7-8; *New Solidarity*, 28 June, 5 July 1919.

15. Fast, "Agricultural Workers' Organization," 115-16.

16. *New Solidarity*, 2 August, 26 July 1919; Fast, "Agricultural Workers' Organization," 116.

17. *New Solidarity*, 16, 23 August, 13 September 1919; Statistics from *One Big Union Monthly* 1 (October 1919), 55 and (November 1919), 58.

18. Weintraub, "The I.W.W. in California," 166-69; *New Solidarity*, 5 July, 2 August, 13, 27 September 1919; Daniel, "Labor Radicalism," 89-90.

19. *Yakima Daily Republic*, 8 July 1919; Daniel, "Labor Radicalism," 90-91.

20. Daniel, "Labor Radicalism," 91; Taylor, *Labor on the Land*, 121; Schwartz, *Seasonal Farm Labor*, 57; *New Solidarity*, 19 April 1919; Fuller, *Hired Hands*, 45-56; Guerin-Gonzales, *Mexican Workers*, 18-19, 71-72.

21. Taylor, *Labor on the Land*, 99; Schwartz, *Seasonal Farm Labor*, 58; Emma Duke, *California The Golden* (New York: National Child Labor Committee, 1921), 1-5, 17-29; Daniel, *Bitter Harvest*, 87, 101-4; Guerin-Gonzales, *Mexican Workers*, 74.

22. *Yakima Daily Republic*, 30 April, 15, 31 May, 7 June, 7 July, 1, 5, 30 September 1919; *Yakima Morning Herald*, 31 May 1919; Carl F. Reuss, Paul H. Landis, and Richard Wakefield, *Migratory Farm Labor and the Hop Industry on the Pacific*

Coast: With Special Application to Problems of the Yakima Valley, Washington (Pullman: State College of Washington, Agricultural Experiment Station), 37; Friday, *Organizing Asian American Labor*, 127-28.

23. *Yakima Daily Republic*, July 24, 14 August 1919; *Yakima Morning Herald*, 1 June 1919; Bates, *Commercial Survey*, 249-62; Schwantes, *Pacific Northwest*, 171; Landis and Brooks, *Farm Labor*, 9; Reuss, et al., *Migratory Farm Labor*, 48.

24. *Yakima Daily Republic*, 10 June, 23 October 1919. See Landis and Brooks, *Farm Labor in the Yakima Valley, Washington*, for the most complete sociological study of region's agricultural workforce.

25. *New York Times*, 13 November 1919; Tyler, *Rebels of the Woods*, 155-84. For a superb scholarly treatment of the Centralia event and the subsequent legal process, see Tom Copeland, *The Centralia Tragedy of 1919: Elmer Smith and the Wobblies* (Seattle: University of Washington Press, 1993); for the Wobbly perspective, see Ralph Chaplin, *The Centralia Conspiracy: The Truth About the Armistice Day Tragedy* (Chicago: General Defense Committee, 1924).

26. *New York Times*, 14 November 1919; *Wenatchee Daily World*, 18, 19, 21, 24 November 1919; *Yakima Daily Republic*, 12, 17 November 1919; *Spokesman-Review*, 13-16, November 1919; Copeland, *Centralia Tragedy*, 91-92.

27. *New Solidarity*, 19 April, 11, 25 October 1919; Fast, "Agricultural Workers' Organization," 119; Short, *Just One American*, 124-25.

28. *New Solidarity*, 22 November 1919; Mat K. Fox, "Agricultural Workers' Industrial Union No. 400, I.W.W. Bulletin No. 56," *One Big Union Monthly* 1 (December 1919), 53-54; Fast, "Agricultural Workers' Organization," 119-20.

29. Preston, *Aliens and Dissenters*; Heale, *American Anticommunism*, 70-78; *New York Times*, 4 January 1919.

30. Thompson and Murfin, *The I.W.W.*, 127-28; Nell Irvin Painter, *Standing at Armageddon: The United States, 1877-1919* (New York: W. W. Norton & Company, 1987), 346-49, 358-62, 368-80; Dubofsky, *We Shall Be All*, 453; Montgomery, *Fall of the House of Labor*, 332; Bernstein, *Lean Years*, 84; Tom Barker, "The Agricultural Workers Union in Argentina," *One Big Union Monthly* 2 (March 1920), 30-31.

31. Fast, "Agricultural Workers' Organization," 121; "Financial Statements," *One Big Union Monthly* 2 (February 1920), 61-62, Fred Fisher, "Agricultural Workers Industrial Union No. 400, I.W.W. Bulletin No. 2," *One Big Union Monthly* 2 (March 1920), 55-56; and "Financial Statements," *One Big Union Monthly* 2 (April 1920), 56-57.

32. *New York Times*, 9 July, 12 September 1920; Lescohier, *Conditions Affecting*, 30-34; Sellars, *Oil, Wheat & Wobblies*, 145-46; Fast, "Agricultural Workers' Organization, 122.

33. "Resolution Regarding Sabotage," *One Big Union Monthly* 2 (April 1920), 56; "The Gruesome Story of American Terrorism, Installment No. 3" *One Big Union Monthly* 2 (May 1920), 51-53; Perlman and Taft, *History of Labor*, vol. 4, 429-30.

34. *New York Times*, 18 February 1920; Fast, "Agricultural Workers' Organization," 123; Dowell, *A History of Criminal Syndicalism*," 17-18, 59; Richard C. Cortner, "The Wobblies and Fiske v. Kansas: Victory Amid Disintegration," *Kansas History: A Journal of the Central Plains* 4 (Spring 1981), 30-31.

35. Dowell, *A History of Criminal Syndicalism*, 60-63; Fisher, "AWIU Bulletin No. 2," 55.

36. Weintraub, "The I.W.W. in California," 95-96; Jamieson, *Labor Unionism*, 59-60; *Report of Commission on Industrial Relations*, vol. 2, 4945; John S. Gambs, *The Decline of the I.W.W.* (New York: Columbia University Press, 1932), 173; John Sandgren, "The I.W.W.: A Statement of Its Principles, Objects and Methods," *One Big Union Monthly* 2 (May 1920), 40.

37. John Engdahl, "The Gruesome Story of American Terrorism, Lest We forget," *One Big Union Monthly* 2 (April 1920), 12-14; *New York Times*, 4 January, 6 August 1919; *Wenatchee Daily World*, 20, 31 January, 7, 14 February, 23 April 1920; *Spokesman-Review*, 3 March, 8 April, 2, 30 May, 10 June, 15 July 1920.

38. Weintraub, "The I.W.W. in California," 95; *Industrial Worker*, 16 October 1920; Jamieson, *Labor Unionism*, 68-69.

39. "Statements of Facts," Court Case #2347, *People of the State of California v. N. Steelik*. California State Archives, Sacramento, California; Bird et al., *Solidarity Forever*, 199-202; Thompson and Murfin, *The I.W.W.*, 149; Kornbluh, *Rebel Voices*, 322; Louis H. Brown, "The Gruesome Story of American Terrorism: Installment No. 4." *One Big Union Monthly* 2 (June 1920), 37.

40. Weintraub, "The I.W.W. in California," 96-98; Mitchell, *Lie of the Land*, 83-94; *Industrial Worker*, 25 February 1925.

41. *Industrial Worker*, 23 October 1920.

42. Sellars, *Oil, Wheat & Wobblies*, 155-56.

43. E. W. Latchem, "The Agricultural Workers Convention," *One Big Union Monthly* 2 (November 1920), 56-57; Fast, "Agricultural Workers' Organization," 123-24.

44. *By-Laws of the Agricultural Workers Industrial Union No. 400: Instructions to Branch Secretaries and Delegates* (Chicago: I.W.W. Publishing Bureau, 1917); *By-Laws of the Agricultural Workers Industrial Union No. 110 of the I.W.W.: Instructions to Members, Job and Stationary Delegates and Branch Secretaries* (Chicago: I.W.W. Publishing Bureau, 1920).

45. E. W. Latchem, "The Aftermath," *One Big Union Monthly* 2 (November 1920), 57-58.

Six: The Resurgence of Harvest Wobblies

1. Thomas Howard McEnroe, "The Industrial Workers of the World: Theories, Organizational Problems, and Appeals, as Revealed Principally in the *Industrial Worker*" (Ph.D. diss., University of Minnesota, 1960), 29-30, 73-93. For a list of English and non-English language newspapers and periodicals, see Brissenden, *The I.W.W.*, 395-99.

2. For a list of pre-1919 flyers and leaflets see Brissenden, *The I.W.W.*, 390-93; Tony Bubka, "Time to Organize!" *American West* 5 (1968), 21-26.

3. *Vegetable and Fruit Workers* (Chicago: Agricultural Workers' Industrial Union No. 110 of the I.W.W., n.d.), no page, Box 161, IWW, WS; *Agricultural Workers Industrial Union No. 110 of the I.W.W. Bulletin No. 11*, 21 April 1922, (hereafter *AWIU, bulletin number* and date) IWW Seattle, UW.

4. *You Need Industrial Unionism*, (n.p., n.d.), Box 44, Folder 35, IWW, WS; Assorted *AWIU Bulletins* from 1922 and 1923, IWW Seattle, UW.

5. *The Two Triple Alliances* Leaflet (n.p.: General Organization Committee of the A.W.I.U. No. 110 of the I.W.W., 1922), Box 44, Folder 35, IWW, WS; *Harvest Time Is Honey Time* Leaflet (Chicago: Agricultural Workers Industrial Union No. 110, n.d.), Box 163, IWW, WS.

6. Ahearn, *Wages of Farm and Factory Laborers*, 91-102; Schwartz, *Seasonal Farm Labor*, 57-59; Lescohier, *Labor Problems*, 18-22; Daniel, *Bitter Harvest*, 67-68.

7. *AWIU Bulletin #1*, 7 February 1922, IWW Seattle, UW.

8. The editors of *Solidarity* changed the publication's name to *Industrial Solidarity* in 1921, but for consistency's sake in the text, the newspaper will be referred to as *Solidarity*; Gambs, *Decline of the I.W.W.*, 249; *AWIU Bulletin No. 6*, 17 March 1922, IWW Seattle, UW.

9. *AWIU Bulletin No. 11*, 21 April, *No. 13*, 5 May, *No. 20*, 14 June 1922, IWW Seattle, UW.

10. *AWIU Bulletin No. 31*, 15 August 1923, IWW, WS; *AWIU Bulletin No. 32*, 13 September 1922, IWW Seattle, UW; *Minutes of the Fifteenth Convention of the Agricultural Workers Industrial Union No. 110 of the I.W.W. Held at Fargo, N. D. October 8-18, 1923* (n.p.: Printing and Publishing Workers' Industrial Union, No. 450, I. W. W., 1923), 5-6, Box 44, Folder 6, IWW, WS; Gambs, *Decline of the I.W.W.*, 166; *Delinquent List of the Agricultural Workers Industrial Union No. 110, of the I. W. W.*, 1 December 1924, Box 44, Folder 30, IWW, WS.

11. Thompson and Murfin, *The I.W.W.*, 95-96; *AWIU Bulletin No. 23*, 12 July 1922, IWW Seattle, UW; *Hang on to Your Life Belt* leaflet (Chicago: The Agricultural Workers' Industrial Union No. 110 of the I.W.W., n.d.), Box 163, IWW, WS; Brissenden, *The I.W.W.*, 349-50.

12. *AWIU Bulletin No. 20*, 21 July, *No. 22*, 28 June 1922, IWW Seattle, UW; Lescohier, "With the I.W.W.," 373.

13. See Abner E. Woodruff, *Evolution of American Agriculture* (n.p.: Agricultural Workers Industrial Union No. 400, 1919?), Box 160, IWW, WS.

14. See Bureau of Industrial Research, *Agriculture: The World's Basic Industry and its Workers* (Chicago: Bureau of Industrial Research, 1921).

15. See *I.W.W. Songs: To Fan the Flames of Discontent* (1923; rpt., Chicago: Charles H. Kerr Publishing Company, 1989).

16. Brazier, "Story," 97-99; De Caux interview, Oral History, UCLA; Stanely Jevery (?) to E. B. Benn, U. S. Marshal, Seattle Washington, 14 September 1922, Dubofsky, *DJF*.

17. *AWIU Bulletin No. 14*, 12 May 1922, IWW Seattle, UW; *Dare To Be Different* leaflet (Chicago: Agricultural Workers' Industrial Union No. 110 of the I.W.W., n.d.), Box 159, IWW, WS.

18. *New York Times*, 10 May 1921; Gambs, *Decline of the I.W.W.*, 158-62; *Minutes of the 12th Convention of the Agricultural Workers Industrial Union No. 110, I.W.W.: Which is the First Annual Delegate Convention Held at Omaha, Neb. October 17, 1921*, 17-18, Box 44, Folder 3, IWW, WS; *Industrial Worker*, 20 March, 13 May 1922.

19. *12th Convention of the Agricultural Workers*, 15, IWW, WS; *Minutes of the 2nd Annual Delegate Convention Which is the 13th Convention of the Agricultural Workers Industrial Union No. 110: Held at Minneapolis, Minn, October 25th to November 7th 1922*, 10, Box 44, Folder 4, IWW Col., WS; *AWIU Bulletin No. 48*, 12 December 1923, IWW, WS. The Work People's College had its origins in the mid-1910s among a community of Finnish socialists in Duluth. The Duluth Finnish community turned to the IWW in large numbers in 1916 and the school became a socialist/Wobbly joint endeavor for Finnish- and English-speaking students of the working class; Gambs, *Decline of the I.W.W.*, 163-64. For a comprehensive study of labor colleges in the U.S., see Richard J. Altenbaugh, *Education for Struggle: The American Labor Colleges of the 1920s and 1930s* (Philadelphia: Temple University Press, 1990).

20. *An Economic Interpretation of the Job* (Chicago: Department of Education of Agricultural Workers Industrial Union No. 110 of the Industrial Workers of the World, June 1922); *What is the I.W.W. Preamble?: A Dialogue* (Chicago: Agricultural Workers Industrial Union No. 110, I.W.W., 1922?).

21. Don D. Lescohier, *History of Labor in the United States, 1896-1932. Volume III: Working Conditions* (New York: The Macmillian Company, 1935), 123; Montgomery, *Fall of the House of Labor*, 398; Bernstein, *The Lean Years*, 52, 60-61.

22. *New York Times*, 20, 27 January 1921; Ahearn, *Wages of Farm and Factory Laborers*, 136-40; Bernstein, *The Lean Years*, 48; Lescohier, "Farm Labor," 11-12.

23. Bernstein, *The Lean Years*, 52-55.

24. Lescohier, "I.W.W. in the Wheat Lands," 380.

25. *Industrial Solidarity*, 7 January 1922; L. C. Gray, Charles L. Stewart, Howard A. Turner, J. T. Sanders, and W. J. Spillman, *Farm Ownership and Tenancy* (1924; rpt., New York: Arno Press, 1976), 509-15, 532-33; Hopkins, *Changing Technology*, 101-13.

26. *Grand Forks Herald*, 11 July 1923; *Industrial Worker*, 26 February, 19 March, 2 April, 1 May, 25 June, 27 August 1921, 21 July, 15 December 1923; *Industrial Solidarity*, 4 March, 13 May, 10 June 1922, 21 March 1923.

27. *Industrial Solidarity*, 10 June 1922, 30 June, 21 July 1923.

28. Lescohier, *Labor Problems*, 18; Lescohier, "Hands and Tools," 382; *Industrial Worker*, 19 March 1921; Lescohier, *Sources of Supply*, 1-5.

29. *Solidarity*, 5 March 1921.

30. *Industrial Worker*, 14 May 1921.

31. *Solidarity*, 30 April 1921. See *Minutes of the Convention of the Agricultural Workers Industrial Union No. 110, I.W.W. Held at Sioux City, Iowa April 18 to 24, 1921*, Box 44, Folder 2, IWW, WS; *AWIU Bulletin, No. 29*, 23 August 1922, IWW, UW; *Minutes of the 2nd Annual Delegate Convention*, 22-23, IWW, WS.

32. *Solidarity*, 4 June 1921.

33. *New York Times*, 12 June, 8 July 1921; *Solidarity*, 25 June, 2 July 1921; Lescohier, *Conditions Affecting*, 35-36.

34. *Solidarity*, 16 July 1921.

35. Sellars, *Oil, Wheat & Wobblies*, 147; Ahearn, *Wages of Farm and Factory Laborers*, 99-102; *Solidarity*, 23 July 1921.

36. Sellars, *Oil, Wheat & Wobblies*, 147; *Solidarity*, 30 July, 6 August 1921; *New York Times*, 17 July 1921.

37. *New York Times*, 19, 21 July 1921.

38. *Industrial Worker*, 6 August 1921; *New York Times*, 16, 17 July 1921.

39. *Industrial Worker*, 13, 20 August, 1 October 1921; *New York Times*, 1 September 1921; *Grand Forks Herald*, 17, 21 July 1923.

40. *Solidarity*, 13, 20 August, 10 September 1921.

41. *Solidarity*, 8 October 1921; *Industrial Worker*, 20 August, 5 November, 3 December 1921; *Wenatchee Daily World*, 20 September, 4 October 1921; *Spokesman-Review*, 21 September 1921.

42. *Wenatchee Daily World*, 8 December 1921; 3, 6, 7, 11, 16 January 1922.

43. *Wenatchee Daily World*, 12 September 1921; *Spokesman-Review*, 11 September 1921; *Industrial Worker*, 3 September, 8 October 1921.

44. *Spokesman-Review*, 25 October 1921; *Solidarity*, 17 December 1921; *AWIU Bulletin No. 41*, 25 October 1921, IWW Seattle, UW; Weintraub, "The I.W.W. in California," 169-73.

45. *Solidarity*, 13, 27 August 1921; *Industrial Workers*, 29 October, 12 November 1921. See *Minutes of the 12th Convention, AWIU*, IWW, WS.

46. *Industrial Worker*, 21 April, 22 July 1922, 11 April 1923; *Industrial Solidarity*, 9 September 1922, 31 March 1923.

47. Lescohier, *Labor Problems*, 17-18; Ahearn, *Wages of Farm and Factory Laborers*, 99-102; *New York Times*, 9 June 1923.

48. *Industrial Solidarity*, 10 June 1922, 18 August 1923; *AWIU Bulletin No. 8*, 7 March 1923, IWW, WS.

49. *AWIU Bulletin No. 32*, 13 September, *No. 35*, 4 October 1922, *No. 49*, 10 January, *No. 1*, 18 January, *No. 20*, 30 May, *No. 34*, 5 September, *No. 42*, 31 October 1923, IWW Seattle, UW; *Industrial Worker*, 28 October, 4 November 19229 June 17 October 1923; *Minutes of the Fourteenth Convention of Agricultural Workers Industrial Union No. 110, I.W.W.: Held at Oklahoma City, Okla., May 20-24, 1923*, 12, Box 44, Folder 5, IWW, WS; *Industrial Solidarity*, 7 October 1922, 30 October 1923.

51. *Industrial Solidarity*, 24 June 1923, 19 August 1922; Sellars, *Oil, Wheat & Wobblies*, 163-66.

53. *Industrial Solidarity*, 7 July 1923; *AWIU No. 31*, 6 September 1922, IWW Seattle, UW; Sellars, *Oil, Wheat & Wobblies*, 165-73; Cortner, "The Wobblies and Fiske v. Kansas," 30-38.

54. Woodrow C. Whitten, "Criminal Syndicalism and the Law in California: 1919-1927," *Transactions of the American Philosophical Society* 59 (March 1969), 55-56.

55. Gambs, *Decline of the I.W.W.*, 69; Weintraub, "I.W.W. in California," 209-10; Preston, *Aliens & Dissenters*, 263-65, 70-72; Whitten, "Criminal Syndicalism in California," 55-56; *Industrial Solidarity*, 30 June 1923.

56. *Minutes of the 2nd Delegate Convention, AWIU*, 22, IWW, WS; *Minutes of the Fourteenth Convention, AWIU*, 13, IWW, WS.

57. *Grand Forks Herald*, 14, 20 July, 4 August 1923; *Industrial Solidarity*, 11 August, 1 September 1923; Ole Evenson, et al., to Secretary of Agriculture, 16 July 1923, Letter, C. W. Pagsley, acting Secretary, Department of Agriculture, to Attorney General, 30 July 1923, and W. D. Riter, assistant Attorney General, to Secretary of Agriculture, 29 August 1923, Dubofsky, *DJF*; *AWIU Bulletin No. 29*, 1 August 1923, *No. 33*, 29 August 1923, IWW, WS; *Industrial Worker*, 5 September 1923.

58. *Wenatchee Daily World*, 27 July, 21, 28 October 1922; *Industrial Worker*, 7 July, 20, 31 October 1923; *Industrial Solidarity*, 5 August, 3 June 1922, 18 August 1923; *Spokesman-Review*, 16 August 1923; *AWIU No. 37*, 26 September 1923, IWW, WS; see the introduction for a detailed account of this strike action.

59. Whitten, "Criminal Syndicalism in California," 56-60; *Industrial Worker*, 18, 28 April, 16 May, 4 August, 4 July, 19 September, 31 October 1923; *New York Times*, 17 July, 24 August, 16 September 1923; Gambs, *Decline of the I.W.W.*, 72-73; *Grand Forks Herald*, 17 July 1923.

60. Preston, *Aliens & Dissenters*, 266; Weintraub, "I.W.W. in California," 199; *Industrial Worker*, 28 November, 1, 8, 22 December 1923; *Industrial Solidarity*, 20 October 1923; *Minutes of the Fifteenth Convention of the AWIU*, 19, IWW, WS; *AWIU Bulletin No. 29*, 1 August, *No. 45*, 21 November, *No. 47*, 5 December 1923, IWW, WS.

Seven: The Road to Oblivion

1. Dubofsky, *We Shall Be All*, 445-68; Patrick Renshaw, *The Wobblies: The Story of Syndicalism in the United States* (Garden City, NY: Doubleday & Company, Inc., 1967), 243-71; Tyler, *Rebels of the Woods*, 185-217; *Industrial Worker*, 25 November 1922; see Sellars, *Oil, Wheat, & Wobblies*, Cole, "Shaping Up and Shipping Out," and Gambs, *Decline of the I.W.W.* for detailed histories of the postwar IWW; Thompson and Murfin, *The I.W.W.*, 139-50; Leland W. Robinson, "Social Movement Organizations in Decline: A Case Study of the IWW" (Ph.D. diss., Northwestern University, 1973), 57-58, 78-79; David Montgomery, "What More To Be Done?" *Labor History* 40 (August 1999), 356-61; Lisa McGirr, "Black and White Longshoremen in the IWW: A History of the Philadelphia Marine Transport Workers Industrial Union Local 8 *Labor History* 37 (Summer 1995), 377-402.

2. Kornbluh, *Rebel Voices*, 232; *Industrial Solidarity* 17 November, 22 December 1923; *AWIU No. 35*, 12 September 1923, IWW, WS; Sellars, *Oil, Wheat & Wobblies*, 144; McEnroe, "Industrial Workers of the World," 381.

3. Gambs, *Decline of the I.W.W.*, 99-100, 112; Sellars, *Oil, Wheat & Wobblies*, 174; *General Office Bulletin*, "The Passing of the A.W.O.," (no date, but probably from 1925), Box 31, Folder 31, IWW, WS.

4. Gambs, *Decline of the I.W.W.*, 113-14; McEnroe, "The Industrial Workers of the World," 381-82; *New York Times*, 11 May 1921; *Minutes of the Fifteenth Convention of the AWIU*, 26, IWW, WS; *Industrial Solidarity*, 3 November 1923; *AWIU Bulletin No. 45*, 21 November 1923, IWW, WS.

5. Gambs, *Decline of the I.W.W.*, 76-78, 80-89; Dubofsky, *We Shall Be All*, 462-63; G. Zinoviev, "The Communist International to the I.W.W.: An Appeal of the Executive Committee of the Third International at Moscow," and "The Communist Party and Industrial Unionism," *One Big Union Monthly* 2 (September 1920), 26-35; McEnroe, "Industrial Workers of the World," 347-53, 358-63, 375-78; Philip S. Foner, *History of the Labor Movement in the United States*. vol. 8. *Postwar Struggles, 1918-1920* (New York: International Publishers, 1988), 233-35; E. W. Latchem, "Where Do We Belong?" *One Big Union Monthly* 2 (October 1920), 28-30; John Sandgren, "Solving the Social Problem Through Economic Direct Action," *One Big Union Monthly* 2 (October 1920), 30-37; *Industrial Worker*, 16 October, 6 November 1920.

6. Gambs, *Decline of the I.W.W.*, 99-116; Thompson and Murfin, *The I.W.W.*, 150-51.

7. McEnroe, "The Industrial Workers of the World," 382-83; Renshaw, *The Wobblies*, 261.

8. Gambs, *Decline of the I.W.W.*, 116-18; Renshaw, *The Wobblies*, 262; McEnroe, "The Industrial Workers of the World," 382-83.

9. Gambs, *Decline of the I.W.W.*, 118-19; McEnroe, "The Industrial Workers of the World," 383; Tyler, *Rebels of the Woods*, 214; *Industrial Worker*, 25, 29 October 1924.

10. Tyler, *Rebels of the Woods*, 214-15; Dubofsky, *We Shall Be All*, 467; Renshaw, *The Wobblies*, 263;

11. Thompson and Murfin, *The I.W.W.*, 151; Dave Roediger, *Fellow Worker: The Life of Fred Thompson* (Chicago: Charles H. Kerr Publishing Company, 1993), 59-60; Robinson, "Social Movement Organizations," 101-2, 80-81, 111, 218; *General Organization Bulletin* (Ypsilanti, MI: The Industrial Workers of the World, October, 1998), 11.

12. *Industrial Solidarity*, 20, 27 May 1925.

13. *AWIU Bulletin No. 54*, 23 January 1924, *No. 55*, 30 January 1924, *No. 30*, 3 September 1924, IWW, WS; *Industrial Solidarity*, 25 June, 9, 16 July, 17 December 1924, 20 May, 3 June, 23 September 1925; *Industrial Worker*, 22 March, 25 June, 23 July, 6 August 1924, 25 February, 11 March 27 June 1925; Barajemes, "The Harvest Message," *Industrial Pioneer* 2 (August 1924), 9-10, 22; "Editorials" *Industrial Pioneer* 2 (July 1925), 2.

14. *Industrial Solidarity*, 10 September 1924, 25 June 1925; *Industrial Worker*, 11 July 1925; *Fifteenth Convention AWIU*, 6, IWW, WS; *Minutes of the Sixteenth Annual Convention of the A.W.I.U. No. 110, I.W.W., Held at Kenmare, North Dakota, October 3-10, 1924*, 5, Box 44, Folder 8, IWW, WS; *Minutes of the Seventeenth Annual Convention of the Agricultural Workers Industrial Union No. 110, of the I.W.W. Held at Minneapolis, Minnesota, October 19-24, 1925*, 9, Box 44, Folder 9, IWW, WS.

15. Roediger, *Fellow Worker*, 56-60; Thompson and Murfin, *The I.W.W.*, 139; *Solidarity*, 27 August, 3 September, 15 October, 12 November 1910; *Industrial Worker*, 1 July 1909, 16 July 1910; Weintraub, "The I.W.W. in California," 253-54; *Sixteenth Convention of the AWIU*, 20-22, IWW, WS; *AWIU Bulletin No. 52*, 9 January 1924, IWW, WS; Whitten, "Criminal Syndicalism," 52-63; *Industrial Solidarity*, 17 June 1925.

16. *Industrial Worker* 9 July 1924, 23 October 1926; *Industrial Solidarity*, 24 May, 11 June 1924, 17 June 1925; Foy, "Migratory Worker's Diary," 29; Card No. X10591, "It's Not Last Year, It's This Year," *Industrial Pioneer* 3 (July 1925), 7-8.

17. AG-1351, "Apples," *Industrial Pioneer* 1 (December 1923), 11-12; Louise F. Shields "Labor Conditions During the 1926 Apple Harvest in the Wenatchee Valley," *Monthly Labor Review* 26 (March 1927), 13-17; *Women in the Fruit-Growing and Canning Industries in the State of Washington: A Study of Hours, Wages and Conditions*, U.S. Department of Labor, Bulletin of the Women's Bureau, No. 47 (Washington, D.C.: GPO, 1926), 39-48.

18. *Industrial Solidarity*, 26 August, 25 November 1925.

19. Evelyne Stitt Pickett, "Hoboes Across the Border: A Comparison of Itinerant Cross-border Laborers between Montana and Western Canada," *Montana* 49 (1999), 19-20, 29-30; Mark Leier, *Where the Fraser River Flows: The Industrial Workers of the World in British Columbia* (Vancouver, BC: New Star Books, 1990), 116-24; Cecilia Danysk, *Hired Hands: Labour and the Development of Prairie Agriculture, 1880-1930* (Toronto, Ontario: McClelland & Stewart Inc., 1995), 106-08, 127-31; "Crossing the Line," *Industrial Pioneer* 2 (October 1924), 26-27; *Industrial Solidarity*, 16 September 1925.

20. Danysk, *Hired Hands*, 112-41; *New York Times*, 11 August, 21 October 1923.

21. *Industrial Worker*, 29 September 1923, 27 May, 15 August, 19 September 1925; Fred Mann, "The Harvest Drive is on Again," *Industrial Pioneer* 3 (July 1925), 5-6; Dubofsky, *We Shall Be All*, 354-55, 357; *Industrial Solidarity*, 5, 12 August 1925.

22. Isern, *Bull Threshers and Bindlestiffs*, 131-36, 159-60; Danysk, *Hired Hands*, 86.

23. *Industrial Worker*, 29 August 1923, 24 July 1926; *AWIU Bulletin No. 39*, 10 October 1923, IWW, WS; Danysk, *Hired Hands*, 104-6, 138, 155; *New York Times*, 17 July 1922, 21 July, 11 August 1923, 21 October 1923; *Industrial Solidarity*, 5 August 1925.

24. Danysk, *Hired Hands*, 100-1, 125-26; *Industrial Worker*, 27 February 1924.

25. Danysk, *Hired Hands*, 107-9, 127-31; *Industrial Solidarity*, 4, 15 October 1924, 17 June, 2, 16 September 1925; *Industrial Worker*, 15 August, 19 September 1925; *Minutes of the Fifteenth Convention of the AWIU*, 23, IWW, WS.

26. *Industrial Solidarity*, 3, 10, 17 September 1924; *Industrial Worker*, 2 August 1924.

27. *Industrial Solidarity*, 8 October 1924; *Minutes of the Sixteenth Convention of the A.W.I.U.*, 16, IWW, WS.

28. *Grand Forks Herald*, 19 August 1925; *Industrial Solidarity*, 12 August 1925; *Industrial Worker*, 29 August 1925.

29. *Industrial Solidarity*, 26 August, 2, 9 September 1925.

30. *Grand Forks Herald*, 25 August 1925; *Industrial Worker*, 5 September 1925; *Industrial Solidarity*, 2 September 1925.

31. *Grand Forks Herald*, 26, 28 August, 2 September 1925; *Industrial Solidarity*, 9, 16 September 1925.

32. *Minutes of the Seventeenth Convention AWIU*, 8-9, IWW, WS; *Minutes of the Eighteenth Convention of the Agricultural Workers Industrial Union No. 110, of the I.W.W. Held at Spokane, Washington October 11th—14th, 1926*, 5-6, Box 44, Folder 11, IWW, WS; *Minutes of the Nineteenth Convention of the Agricultural Workers Industrial Union No. 110, of the I.W.W. Held at Williston, N. Dak. October 10, 1927*, 4-5, Box 44, Folder 12, IWW, WS; *Minutes of the Twentieth Convention of the Agricultural Workers Industrial Union No. 110, of the I.W.W. Held at Williston, N. Dak. October 10, 1928*, 5-6, IWW Seattle, UW; *Twenty-First Annual Convention of the A.W.I.U. No. 110 of the I.W.W. held November 4, 1929 at Seattle, Washington*, 3-4, IWW Seattle, UW; *Industrial Worker*, 18 September 1926.

33. *Industrial Worker*, 9 January 1924, 26 December 1925; "The Harvest Drive Is On!" *Industrial Pioneer* 2 (July 1924), n.p.; Fred Mann, "The Old 400," *Industrial Pioneer* 4 (July 1926), 10; James Sullivan, "Reviewing the 1925 Harvest Drive" *Industrial Pioneer* 3 (November 1925), 6-7; Sellars, *Oil, Wheat & Wobblies*, 180-81; John J. Hader, "Honk Honk Hobo," *The Survey* 60 (1 August 1928), 454-55; *Grand Forks Herald*, 29 August 1925.

34. *Industrial Worker*, 16 October 1926; Sullivan, "1925 Harvest Drive," 6-7; Sellars, *Oil, Wheat & Wobblies*, 180; *Industrial Solidarity*, 19 August 1925; Hader, "Honk Honk Hobo," 454-55.

35. Hader, "Honk Honk Hobo," 453; *Minutes of the Fifteenth Convention of the AWIU*, 24, IWW, WS; *Minutes of the Seventeenth Convention of the AWIU*, 7, 23 27, IWW, WS; *Minutes of the Eighteenth Convention of the AWIU*, 13-18, IWW, WS; *Minutes of*

the Nineteenth Convention of the AWIU, 11, IWW, WS; *Minutes of the Twentieth Convention of the AWIU,* 11-12, IWW Seattle, UW; *Industrial Worker,* 25 September, 23 October 1926.

36. *Industrial Worker,* 9 April 1924, 1 October 1921, 13 May 1922, 20 October, 21 November 1923; *Industrial Solidarity,* 17 June 1925; *AWIU Bulletin No. 5,* 14 February 1923, IWW, WS; *Minutes of the Nineteenth Convention of the AWIU,* 9, IWW, WS.
37. Thompson and Murfin, *The I.W.W.,* 130, 149; *Industrial Solidarity,* 17 September 1924.
38. Applen, "Migratory Harvest Labor," 178-79; Frank Thorpe, "All Together for a Banner Drive!" *Industrial Pioneer* 4 (June 1926), 3-4; Sullivan, "1925 Harvest Drive," 29; Mann, "Old 400," 10-11; Sellars, *Oil, Wheat, and Wobblies,* 179-180; Hopkins, *Changing Technology,* 55-68.
39. Applen, "Migratory Harvest Labor," 176-77; Isern, *Bull Threshers and Bindlestiffs,* 185; Taylor, *Labor on the Land,* 93; *Industrial Worker,* 8 October 1927; Danysk, *Hired Hands,* 162-71; *Industrial Worker,* 9 April 1927, 21 July 1928; Hopkins, *Changing Technology,* 70-76, 119-23.
40. Applen, "Migratory Harvest Labor," 177-78; Hopkins, *Changing Technology,* 43-46; Isern, *Bull Threshers and Bindlestiffs,* 185-99.
41. *Industrial Worker,* 19 March, 18 August 1927; Gambs, *Decline of the I.W.W.,* 178-82.

Epilogue

1. *Nineteenth Convention,* 11; *Twentieth Convention of the AWIU,* 11, IWW Seattle, UW; Mary E. Gallagher, Interview, 18 December 1955, Oral History, UCLA; Charles and Jennie Velsek Papers, Walter Reuther Library and Archives of Labor and Urban Affairs, Wayne State University, Detroit, Michigan (hereafter Velsek Papers, WS); Frederick Thompson Papers, Walter Reuther Library and Archives of Labor and Urban Affairs, Wayne State University, Detroit, Michigan (hereafter Thompson Papers, WS); Request for charter, IWW Collection, Box 44, Folder 31, IWW, WS; Dubofsky, *We Shall Be All,* 113-14; *Twenty-Third Annual Convention of the A.W.I.W. No. 110 of the I.W.W.,* 11, Box 44, Folder 16, IWW, WS.
2. For AWIU conventions and special meetings from 1931-1939 see Box 44, IWW, WS; "Fruit Pickers Attention," Box 161, IWW, WS; "Attention Apple Knockers," Box 156, IWW, WS; Sellars, *Oil, Wheat & Wobblies,* 182; Schwartz, *Seasonal Farm Labor,* 134; *Industrial Worker,* 5, 19 March, 11 June, 18 August, 10 September, 8 October 1927, 22 September 1928; *Twenty-First Convention of the AWIU,* 28, IWW Seattle, UW.
3. Jamieson, *Labor Unionism,* 236-39; McWilliams, *Ill Fares the Land,* 111-12; Thompson and Murfin, *The I.W.W.,* 152-53; Gambs, *Decline of the I.W.W.,* 150-53.
4. See James G. Newbill, "Farmers and Wobblies in the Yakima Valley, 1933," *Pacific Northwest Quarterly* 68 (April 1977), 80-87; Cletus E. Daniel, "Wobblies on the Farm: The IWW in the Yakima Valley," *Pacific Northwest Quarterly* 65 (October 1974), 166-75. Also for personal recollections of the Yakima organizing effort of 1933, see the Velsek Papers, WS and the Frederick Thompson Papers, WS.
5. The only other harvest Wobbly agricultural organizing efforts of note after 1933 took place in the mid-1960s in the Michigan berry harvests and in the Yakima Valley harvests. These efforts were not successful enough to reestablish the AWIU as a force in migrant farm labor organizing. For the best analysis of the IWW during its declining years see Robinson, "Social Movement Organizations." For an analysis of farm worker unionizing in California during the 1930s, see Daniel, *Bitter Harvest.*

Bibliography

Primary Sources

Archival Materials:

Minnesota State Historical Society, Saint Paul
- Northern Information Bureau (Minneapolis, MN)
- E. W. Latchem Papers
- Arthur Le Sueur Papers

Nebraska State Historical Society, Lincoln, Nebraska
- State Council of Defense Papers, Ser. 3

North Dakota State University, Fargo
- Institute for Regional Studies

State Historical Society of Wisconsin, Madison
- Deborah Shaffer Papers
- Fred Thompson Interview

University of California, Berkeley, Bancroft Library
- Simon Julius Lubin Papers
- Stuart Marshall Jamieson Collection of Field Notes

University of California, Los Angeles, Research Library, Department of Special Collections
- Oral History Program

University of Michigan, Ann Arbor, Special Collections
- Joseph Labadie Papers

University of Washington, Seattle, Allen Library, Archives and Manuscripts
- John L. Miller Papers
- IWW Seattle Office
- IWW California Office

Washington State Archives, Olympia, Washington
- Governor Ernest Lister Papers
- Washington State Secret Service

Washington State University Libraries, Manuscripts, Archives, and Special Collections, Pullman
- Agricultural Economics Survey and Studies, 1912-1965

Wayne State University, Detroit, Michigan, Walter P. Reuther Library, Archives of Labor and Urban Affairs
- Industrial Workers of the World Collection
- Charles and Jennie Velsek Papers
- Frederick W. Thompson Papers
- E. W. Latchem Papers

Government Documents:

Adams, R. L. and T. R. Kelly. *A Study of Farm Labor in California.* Agricultural Experiment State Circular No. 193. Berkeley: University of California, 1918.

Bates, Edwin. *Commercial Survey of the Pacific Northwest.* U.S. Department of Commerce. Domestic Commerce Series, No. 51. Washington, D.C.: GPO, 1932.

California Commission of Immigration and Housing. *First Annual Report.* Sacramento, 2 January 1915.

Clark, Victor S. "Mexican Labor in the United States" (from Department of Commerce and Labor, Bureau of Labor *Bulletin*, No. 78). Washington, D.C., 1908 in *Mexican Labor in the United States.* New York: Arno Press, 1974.

Cooper, T. P., F. W. Peck, and Andrew Boss. *Labor Requirements of Crop Production.* Agricultural Experiment Station, Bulletin No. 157. Saint Paul: University of Minnesota, 1916.

Country Life Commission. *Report of the Country Life Commission.* Washington, D.C.: GPO, 1909.

Dubofsky, Melvyn, ed. *Department of Justice Investigation Files. Part I: The Industrial Workers of the World.* Frederick, MD: University Publications of America, 1989.

Holmes, George K. *Supply of Farm Labor.* U.S. Department of Agriculture, Bureau of Statistics, Bulletin 94, 1912.

Hopkins, John A. *Changing Technology and Employment in Agriculture.* U.S. Department of Agriculture, Bureau of Agricultural Economics, 1941. Rpt., New York: Da Capo Press, 1973.

Jamieson, Stuart. "Labor Unionism in American Agriculture." *Monthly Labor Review* 62 (January 1946) U.S. Department of Labor.

——. *Labor Unionism in American Agriculture.* Department of Labor Bulletin No. 836, 1945. Rpt., New York: Arno Press, 1976.

Landis, Paul H. and Melvin S. Brooks. *Farm Labor in Yakima Valley, Washington.* Washington Agricultural Experiment Station Bulletin No. 343. Pullman: State College of Washington, 1936.

Lescohier, Donald D. *Harvest Labor Problems in the Wheat Belt.* U.S. Department of Agriculture Bulletin No. 1020. Washington, D.C.: GPO, 1922.

——. *Conditions Affecting the Demand for Harvest Labor in the Wheat Belt.* U.S. Department of Agriculture Bulletin No. 1230. Washington, D.C.: GPO, 1924.

——. *Sources of Supply and Conditions of Employment of Harvest Labor in the Wheat Belt.* U.S. Department of Agriculture Bulletin No. 1211. Washington, D.C.: GPO, 1924.

Murray, Nat C. "The Wheat Crop of 1913-14." *Farmers' Bulletin No.629.* United States Department of Agriculture, 16 October 1914.

Rasmussen, Wayne D. *Agriculture in the United States: A Documentary History.* Vols. 1-4. New York: Random House, 1975.

Reuss, Carl F., Paul H. Landis, and Richard Wakefield. *Migratory Farm Labor and the Hop Industry on the Pacific Coast: With Special Application to Problems of the Yakima Valley, Washington.* Pullman: State College of Washington, Agricultural Experiment Station, 1938.

Shaw, Eldon E. and John A. Hopkins. *Trends in Employment in Agriculture, 1909-1936.* Philadelphia: Works Progress Administration, National Research Project, 1938.

Shields, Louise F. "Labor Conditions During the 1926 Apple Harvest in Wenatchee Valley." *Monthly Labor Review* 26 (March 1927): 13-17. U.S. Department of Labor.

State Board of Control of California. *California and the Oriental.* Sacramento: California State Printing Office, 1920.

United States Commission on Industrial Relations. *Report of the Commission on Industrial Relations.* Vols. 2, 3, 5, 6. Washington, D.C.: GPO, 1916.

United States Industrial Commission. *Report of the Industrial Commission on Agriculture and Agricultural Labor.* Vol. 10. Washington, D.C.: GPO, 1901.

U.S. Military Intelligence Reports: Surveillance of Radicals in the United States, 1917-1941. Frederick, MD: University Publications of America, 1984.

Veblen, Thorstein. "An Unpublished Paper on the I.W.W." *Journal of Political Economy* 40 (December 1932): 796-807.

Washington Agriculture: Parts 3 to 10, Inclusive, Bulletin 134. Pullman: State College of Washington, 1929.

Women in the Fruit-Growing and Canning Industries in the State of Washington: A Study of Hours, Wages and Conditions. Washington, D.C.: GPO, 1926.

Federal and State Trial Proceedings and Testimony:

From *United States v. William D. Haywood, et al.* IWW Collection, Archives of Labor and Urban Affairs, Walter P. Reuther Library, Wayne State University:

Banks, Jesse N. Testimony.
Burdell, Joe. Testimony.
Carlson, C. O. Testimony.
Casebolt, William. Testimony.
Cole, William. Testimony.
Edenstorm, John. Testimony.
Edwards, Forrest. Testimony.
Gibson, Frank B. Testimony.
Grannat, William. Testimony.
Maloney, James. Testimony.
Pierce, Henry A. Testimony.
Selby, Charles. Testimony.
Wermke, Frank E. Testimony.

From *People of the State of California against Richard Ford and H. D. Suhr. Appellants.* Vol. 2. IWW Seattle Office, Allen Library, Manuscripts and Archives, University of Washington:

James, Alvin W. Testimony.
James, Percy H. Testimony.
Smith, Earl. Testimony.

People v. Richard Ford, et al. Vol. 4. Superior Court. County of Yuba, California. IWW Seattle Office. Allen Library, Manuscripts and Archives, University of Washington.

"Statements of Facts." Court Case #2347, *People of the State of California v. N. Steelik.* California State Archives, Sacramento, California.

Oral Histories and Interviews:

Bird, Stewart, Dan Georgakas, and Deborah Shaffer, eds. *Solidarity Forever: An Oral History of the IWW.* Chicago: Lake View Press, 1985.

De Caux, Len. Interview, 1985. Oral History Program, University of California, Los Angeles.

Ferguson, Mrs. O. L. Interview, 9 October 1954. Institute for Regional Studies, North Dakota State University.

Foner, Philip S., ed. *Fellow Workers and Friends: I.W.W. Free-Speech Fights as Told by Participants.* Westport, CT: Greenwood Press, 1981.

Krieger, Sam. Interview, 24 September 1978. Deborah Shaffer Papers, State Historical Society of Wisconsin.

Miller, John L. Interview, 11 March 1974. John L. Miller Papers, Manuscripts and Archives, University of Washington.

Miller, Jack. Interview, 21 February 1978. Deborah Shaffer Papers, State Historical Society of Wisconsin.

Murphy, Joe. Interview, 23 September 1978. Deborah Shaffer Papers, State Historical Society of Wisconsin.

Peterson, Nels. Interview, 23 February 1978. Deborah Shaffer Papers, State Historical Society of Wisconsin.

Spies, Jack. Interview, 27 October 1967. Minnesota State Historical Society.

Terry, Alfred N. Interview, 17 August 1954. Institute for Regional Studies, North Dakota State University.

Thompson, Fred. Interview, 26 May 1973. State Historical Society of Wisconsin.

The Wobblies. Directed by Stewart Bird and Deborah Shaffer. 89 minutes, color. 1979. Distributed by First Run Features, New York.

IWW Convention Proceedings and Special Conference Reports:

Minutes of the 12th Convention of the Agricultural Workers' Industrial Union No. 110, I.W.W.: Which is the First Annual Delegate Convention Held at Omaha, Neb. October 17, 1921. n.p., n.d.

Minutes of the 2nd Annual Delegate Convention Which is the 13th Convention of the Agricultural Workers Industrial Union No.110: Held at Minneapolis, Minn, October 25th to November 7th 1922. n.p., n.d.

Minutes of the Convention of the Agricultural Workers Industrial Union No. 110, I.W.W. Held at Sioux City, Iowa, April 18 to 24, 1921. n.p.: Printing and Publishing Workers' Industrial Union No. 450, I.W.W., n.d.

Minutes of the Eighteenth Convention of the Agricultural Workers Industrial Union No. 110, of the I.W.W. Held at Spokane, Washington, October 11th-14th, 1926. n.p., n.d.

Minutes of the Fifteenth Convention of the Agricultural Workers' Industrial Union No. 110 of the I.W.W. Held at Fargo, N.D. October 8-18, 1923. n.p.: Printing and Publishing Workers' Industrial Union, No. 450, I.W.W., n.d.

Minutes of the Fourteenth Convention of the Agricultural Workers' Industrial Union No. 110, I.W.W.: Held at Oklahoma City, Okla., May 20-24, 1923. n.p.: Printing and Publishing Workers Industrial Union, No. 450, I.W.W., n.d.

Minutes of the Nineteenth Convention of the Agricultural Workers Industrial Union No. 110, of the I.W.W. Held at Williston, N. Dak. October 10, 1927. n.p., n.d.

Minutes of the Seventeenth Annual Convention of the Agricultural Workers Industrial Union No. 110, of the I.W.W. Held at Minneapolis, Minnesota, October 19th-24th, 1925. n.p., n.d.

Minutes of the Sixteenth Annual Convention of the A.W.I.U. No.110, I.W.W. Held at Kenmare, North Dakota, October 3-10, 1924. n.p.:

Printing and Publishing Workers' Industrial Union No. 450, I.W.W., n.d.

Minutes of the Twentieth Convention of the Agricultural Workers Industrial Union No. 110, of the I.W.W. Held at Williston, N. Dak. October 10, 1928. n.p., n.d.

Proceedings, The Founding Convention of the IWW. New York: Merit Publishers, 1969.

Stenographic Report of the Eighth Annual Convention of the Industrial Workers of the World. Chicago, 15-29 September 1913.

Twenty-First Annual Convention of the A.W.I.U. No. 110 of the I.W.W. Held November 4, 1929 at Seattle, Washington. n.p., n.d.

Books, Articles, Pamphlets, Leaflets:

AG-1351. "Apples." *Industrial Pioneer* I (December 1923): 11-12.

An Economic Interpretation of the Job. Chicago: Industrial Workers of the World, 1922.

Anderson, Nels. *The American Hobo: An Autobiography.* Leiden, Netherlands: E. J. Brill, 1975.

Barajemes. "The Harvest Message." *Industrial Pioneer* II (August 1924): 9-10, 22.

Brazier, Richard. "The Story of the I.W.W.'s 'Little Red Songbook.'" *Labor History* (Winter 1968): 91-105.

Brown, Louis H. "The Gruesome Story of American Terrorism: Installment No. 4." *One Big Union Monthly* 2 (June 1920): 37-39.

Bruere, Robert W. "Following the Trail of the I.W.W." n.p. New York Evening Post, 1918.

Bureau of Industrial Research. *Agriculture: The World's Basic Industry and Its Workers.* Chicago: Bureau of Industrial Research, 1921.

By-laws of the Agricultural Workers Industrial Union No. 400: Instructions to Branch Secretaries and Delegates. Chicago: I.W.W. Publishing Bureau, 1917.

By-laws of the Agricultural Workers Industrial Union No. 110 of the I.W.W.: Instructions to Members, Job and Stationary Delegates and Branch Secretaries. Chicago: I.W.W. Publishing Bureau, 1920.

"The Campaign of the Agricultural Workers." *One Big Union Monthly* 1 (August 1919): 7-8.

Card No. X10591. "It's Not Last Year, It's This Year." *Industrial Pioneer* III (July 1925): 7-8.

Chaplin, Ralph. *Wobbly: The Rough-and-Tumble Story of an American Radical.* Chicago: University of Chicago Press, 1948.

Connors, Tom. "The Industrial Union in Agriculture." In *Twenty-five Years of Industrial Unionism.* Chicago: Industrial Workers of the World, 1930.

"Crossing the Line." *Industrial Pioneer* II (October 1924): 26-27.

Dare To Be Different. Chicago: Agricultural Workers' Industrial Union No. 110 of the I.W.W., n.d.

De Caux, Len. *The Living Spirit of the Wobblies.* New York: International Publishers, 1978.

Delinquent List of the Agricultural Workers' Industrial Union No.110, of the I.W.W. n.p., 1 December 1924.

Douglas, William O. *Go East, Young Man: The Early Years.* New York: Random House, 1974.

"Editorials." *Industrial Pioneer* VII (July 1925): 2.

Engdahl, John. "The Gruesome Story of American Terrorism, Lest We Forget." *One Big Union Monthly* 2 (April 1920): 12-14

"Financial Statements." *One Big Union Monthly* 2 (March 1920): 61-62.

——. *One Big Union Monthly* 2 (April 1920): 56-57.

Fisher, Fred. "Agricultural Workers' Industrial Union No. 400, I.W.W. Bulletin No. 2." *One Big Union Monthly* 2 (April 1920): 55-56.

Flynn, Elizabeth Gurley. *Sabotage: The Conscious Withdrawal of the Workers' Industrial Efficiency.* Cleveland: I.W.W. Publishing Bureau, 1916.

Fox, Mat K. "The Story of No. 400." *One Big Union Monthly* 1 (September 1919): 49.

——. "Agricultural Workers' Industrial Union No. 400 I.W.W." *One Big Union Monthly* 1 (March 1919): 58-59.

——. "Agricultural Workers' Industrial Union No. 400, I.W.W. Bulletin No. 29." *One Big Union Monthly* 1 (May 1919): 56-58.

——. "Agricultural Workers' Industrial Union, No. 400 Bulletin No. 32." *One Big Union Monthly* 1 (June 1919): 56-59.

——. "Agricultural Workers' Industrial Union, No. 400 Bulletin No. 37." *One Big Union Monthly* 1 (July 1919): 57-59.

——. "Agricultural Workers' Industrial Union No. 400, I.W.W. Bulletin No. 56." *One Big Union Monthly* 1 (December 1919): 53-54.

Foy, James. "A Migratory Worker's Diary," *Industrial Pioneer* 1 (February 1924): 29.

——. "More About the Migratory Worker's Diary." *Industrial Pioneer* 1 (April 1924): 14.

General Organizing Bulletin. Ypsilanti, MI: The Industrial Workers of the World, October 1998.

"The Gruesome Story of American Terrorism, Installment No. 3." *One Big Union Monthly* 2 (May): 51-53.

Hang on to Your Life Belt. Chicago: Agricultural Workers' Industrial Union No. 110 of the I.W.W., n.d.

"The Harvest Drive Is On." *Industrial Pioneer* 2 (July 1924): n.p.

Harvest Time Is Honey Time. Chicago: Agricultural Workers' Industrial Union No. 110, n.d.

Haywood, William D. *Bill Haywood's Book: The Autobiography of William D. Haywood.* New York: International Publishers, 1929.

H. E. H. "An Ill Wind in the Palouse." *Industrial Pioneer* 1 (October 1921): 43-44.

I.W.W. Songs: To Fan the Flames of Discontent. Chicago: I.W.W. Publishing Bureau, 1917.

I.W.W. Songs: To Fan the Flames of Discontent. General Defense Edition. Chicago: I.W.W. Publishing Bureau, 1918.

I.W.W. Songs: To Fan the Flames of Discontent. 1923; Rpt., Chicago: Charles H. Kerr Publishing Company, 1989.

Koeltgen, Ewald. "I.W.W. Convention." *International Socialist Review* 14 (November 1913): 275-76.

Kornbluh, Joyce L. *Rebel Voices: An IWW Anthology.* Chicago: Charles H. Kerr Publishing Company, 1988.

Latchem, E. W. "The Modern Agricultural Slave." *One Big Union Monthly* 7 (August 1920): 54-56.

——. "Where Do We Belong?" *One Big Union Monthly* 2 (October 1920): 28-30.

——. "The Agricultural Workers' Convention." *One Big Union Monthly* 2 (November 1920): 56-57.

——. "The Aftermath." *One Big Union Monthly* 2 (November 1920): 57-58.

Lescohier, Donald D. "The Farm Labor Problem." *Journal of Farm Economics* 3 (January 1921): 10-15

——. "With the I.W.W. in the Wheat Lands." *Harper's Magazine* 147 (August 1923): 371-80.

——. "Harvesters and Hoboes." *Survey* 50 (July 1923): 482-87, 503-04.

——. "Hands and Tools of the Wheat Harvest." *Survey* 50 (August 1923): 376-82, 409-12.

Lewis, Austin. "The Drift in California." *International Socialist Review* 12 (November 1911): 272-74.

Mann, Fred. "The Harvest Drive is on Again." *Industrial Pioneer* III (July 1925): 3-6.

——. "The Old 400." *Industrial Pioneer* 4 (July 1926): 10-12.

McDonald, Edward. *The Farm Laborer and the City Worker: A Message to Both.* Cleveland: I.W.W. Publishing Bureau, n.d.

McGuckin, Henry E. *Memoirs of a Wobbly.* Chicago: Charles H. Kerr Publishing Company, 1987.

O'Connor, Harvey. *Revolution in Seattle: A Memoir.* New York: Monthly Review Press, 1964.

Parker, Carleton H. *The Casual Laborer and Other Essays.* New York: Harcourt, Brace, and Howe, 1920.

Plotting to Convict Wheatland Hop Pickers. Oakland: International Press, 1914.

Powderly, Terence V. *Thirty Years of Labor: 1859-1889.* 1890; Rpt., New York: August M. Kelley Publishers, 1967.

"Resolution Regarding Sabotage." *One Big Union Monthly* 2 (April 1920): 56.

Riebe, Ernest. *Mr. Block: Twenty-Four IWW Cartoons.* Chicago: Charles H. Kerr Publishing Company, 1984.

Roediger, Dave. *Fellow Worker: The Life of Fred Thompson.* Chicago: Charles H. Kerr Publishing Company, 1993.

Sandgren, John. "The I.W.W.: A Statement of Its Principles, Objects and Methods." *One Big Union Monthly* 2 (May 1920): 36-41.

———. "Solving the Social Problem Through Economic Direct Action." *One Big Union Monthly* 2 (October 1920): 30-37.

Short, Mrs. Wallace M. *Just One American.* n.p.: Mrs. Wallace M. Short, 1943.

Songs of the Workers: On the Road, In the Jungles and In the Shops. Spokane, WA: Spokane Local of the I.W.W. 1912?

St. John, Vincent. *The I.W.W.– Its History, Structure and Methods.* Chicago: I.W.W. Publishing Bureau, 1917.

Stromquist, J. A. "California Oranges." *Industrial Pioneer* 1 (March 1921): 23-26.

Sullivan, James. "Reviewing the 1925 Harvest Drive." *Industrial Pioneer* 3 (November 1925): 5-7, 29-30.

The Two Triple Alliances. n.p.: General Organization Committee of the A.W.I.U. No. 110 of the I.W.W., 1922.

Thorpe, Frank. "All Together for a Banner Drive!" *Industrial Pioneer* 4 (June 1926): 2-4.

Vegetable and Fruit Workers. Chicago: Agricultural Workers' Industrial Union No. 110 of the I.W.W., n.d.

What is the I.W.W. Preamble?: A Dialogue. Chicago: Industrial Workers of the World, n.d.

Woirol, Gregory R. *In the Floating Army: F. C. Mills on Itinerant Life in California, 1914.* Urbana: University of Illinois Press, 1992.

Woodruff, Abner E. *Evolution of American Agriculture.* n.p.: Agricultural Workers' Industrial Union No. 400.

You Need Industrial Unionism. n.p.: Industrial Workers of the World, n.d.

Zinoviev, G. "The Communist International to the I.W.W.: An Appeal of the Executive Committee of the Third International at Moscow" and "The Communist Party and Industrial Unionism." *One Big Union Monthly* 2 (September 1920): 26-35.

Newspapers:

Defense News Bulletin (Chicago)
Fresno Republican (California)
Grand Forks Herald (North Dakota)
Industrial Solidarity (Chicago)
Industrial Worker (Spokane and Seattle, Washington)
Industrial Union Bulletin (Chicago)
Mankato Free Press (Minnesota)
Minneapolis Morning Tribune (Minnesota)
New Solidarity (Chicago)
New York Times (New York)
Pacific Rural Press (San Francisco, California)
Pullman Herald (Washington)
San Francisco Chronicle (California)
Solidarity (New Castle, Pennsylvania; Cleveland, Ohio; Chicago)
Spokane Daily Chronicle (Washington)
Spokane Press (Washington)
Spokesman-Review (Spokane, Washington)
Wenatchee Daily World (Washington)
Yakima Daily Republic (Washington)
Yakima Morning Herald (Washington)

Secondary Sources
Books:

Ahearn, Daniel J. *The Wages of Farm and Factory Laborers, 1914-1944.* New York: Columbia University Press, 1945.

Anderson, Nels. *The Hobo: The Sociology of the Homeless Man.* 1923; Rpt., Chicago: Midway Reprint, 1975.

Bernstein, Irving, *The Lean Years: A History of the American Worker, 1920-1933.* Boston: Houghton Mifflin Company, 1966.

Brissenden, Paul F. *The I.W.W.: A Study of American Syndicalism.* 2nd ed. New York: Russell & Russell, Inc., 1957.

Bruce, Andrew A. *Non-Partisan League.* New York: The Macmillian Company, 1921.

Buenker, John D. and Edward R. Kantowicz, eds. *Historical Dictionary of the Progressive Era, 1890-1920.* New York: Greenwood Press, 1988.

Carlson, Peter. *Roughneck: The Life and Times of Big Bill Haywood.* New York: W. W. Norton & Company, 1983.

Chan, Sucheng. *This Bittersweet Soil: The Chinese in California Agriculture, 1860-1910.* Berkeley: University of Caklifornia Press, 1986.

Chaplin, Ralph. *The Centralia Conspiracy: The Truth About the Armistice Day Tragedy.* Chicago: General Defense Committee, 1924.

Conlin, Joseph R. ed. *At the Point of Production: The Local History of the I.W.W.* Westport, CT: Greenwood Press, 1981.

———. *Bread and Roses Too: Studies of the Wobblies.* Westport, Connecticut: Greenwood Publishing Corporation, 1969.

Copeland, Tom. *The Centralia Tragedy of 1919: Elmer Smith and the Wobblies.* Seattle: University of Washington Press, 1993.

Daniel, Cletus E. *Bitter Harvest: A History of California Farmworkers, 1870-1941.* Ithaca: Cornell University Press, 1981.

Danysk, Cecilia. *Hired Hands: Labour and the Development of Prairie Agriculture, 1880-1930.* Toronto, Ontario: McClelland & Stewart Inc., 1995.

Dos Passos, John. *The 42nd Parallel.* 1930; Rpt., Boston: Houghton Mifflin Company, 1946.

Dowell, Eldridge Foster. *A History of Criminal Syndicalism Legislation in the United States.* Baltimore: Johns Hopkins Press, 1939.

Drache, Hiram M. *The Day of the Bonanza: A History of Bonanza Farming in The Red River Valley of the North.* Fargo: North Dakota Institute for Regional Studies, 1964.

Dubofsky, Melvyn. *We Shall Be All: A History of the Industrial Workers of the World.* 2nd ed. Urbana: University of Illinois Press, 1988.

Duke, Emma. *California The Golden.* New York: National Child Labor Committee, 1921.

Ebeling, Walter. *The Fruited Plain: The Story of American Agriculture.* Berkeley: University of California Press, 1979.

Ficken, Robert E. and Charles P. LeWarne. *Washington: A Centennial History.* Seattle: University of Washington Press, 1988.

Fink, Leon. *In Search of the Working Class.* Urbana: University of Illinois Press, 1994.

Fite, Gilbert C. *The Farmers' Frontier, 1865-1900.* Norman: University of Oklahoma, 1987.

———. *American Agriculture and Farm Policy Since 1900.* New York: Macmillian Company, 1964

Foner, Philip S. *History of the Labor Movement in the United States.* Vol. 4. *The Industrial Workers of the World, 1905-1917.* New York: International Publishers, 1965.

———. *History of the Labor Movement in the United States.* Vol. 7. *Labor and World War I, 1914-1918.* New York: International Publishers, 1987.

———. *History of the Labor Movement in the United States.* Vol. 8. *Postwar Struggles, 1918-1920.* New York: International Publishers, 1988.

Friday, Chris. *Organizing Asian American Labor: The Pacific Coast Canned-Salmon Industry, 1870-1942.* Philadelphia: Temple University Press, 1994.

Fuller, Varden. *Hired Hands in California's Farm Fields: Collected Essays on California's Farm Labor History and Policy.* Oakland: Division of Agriculture and Natural Resources, California Experiment Station, 1991.

Gambs, John S. *The Decline of the I.W.W.* New York: Columbia University Press, 1932.

Glickman, Lawrence B. *A Living Wage: American Workers and the Making of*

Consumer Society. Ithaca: Cornell University Press, 1997.

Gonzalez, Gilbert G. *Labor and Community: Mexican Citrus Worker Villages in a Southern California County, 1900-1950.* Urbana: University of Illinois Press, 1994.

Gomez-Quinones, Juan. *Mexican American Labor, 1790-1990.* Albuquerque: University of New Mexico Press, 1994.

Gray, L. C., Charles L. Stewart, Howard A. Turner, J. T. Sanders, and W. J. Spillman. *Farm Ownership and Tenancy.* 1924; Rpt., New York: Arno Press, 1976.

Guerin-Gonzales, Camille. *Mexican Workers and American Dreams: Immigration, Repatriation, and California Farm Labor, 1900-1939.* New Brunswick, NJ: Rutgers University Press, 1994.

Hargreaves, Mary Wilma M. *Dry Farming in the Northern Great Plains, 1900-1925.* Cambridge: Harvard University Press, 1957.

Heale, M. J. *American Anticommunism: Combating the Enemy Within,1830-1970.* Baltimore: Johns Hopkins University Press, 1990.

Hurt, Douglas A. *American Agriculture: A Brief History* (Ames: Iowa State University Press, 1994);

Isern, Thomas D. *Bull Threshers and Bindlestiffs: Harvesting and Threshing on the North American Plains.* Lawrence: University Press of Kansas, 1990.

Yuji Ichioka, *The Issei: The World of the First Generation Japanese Immigrants, 1885-1924* (New York: The Free Press, 1988)

Jensen, Vernon H. *Lumber and Labor.* New York: Farrar & Rinehart, Inc., 1945.

Kennedy, David M. *Over Here: The First World War and American Society.* Oxford: Oxford University Press, 1980.

Leier, Mark. *Where the Fraser River Flows: The Industrial Workers of the World in British Columbia.* Vancouver, British Columbia: New Star Books, 1990.

Leschoier, Don. D. *History of Labor in the United States, 1896-1932.* Vol. 3. *Working Conditions.* New York: The Macmillian Company, 1935.

Lindemann, Albert S. *A History of European Socialism.* New Haven: Yale University Press, 1983.

Martin, Philip L. *Harvest of Confusion: Migrant Workers in U.S. Agriculture.* Boulder, CO: Westview Press, 1988.

McGregor, Alexander Campbell. *Counting Sheep: From Open Range to Agribusiness on the Columbia Plateau.* Seattle: University of Washington Press, 1982.

McWilliams, Carey. *Factories in the Field: The Story of Migratory Farm Labor in California.* Boston: Little, Brown and Company, 1939.

——. *Ill Fares the Land: Migrants and Migratory Labor in the United States.* Boston: Little, Brown, and Company, 1942.

Meinig, D. W. *The Great Columbia Plain: A Historical Geography, 1805-1910.* Seattle: University of Washington Press, 1968.

Mighell, Ronald L. *American Agriculture: Its Structure and Place in the Economy.* New York: John Wiley & Sons, Inc., 1955

Mitchell, Don. *The Lie of the Land: Migrant Workers and the California Landscape.* Minneapolis: University of Minnesota Press, 1996.

Montgomery, David. *The Fall of the House of Labor: The Workplace, the State, and American Labor Activism, 1865-1925.* Cambridge: Cambridge University Press, 1987.

Novack, George, Dave Frankel, and Fred Feldman. *The First Three Internationals: Their History and Lessons.* New York: Pathfinder Press, Inc., 1974.

Painter, Nell Irvin. *Standing at Armageddon: The United States, 1877-1919.* New York: W. W. Norton & Company, 1987.

Perlman, Selig and Philip Taft. *History of Labor in the United States, 1896-1932.* Vol. 4. *Labor Movements.* New York: Macmillian Company, 1935.

Peterson, H. C. and Gilbert C. Fite. *Opponents of War, 1917-1918*. Madison: University of Wisconsin Press, 1957.

Preston Jr., William. *Aliens and Dissenters: Federal Suppression of Radicals, 1903-1933*. 2nd ed. Urbana: University of Illinois Press, 1994.

Renshaw, Patrick. *The Wobblies: The Story of Syndicalism in the United States*. Garden City, NY: Doubleday & Company, Inc., 1967.

Robbins, William G. *Colony and Empire: The Capitalist Transformation of the American West*. Lawrence: University Press of Kansas, 1994.

Roediger, David. *Towards the Abolition of Whiteness: Essays on Race, Politics, and Working Class History*. London: Verso, 1994.

—— and Philip S. Foner. *Our Own Time: A History of American Labor and the Working Day*. New York: Greenwood Press, 1989.

Salerno, Salvatore. *Red November Black November: Culture and Community in the Industrial Workers of the World*. Albany: State University of New York Press, 1989.

Salvatore, Nick. *Eugene V. Debs: Citizen Socialist*. Urbana: University of Illinois Press, 1982.

Sargent, Noel. *Non-Partisan League Leaders Work with the I.W.W.* St. Paul: Minnesota Sound Government Association, 1920.

Schaffer, Ronald. *America in the Great War: The Rise of the War Welfare State*. New York: Oxford University Press, 1991.

Schob, David E. *Hired Hands and Plowboys: Farm Labor in the Midwest, 1815-60*. Urbana: University of Illinois Press, 1975.

Schwantes, Carlos A. *The Pacific Northwest: An Interpretive History*. Lincoln: University of Nebraska Press, 1989.

——. *Hard Traveling: A Portrait of Work Life in the New Northwest*. Lincoln: University of Nebraska, 1994.

Schwartz, Harry. *Seasonal Farm Labor in the United States: With Special Reference to Hired Workers in Fruit and Vegetable and Sugar-Beet Production*. New York: Columbia University Press, 1945.

Sellars, Nigel Anthony. *Oil, Wheat & Wobblies: The Industrial Workers of the World in Oklahoma, 1905-1930*. Norman: University of Oklahoma Press, 1998.

Shannon, Fred A. *The Farmer's Last Frontier: Agriculture, 1860-1897*. New York: Harper Torchbooks, 1968.

Taylor, Paul S. *Labor on the Land: Collected Writings, 1930-1970*. New York: Arno Press, 1981.

——. *Mexican Labor in the United States*. Vol. 1. Berkeley: University of California Press, 1930.

Thompson, Fred W. and Patrick Murfin. *The I.W.W.: Its First Seventy Years, 1905-1975*. Chicago: Industrial Workers of the World, 1976.

Thorne, Florence Calvert. *Samuel Gompers–American Statesman*. 1957; Rpt., New York: Greenwood Press Publishers, 1969.

Todes, Charlotte. *Labor and Lumber*. New York: Arno Press, 1975.

Trachtenberg, Alan. *The Incorporation of America: Culture and Society in the Gilded Age*. New York: Hill and Wang, 1982.

Tyler, Robert L. *Rebels of the Woods: The I.W.W. in the Pacific Northwest*. Eugene: University of Oregon Books, 1967.

Wenzer, Kenneth C. *Anarchists Adrift: Emma Goldman and Alexander Berkman*. St. James, NY: Brandywine Press, 1996.

Werstein, Irving. *Pie in the Sky: An American Struggle, the Wobblies and Their Times*. New York: Delacorte Press, 1969.

Workman, E. *History of "400" A.W.O.: The One Big Union Idea in Action*. New York: One Big Union Club, 1939.

——. *The Agricultural Workers' Organization: A Story of Class Union in the Making*. New York: One Big Union Club, 1939.

Worster, Donald. *Rivers of Empire: Water, Aridity, and the Growth of the*

American West. New York: Oxford University Press, 1985.

Articles, Chapters:

Barker, Tom. "The Agricultural Workers' Union in Argentina." *One Big Union Monthly* 2 (March 1920): 30-31.

Brissenden, P. F. "Lively Corpse." *The New Republic* 18 (26 August 1916): 95.

Bubka, Tony. "Time to Organize!" *American West* 5 (1968): 21-26.

Carter, David A. "The Industrial Workers of the World and the Rhetoric of Song." *The Quarterly Journal of Speech* 66 (1980), 365-74.

Cortmer, Richard C. "The Wobblies and Fiske v. Kansas: Victory Amid Disintegration." *Kansas History: A Journal of the Central Plains* 4 (Spring 1981): 30-38.

Daniel, Cletus E. "Wobblies on the Farm: The IWW in the Yakima Valley." *Pacific Northwest Quarterly* 65 (October 1974): 166-75.

———. "In Defense of the Wheatland Wobblies: A Critical Analysis of the IWW in California." *Labor History* 19 (Fall 1978): 485-509.

DiGirolamo, Vincent. "The Women of Wheatland: Female Consciousness and the 1913 Wheatland Hop Strike" *Labor History* 34 (1993), 236-55

Downing, Mortimer. "The Case of the Hop Pickers." *International Socialist Review* 14 (October 1913): 210-13.

Hader, John J. "Honk Honk Hobo." *The Survey* 60 (1 August 1928): 453-55.

Hanson, Tim. "Wobblies in the Woods: The 1917 Lumber Strike in the Inland Empire." *Pacific Northwest Forum* 4 (1991): 69-80.

Haug, Charles James. "The Industrial Workers of the World in North Dakota, 1913-1917." *North Dakota Quarterly* 39 (Winter 1971): 85-103

Higbie, Toby. "Indispensable Outcasts: Harvest Laborers in the Wheat Belt of the Middle West, 1890-1925." *Labor History* 38 (Fall 1997): 393-412.

Newbill, James G. "Farmers and Wobblies in the Yakima Valley, 1933." *Pacific Northwest Quarterly* 68 (April 1977): 80-87.

Pickett, Evelyne Stitt, "Hoboes Across the Border: A Comparison of Itinerant Cross-border Laborers between Montana and Western Canada." *Montana* 49 (1999), 19-31.

Pratt, William C. "Socialism on the Northern Plains, 1900-1925." *South Dakota History* 18 (Spring/Summer 1988): 1-35.

Rasmussen, Wayne D. "A Century of Farming in the Inland Empire." in *Spokane & the Inland Empire: An Interior Pacific Northwest Anthology*, edited by David H. Stratton. Pullman: Washington State University Press, 1991.

Reis, Elizabeth. "The AFL, the IWW, and Bay Area Italian Cannery Workers." *California History* 64 (Summer 1985): 174-242.

Reuss, Carl F. "The Farm Labor Problem in Washington, 1917-1918." *Pacific Northwest Quarterly* 34 (October 1943): 339-52.

Rosenberg, Daniel. "The IWW and Organization of Asian Workers in Early 20th Century America." *Labor History* 36 (Winter 1995): 77-87.

Schneider, John C. "Tramping Workers, 1890-1920: A Subcultural View." in *Walking to Work: Tramps in America, 1790-1935*, edited by Eric H. Monkkonen. Lincoln: University of Nebraska Press, 1984.

Schwantes, "Spokane and the Wageworkers' Frontier: A Labor History to World War I," in *Spokane and the Inland Empire: An Interior Pacific Northwest Anthology*. Ed. David H. Stratton. Pullman: Washington State University Press, 1991.

Schwartz, Harry. "Agricultural Labor in the First World War." *Journal of Farm Economics* 24 (February 1924): 178-87.

Street, Richard Steven. "Tattered Shirts and Ragged Pants: Accomodation, Protest, and the Coarse Culture of California Wheat Harvesters and Threshers, 1866-1900." *Pacific Historical Review* (November 1998): 573-608.

Sprunk, Larry J. "Hugh O'Connor–New Rockford" *North Dakota History* 44 (1977): 46-50.

Taft, Philip. "The I.W.W. in the Grain Belt." *Labor History* 1 (Winter 1960): 53-67.

——. "The Federal Trials of the IWW." *Labor History* 3 (Winter 1962): 57-91.

Philip Taft, "Mayor Short and the I.W.W. Agricultural Workers" *Labor History* 7 (1966): 173-77.

Taylor, Paul S. "Mexican Labor in the United States. Migrations Statistics II," in *University Publications in Economics.* Vol. 12. Berkeley: University of California Press, 1929.

Van Valen, Nelson. "The Bolsheviki and the Orange Growers." *Pacific Historical Review* 22 (February 1953): 39-50.

Whitten, Woodrow C. "The Wheatland Episode." *Pacific Historical Review* 17 (February 1948): 37-42.

——. "Criminal Syndicalism and the Law in California: 1919-1927." *Transactions of the American Philosophical Society* 59 (March 1969): 3-73.

Dissertations and Theses:

Applen, Allen G. "Migratory Harvest Labor in the Midwestern Wheat Belt, 1870-1940." Ph.D. diss., Kansas State University, 1974.

Barnes, Donald M. "The Ideology of the Industrial Workers of the World: 1905-1921." Ph.D. diss., Washington State University, 1962.

Clark, Douglas M. "The Wheatland Hop Field Riot." Master's thesis, Chico State College, 1963.

Cole, Peter. "Shaping Up and Shipping Out: The Philadelphia Waterfront During and After the IWW Years, 1913-1940." Ph.D. diss., Georgetown University, 1997.

Daniel, Cletus Edward. "Labor Radicalism in Pacific Coast Agriculture." Ph.D. diss., University of Washington, 1972.

Dembo, Jonathan. "A History of the Washington State Labor Movement, 1885-1935." Ph.D. diss., University of Washington, 1978.

Fast, Stanley P. "The Agricultural Workers' Organization and the Harvest Stiff in the Midwestern Wheat Belt, 1915-1920." Master's thesis, Mankato State College, 1974.

Fisher, J. Donald. "A Historical Study of the Migrant in California." Master's thesis, University of Southern California, 1945.

Garey, Lewis Farr. "Relation of Labor Income to Size and Type of Farming in Madison County, Nebraska." Master's thesis, University of Nebraska, 1915.

Knight, Jonathan David. "The Spokane and Fresno Free-Speech Fights of the Industrial Workers of the World, 1909-1911." Master's thesis, Washington State University, 1991.

Krissman, Fred. "Californian Agribusiness and Mexican Farm Workers (1942-1992): A Binational Agricultural System of Production/Reproduction." Ph.D. diss., University of California, Santa Barbara, 1996.

McEnroe, Thomas Howard. "The Industrial Workers of the World: Theories, Organizational Problems, and Appeals, as Revealed Principally in the *Industrial Worker*. Ph.D. diss., University of Minnesota, 1960.

Robinson, Leland W. "Social Movement Organizations in Decline: A Case Study of the IWW." Ph.D. diss., Northwestern University, 1973.

Sideman, Michael Samuel. "The Agricultural Labor Market and the Organizing Activities of the I.W.W., 1910-1935." Master's thesis, Northwestern University, 1965.

Weintraub, Hyman. "The I.W.W. in California: 1905-1931." Ph.D. diss., University of California, Los Angeles, 1947.

Index

❉❉❉

AG-1351 (AWIU member), 215
Agrarianism, 32
Agricultural labor,
    in American West, 4, 8-9
    in California, 6, 30-40, 48-54, 156,
        158, 164-65, 173-74, 200, 214-15
    farm hands, 5, 30-31, 33, 39, 43
    and federal government, 24, 33, 81,
        89, 126-34, 136, 146-48, 159, 161,
        170, 218, 220
    on Great Plains, 6, 15-29, 133-38, 156,
        162-63, 170, 174, 176-77, 181, 189,
        191, 193, 214, 222-24, 226-29, 232-
        33
    and immigrants, 20-21, 30-37, 47-48,
        158, 181
    migrants and seasonal workers, 5, 8-
        9, 10, 18-29, 30-40, 43-51, 63, 67-
        68, 72, 79, 133-38, 147-49, 156,
        158, 162-67, 170, 173-74, 177, 180,
        184-85, 190-91, 193, 200-202, 215-
        17, 222-24, 226-29, 232-33
    in Pacific Northwest, 40, 43, 45-46,
        165-66, 200, 215-16
    shocking, 15-16, 227
    and state governments, 24, 34-35, 80-
        81, 133-34
    threshing, 16, 19-20, 227
    and transportation, 18, 23-24, 36, 39,
        45-46, 99, 110, 156, 164-66, 174,
        176-77, 196, 220, 224, 232-33
    wages of, 24-25, 35-37, 39, 47, 49-50,
        123, 136, 138, 147, 149, 162-63,
        170, 172, 173, 176, 195-97, 202. *See
        also* Agricultural Workers'
        Industrial Union; Agricultural
        Workers' Organization; Industrial
        Workers of the World, agricultural
        labor organizing by
    in Washington, 6, 43-46, 63, 67-68,
        102, 147, 156, 158, 165-67, 173,
        189-90
    and women and families, 37-40, 45,
        48-50, 134, 156, 165-167, 174, 181,
        201-2, 232-33

    working and living conditions of, 25-
        26, 31, 38-40, 47-52, 147, 156, 181,
        185, 202
    worklife culture of, 10, 47, 81, 83,
        113-16, 118, 156, 180-81, 185-86
        Great Plains harvesters, 20-29,
            177, 222-24
        California harvesters, 29-40,
            164-65
        Pacific Northwest harvesters,
            43-46, 165-66, 200, 215-16
Agricultural Workers' Industrial
    Organization (AWIO) California,
    97
Agricultural Workers' Industrial Union
    (AWIU), 84, 128, 142, 149, 177,
    207, 213. *See also* Harvest
    Wobblies
    in Arkansas, 182
    boycotts, 198, 221
    and Construction Workers' Industrial
        Union (CWIU), 144
    in California, 140, 147, 156, 158-59,
        164-66, 171-74, 182-13, 200, 204-
        7, 213-15, 230
    in Canada, 216-19, 221, 225
    in Colorado, 230-31
    and economic theory, 184-85, 189-93,
        202, 207, 232
    and education, 177-89, 193, 196, 201-
        2, 207
    and Emergency Program, 213
    and federal government, 120, 136,
        138-43, 145, 150-1, 160-62, 194
    founding of, 109
    and Fruit Workers' Union of Yakima
        (FWUY), 146
    on Great Plains, 133-35, 136, 140-11,
        147-10, 155-16, 161-63, 171-72,
        174, 176, 186, 189, 193-98, 201-4,
        207, 213-14, 225
    in Illinois, 182-83
    in Iowa, 159-61, 168, 170, 182, 194,
        202, 205
    and IWW, 3-4, 109, 155, 159, 168-69,
        177-78, 187, 205, 208-13